INJUSTICE

Rakaia Bridge, New Zealand, as first mentioned on page 54

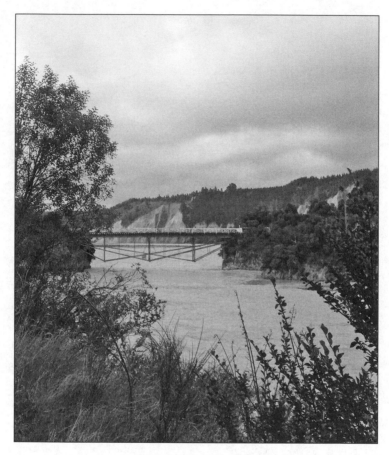

INJUSTICE
Why social inequality persists

Daniel Dorling

First published in Great Britain in 2010 by

The Policy Press
University of Bristol
Fourth Floor
Beacon House
Queen's Road
Bristol BS8 1QU
UK

Tel +44 (0)117 331 4054
Fax +44 (0)117 331 4093
e-mail tpp-info@bristol.ac.uk
www.policypress.co.uk

North American office:
The Policy Press
c/o International Specialized Books Services (ISBS)
920 NE 58th Avenue, Suite 300
Portland, OR 97213-3786, USA
Tel +1 503 287 3093
Fax +1 503 280 8832
e-mail info@isbs.com

British Library Cataloguing in Publication Data
A catalogue record for this book is available from the British Library

Library of Congress Cataloging-in-Publication Data
A catalog record for this book has been requested

ISBN 978 1 84742 426 6 hardcover

Cover design by The Policy Press
Front cover: photograph kindly supplied by www.istock.com
Printed and bound in Great Britain by TJ International, Padstow

FSC
Mixed Sources
Product group from well-managed
forests and other controlled sources
Cert no. SGS-COC-2482
www.fsc.org
© 1996 Forest Stewardship Council

To my parents,

Bronwen and David Dorling

Other related titles from The Policy Press

Gordon, D., Davey Smith, G., Dorling, D. and Shaw, M. (eds) (1999) *Inequalities in health: The evidence presented to the Independent Inquiry into Inequalities in Health, chaired by Sir Donald Acheson*

Shaw, M., Dorling, D., Gordon, D. and Davey Smith, G. (1999, 2000) *The widening gap: Health inequalities and policy in Britain*

Mitchell, R., Dorling, D. and Shaw, M. (2000) *Inequalities in life and death: What if Britain were more equal?*

Davey Smith, G., Dorling, D. and Shaw, M. (eds) (2001) *Poverty, inequality and health: 1800–2000 – A reader*

Dorling, D. and Thomas, B. (2004) *People and places: A 2001 Census atlas of the UK*

Wheeler, B., Shaw, M., Mitchell, R. and Dorling, D. (2005) *Life in Britain: Using Millennial Census data to understand poverty, inequality and place: Ten summary reports and a technical report*

Dorling, D., Rigby, J., Wheeler, B., Ballas, D., Thomas, B., Fahmy, E., Gordon, D. and Lupton, R. (2007) *Poverty, wealth and place in Britain, 1968 to 2005*

Thomas, B. and Dorling, D. (2007) *Identity in Britain: A cradle-to-grave atlas*

Shaw, M., Davey Smith, G., Thomas, B. and Dorling, D. (2008) *The Grim Reaper's road map: An atlas of mortality in Britain*

Contents

List of figures and tables

Figures

Tables

Acknowledgements

Alison Shaw at The Policy Press rewrote the structure of this book and very tactfully persuaded me to at least try to be less self-indulgent and wordy; I am very grateful to her, to three anonymous reviewers for their critical comments on an early draft, to Jo Morton, who oversaw the production of this volume, to Dave Worth, for typesetting it and to Margaret Vaudrey for compiling the index. Dawn Rushen copy-edited the book and convinced me to stop repeating myself so much. Paul Coles at the University of Sheffield redrew all the figures, more than once. Thank you all.

Dimitris Ballas, John Bibby, Stacey Hewitt, Bob Hughes, Steve Kidd, Bill Lodge, Charles Pattie, Kate Pickett, Molly Scott Cato, Ludi Simpson, Judith Watson and Richard Wilkinson also commented constructively on all or parts of earlier versions. The British Academy and the Leverhulme Trust funded most of the time out needed to begin and end the work, and I am very grateful to them. My colleagues in the Departments of Geography at both the University of Sheffield (UK) and the University of Canterbury (New Zealand) have also been extremely understanding. In particular this book draws on the experiences of working with the Social and Spatial Inequalities Group at Sheffield, with colleagues from the Department of Social Medicine at the University of Bristol, with many other colleagues who have been producing reports on poverty and wealth for the Joseph Rowntree Foundation and the British government, and with those with whom I am working internationally on inequality, often as a result of the Worldmapper project (www.worldmapper.org).

Dave Gordon of the University of Bristol kindly provided the contemporary statistics on poverty used in Chapter 4, and I am grateful to Dan Vale of The Young Foundation who did me a similar service as regards the statistics on mental health used in Chapter 7. Helena Tunstall at the University of York helped draw up an earlier version of Table 7 and pointed me to the original source. Jon Minton, also from York, introduced me to the literature combining social evil, social control and war. Tomoki Nakaya of

Ritsumeikan University introduced me to social statistics on Japan, and Kjartan Sveinsson, of the Runnymede Trust, kindly pointed me to information on Iceland I would not otherwise have found, as also did Ben Hennig. I am also grateful to Dimitris Ballas, Anna Barford, Ben Hennig, John Pritchard, Mark Ramsden, Jan Rigby, Bethan Thomas, Dan Vickers and Ben Wheeler for their collaboration over recent years in Sheffield. Half a dozen former PhD students feature in these lists; I have almost certainly learnt more from them (and others I have 'taught') than they have learnt from me: thank you.

Observers of social change in Britain know that when times get desperate the people you fall back on are your mother and your lover. Bronwen Dorling and Alison Dorling both helped turn my initial dyslexic encodings into slightly more readable text, and have had to put up with my attempts to write for far too long. I am very grateful and will probably be buying them flowers, because that is what we do. All the mistakes remain mine, although they are also partly a collection of other men and women's posies.[1]

Danny Dorling, Sheffield

A full bibliography, tables and the Excel spreadsheets that were used to create the figures in this book are available on the Injustice webpages at www.policypress.co.uk

---

[1] See pages 9 to 11 for an explanation of 'posies'. All other notes appear at the end of the book (pages 321-72) rather than as footnotes and so can be skipped (although you won't know what you're missing if you do).

1

Introduction

Although few say they agree with injustice, nevertheless we live in an unjust world. In the world's richest countries injustice is caused less and less by having too few resources to share around fairly and it is increasingly being maintained by widespread adherence to beliefs that actually propagate it. These beliefs are often presented as natural and long-standing, but in fact they are mostly modern creations. What appeared fair and normal yesterday will often be seen as unjust tomorrow. Changing what is understood by injustice today means telling some people, usually those in positions of power, that what they consider to be fair is in fact in many ways unjust.

This book aims to help redefine injustice. While no one would claim to be on the side of injustice, without the continued spread of beliefs in support of injustice it would not survive long in its present form. Now that we have enough resources for all, much that was previously seen as unfortunate has become unjust.

The five tenets of injustice are that: elitism is efficient, exclusion is necessary, prejudice is natural, greed is good and despair is inevitable. Because of widespread and growing opposition to the five key unjust beliefs, including the belief that so many should now be 'losers', most of those advocating injustice are careful with their words. And those who believe in these tenets are the majority in power across almost all rich countries. Although many of those who are powerful may want to make the conditions of life a little less painful for others, they do not believe that there is a cure for modern social ills, or even that a few inequalities can be much alleviated. Rather, they believe that just a few children are sufficiently able to be fully educated and only a few of those are then able to govern; the rest must be led. They believe that the poor will always be with us no matter how rich we are. They have also come to believe that most others are naturally, perhaps genetically, inferior to them. And many of this small group believe that their friends' and their own greed is helping the rest of humanity as much as humanity can be helped; they are convinced that to argue against such a counsel of despair is foolhardy. It is their beliefs that uphold injustice.

This book brings together evidence which shows that these beliefs are unfounded. The evidence also shows how people who end up in power come so easily to hold these beliefs, or become converted to them, and how their beliefs provide false justification for those who benefit most from injustice.

1.1 The beliefs that uphold injustice

Within affluent countries, especially the more economically unequal of affluent countries,[1] social injustices are now being recreated, renewed and supported by five new sets of beliefs. These beliefs have old origins, but have taken new faces. Although they are beliefs which have now been publicly condemned as wrong, beliefs which most individuals claim not to support, the acceptance of these beliefs by just a few, and the reluctance of many others to confront those few, is crucial to maintaining injustice in such times and lands of plenty. This book brings together and updates many of the arguments against upholding these beliefs. It suggests that if injustices are to be reduced for all, it is important not just to claim that you do not hold these beliefs, but to positively reject them. But if the existence of injustice is actually at the heart of what you believe to be correct, then simply saying you reject the labels attached to these beliefs (elitism, exclusion, prejudice, greed and despair) will not be sufficient to reduce injustice. If you think that the beliefs themselves about each label are correct, then you must also believe that injustice is good.

The beliefs that uphold injustice in its contemporary form have been given many names and categorised in many ways,[2] but most of the categorisations can be simplified to the five beliefs: elitism is efficient, exclusion is necessary, prejudice is natural, greed is good and despair is inevitable. Each belief also creates a distinct set of victims – the delinquents, the debarred, the discarded, the debtors and the depressed. Those who uphold these beliefs find it hard to see

–

possibilities beyond the current situation; they are, in effect, advocates for the continuation of injustice, arguing that the victims will always be with us in large numbers, the numbers suggested in Table 1.

Table 1: Proportions that suffer injustices of different kinds in affluent nations

Fraction	Subjects	Labelled	Description of group who suffer the injustice	%	Year
A seventh	Children	Delinquent	Found limited or simple at learning when tested	13	2006
A sixth	People	Debarred	Excluded from social norms in at least two ways	16	1999/ 2001
A fifth	Adults	Debtors	Admit not managing to get by financially (if asked)	21	1984– 2004
A quarter	Households	Discarded	Have no car where car use has become assumed	26	2006/ 07
A third	Families	Depressed	Member suffers depression/chronic anxiety disorder	33	2000
A half	Citizens	Disenfranchised	Adults who did not or could not vote in the latest US presidential election	46	2008

Notes and sources: Data on children are taken from an OECD survey of the Netherlands and represent 13% as limited or simple, nearly an eighth, but in Britain the proportion is a sixth; the figure of a seventh is a geographically wider average (see Section 3.1 of this book). The next four rows are derived from British studies of poverty (Section 4.1), society (Section 5.1), wealth (Section 6.1) and psychiatric morbidity (Section 7.1) from surveys taken in the years shown. The final row is derived from dividing the 131 million people who voted in the US presidential election of 2008 by the population aged 15+, some 243 million (www.census.gov), equivalent to an 18+ estimate including all those not counted as resident in the US.

It is a sign of the duplicity of our times that institutions which often say they are against elitism do most to promote it; that governments which say they aim to reduce social exclusion actually create it; that movements which pretend not to be prejudiced foster hate; that academic disciplines where the orthodoxy is to advocate greed cannot say so explicitly; and that many experts argue that the best that most can hope for is a life of which they themselves would despair. They do not say this explicitly, but it is implied in their accusation that those who argue against them are being utopian.

As those with most power continue to promote elitism, exclusion, prejudice, greed and despair, injustice will not be reduced – it is described as inevitable and as 'practical' politics. It is only in the most unequal of rich nations that those with power can explicitly say that they believe there is good in the inequalities sustained by this injustice. Elsewhere in the rich world most who favour injustice are more circumspect, but as the examples in this book show, the powerful have been effective in many countries where life chances are now less fair than they were just a few decades ago. However, those who support injustice are being opposed and exposed more and more as time passes, and social movements are gathering momentum to challenge their views.

Because belief in the five tenets of injustice is so widespread among people in power, these beliefs are then propagated through what they control. For instance, many of those who fund and manage educational institutions encourage teachers to present these beliefs as truths. The beliefs are also propagated by governments whose departments for social security increasingly label the poor as wanting, feckless, immoral and criminal. The beliefs are supported by the media, where stories are common which imply that some people are less deserving, where great city businessmen (and a few businesswomen) are lauded as superheroes and where immigrants looking to work for a crumb of the City's bonuses are seen as scroungers. The beliefs are supported by a politics whose mantra is that without greed there would be no growth, and without growth we would all be doomed.[3] These beliefs are supported by industries, whose spokespeople say we must continue to consume more and more and which now manufacture pharmaceutical treatments to cope with the consequent despair on a mass scale – within rich countries and worldwide, mental distress and despair is the largest growth industry for pharmaceutical companies and frontline medical practitioners.[4] So in various ways academia, government, the media, politics and industry are each a key element in promoting injustice.

1.2 The five faces of social inequality

This book is concerned mainly with injustice in affluent countries, but it does touch on wider debates. If you had to choose one word to characterise the nature of human society as it is currently arranged worldwide, there is no better word than 'injustice'. Across all walks of life, between continents and over the decades, injustice has been constantly prevalent. Chapter 2 provides a summary of the recent history and current extent of injustice in general in affluent countries, before Chapters 3–7 examine the domains most affected by each face of inequality, starting with education.

'Elitism is efficient'

The origins of the ideas that currently constitute the core beliefs of injustice can be traced back to when we last lived in times as unequal as today, during the last 'gilded age', which began at the end of the American Civil War in 1865 and ended in 1914 in Europe, and in the 1920s in the United States.[5] Chapter 3 suggests that elite prizes such as those established by Alfred Nobel came about when they did, along with the first intelligence (IQ) tests, because it was only at that point that there were spoils great enough to be shared out in rich countries, and those who had gained most needed to justify their positions in newly created hierarchies. Nobel prizes were first awarded in 1901 in the midst of that first gilded age of great wealth concentration, when it was unimaginable that there would not be a 'natural' elite.

The statistics produced by some international bodies, such as the Organisation for Economic Co-operation and Development (OECD), suggest that they still continue the tradition of trying to defend elitism as natural (see Figure 2, page 74, and the discussion of its derivation in Chapter 3), but these bodies are now far more coy about their intent than those in the 1890s who first used social statistics to suggest that paupers mainly bred more paupers. That coyness suggests that in recent years some progress against rising elitism has been made because elitists now know to hide their core beliefs about the distribution of human ability in obscure technical notes. Although elitist views still underlie the beliefs of many in

–

power, they have also now been institutionalised in the form of bodies such as the OECD. Those destined to be paupers today are labelled children 'limited in their ability' (see Section 3.1) – a staggering seventh of all children born in the richest of countries are given this label today. Almost 70 years ago in the UK, William Beveridge named 'ignorance' as one of his five social evils, but as ignorance has been overcome across the rich world, widespread elitism has taken its place, and children who would have appeared of normal ability in the 1940s are now called 'limited' today.

'Exclusion is necessary'

The most terrible result of elitism is that it can be used to justify the exclusion of so many people from normal social activity. Chapter 4 suggests that it was in the most affluent of countries a century ago that the supposed scientific theories defending inequality began to be drawn up. The modern origins of exclusion can be traced to an academic paper of 1895 when data were first presented that showed the geographical distribution of English and Welsh paupers in a way that was designed to suggest that pauperisation was some kind of natural phenomenon.[6] The timing of this was no coincidence – this was the first time under a market system that such an abundance of wealth had emerged. It then became necessary to try to update feudal justifications for the unequal distribution of that wealth and to explain why so many should have to live with so little. The new justifications became dominant beliefs between the 1890s and the 1930s, but were then rejected for a generation before gaining ground again as social exclusion rose from the late 1960s onwards, alongside the great growth in personal debt when the old social evil described by Beveridge as 'want' was cut down in size. The cycles through which people fell into exclusion due to having too little were first established as we currently see them only in the 1960s.[7] Before then, to be truly rich was to be landed. To be poor was, for many, normal. Today, one in six of all households in rich countries are again excluded from social norms due to poverty and are poor in at least two ways of counting poverty.[8] What now makes those households poor is the effects of the riches of others.

'Prejudice is natural'

Elitism and exclusion have further causes and corollaries, and chief among these is prejudice. As elitism and inequality rise, and as more people become socially excluded, or are able to exclude themselves by using their wealth, those at the top more often look down on others with ever greater disdain and fear, as evidenced by growing social segregation.[9] Those at the bottom are also less likely to trust others and more likely to become fearful in a society that so clearly values them so little. Racism rises in just these kinds of circumstances, and a wider form of racism (a new social Darwinism) quietly spreads.[10] Chapter 5 documents this process. It shows how, over time, inequalities in wealth and health, and the widespread acceptance of bigoted views, all shrank from their height in the 1920s to reach minima in the early 1970s, before rising up again in that fateful decade of oil shock, inflation and overseas intervention (war). Just as one in seven have been marked as 'limited' by elitist labels and one in six as 'poor' by the economic circumstances of exclusion, as a result of new prejudices about how it is acceptable to treat others (which has overtaken the old social evil of 'idleness' in importance and effect), an even higher proportion of one in five households in rich countries were only just managing to get by with great difficulty, even before the financial crash of 2008. Chapter 5 outlines the material mechanism through which prejudice is transmitted between generations, how it is maintained by inherited wealth and the deep social polarisation that results.

'Greed is good'

The rise of elitism, exclusion and prejudice were all precursors of the age of greed, ushered in during the 1980s, seen as good, and not questioned seriously until 2008. Chapter 6 shows how at least a quarter of households are now disregarded in what is considered access to normal infrastructure, whether it be simply the ability to own and drive a car or having the means to access the internet.

In the US not to have a car these days is not to live as a 'normal' human being.[11] But in Britain almost half the children of lone parents have no access to a car.[12] Many people who need a car, because they have young children or find it hard to walk or no longer live near shops, have no car, but many of the car journeys made by others are non-essential and the majority of cars contain only one person, the driver. There are actually enough cars currently owned for all those who need a car to have one.

Mass car driving is the simplest example of what happens when greed begins to be valued in its own right. When you next look at a congested street, with cars jostling to move a few metres forward, pedestrians dodging in between, cyclists weaving dangerously around them, children walking past at the level of exhaust pipes, no one getting anywhere fast, and all those petrol engines continuously running, this is both the symbolic but also the very real collective outcome of individual greed encouraged to grow by the mantra of personal freedom.

'Despair is inevitable'

Unsurprisingly, growing despair is the result for those living in the most elite of affluent societies, where inequalities are allowed and encouraged to rise untrammelled, where more and more are excluded or live partly in fear of being ostracised, where prejudice towards the 'lower orders' begins again to become normal and where greed is commonly referred to implicitly (if not often explicitly) as good. Chapter 7 recounts how in the 1990s the fastest rise in despair occurred. This rise was not just in the growing use of prescription medicines, but in the growth of feelings that there must be more to life.[13] Even children were hit with a feeling of despair, with the fastest increases in adolescent depression being recorded in North America in the 1990s, a rise found not to be due to changing diagnostic practice.[14] In Britain this despair reached such levels that by 2006 it was being reported that a third of families had at least one family member who was suffering from depression or a chronic anxiety disorder.[15] The despair was also public, as shown by the publication of so many books criticising modern trends, the rise of the green movement and of new forms of social protest. Across Europe the majority of best-selling books on subjects such as economics were not business manuals but alternative treatises on the woes of capitalism. By 2004 anti-globalisation books were almost the only books on business or economics that sold well in Europe.[16] The US was slower to catch the trend, but in 2008 voted in a president on a very different ticket to the usual. The promoters of individualism and acquisition were themselves beginning to be greeted with despair.

Chapter 8 brings the argument to a conclusion. It concentrates on the 2000s, on how we stumbled into a crisis that no one now denies was of our own making. In Chapters 3–7 questions are asked as to who, why, where, what and when each new injustice hit, while Chapter 8 instead just asks *how* it is possible to be optimistic in the face of rising social injustices and a financial crash. It concentrates on what is now different, on what we now know and on how many more people are now involved in the arguments about what happens next. Out of the many things that are different, the increase in education is the most important, with a majority of young people in the world being literate, and near majorities in more equitable rich countries now attending university. Compared with the end of the last gilded age it is now much harder to see who or what there is left to exploit, and how much harder it will be to fool so many better informed people this time round.

1.3 A pocket full of posies

With injustice, all is connected. From the depicting of 19th-century paupers, to the awarding of 20th-century peace prizes, and the mapping of 21st-century global income distributions, injustice is the common denominator. The same patterns of gross inequality are seen again and again. They appear when health inequalities are calculated and wealth inequalities are tabulated. Within rich countries, the portrayal of children's abilities as lying along bell curves (as if these are natural things) is unjust. The consequent curving upwards of rates of depression and anxiety is closely connected to how children are treated, are ranked, and expect to be treated as adults. Portraying large groups of adults as inferior is similarly unjust, as is promoting greed among a few as some kind of benefit to the many, or seeing the distress of so many as a reflection of their ascribed failings. Injustice has always survived because of its support by the powerful. The same is true today, but never have the powerful had so little to fall back on.

Arguments against injustice used to be rare treatises. A single essay against slavery written in 1785 could be held up high as a shining example of such work two centuries later,[17] but it has largely only been within living memory that we have started to learn that it was not the essays of aristocrats that made differences in the past; it was the fact that their contributions were far more often recorded and preserved. Slaves made slavery uneconomic by not adapting willingly to slavery; they revolted. Similarly, it is only within the last century that the lives of the 'great men' of science, politics and business (men who are still so often put on pedestals) have been re-examined and found not to produce biographies of awe.[18] Their fallibilities, failings and, most importantly, their luck are all being revealed more frequently. In each case they are remembered for an achievement that was always just about to be made because of the circumstances or the actions of others around them, now mostly forgotten. The belief that human advancement is achieved by a few great people themselves standing on the shoulders of giants is misplaced. There is no such thing as superhuman people, and to say that they exist and to say that some people are more human than others is unjust.[19]

Men still pay homage to other men. The vast majority of that tiny group of humans who have had their histories recorded has been male, but a new generation of men and women is beginning to realise how it is both unjust and unrealistic to claim more than an immeasurably small impact as their personal contribution. One American scholar, Elvin Wyly, who was among the early group to document how sub-prime lending was unsustainable in the US, wrote of his writings recently that all he had done was to have '… gathered a posie of other men's flowers, and only the thread that binds them is my own'.[20] Even that phrase was not his own, he admitted. It was attributed to the title page of Peter Gould's book (on medical geography), who in turn was quoting from the title page of a book of poems collected during the Second World War, who in turn…. The earliest recorded version dates from over 400 years earlier and reads: 'I have here only made a nosegay of culled flowers, and have brought nothing of my own but the thread that ties them together'.[21] And the only reason that this is the first recording is that printing had only just been invented then. The idea that we do little more than collect the flowers of others' ideas and simply tie them together in slightly different ways will have begun with the first picking of flowers, long before it could be recorded on paper.

Several years' careful research across many academic disciplines and the consequent documentation of many others' ideas and comments have come together in this book, which is the bringing together of others' posies with a few of my own thoughts to add to the call for greater levels of social justice. True social justice will both create and require much greater equality than is as yet widely accepted.[22]

2

Inequality: the antecedent and outcome of injustice

Social inequality within rich countries persists because of a continued belief in the tenets of injustice, and it can be a shock for people to realise that there might be something wrong with much of the ideological fabric of the society we live in. Just as those whose families once owned slave plantations will have seen such ownership as natural in a time of slavery, and just as not allowing women to vote was once portrayed as 'nature's way', so too the great injustices of our times are, for many, simply part of the landscape of normality. For instance, while it is still accepted and seen as acceptable that there should be a few Ivy League universities for those with the 'greatest minds' to study at, below them prestigious institutions for the next tier, lesser institutions for the next tier, intermediate training for the next, school certificates for those below and possibly prison for those below them, all because of what is thought to be inherently within people, then there is little hope for greater justice. What matters most is not just how deep those beliefs of inherited difference remain, but how coded is the language we now use to talk of them, and how many who do not superficially think of themselves as elitist clearly believe in elitism.

Books on injustice, of which there have been many, usually begin by listing the books' antecedents: the great thinkers who have gone before, works that have inspired. This book makes no claim to be visionary or novel; it pulls together a small collection from a large array of mostly very recent writing about a greater argument, the case for which is slowly becoming widely accepted. This is the case about the nature of, and widespread harm caused by, injustice, of new social evils and of the rising inequality that both results from injustices and also underlies their rise.

It has already been well established that the dividing of labour into smaller and smaller parts both minimises wages and generates monotony.[1] We also know that the world has enough for everyone's needs but not for their greed.[2] There is no utopian revelation here because we are no longer living in a world where the people who argue for justice are in a tiny minority.[3] Most great utopian visions came about during times when far fewer people were permitted to voice opinions, and most who were so permitted believed that the day would never come when we would really hold it as a self-evident truth that all people are created equal. Most of us now say we hold that truth but, as I pull evidence together in what follows, I demonstrate that those with power increasingly do not mean it when they say it, because such belief is inconsistent with what else they say they believe about other people. Often stated beliefs in equality and justice are mere platitudes or refer to a very limited definition of the concepts.

The new injustices in affluent countries have several things in common: all are aspects of rising social inequalities; all have arisen from a surplus of riches; and all suggest that so far we have come up with the wrong answer to the question of what we should do now that we are so rich. In rich countries we are almost all well off compared with our parents. On a worldwide level we would all be well off if only we could share the surplus.[4]

2.1 The inevitability of change: what we do now that we are rich

We now know that we have enough for everyone's needs, as we know with some precision how many of us there are on the planet, and we have a good idea of how many of us there soon will be – the central projection of the United Nations' (UN's) world population estimates show human population growth is coming to an end within the lifetime of most people alive today.[5] It will be the result not of pandemic or war but simply of most women today having three offspring, and of their daughters being expected to have two.

As we become fewer in rich countries, many are now arguing that further increases in our wealth are not necessarily producing greater happiness, longer healthy lives, a better informed population or a freer society.[6] We live in times when we are now told very different stories about our history as a species and its 'progress' than those told to our parents. For instance, we now know that we are only just today regaining the average heights of humans 13,000 years ago because we are at last again able to eat a wide enough variety of nutrients (with enough reliability of supply) for our bodies to grow to full height. The hunger began when we first farmed, and harvests periodically failed – past skeletons show this. We then shrank in stature even further due to the privations and famines that came with early industrialisation and lives increasingly lived on factory floors, in slums or as peasants in the country.

In 1992 it was claimed, using the examples of ancient skeletons found in what is now Greece and Turkey, that modern Greeks and Turks had still not regained the average heights of our hunter-gatherer ancestors due to average nutritional levels still not being as good as those found *before* antiquity. The heights to be re-attained were 5'10" (178 cm) for men and 5'6" (168 cm) for women.[7] These average heights had fallen by 7 and 5 inches respectively when agriculture was introduced.[8] By 2004, however, the average heights of people living in Greece and Turkey had grown; although women were still an inch behind the average heights of those alive 13,000 years earlier,[9] Greek men had finally regained the average height that our ancestors reached.[10]

We can be optimistic about the possibility of change because today we are living in very different circumstances compared with just one generation ago. In rich countries average human heights have shot up only very recently to be back to what our skeletons evolved to support. Even the middle class only one generation ago were mostly slightly stunted; the upper classes a generation before that also were and lost a tenth of their infants to disease in the richest countries of the world.[11] Those nine tenths of upper-class infants who survived were not as well fed or cared for medically as are many poorer people in more equitable rich countries today.

If you wrote about injustice in 1910 or in 1960 you were writing in remarkably different times. *Write now, and for the first time in human history a majority of people worldwide can read what you write.* Some five out of every six children in the world are now taught to read and write to a degree that only a minority of their parents were; a majority of their children will probably have internet access.[12] A hundred million young adults worldwide now study in universities each year.[13] Education may still be hugely unjust in how it is distributed, but there are many more people alive in the world today who have been given the freedom to learn right through to college. This is not just many more than before, it is many more than all those who ever went to university before combined.

University degrees are wonderful things; it is the arranging and valuing of them by hierarchy of institution that is problematic, when people study for the label, for the university brand, rather than actually to learn. Because there were so few of them, the forerunners of today's university graduates almost all became part of a tiny elite, governing others and being rewarded with riches as a result. Because there are so many more graduates now, only a very small minority of today's university graduates can become rich at the expense of others.

Table 2 shows the categorisation of injustices described in this book in 2010 and how it relates to categorisations made in 1942, and various subsequent attempts to update them made in 1983, 2007 and 2008. The 10 examples of social woes that respond most closely to social inequalities listed in 2009 under the headline of 'Inequality: mother of all evils' in one newspaper[14] could also be slotted into the table, with a little stretching. The old social evils were: lack of education (ignorance), lack of money (want), lack of work (idleness), lack of comfort (squalor) and lack of health (disease). The new injustices have arisen out of a glut of: education (elitism), money (exclusion), scorn (prejudice), wealth (greed) and worry (despair).

The five forms of injustice are each in turn amalgams of others' lists of concerns and perils. For simplicity each new injustice can be said to have arisen most strongly a decade after the last (in the 1950s, 1960s, 1970s, 1980s and 1990s respectively), and out of the ashes of past evils that have largely been overcome in material terms. Tolerance of, acceptance of (even advocating) the new injustices is at the heart of social injustice in rich countries today. Poor countries remain bedevilled by the old social evils, not because they are on some developmental ladder waiting for their problems to become problems of riches, but increasingly because of the ignorance, want,

Table 2: Injustices, social evils, political, philosophical and public labels combined

2010 Injustice	1942 Past	1983 Political	2007 Philosophical	2008 Public
Elitism	Ignorance	6. Differences in skills and ability	4. Threats to sense, using imagination, and thought 5. Threats to experiencing and expressing emotions freely	3. A decline in values, lack of tolerance, compassion and respect 4. Problems concerning young people, family breakdown and poor parenting
Exclusion	Want	1. The exploitation of those who work	3. Threats to bodily integrity 9. Threats to play, ability to relax, to take Sabbaths and holidays	1. Problems caused by individualism, consumerism, decline in community life 2. Excessive use of drugs and alcohol, both as consequence and causes 5. Inequality and poverty, corrosive evil in an affluent society
Prejudice	Idleness (sexism and racism)	3. Unemployment 5. The economic subordination of women	6. Threats to being able to use practical reason (to be able to contribute) 7. Threats to affiliation, to belonging, having mutual respect	7. Violence and crime, child abuse and exploitation 8. Gender inequality, inequalities embedded in current thinking 9. Intolerance resulting from the beliefs of many religions, and similar ideas 10. Problems of attitudes to social diversity and immigration
Greed	Squalor	2. The inheritance of wealth by a minority	10. Threats to having control over one's environment (to having rights) 8. Threats to other species, lack of concern sure to backfire	6. Problems caused by big business, apathy and a democratic deficit 12. Environmental issues, selfishness and insularity
Despair	Disease	4. Infirmity and problems of old age	1. Threats to life 2. Threats to bodily health	11. Health problems, especially lack of care for older people

Sources: First column: this book. Second column: past evils, William Beveridge's well-known labels and popular additions in brackets. Third column: political labels from socialists (Cockshott, W.P. and Cottrell, A. [1983] *Towards a new socialism*, Nottingham: Spokesman, pp 11, 12). Fourth column: philosophical labels from philosophers (Wolff, J. and de-Shalit, A. [2007] *Disadvantage*, Oxford: Oxford University Press, pp 38-9). The most important are claimed to be: 1, 2, 3, 4, 7 and 10, see pp 106 and 191, and for some extra ones, 11-14, see p 198, footnote 9). Fifth column: public labels from newspapers (Mackay, N. [2008] 'Our 10 modern evils', *Sunday Herald*, 20 April) and think-tank projects and surveys (Watts, B. [2008] *What are today's social evils? The results of a web consultation*, York: Joseph Rowntree Foundation, p 6). Numbering is from original publications.

idleness, squalor and disease caused in most of the poor world as a side effect of the elitism, exclusion, prejudice, greed and despair which are now endemic within rich countries.

2.2 Injustice rising out of the ashes of social evils

'Elitism is efficient'

Well-meaning attempts to eliminate very poor education have had the unintended by-product of fuelling the rise of a new injustice by beginning to promote the widespread acceptance of elitism.This has occurred over many years through providing most extra educational resources to those whose parents had generally themselves received the most – in Britain this took place through the provision of more grammar schools, then sixth form colleges, new and expanded universities and now a multitude of new postgraduate degrees. All these extra resources were provided following the introduction of secondary education for all, and then, comprehensive education for most.Those whose families had in the past secured slight educational advantages were now able to secure much greater advantages through amassing more and more qualifications within selective awarding institutions. In 1942 a tiny minority of adults had a university degree and it was normal to have no formal qualifications. Now, although many young adults still have no or few formal qualifications, there are also many who hold a long list of school and university certificates. Pick two young people at random and they are far more likely to be qualified to very different levels today as compared to any point in the past.

The mass schooling of children through to their late teens in rich countries marked an end to the acceptance of illiteracy as normal. This school movement grew in strength right through the gilded age, through the crash and depression, and came out of the SecondWorld War with a victory for children, especially for girls, who became seen as educable through secondary school age. However, almost immediately after the war, in the beginnings of the ColdWar (and in an era of vehement anti-communism), with men feeling threatened by women who had shown that they could do men's jobs, and with the well-off feeling threatened by the poor who had shown that, if taught, they too could read and write, the injustice of elitism began to be propagated. It was more pernicious than previous class, religion, 'race' and gender bars to advancement because it was claimed that the elite should rule and be differently rewarded because they were most able to rule due to their advanced knowledge and skill rather than because of some feudal tradition (because their father was part of the elite too). Elitism became a new justification for inequality.

Before the 1950s there was no need to argue for elitism. Women were rarely admitted to college, and girls very often left school earlier than boys. It was often said that girls were a different breed – in actual fact, everyone was a different breed from the few allowed to talk about 'breeds' of human then.[15] However, as Table 2 shows, by the 1980s the fact that people were paid differentially according to perceived differences in their skills and supposed abilities had been identified as a new social evil. A quarter of a century after that, contemporary philosophers listed threats to people being able to use their imagination or being able to express emotion as 'disadvantages' that could easily be placed under this same heading. This illustrates just how quickly our demands can be raised, even to the point of including as part of what is new about social evils being denied the opportunity to use imagination and express emotion. There are many bad jobs where these disadvantages prevail.[16] However, when surveyed,[17] the public talked less of this and more of a fall in compassion and respect, and of problems emerging for young people caused by poor parenting, which resulted in seeing some as inferior, as nowhere near part of 'the elite'. In affluent nations which have become even more unequal, following the rise of elitist thinking in the 1950s, people came to be socially segregated more and more by educational outcome.

Elitist thinking not only determines children's life chances but also has an effect on everything that is seen as decent or acceptable in a society.

—

'Exclusion is necessary'

Where elitist thinking was allowed to grow most strongly, social exclusion became more widespread. Again, as Table 2 illustrates, social exclusion is a new face of injustice that grew out of the general eradication of the bulk of an old social evil, 'want', going hungry, wanting for clothes and other basic possessions, warmth and other essentials. It was in the 1960s that the widespread eradication of old wants, which came with near full employment, pensions and more decent social security benefits, inadvertently resulted in new forms of exclusion, such as trying to exclude people for 'not being like us'; this was seen most clearly in rising racism during the 1970s.[18]

By the 1980s the categories of new injustices included 'the exploitation of those who work'. Those in work were almost all able to eat enough, but as wages at the bottom declined in relation to those above, although those with no work did worst, many families of people in work but in bad jobs also began to become excluded from the norms of society, such as not having an annual holiday or not always getting breakfast before going to school. Being excluded from the norms of society was first seriously suggested as a definition of poverty in the 1960s by Peter Townsend.

As income inequalities grew, the numbers excluded by having too little also grew and the numbers who could afford to exclude themselves grew slightly too. Those who categorised injustices in 2006 saw how such exclusions threatened people's well-being, their bodily integrity and their ability to play, to relax and to take holidays (Table 2, column 4). The public defined the problems of social exclusion as being caused by individualism and consumerism, which had then led to more problems of drugs and alcohol corroding society (Table 2, column 5). To look at the wider context in the rich countries, which have become more consumerist, more people have been made poorer as the need to get into debt to try to keep up rises.

The tendency for the affluent in rich countries to exclude themselves from social norms results in ever greater consumption, both as these people buy more and as they raise the expectations of others. That, in turn, causes want to rise elsewhere, including the old evil of the most basic of wants rising as peasants are made into paupers in poor countries when poor countries are impoverished to satisfy the desires for wealth within rich nations. Many now see pauperisation as the direct end result of massive economic polarisation on a world scale,[19] and part of this pauperisation is the conscious de-linking of a few countries from the world economy in attempts to evade such polarisation.[20]

'Prejudice is natural'

Prejudice grows like mould, based on elitist myths in times of exclusion.[21] As inequalities began to fall after the last gilded age, it became radical and then acceptable to argue in the 1930s that 'It is the mark of a civilised society to aim at eliminating such inequalities as have their source, not in individual differences, but in its own organisation'.[22] What was unforeseen in such arguments was that 40 years later, as the trend in inequality turned upward once again in the 1970s, creating the antecedents for what would later be a new gilded age, the argument would be reversed and some people would begin to preach that inequalities were simply reflections of individual differences in ability, and if inequalities grew wider, well, that was just a clearer expression of those inherent differences.

By the 1990s prejudice had reached such heights that it needed to be more and more clearly explained by those opposed to elitism that human beings were not born with inherent differences. Rather, people were born with plasticity – unlike other species, human infants have very few of their '... neural pathways already committed'[23] at birth; they are then able (and have) to adapt to the conditions they find themselves born into. Those human beings born with fixed inherent traits would have been less likely to survive through the rapidly changing environments that they found themselves in over the course of (human) history. We evolved to become more flexible. We inherited the ability *not* to inherit particular abilities! Those now born into times of scarcity and brutality are malleable infants who quickly learn to be selfish and to grab what they can, if that is what they learn from watching the actions of others. Born into times, or just into families, of good organisation and plenty, infants are capable of growing up to be cooperative and altruistic. But born into times

—

of free market organisation and plenty, we often just learn to want more and more and more. And there is more and more to want.

The same flexibility that allows newborn infants to learn in a few years one of thousands of possible languages, and in most of the world two or more languages, also allows them to adapt to finding themselves born into one of thousands of different cultures where survival was and remains best protected by new members quickly and inherently learning to behave in a way which fits their surrounding environment. Because so few of our neural pathways are committed at birth we respond well to being nurtured, whether that nurturing is brutal or caring. Where nurturing is caring, growing up to care too has become a more cherished trait. More survive when there is wider caring, and so caring survives by being among the most appropriate behaviours to be taught and to evolve, including evolution beyond our genes, cultural evolution.

It is the very fact that human societies can change in collective behaviour over such short times that suggests that our destinies are not in our genes. We can move in just a few generations from being feudal or cooperative, to being competitive or totalitarian. We move within lifetimes from seeing large groups of people persuaded to take part in wars, to not resisting conscription, to marching and singing for others' rights. Prejudices rise and fall as people preach to promote them or teach against them. Prejudice is nurtured, a product of environments of fear, which is easily stoked up and takes years to quench. One manifestation of prejudice is that when great numbers are seen as less deserving, as slaves, paupers, or just 'average', a minority can describe their own behaviour not as greed but as simply receiving higher rewards because they are different kinds of human beings, who deserve to be put on a pedestal above those they view with prejudice.

'Greed is good'

Parts of our destinies can be swayed by our genes if the environment does not mitigate their influence. Greed has been excused as a side effect of otherwise beneficial evolutionary traits. This suggests that just as our hunter-gatherer desire to store calories by stuffing ourselves with fats and sugars was at one time usually beneficial, so too was our 'cave fire' interest in the stories of others, reflecting a then vital desire to understand the minds of all those around us. Unfortunately these traits of obsessing over what others nearby have and what they are doing, while beneficial in times of scarcity, leads to greed where and when there is abundance. A preoccupation with the minutiae of others' lives helped us to survive in small groups, but has now gone awry as we 'max out' on celebrity watching, gorging on and mimicking soap operas.[24] Similarly, we are said to be trapped by our genes to take perceived status deadly seriously again. Slights to our status cause hurt that possibly has evolutionary origins because they cause us to fear that we are about to lose our position in ancient rank orders with deadly effect. The status syndrome may well have preserved sustainable, if claustrophobic, patriarchal and matriarchal village hierarchies where everyone knew their place. Outside village life it causes misery, but gives us a biological reason to see why it would be to the greater good for all of us to behave justly and to minimise status hierarchies, which we may otherwise have a natural inclination to exacerbate.[25] Biologically we come programmed for tribal and village life, alongside our plasticity.

As feudalism ended, our acute abilities to notice slights and our innate fear of being ostracised led, in the new worlds of cities and strangers, to a few seeking to rise ever upwards to be 'the big man', and to many feeling abandoned as if they had been placed outside the village to die. Some argue that these traits in turn came from pre-human ranking systems common in mammals that live in groups.[26] However, stories conjured up through musing over evolutionary biology only take us so far and are of themselves evidence that all is far from genetic, given how we only recently thought up these stories. Discovering our genes was a product of our cultures. Cultures developed not just to reward work, exploration and discovery but also to protect leisure time through inventing Sabbaths and to prevent the hoarding of wealth; these inventions are as old as cave fires and village hearths. In contrast, it took the early spread of city living before many of our cultures developed enough to see usury, the taking of interest on others' debts, as a sin.

—

People have been making their own history for quite some time, despite repeatedly lamenting and finding themselves in circumstances not of their choosing.[27] And the histories are made collectively – we collectively gorge now on shopping and soap operas. Status paranoia is reinforced as our people watching is now done through watching television and surfing the internet. Being greedy is offered to us collectively through advertising as a lure to wanting more. Work harder, they say, if you want more, but greed divides people as a result of unequal reward. The rich in greedy societies did not become happier as greed came to be seen again as so good by so many in the 1980s.[28] We easily forget that the phrase 'greed is good' was evoked in resistance to the mantra that it *was* supposedly good! Even Hollywood took part in the attempts to resist, to make a different history, to tell a different story, to get a different future. The greedy do not gain happiness but they do fuel others' misery by reducing everyone's sense of adequacy.

The rise again of greed was the unforeseen outcome of victory over squalor. Greed and squalor have coexisted for centuries, but it was with the widespread eradication of the worst aspects of material squalor in affluent nations that basic checks and balances on greed were lost. The rise in greed occurred not just because a few might be a little more programmed to be greedy, and a tiny number have always been scurrilous enough to do better in business and then hoard gains. Greed rose because the circumstances were right; what had been in place to control greed had been removed in attempting to eradicate squalor. We pumped out oil to drive cars so we no longer needed to live on streets full of horse manure, to make plastics to wrap around food and slow down its rotting. We mass-produced chickens and refrigerators, so that we could eat better, but also greedily, eating meat almost every day as a result. We ushered in mass consumption, removed the Sabbath and other high-days and declared usury a virtue, and then found there were almost no limits to individual desire for more cars, for more chicken and for more fridges. We ended up with more than people could possibly need in any one home and, for those who could afford them, more homes than they could possibly use, containing yet more fridges, more cars, more chicken, all seen as signs of success. And we ended up with widespread quiet despair.[29]

—

24

'Despair is inevitable'

Despair is the final injustice of the five new faces of inequality, mutating from the old social evil of widespread physical disease. Health services now exist that effectively treat and contain most physical disease in affluent countries. However, while most physical maladies are now well treated with high-quality care in all but the most unequal of these rich countries, mental illness (including a form of 'affluenza') has been rising across the rich world.[30] In Britain depression is the most common cause of long-term sickness (followed by a bad back),[31] and clinical depression has been growing most quickly among adolescents (see Figure 21, Chapter 7, page 276). Corporate profiteering and the strengthening of paradigms of competition have both been shown to have influenced this rise, and to cause worldwide inequalities in health to be rising, as life expectancy is lower everywhere where economic inequalities are greater.[32] A more general malaise of despair has also settled over the populations of rich countries as elitism has strengthened, exclusion has grown, prejudice has been raised a level and greed has expanded. This is despair for the future, a despair that was felt throughout what were seen as the best of economic times, the late 1990s boom, despair which is now very much more palpable since those times have ended.

2.3 So where do we go from here?

It can be annoying to read a book with the expectation that it will end in one way, only to find that it ends in an altogether different way. Having our expectations satisfied is part of what makes life good. So you should know now that the argument at the end of this book is that recognising the problem is the solution.

Elitism

No amount of affirmative action schemes, good schooling, money for computers or textbooks, different curricula or improved parenting methods are going to help improve how we are educated and think if, in our heart of hearts, those who do most of the deciding as to how the rest get to learn harbour elitist pretensions. We should not expect to see any reduction in the numbers of children labelled as 'modern-day delinquents' wherever enough of the people who have more control over how others are treated still believe strongly enough that they themselves and their offspring are a little more inherently able than most.[33] If you think that you are somehow more than simply the product of your upbringing and the environment into which the little plastic, neurally uncommitted you was thrust, that you might carry some inherited trait that makes you special (not just having a few idiosyncrasies), then you too are part of the problem. Of course, because of differences in upbringing, environment and individual idiosyncrasies, different people do become better suited to doing different jobs by the time they are adults, and they need different training. However, even acknowledging this, it is very hard to justify the extent of educational apartheid we currently tolerate, and we could easily reduce differences dramatically among children if fewer were excluded from birth from what is normal life for most.

Exclusion

Social exclusion cannot be ended by complex schemes of tax credits, child benefits and local area funding when those with most are allowed to accrue even more. In the more unequal of rich countries, as long as we are happy to tolerate wide inequalities in income and wealth, there will always be large numbers of poor people. However, it is not easy to take the step of accepting this fact. We know this because it has not happened. Instead it is easy to divide those with the least into two groups: one you think might be deserving of a little more, and the rest undeserving.

Infants born into poverty almost always feature in the 'deserving of a little more' group, unless they were born in the back of a lorry crossing from France to Britain, or Mexico to the US (see Section 5.2). While the lone young feckless woman, sleeping around, stealing and injecting herself with heroin to escape reality is almost always put in the undeserving category, in most cases it is women in her position who give birth to the infants who will have the worse chances in life, and whose deaths cause the greatest outcry when the circumstances are revealed in court. However, understanding that child poverty will not end while we tolerate poverty for anyone is far from simple, otherwise we would have eradicated child poverty by now.

It is not a matter of money but of belief. Eradicating poverty is cheap because a little money goes a long way when you are poor. Poverty, as defined by social exclusion, is a relative measure; people are poor because they cannot afford to take part in the norms of society, and these norms only become unaffordable because the better-off have been allowed to become even better off. This happens, for example, when taxes are reduced, as taxes provide a source of redistribution from rich to poor. What is most costly is maintaining a small group of extremely wealthy people who are able to exclude themselves from the norms of society at great expense, and this is what we do manage to do, despite the huge costs to everyone else. We do this as long as we continue to be convinced that these people are especially worthy of so much wealth. The last time we stopped being so convinced, at the end of the last gilded age following the 1920s excesses, we started to spread out what we all had more fairly and we did not stop spreading it for nearly 40 years.

Although between 1968 and 1978 poverty was far from eradicated, people could at least appreciate each others' fears, concerns and lives more than many generations had before and any have done since. In the US, the UK and a few similarly rich countries we then did the opposite for the next 30 years, and allowed the rich to take more each year than they had before.[34] We need to understand this history before considering what might be sufficient to reverse this growth of injustice.

Prejudice

The argument in this book does not end with a suggestion of how prejudice can be ended; it is not the kind of map of utopia that says 'turn left at hill marked "recognise institutional racism", then march up the valley of "reducing the gender gap", following "gay and lesbian rights" river to find "nirvana" mountain'. What I try to show is how the kinds of prejudices which were previously applied to specific groups, of people said not to be 'one of us', have now become expanded to the much wider populace who are now 'not like us', as 'us' has again shrunk to a small group of winners who excuse their winning as being a mixture of their extra hard work and the inherent failings of others. The poor in particular are now subject to a widespread prejudice whereby, it is nastily and quietly said, they must have something wrong with them if they are not able to work their way out of poverty. In the end the rich have to believe there is something wrong with other people in order for them to believe it is fair to leave so much of their money to their own children rather than do something more useful with it. Historically most people have inherited very little because their parents had very little to leave. To see inheritance as normal we have to behave as only aristocracy once did. To draw maps of the roads to utopia is to foster the belief that a better collective inheritance is possible.

You can love your children and desperately want to spare them hardship, but in aggregate you do not make their world safer if you are rich and leave your money to them as inheritance. Wealth is a measure of inequality, and most wealth in the world is amassed through inheritance and usury, not through work.[35.] This is wealth that has not been earned by those who inherit and almost all of it was not fairly earned by those who give it. That tiny amount which was originally collected through the sweat of the holder's own labour is only a miniscule fraction of the wealth of the world. Most wealth comes from routes such as former plantation holdings that cascaded down to families in the US, or from parents finding their home had increased in value because it was located in London, and London contained the bankers who had found a new way of making money, which for a time indirectly increased house prices there. Relying on wealth indirectly amassing through the guile of bankers is not a safe way to live.

Greed

Most inheritance of great wealth is justified on the basis of prejudice, of rich people believing that their children have a special right to more because it is somehow their 'duty' to be set up to be above others, to pass on the family estate in turn. In this book I argue that it is a myth that the wealthy are the children of those who work hard, take risks, make money and just want to leave it to their family. Not too long ago only a small minority believed this myth about the wealthy. What is new today is how that belief has spread to the middle classes and to many of the poor who (especially in the US) would also repeal inheritance tax laws, not in case they win the lottery, but because they have swallowed the myth that hard work and a little risk-taking makes you wealthy.

Fear has grown as wealth inequalities have grown, resulting in heightened prejudice in deciding who marries whom, how much we collectively care and who now dies youngest in times of plenty. However, often the children of the very rich suffer high mortality rates even in countries we currently see as quite equitable,[36] although if you try to argue today that children would be better off not with inherited money but if society as a whole provided better support for all, there will usually be disbelief. It was easier in the past to argue against inheritance, to have the great houses made accessible to the public and to secure land reform around much of the globe. Unlike in the 1940s, many people in affluent countries today are told that they have riches, that their houses are worth a great deal, or they believe that they will have money gained from some other source to inherit. If you point to other societies that are more equal – in Japan, in most of Western and Northern Europe, even in Canada – and show the outcomes to be better, they may suggest that those societies are more equal due to special historical circumstances that cannot easily be replicated in their more unequal country.[37] They say they cannot replicate the kind of land redistribution that occurred in Japan after the war, or the stronger sense of trust and belonging that exist in most affluent nations; but why not? All that is required to redistribute land is a significant land value tax, and we now know that trust rises in societies that become more equal.

We have to say again and again that there are no beneficial side effects of one man's greed. It does not create worthwhile work for others;[38] it is not efficient; it does not curtail waste; in fact it causes huge amounts to be wasted. Greed also corrupts thinking, as those who take most simultaneously argue that they fund state services the most through those taxes they cannot avoid. Greed must be seen as an injustice before it is even possible to imagine reining it in, as it has been reined in before. A common theme in the saga of human history is the story of constraining greed, learning to store grain, preaching against usury, cooperating. We last did this when we benefited from contracting inequalities in wealth, as occurred between 1929 and 1978 across the rich world. However, this time the circumstances are different.

Whenever greed has been reined in before, there has later been some foreign land, some internal group, some other way in which exploitation and dominance could rise again. This time every last land has already been colonised in one way or another. There is no one left to have their days brought into the paid labour market; there are no more schemes where you whizz money around the world and pretend more exists in transit than at any one location (as was occurring at the point the banking system crashed in 2008). That was only possible when so many were still illiterate and innumerate. It is harder to sell dodgy home loans, which start off cheap but where interest payments rise greatly later, to a better-educated consumer. That is why such loans could only be sold in large numbers in the most unequal of rich countries where, according to Richard Wilkinson and Kate Pickett's 2009 book *The spirit level*, there lived the worst educated and most desperate of consumers, in the US and UK. There should be fewer dupes next time but there need not be a next time – another boom to lead to bust in future. It is precisely to ward off forgetting and being duped again that so many write, and say, and shout, and argue, and cry so much today that another future is possible. That conserving, recycling, sharing counter-culture of our recent past is now presented as a preferable general culture to the return of such greed.

Despair

And lastly, what solution is there to despair? Again, simply recognising that there is a problem is the first step. Count the pills, measure the anxiety, the alcohol consumption, the nervousness, the thoughts in the middle of the night when it doesn't all seem possible. Look at the mental state of children today in rich countries and compare that to the recent past, and then ask yourself if this is the progress you had hoped for. Look at levels of self-harm. You may be lucky yourself, fortunate with your friends or family, your simple life or your high degree of self-confidence. But if you are not, and if despite that you just say 'it isn't that bad', 'get a grip', 'grow a stiff upper lip', if you don't go back to look at what is wrong in your life but just try to tackle the symptoms of those wrongs, to wash away the worries, then there is no solution to despair. There are many facets to despair: anxiety, fear, mistrust, anger, not quite knowing what might happen to you if you do not perform well enough or fit in neatly enough. How secure do you feel?

You either have to have a remarkably tranquil life by modern standards, a close and highly supportive set of friends and family, or a very high level of self-belief not to worry, not to often feel under strain. There are a set of standard questions routinely asked of people to see if they might be suffering from depression in affluent countries.[39] It is an interesting exercise to de-personalise these questions and ask them of those around you.

Are the people where you live, the people who run your country and those not as well off as you, able to concentrate on whatever they are doing? Do they lose much sleep through worry? Do they think they are playing a useful part in things? Are most capable of making decisions about things? Do most feel constantly under strain? Do they often feel that they cannot overcome their difficulties? Are they able to enjoy their normal day-to-day activities? Are they able to face up to their problems? Have they been feeling unhappy and depressed? Are they losing confidence in themselves? Do some see themselves as worthless? Have most been feeling reasonably happy, all things considered? Or not?

As a sign of the times, and certainly a cause for despair, the precise wording of the questionnaire that these questions are derived from is subject to copyright conditions and cannot be reproduced here because a corporation wants to profit from them.[40] Nor am I able to reproduce the scoring system that lets you decide if you are depressed. This, the owning of copyright on a test for depression, is yet another of those facets of modern society that our recent ancestors could not have made up as a sick joke. Future generations may find it hard to understand that we ever tolerated this. Nevertheless, although the scoring system cannot be revealed it is unlikely that, if you knew them well, you would describe the lives of many around you as being particularly happy and fulfilled. It is only because we do not know each other well that we can imagine that most around us do appear happier and (at a superficial glance) many appear fulfilled. It is, after all, often because everyone else around you appears to be having so much fun, especially those who live and smile on the television screen, that you blame yourself for not being as apparently fulfilled as them. But do you admit it to others?

In more unequal affluent countries, when asked a single question about their mental condition, most people say they are doing fine, even great, 'never been better'. In contrast, it is in those more equitable affluent countries where people live the longest, where social conditions are most favourable, that people are most likely to admit to not feeling so great all the time, because they can afford to admit to it.[41] In the most unequal of countries, admitting to yourself that you are down is the beginning of a journey on a slippery slope where you can expect little help other than 'therapy' at a high financial price and where your 'therapist' has no financial incentive for you to quickly recover. The start of the solution to living in places and times of despair is to collectively and publicly admit to despair. The worst thing you and those around you can do is to pretend that all is fine. This just perpetuates injustice.

This book has no great single solution save 'the impossible', to offer a map of part of a route to end the injustices of elitism, exclusion, prejudice, greed and despair as the latest incarnations of rising inequality. No suggestion is made for a global jubilee where, not just between countries but also within them, debt is written off and the rich are helped to agree to end their claims on so much of the lives of so many of the poor. Such events are absolutely impossible, at least until the moment they happen. However, many people worked hard the last time a gilded age ended to reduce social inequalities and to secure more justice, so the 'impossible' has happened before.

3

'Elitism is efficient': new educational divisions

People in poorer parts of the world today may easily be the first in their family to have graduated from a secondary school. At the same time many children still never attend a primary school, let alone persevere through what is considered in rich countries to be a basic education. And university education is rare. In contrast, the affluent world is characterised by long-standing and ever-improving compulsory primary and secondary education for all children, with rates of university access rising almost continuously. Despite this, many young people are not presented as well educated in most affluent nations, but as failing to reach official targets. This chapter brings together evidence which shows how particular groups are increasingly seen as 'not fit' for advanced education, as being limited in their abilities, as requiring less of an education than the supposedly more gifted and talented.

The amassing of riches in affluent countries, the riches which allowed so much to be spent on education, has not resulted in an increased sense of satisfaction in terms of how young people are being taught and are learning. Instead, it has allowed an education system to be created which now expresses ever-increasing anxiety over how pupils perform, in which it has become common to divide up groups of children by so-called ability at younger and younger ages to try to coach them to reach 'appropriate' targets. This has a cumulative effect, with adolescents becoming more anxious as a result. Despite the abandonment of the former grammar school system in Britain, children are still being divided among and within schools. This is also evident in the US, but in Britain it is more covert. Parents have been moving home in order to get their children into their chosen state school, they may pretend to be religious to gain access to faith schools, and slightly more of them were paying for private education by 2007 than had done so before. As more resources are concentrated on a minority the (perceived) capabilities of the majority are implicitly criticised.

In this chapter evidence is brought together to show how myths of inherent difference have been sustained and reinforced by placing a minority on pedestals for others to look up to. Such attitudes vary in degree among affluent nations but accelerated in intensity during the 1950s (to be later temporarily reversed in the 1960s and 1970s). In the 1950s, in countries like Britain, the state enthusiastically sponsored the division of children into types, with the amounts spent per head on grammar school children being much higher than on those at the alternative secondary moderns. Such segregationist policies are still pursued with most determination in the more unequal rich countries. More equitable countries, and the more equitable parts of unequal countries (such as Scotland and Wales in Britain), have pushed back most against this tide of elitism since it rose so high in the 1950s.

Elitism in education can be considered a new injustice because, until very recently, too few children even in affluent countries were educated for any length of time. All are now at risk of being labelled as 'inadequate' despite the fact that the resources are there to teach them, of being told that they are simply not up to learning what the world now demands of them. Those who are elevated also suffer.

All will fail at some hurdle in an education system where examination has become so dominant. To give an example I am very familiar with, in universities, professors, using elitist rhetoric, try to tell others that the world is complicated and only they are able to understand or make sense of it; they will let you see a glimpse, they say, if you listen, but you cannot expect to understand; it takes years of immersion in academia, they claim; complex words and notions are essential, and they see understandable accounts as 'one-dimensional'.[1]

Occasionally there is no alternative to a complex account of how part of the world appears to work, but often a complex account is simply a muddled account. Professors often say that an aspect of the world is too complex for them to describe clearly because they themselves cannot describe it in a clear way, not because it cannot be described clearly. Suggesting such widespread complexity justifies the existence of academia because elitism forces those it puts on pedestals to pretend

—

to greatness, but if you talk to academics it thankfully becomes clear that most are, to some extent, aware of this pretence. They are aware, like the Wizard of Oz, of how humdrum they really are.

People are remarkably equal in ability. However, if you spend some time looking you can find a few people, especially in politics, celebrity (now a field of work) or business, who appear to truly believe they are especially gifted, that they are a gift to others who should be grateful for their talents and who should reward them appropriately. These people are just as much victims of elitism as those who are told they are, in effect, congenitally stupid, fit for little but taking orders and performing menial toil despite having been required to spend over a decade in school. Under elitism education is less about learning and more about dividing people, sorting out the supposed wheat from the chaff and conferring high status upon a minority.

The old evil of ignorance harmed poorer people in particular because they could not read and write and were thus easily controlled, finding it harder to organise and to understand what was going on (especially before radio broadcasts). What differentiates most clearly the new social injustice of elitism from the old evil of ignorance is that elitism damages people from the very top to the very bottom of society, rather than just being an affliction of the poor. Those at the top suffer because the less affluent and the poor have their abilities denounced to such an extent that fewer people end up becoming qualified in ways that would also improve the lives of the rich. For example, if more people were taught well enough to become medical researchers then conditions that the rich may die of could be made less painful, or perhaps even cured, prolonging their lives. If more are taught badly at school, because it is labourers and servants that the rich think they lack, then cures for illnesses may not be discovered as quickly.

The British education system has been described as 'learning to labour' for good reason. But it is, however, the poorest who are still most clearly damaged by elitism, by the shame that comes with being told that their ability borders on illiteracy, that there is something wrong with them because of who they are, that they are poor because they have inadequate ability to be anything else.

—

3.1 The 'new delinquents': those most harmed by elitism, a seventh of all children

Although nobody officially labels a seventh of children as 'delinquent', they might just as well because that is the stigmatising effect of the modern labels that are applied to children seen as the 'least able'. A century ago delinquency was an obsession and thought to lead to criminality; education was the proffered antidote. However, it was not lack of education that caused criminality in the young, at least not a lack of the mind-numbing rote-and-rule learning that so commonly used to be offered as education; it was most often necessity. Today it is money for drugs rather than food, as the nature of the need has changed, but old labels such as 'delinquent' are retained in the popular press, and a new form of what can still best be described as 'delinquency' has arisen.

Increased educational provision that has been increasingly unequally distributed has led to the rise of this new elitism. Where once there had been the castle on the hill and the poor at the gates, the castle grounds were then subdivided into sections, places up and down the hill, neatly ordered by some supposed merit. And today an even neater ordering of people has been achieved – to demarcate social position and occupation all now have numbers and scores, exam passes, credit ratings, postcodes and loyalty cards, rather than simply titles and surnames.

Scoring all individuals in affluent societies is a very recent affair. Giving all children numbers and grades throughout their schooling and yet more grades afterwards (at university or college) was simply not affordable before the Second World War in even the most affluent of countries. It was a luxury confined to the old grammar schools and universities. At that time, most children would simply be given a certificate when they left school to say that they had attended. This system changed when compulsory secondary education for all swept the affluent world following the war, although with the belief that all could be educated came the caveat that most of those who believed this did not see all the children that they were about to allow through to secondary school as equal in potential ability.

—

Ranking children according to 'ability'

Some of the best evidence of policy makers seeing different groups of children as so very different comes from the work of educational economists. Half a century ago the rich countries created a club, the OECD, effectively a rich country club which is now dominated by economists. It was partly the rise in power of economists belonging to clubs like the OECD which resulted in elitism growing, and through which the beliefs of elitism were spread. That club published the figures used to draw Figure 1 (below), figures that suggest that one in seven children growing up in one particular rich country today (the Netherlands) have either no or very limited knowledge.[2]

We used to see the fate of children as being governed by chance, with perhaps even the day of their birth influencing their future life. Rewriting the old rhyme, the OECD would say of children today (in the Netherlands) that they can be divided into seven differently sized groups by their supposed talents and future prospects:

> **The educational ode of the OECD***
> *Monday's child has limited knowledge,*
> *Tuesday's child won't go to college,*
> *Wednesday's child is a simple soul,*
> *Thursday's child has far to go,*
> *Friday's child can reflect on her actions,*
> *Saturday's child integrates explanations,*
> *But the child that is born on the Sabbath day*
> *Has critical insight and so gets the most say.*

The OECD economists and writers do not put it as crudely as this, however. It is through their publications (from which come the labels that follow)[3] that they say in effect that there is now a place where a seventh of children are labelled as failures by the time they reach their 15th birthday.

* *by author (aged 41½)*

—

37

Using OECD data, if we divide children into seven unequally sized groups by the days of the week and start with those most lowly ordered, then the first group are Monday's children (from Figure 3.1, 11%+2%=13%). They are those who have been tested and found to have, at most, only 'very limited knowledge'. Tuesday's children (21%) are deemed to have acquired only 'barely adequate knowledge' to get by in life. Wednesday's and Thursday's children (27%) are labelled as being just up to coping with 'simple concepts'. Friday's and Saturday's children (26%) are assessed as having what is called 'effective knowledge', enough to be able to reflect on their actions using scientific evidence, perhaps even to bring some of that evidence together, to integrate it. The remaining children (11%+2%=13%), one in every seven again, are found by the testers to be able to do more than that, to be able to use well-'developed inquiry abilities', to link knowledge appropriately and to bring 'critical insights' to situations. But although these children may appear to be thinking along the lines that those setting the tests think is appropriate, even they are not all destined for greatness. According to the testers they will usually not become truly 'advanced thinkers'. It is just one in seven of the Sabbath children (100%÷7÷7=2%) who is found to be truly special. Only this child, the seventh born of the seventh born, will (it is decreed) clearly and consistently demonstrate 'advanced scientific thinking and reasoning', will be able to demonstrate a willingness to use scientific understanding 'in support of recommendations and decisions that centre on personal, socio-economic, or global situations'.[4] This child and the few like them, it is implied, are destined to be our future leaders.

Figure 1 shows the proportions of children in the Netherlands assigned to each ability label from 'none' clockwise round to 'advanced'. The Netherlands is a place you might not have realised had brought up over 60% of its children to have only a simple, barely adequate, limited education, or even no effective education at all (according to OECD statistics).

Figure 1: Children by ability in the Netherlands, according to the OECD, 2006 (%)

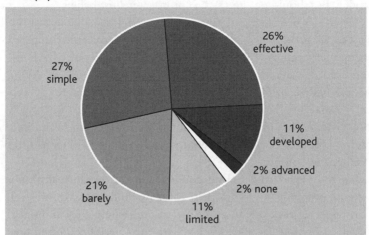

Notes: 'None' implies possessing no knowledge as far as can be measured. 'Limited' implies possessing very limited knowledge. 'Barely' stands for barely possessing adequate knowledge in the minds of the assessors. 'Simple' means understanding only simple concepts. 'Effective' is a little less damning. 'Developed' is better again; but only 'advanced' pupils are found to be capable, it is said, of the kind of thinking that might include 'critical insight'.

Source: OECD (2007) *The Programme for International Student Assessment (PISA), OECD's latest PISA study of learning skills among 15-year-olds,* Paris: OECD, derived from figures in table 1, p 20

Fixing the results to a bell curve

The OECD, an organisation of economists (note not teachers), now tells countries how well or badly educated their children are. And it is according to these economists that the Netherlands is the country which best approximates to the 1:1:2:2:1 distribution of children having what is called limited, barely adequate, simple, effective and developed knowledge, by having reached the OECD's international testing levels 1, 2, 3, 4 and 5 respectively. This is not how children in the Netherlands actually are, nor how they appear to any group but the OECD; it is not how the majority of their parents think of them; it is not even how their teachers, school inspectors or government rank them; but it is how the children of the Netherlands, and all other children in the richer countries of the world, have slowly come to be seen by those who carry out these large-scale official international comparisons. Large-scale international comparisons can be great studies, but should not be used to propagate elitist beliefs.

Given this damning description of their children it may surprise you to learn that the Netherlands fare particularly well compared with other countries. Only half a dozen countries out of over 50 surveyed did significantly better when last compared (in 2006). More children in the UK were awarded the more damning levels of 1, 2 and 3 – 'limited', 'barely adequate' and 'simple'. In the US both Monday's and Tuesday's children were found to be limited, and only half of Sunday's children were 'developed' – just half the Netherlands' proportion.

Do the best of the richest countries in the world really only educate just under a seventh (13%) of their children to a good level, and just a seventh of those (2%) to a level where they show real promise? Are just 2% of children able, as the OECD definition puts it, to 'use scientific knowledge and develop arguments in support of recommendations and decisions that centre on personal, socio-economic, or global situations'? In Finland and New Zealand this 'genius strand' is apparently 4%, in the UK and Australia 3%, in Germany and the Netherlands 2%, in the US and Sweden 1%, and in Portugal and Italy it is nearer to 0%. These are children who, according to the educational economists, show real promise. They are the children who have been trained in techniques so as to be able to answer exam questions in the ways the examiners who operate under what are called 'orthodox economic beliefs' would most like them to be answered. The proportions are so low because the international tests are set so that the results are distributed around a 'bell curve'. This is a bell curve with smoothly tapering tails, cut off (internationally and intentionally) so that 1.3% are labelled genii and 5.2% as know-nothings (see Figure 2 on page 47 below).

Engineering competition in place of cooperation

Economists use the results of their international comparative exercises for the purpose of making claims, such as '... having a larger number of schools that compete for students was associated with better results'.[4] Many of the people who work for organisations such as the

OECD feel they have a duty to suggest that competition between countries, schools and pupils is good, and to encourage it as much as they can.

According to this way of thinking, science education, which is usually extended to include technology, engineering, maths and (quietly) economics,[5] is the most important education of all. Supporting such science education, its promotion and grading in these ways, is seen as working in support of recommendations and decisions that centre on best improving personal, socioeconomic and global situations to engineer the best of all possible worlds. This imagined world is a utopia with all benefiting from increased competition, from being labelled by their apparent competencies. This is a world where it is imagined that the good of the many is most enhanced by promoting the ability of the few.

Although the OECD tables, and almost all other similar performance tables, are presented explicitly as being helpful to those towards the bottom of their leagues, as being produced to help pull up those at the bottom, this is rarely what they achieve. Educational gaps have not narrowed in most places where such tables have been drawn up. This is partly because they suggest how little hope most have of ever being really competent; 'leave competency to the top 2%' is the implicit message, for, unless you are in the top seventh, you cannot hope to have a chance of succeeding, where success means to lead. Even when standards improve and most level 1 children are replaced by level 2, level 2 by 3, and so on, the knowledge which is judged to matter will also have changed and become ever more complex. If we accept this thinking, the bell curves will be forever with us.

This bell curve thinking (Figure 2, page 47) suggests that right across the rich world children are distributed by skill in such a way that there is a tiny tail of truly gifted young people, and a bulk of know-nothings, or limited, or barely able or just simple young people. It is no great jump from this to thinking that, given the narrative of a shortage of truly gifted children, then as young working adults those children will be able to name their price and will respond well to high financial reward. In contrast, the less able are so numerous they will need to be cajoled to work. These masses of children, the large majority, will not be up to doing any interesting work, and to

—

get people to do uninteresting work requires the threat of suffering. This argument quickly turns then to suggest that they will respond best to financial rewards sufficiently low as to force them to labour. It is best to keep them occupied through hours of drudgery, it has been argued, admittedly more vocally in the past than now.

But what of those in between, of Friday's and Saturday's children, with effective but not well-developed knowledge – what is to be done with them? Offer them a little more, an average wage for work, a wage that is not so demeaning, and then expect them to stand between the rest of weekday children and those of the Sabbath, a place half way up the hill. Give them enough money for a rest now and again, one big holiday a year, money to run a couple of cars, enough to be able to struggle to help their children get a mortgage (the middle-class aspiration to be allowed to have a great debt).

Nature or nurture, or neither?

But surely (you might think) there are some groups of children who are simply born less able than others, or made so by the way they have been brought up in their earlier years? Most commonly these are infants starved of oxygen in the womb or during birth, denied basic nutrients during infancy. Such privations occur early on in the lives of many of the world's poorest children. But this physical damage, mostly preventable and due in most cases to absolute poverty, now rarely occurs in North America, affluent East Asia or Western Europe. When serious neglect does occur the results are so obvious in the outcomes for the children that they clearly stand out. The only recent European group of children treated systematically in this way were babies given almost no human contact, semi-starved and confined to their cots in Romanian orphanages. They have been found to have had their fate damaged irreparably. Medical scanning discovered that a part of their brain did not fully develop during the first few years of their lives, and their story is now often told as potential evidence of how vital human nurturing is to development.[6]

Two generations earlier than the Romanian orphanages, from Germany and Austria, come some of the most telling stories of the effects that different kinds of nurturing can have on later behaviour.

There are worse things you can do to children than neglect them. It is worth remembering the wartime carnage that resulted in the creation of the institutions for international solidarity. We easily now forget where the idea that there should be economic cooperation in place of competition came from. The most studied single small groups of individuals were those who came to run Germany from the mid-1930s through to the end of the Second World War. To understand why the word 'co-operation' remains in the title of the OECD, it is worth looking back at the Nazis (and their elitist and eugenicist beliefs) when we consider what we have created in the long period of reconstruction after that carnage.

The childhood upbringings of the men who later became leading members of the Nazi party have been reconstructed and studied as carefully as possible. Those studies found that as children these men were usually brought up with much discipline, very strictly and often with cruelty. They were not born Nazis – the national social environment and their home environment both had to be particularly warped to make them so. Warped in the other direction, it has been found, were the typical home environments of those equally rare German and Austrian children who grew up at the same time and in the same places but went on to rescue Jewish people from the Nazi regime. Their national social environment was identical. Their home environment also tended to revolve around high standards, but standards about caring for others; the home was rarely strict and as far as we know, never cruel. It was '… virtually the exact opposite of the upbringing of the leading Nazis'.[7] Further studies have found that many of the rescuers discovered that they had no choice but to help, it having been instilled in them from an early age. 'They would not be able to go on living if they failed to defend the lives of others.'[8]

Across Europe in the 1940s there were too few rescuers, and most Jews targeted for persecution were killed. The fact that people in mainland Europe[9] were largely complicit in the killing, and are still reluctant to accept this truth, is claimed as part of the reason for current silences about 'race'; it remains '… an embarrassment'.[10] However, out of that war came a desire to cooperate better internationally.

A particular kind of knowledge

The OECD, later so widely criticised as a rich country club, was not set up to preserve privilege, reinforce stereotypes and encourage hierarchy. Originally called the Organisation for European Economic Co-operation (OEEC), it was established to administer US and Canadian aid to war-ravaged Europe. That thinking changed in the 1950s, and it was renamed the Organisation for Economic Co-operation and Development (OECD) in 1961. Its remit gradually gravitated towards concentrating on what was called improving efficiency, honing market systems, expanding free trade and encouraging competition (much more than cooperation). By 2008 the OECD was being described in at least one textbook as a '... crude, lumbering think-tank of the most wealthy nations, bulldozing over human dignity without pause for thought. Its tracks, crushed into the barren dereliction left behind, spell "global free market"'.[11] The organisation describes its future a little differently, as '... looking ahead to a post-industrial age in which it aims to tightly weave OECD economies into a yet more prosperous and increasingly knowledge-based world economy'.[12]

The knowledge base that the OECD refers to is a particular kind of knowledge that comes from a particular way of valuing people, of seeing the world, a way that came to dominate the thinking of those appointed to high office in the rich world by the start of the 21st century. From the late 1970s onwards, if you did *not* think in this particular way you would be quite unlikely to be appointed to work for bodies such as the OECD, or to rise high within any government in an unequal affluent nation, even less likely to do well in business. This way of thinking sees money as bringing dignity, sees children as being of greatly varying abilities and sees its own educational testers as knowing all the correct answers to its battery of questions, which include questions for which there is clearly no international agreement over the correct answers.[13] It is not hard to devise a set of questions and a marking scheme that results in those you test appearing to be distributed along a bell curve. But to do this, you have to construct the world as being like this in your mind. It is not revealed as such by observation.

—

Constructing and measuring intelligence

What observation reveals is that ever since we have been trying to measure 'intelligence' we have found it has been rising dramatically.[14] This is true across almost all countries in which we have tried to measure it.[15] This means that the average child in 1900 measured by today's standards would appear to be an imbecile, 'mentally retarded' (the term used in the past), a 'virtual automaton'.[16] When we measure our intelligence in this way it appears so much greater than our parents' that you would think they would have marvelled at how clever their children were (but they didn't).[17] What this actually means is that in affluent countries over the course of the last century we have become better educated in the kind of scientific thinking which scores highly in intelligence tests. More of us have been brought up in small households and therefore given more attention. We have been better fed and clothed. Parenting did improve in general, but we were also expected to compete more and perform better at those particular tasks measured by intelligence tests.

If our grandparents had been the 'imbeciles' their test results would (by today's standards) now suggest, they would not have been able to cooperate to survive. Although today's young people have been trained to think in abstract ways and to solve theoretical problems on the spot (it would be surprising if they could not, given how many now go on to university), there are other things they cannot do which their grandparents could. Their grandparents could get by easily without air conditioning and central heating, and many grew their own food, while their grandchildren often do not know how to mend things and do more practical work. Our grandparents might not have had as much 'critical acumen' on average, but they were not exposed to the kind of mental pollution that dulls acumen such as television advertising, with all the misleading messages it imparts. Observation tells us that intelligence merely reflects environment and is only one small part of what it means to be clever. Despite this, 'critical acumen', the one small highly malleable part of thinking that has become so much more common over the course of recent generations, has mistakenly come to be seen both as all important and as unequally distributed within just one generation.

—

3.2 IQism: the underlying rationale for the growth of elitism

A new way of thinking, a theory, was needed to describe a world in which just a few would be destined to have minds capable of leading the rest and in which all could be ordered along a scale of ability. That new way of thinking has come to be called 'IQism'. This is a belief in the validity of the intelligence quotient (IQ), and in the related testing of children resulting in their being described as having ability strung along a series of remarkably similar-looking bell curves, as shown in Figure 2. The merits of thinking of intelligence as having a quotient came out of wartime thinking and were pushed forward fastest in the 1950s when many young children and teenagers were put through intelligence tests. In Britain almost all 11-year-olds were subjected to testing (the '11 plus'), which included similar 'intelligence' tests, to determine which kind of secondary school they would be sent to. Although such sorting of children is no longer so blatantly undertaken, the beliefs that led to this discrimination against the majority are now the mainstream beliefs of those who currently make recommendations over how affluent economies are run. And, just as we no longer divide children so crudely by subjecting them to just one test, the educational economists are now careful not to draw graphs of the figures they publish – this would present a miserable picture of the futures of those for whom the bell curves toll. There are no histograms of these results in the OECD report in which the data used here are presented.

If children had a particular upper limit to their intellectual abilities, an IQ, and that limit was distributed along a bell curve, then it would be fair to ascribe each to a particular level, to suggest that perhaps in some countries children were not quite performing at the levels they could be. But is it really true that in no country do more than 4% of children show signs of being truly able?[18]

Graphs that arouse suspicion

Almost identical curves could be drawn for different countries if human ability were greatly limited, such as those curves shown in Figure 2. This figure is drawn from the key findings of the 2007

—

46

Figure 2: Distribution of children by ability, according to the OECD, 2006 (%)

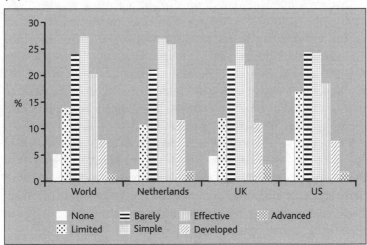

Source: Data given in OECD (2007) *The Programme for International Student Assessment (PISA), OECD's latest PISA study of learning skills among 15-year-olds*, Paris: OECD, derived from figures in table 1, p 20

OECD report, which includes six graphs. None of those graphs show a single bell curve. Figure 2 reveals how the OECD economists think ability is distributed among its member countries, and in three particular places. It is possible that the OECD economists were themselves reluctant to draw the graph because they knew it would rightly arouse suspicion. However, it is far from easy to guess at motive. What it is possible, if extremely tedious, to do is to read the technical manual and find hidden, after 144 pages of equations and procedures, the fact that those releasing this data, when calibrating the results (adjusting the scores before release), '... assumed that students have been sampled from a multivariate normal distribution'.[19] Given this assumption, almost no matter how the students had 'performed', the curves in Figure 2 would have been bell shaped. The data were made to fit the curve.

There is very little room under a bell curve to be at the top. Bell-curved distributions suggest that, at best, if most were destined to have their abilities lifted the vast majority (even if improved) would remain 'limited', or barely 'adequate', or just able to understand 'simple things'. The implication of ability being strung out like this is that even following educational gain, the many would always have to be governed by the few, the elite, 'the advanced'. If this testing is producing scores with any kind of validity concerning underlying ability, then only a very few children will ever grow up to understand what is going on. If this is not the case, if there is not just a tiny minority of truly able children, then to describe children in this way, and to offer prescriptions given such a description (and the subsequent outcomes), is deeply unjust.

Those people who believe in IQ have been thinking and writing about it for less than a century. It is not an old idea. The concept was first proposed in 1912 with the German name *Intelligenz-Quotient*, derived from testing that occurred just a few years earlier in 1905 in France, but testing that did not, initially, assume a limit. The concept of assuming a limit to children's intellectual potential was subsequently developed by those with a taste for testing. The assumption was that intellectual ability was limited physically, like height. Different children would grow to different heights, which tended to be related to their parents' heights, but also to the wider social environment which influenced their nutrition, their exercise and their well-being.

The idea that intellectual ability is distributed like height was proposed within just a few years of the bell curve itself first being described mathematically. It is now easy to see how it could have been imagined, why the idea of IQ and the concept of its hereditability came to flourish. Most people who were told of the idea were also told that their IQ was high. People who propagated the idea thought that their IQs were even higher. People enjoy flattery – it makes us feel safe and valued. But, tragically, in the round, the concept of IQ made no individuals actually safer or more valued for who they really were. Great evils of genocide were carried out under IQism (and related beliefs). But as those evils become memories, as the stories of early elitism are forgotten, as the old-fashioned social evil of illiteracy is largely overcome in affluent nations, IQism is growing again as an ideological source for injustice.

Those recognised as making progress in the study of education suggest that thinking is as much like height as singing is like weight. You can think on your own, but you are best learning to think with others. Education does not unfold from within but is almost all '... induction from without'.[20] There are no real 'know-nothings'; they could not function. Children are not limited, or barely able, or simple. We are all occasionally stupid, especially when we have not had enough sleep, or feel anxious and 'don't think'.

If you use singing as a metaphor for education, we are similarly all capable of singing or not singing, singing better or worse. What is seen as good singing is remarkably culturally specific, varying greatly by time and place. Work hard at your singing in a particular time and place, and people will say you sing well if you sing as you are supposed to. It is possible to rank singing, to grade it and to believe that some singing is truly awful and other singing exquisite, but the truth of that is as much in the culture and ears of the listener as it is in the vocal cords of the performer. Someone has almost certainly been silly enough to propose that human beings have singing limits which are distributed along a bell-shaped curve.[21] After all is said, despite the fact that we are all capable of being stupid, the bell-curve-of-singing idea did not catch on. We are not as vain about how good we are at yodelling in the shower as we are about being told we are especially clever. We can all sing, we can all be stupid, we can all be clever, we can learn without limits.

Learning without limits

It is only recently that it has been possible to make the claim that almost all children in rich countries are capable of learning without limits. The same was not true of many of their parents and of even fewer of their grandparents. And the same is not true of almost a tenth of children worldwide, some 200 million five-year-olds. These children are the real 'failures', failing to develop all their basic cognitive functions due to iodine or iron deficiency, or malnutrition in general leading to stunting of the brain as well as the body, and/ or having received inadequate stimulation from others when very young.[22] Children need to be well fed and cared for both to learn to think well and to be physically able enough to think well, just as they do to be able to sing well. But well fed and loved, there is no subsequent physical limiting factor other than what is around them. If you grow up in a community where people do not sing, it is unlikely that you will sing. If you grow up where singing is the norm, you are likely to partake.

Much of what we do now our recent ancestors never did. They did not drive cars, work on computers; few practised the violin, and hardly any played football, so why do we talk of a violinist or a footballer having innate talent? Human beings did not slowly evolve in a world where those whose keyboard skills were not quite up to scratch were a little less successful at mating than the more nimble fingered. We learn all these things; we were not born to them, but we are born elastic enough to learn. How we subsequently perform in tests almost entirely reflects the environment we grew up in, not differences in the structures of our brains.[23] However, there remains a widespread misconception that ability, and especially particular abilities, are innate, that they unfold from within, and are distributed very unevenly, with just a few being truly talented, having been given a gift and having the potential to unfold that gift within them, hence the term 'gifted'.

The misconception of the existence of the gifted grew out of beliefs that talents were bestowed by the gods, who each originally had their own special gifts, of speed, art or drinking (in the case of Dionysus). This misconception was useful for explaining away the odd serf who could not be suppressed in ancient times or the few poor boys who rose in rank a century ago. But then that skewed distribution of envisaged talent was reshaped as bell curved. The results of IQ tests were made into a bell-curved graph by design, but people were told (what turned out to be) the lie that the curve somehow emerged naturally.[24] Apply an IQ test to a population for which that test was not designed specifically, and most people will either do very badly or very well at that test, rather than perform in a way that produces a 'bell curve' distribution. Tests have to be designed and calibrated to result in such an outcome. The bell curve as a general description of the population became popular as more were required to rise in subsequent decades to fill social functions that had not existed in such abundance before: engine operator, teacher, tester. Today educators are arguing to change the shape of the perceived curve of ability again, to have the vast majority of results skewed to the right, put in the region marked 'success', as all begin to appear so equally able. The conclusions of those currently arguing against the idea of there being especially gifted children make clear how '… categorizing some children as innately talented is discriminatory … unfair … wasteful … [and] unjustified…'.[25] It contributes to the injustice whereby social inequality persists.

The gifted, the talented and the ugly

Although we are now almost all fed well enough not to have our cognitive capabilities limited physically through the effects of malnutrition on the brain, and more and more children are better nurtured and cared for as infants in affluent countries, and although we are now rich enough to afford for almost all to be allowed to learn in ways our parents and grandparents were mostly not allowed, we hold back from giving all children that encouragement and, instead, tell most from a very early age that they are not up to the level of 'the best in the class', and never can be. We do this in numerous ways, including where we make children sit at school, usually on a table sorted by ability if primary school teachers are following Ofsted guidance. Within our families all our children are special, but outside the family cocoon they are quickly ranked, told that to sing they need to enter talent shows that only a tiny proportion can win, told that to learn they need to work harder than the rest and, more importantly, that they need to be 'gifted' if they are to do very well.

It is now commonly said that children need to be 'gifted', to become Sunday's well-developed 'level 5' child. They need to be 'especially gifted' to be that seventh of a seventh who reach 'level 6', and it is harder still to win a rung on the places stacked above that scale. Most are told that even if they work hard they can at best only expect to rise one level or two, to hope to be simple rather than know-nothings, or to have effective knowledge, to be a useful cog in a machine, rather than just being a 'simpleton' (if you do particularly well). Aspiring to more than one grade above your lot in life is seen as fanciful. Arguing that there is not a mass of largely limited children out there is portrayed as misguided fancy by the elitists. Most say this quietly, but I have collected some of their musings here, and I give many examples later in this book to demonstrate this; occasionally a few actually say what they think in public: "'Middle-class children have better genes", says former schools chief, "... and we just have to accept it"'.[26] Such public outbursts are not the isolated musings of a few discredited former schools' inspectors or other mavericks. Instead they reveal what is generally believed by the kinds of people who run governments that appoint such people to be schools' inspectors. It is just that elitist politicians tend to have more sense than to tell their electorate that they believe most of them to be so limited in ability.

You might think that what the OECD educationalists are doing is trying to move societies from extreme inequality in education, through a bell curve of current outcome, to a world of much greater equality. However, the envisaged distribution of ability is not progressively changing shape from left-skewed, to bell-shaped, to right-skewed uniformly across the affluent world. In countries such as the Netherlands, Finland, Japan and Canada people choose to teach more children what they need to know to reach higher levels. In those countries it is less common to present a story of children having innate differences. In other countries, such as the UK, Portugal, Mexico and the US, more are allowed to learn very little, and children are more often talked about as coming from 'different stock'.[27] The position of each country on the scale of how elitist their education systems are has also varied over time.

How different groups are treated differently within countries at different times can be monitored by looking at changes in IQ test results. This evidence shows that these tests measure how well children have been taught in order to pass tests. So the generation you are born into matters in determining IQ. Intelligence tests have nothing to do with anything innate. Take two identical twins separated at birth and you will find that their physical similarities alone are enough for them to be similarly treated in their schools, given in effect similar environments to each other, in a way that accounts for almost all later similarities in how they perform in IQ tests. If both are tall and good-looking, for instance, they are more likely to become more confident, receive a little more attention from their teachers, a little more praise at their performance from their adoptive parents, a little more tolerance from their peers; they will tend to do better at school. These effects have been shown to be enough by themselves to account for the findings in studies of identical twins who have been separated at birth, but usually brought up in the same country, and who follow such similar trajectories. The trajectories also tend to be so similar because, of course, the twins are brought up over exactly the same time span.[28]

Many rivers to cross

In the US the 'IQ' gap between black and white Americans fell from the 1940s to the 1970s, but rose subsequently back to the 1940s levels of inequality by the start of the 21st century. This move away from elitism and then back occurred in tandem with how the social position and relative deprivation of black versus white Americans changed.[29] From the 1940s to the 1970s black Americans won progressively higher status, won the right to be integrated more into what had become normal economic expectations; wages equalised a little. Then, from the 1970s onwards, the wage gap grew; segregation increased again; civil rights victories were transformed into mass incarceration of young black men. No other country locks up as many of its own people as the US. In 1940 *10 times* fewer were locked up in jail in the US as now, and 70% of the two million now imprisoned are black.[30] This huge rise in imprisonment in the US, and its acceptance as normal because of who is now most often imprisoned, is perhaps the starkest outcome of the growth of elitism in any single rich country.

Treating a few people as especially able inevitably entails treating others as especially unable. If you treat people like dirt you can watch them become more stupid before your eyes, or at least through their answers to your multiple choice questions in public examinations. From the 1970s onwards poor Americans, and especially poor black Americans, were progressively treated more and more like dirt. Literally just a few were allowed to sing.[31] To a lesser extent similar trends occurred in many other parts of the affluent world, in all those rich countries in which income inequalities grew. And they grew most where IQism became most accepted.

IQism can be a self-fulfilling prophecy. If you believe that only a few children are especially able, then you concentrate your resources on those children and subsequently they will tend to appear to do well. They will certainly pass your tests, as the tests are designed for a certain number to pass, and the children you selected will have been chosen and then taught to pass such tests. Young people respond well to praise to learn, and get smarter when they learn as a result. They respond badly to disrespect, which reduces their motivation to learn, so they perform badly in tests. People, and especially children, crave recognition and respect. Telling children they rank low in a class is a way of telling them that they have not earned respect. Children are not particularly discerning about what they are taught. They will try to do well at IQ tests if you train them to try to do well at IQ tests. However, almost everyone wants to fit in, to be praised, not to rank towards the bottom, not to be seen as a liability, as those at the bottom are seen.

There is a river in New Zealand called the Rakaia that is spanned by a suspension bridge of novel design. (A photograph of it is included on page ii.) There is a notice by the bridge that tells its history and that of the ford that existed before the bridge. The river is wide and fierce, draining water from the Southern Alps. The notice says that before the bridge was built, the Maori would cross the river in groups, each group holding a long pole placed horizontally on the surface of the water so that the weakest would not be swept off their feet. The notice was written by the people who came after the Maori, who knew how to build a bridge of iron supported from beneath, but who did not understand why a group of people would cross a river with a pole. It was in fact not to protect the weakest, but to protect the entire group. Any individual trying to ford a fast-flowing river draining glacial waters runs a great risk. If you hold onto a long horizontal pole with others, you are at much lower risk. The concept of 'from each according to his abilities, to each according to his needs' was a concept that took shape in places and times when it was better understood that all benefited as a result. When crossing a freezing river with a pole, you need as many others holding onto that pole with you as can fit.

—

All children are different. They grow up to be adults with differing idiosyncrasies, traits (often mistaken as talents or natural endowments) both peculiar to them and peculiar to the types of societies they are raised in. Some will turn out to be considered great singers, others to sing well in choirs, if brought up where it is normal to sing. Some of these idiosyncrasies are related to physical features – taller people may have held on better to that pole, for example. Because of what was allowed at the time, and not any genetic trait, it will almost certainly have been a man, but it will not necessarily have been an especially tall man, who grew up to think of suspending a bridge across the Rakaia. Almost every adult who thinks of building a suspension bridge was a child who had seen it done before, and almost none of the children who have never seen a bridge made that way will work out how to do so without prompting by someone who has. No one had the 'unique' idea in the first place. Or, to put it another way, every slight change that was made, from the earliest tree-trunk bridge to the latest design, was 'unique', as are all our thoughts. We are, none of us, superhuman. We are not like the gods with their gifts. We can all be stupid. We hold onto the pole to cross the river having faith in the strength of others. This is a much safer way to proceed than having a few carried by others who are not joined together. If, in the short term, you value being dry above solidarity or if you are led to believe that you are destined to carry others who are your superiors, then all are at greater risk of drowning.

3.3 Apartheid schooling: from garaging to hot housing

Before we had suspension bridges many people drowned crossing rivers. And many also died in the process of building the bridges. Suspension bridges were first built using huge amounts of manual labour to dig out the ironstone needed, and the coal to forge the iron, to construct the girders and rivet everything in place. Almost everything was originally made by hand, and even the job of constructing each rivet, as in Adam Smith's idealised pin factory, was initially done by dividing the process into as many small processes as possible and then giving responsibility for a particular part of the work, the flattening of the head of the rivet, say, to a particular man, woman or child labourer.

When pin factories were first created they initially mostly employed adult men – it did not take much schooling to teach a man how to squash a hot rivet in a vice so that its head was flattened. It took even less schooling to teach the woman who fed him at night how to cook the extremely limited rations available to those who first worked in factories. But it took a little more schooling to teach the foreman in charge of the factory how to fill in ledgers to process orders. It took even more schooling to train the engineer who decided just how many rivets were needed to make the bridge safe. If you look at the bridge currently spanning the gorge of the Rakaia River you will see that whoever made that decision erred on the side of caution – there tend to be a lot of rivets in old bridges. A lot of rivets meant a lot of rivet makers. If reasonably fed, then rivet makers and their wives made many children, little future rivet makers, almost none of whom, living in the towns where rivets were made, grew their own food, and so there were a great many new hungry mouths to feed and not enough time or people to spare to teach most of the little ones, who, after all, were destined to make yet more rivets for yet more bridges. But incrementally a surplus of wealth was amassed and a small part of that surplus was used to build schools, especially in the countries to where most of the surplus came, such as Britain.

A good age for education

Slowly a little more time was found, won and forged out of lives of great drudgery. Women gained a little power, managed to say 'no' a little more, and have six children each rather than eight. By 1850 in a country like Britain, most children attended some kind of school, often just Sunday school. By the 1870s it became law that all children should attend school until the age of 10; that age was ratcheted up steadily until the 1970s, after which there was a hiatus. By the 1970s women in Britain were having on average two children with the help both of the pill and of not insignificant liberation (just a century earlier people had been imprisoned for teaching about condoms). Educational equality rose, ignorance was slowly abated, and (as fertility fell) there were fewer children to teach and it was increasingly felt that there was more to teach to all of them. But that trend of increased equality came to an end in the 1970s as 1950s elitism began to outweigh earlier progress. The latter half of Figure 3 shows, as far as university entry is concerned, a curtailing of hope and opportunity as the belief that we did not all inherently have the same potential gained sustenance from arguments over IQ and aspects of intellectual 'potential'. Mostly recently, however, as the very final years in the figure show, those elitist arguments have been partly lost concerning school-leaving age in at least one unequal rich country – all will now be in education until the age of 18 in Britain, although whether all, if not in the 'top streams', will be thought educable till then and treated with respect in schools is a battle still being fought.

Increased elitism might tolerate raising the school-leaving age to 18, but it is not commensurate with providing more education for all after that. In contrast to the recent acceleration in school-leaving age, the

Figure 3: School-leaving age (years) and university entry (%), Britain, 1876-2013

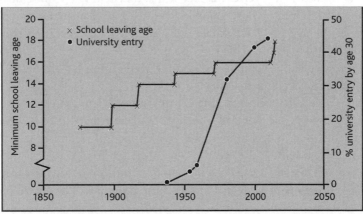

Sources: BBC (2007) 'School leaving age set to be 18', report, 12 January; Meikle, J. (2007) 'Education dropouts at 16 will face sanctions', *The Guardian*, 23 March; Timmins, N. (2001) *The five giants: A biography of the welfare state* (new edn), London: HarperCollins, pp 2, 73, 198 and 200); and for latest official estimates, see Higher Education Funding Council for England website on widening participation of local areas: www.hefce.ac.uk/Widen/polar/

rapid rise in university entry that peaked around the late 1960s is now decelerating, and decelerated most quickly in the most recent decade, as Figure 3 makes clear. Any further increases in school-leaving age would require compulsory university attendance, as tertiary education would be provided for all, just as secondary education was to current students' grandparents. Comprehensive universities would be as different to current universities as comprehensive schools are to grammar schools. Such a thing is hard to imagine today, but no harder than it was to imagine compulsory secondary school attendance just one lifetime ago, and a welfare state to go with it. That welfare state was first created in New Zealand.

Progress and rationing

Eventually all the great gorges had been spanned, even as far south in the world as the Rakaia River. Roads were built, agriculture further mechanised. Food was preserved, chilled, shipped abroad; mouths in Europe were fed; money from Europe was returned (with 'interest'); within just a decade of the first IQ test being christened on the other side of the planet. Rivet making was automated. The requirement for all children in rich countries to attend an elementary school until the age of 14 was finally fully enforced, occurring less than the length of a human lifetime ago (see Figure 3). That requirement was extended to compulsory secondary education for girls as well as boys, in all affluent nations.

In early 1950s Britain, young mouths were still being fed by rations even though the war had ended. It was then that IQ tests were initially used to decide, to 'ration', which kind of secondary school children would be allowed to go to. Although food and education were not directly related, the ideas of how you could rationally plan the allocation of both had arisen during wartime. For education the future rationing of what were then scarce resources (graduate teachers) was based on how those children performed on one day with pen and paper at a desk around the time of their 11th birthday. For some involved the intention was altruistic, to secure the best for the 'brightest' of whatever background, but the result was gross injustice. Similar injustices occurred in most other newly affluent nations. These injustices were resisted, seen as segregation by 'race' in the US, and by social class in Britain, and within just another couple of decades almost all children went to their nearest school, with no continuing distinction between grammar or secondary modern.

The phenomenon of almost all children going to their nearest secondary school, to the same school as their neighbours' children, had occurred hardly anywhere in the world before the 1970s. When all local children go to the same neighbourhood state school it is called a 'comprehensive' school because it has to provide a comprehensive education for all. The main alternatives to comprehensive schools are selective schools where most children are selected to go to a school for rejects (called 'secondary moderns' in Britain) and only a few are allowed to go to schools for those not rejected by a test ('grammar schools'). Before there was a change to the system, three quarters of children would typically be sent to schools for 'rejects', those secondary moderns. In Britain in 1965, 8% of all children of secondary school age attended a comprehensive school, 12% in 1966, 40% in 1970, 50% in 1973, 80% by 1977 and 83% by 1981.[32]

It was under the Conservative administration led by Margaret Thatcher that the final cull of over a third of the 315 remaining grammar schools still functioning in 1979 was undertaken, with 130 becoming comprehensives by 1982.[33] However, the Conservative government then introduced 'assisted places' in 1979, the scheme whereby they began to sponsor a small group of select children chosen by private schools. And so, just at the time when it looked as if divisive state education was ending, the state itself sponsored an increase in division, which was the first major increase in private school entry in Britain in decades. Britain was not alone in seeing such elitism rise.

In 1979 Britain was following events that had first had their immediate impact elsewhere. In California, where Ronald Reagan was governor until 1975 (later becoming US president in 1980), private school entry first rose rapidly after years of decline. Between 1975 and 1982, in just seven years, the proportion of children attending private schools in California rose, from 8.5% to 11.6%.[34] This occurred when, as a result of Ronald Reagan's failure to fund properly the poorest of schools before he lost office, the state reduced the funding of all maintained schools to a level near that of the lowest funded school, following a Californian Supreme Court ruling of 1976. The ruling stated that it was unconstitutional to fund state schools variably between areas in relation to the levels of local property taxes. Before the court ruling, state schools in affluent areas were better funded than state schools in poorer parts of California, just as before the abolition of almost all selective grammar schools in Britain, affluent parents whose children were much more likely to attend such schools had seen much higher state funding of their children's education compared with that of the majority. In both the US and Britain the advent of much greater educational equality was accompanied by a significant growth in the numbers of parents choosing to pay so that their children would not have to be taught alongside certain others, nor given the same resources as those others.

The rise in private school places occurred with the fall in grammar school places in Britain, and was much greater in the US with the equalising down of state education resources in California. In Britain the greatest concentration of private school expansion occurred in and on the outskirts of the most affluent cities such as London, Oxford and Bristol – not where local schools did worse, but where a higher proportion of parents had higher incomes. Educational inequalities had been reduced to a historic minimum by the 1970s in the US, just as income inequalities had. In education this trend was turned around by the reaction to the notorious[35] *Serrano verses Priest* California court cases of 1971, 1976 and 1977. Similarly in Britain half of all school children were attending non-selective secondary schools by 1973: again, educational inequalities fell fastest when income inequalities were most narrow. These were crucial years where issues of equality between rich and poor were being fought over worldwide as well as between local schools. Internationally, poorer countries that controlled the supply of oil worked together to raise the price of oil dramatically in that same turbulent year (during the October Yom Kippur war). International inequalities in wealth fell to their lowest recorded levels; worldwide inequalities in health reached a minimum a few years later.[36] Within Britain and the US such health and wealth inequalities had reached their lowest recorded levels a little earlier, around the start of the 1970s.[37] This was a wonderful time for people in affluent countries, who had never had it so good. Wages had never been as high; even the US minimum wage was at what would later turn out to be its historic maximum.[38]

Before the jobs went at the end of the decade, before insecurity rose, it was a great time to be ordinary, or to be average, or even above average, but the early 1970s were a disconcerting time if you were affluent. Inflation was high; if you were well off enough to have savings then those savings were being eroded. People began to realise that their children were not going to be as cushioned as they were by so much relative wealth, by going to different schools. When politicians said that they were going to eradicate the evil of ignorance by educating all children in Britain, or that they were going to have a 'Great Society' in the US, they did not mention that this would reduce the apparent advantages of some children. Equal rights for black children, a level playing field for poor children – these can be seen as threats as more compete in a race where proportionately fewer and fewer can win.

Because you're worth it?

In 2009 the OECD revealed (through its routine statistical publications) that Britain diverted a larger share of its school education spending (23%) to a tiny proportion of privately educated children (7%) than did almost any other rich nation. That inequality had been much less 30 years earlier.

It is not hard for most people to know that they are not very special. Even affluent people, if they are not delusional, know in their heart of hearts that they are not very special; most know that they are members of what some call the 'lucky sperm club', born to the right parents in their turn, or just lucky, or perhaps both lucky and a little ruthless. However, you don't carry on winning in races that have fewer and fewer winners if you don't have a high opinion of yourself. Only those who maintain the strongest of narcissistic tendencies are sure that they became affluent because they were more able. A few of those who couple such tendencies with eugenicist beliefs think that their children will be likely to inherit their supposed acumen and do well in whatever circumstances they face. The rest, the vast majority of the

—

rich, who are not cocksure, had a choice when equality appeared on the horizon. They could throw in their lot with the masses, send their children to the local school, see their comparative wealth evaporate with inflation and join the party, or they could try to defend their corner, pay for their children to be segregated from others, look for better ways to maintain their advantages than leaving their savings to the ravages of inflation, vote and fund into power politicians who shared their concerns, and encourage others to vote for them too. They encouraged others to vote by playing on their fears, through making donations to right-wing parties' advertising campaigns (see Section 5.1). They convinced enough voters that the centre-left had been a shambles in both the US and the UK. The opposition to the right-wing parties was too weak, campaign funding too low, and in 1979 in Britain and 1980 in the US the right wing won.

Although not as rare as the wartime rescuers of the 1940s, the effective left-wing idealists of the 1970s were too few and far between, although there were more of these idealists in some countries than in others. In Sweden, Norway and Finland left-wing idealists won, but society also held together in Japan, Germany, Austria, Denmark, Belgium, the Netherlands and France, in Spain after Franco, in Canada, to an extent in Greece (once the generals were overthrown), in Switzerland and in Ireland. It was principally in the US, but also in Britain, Australia and New Zealand, Portugal and Singapore, that those who were rich had the greatest fears, and the greatest influence. It was there that the political parties and idealists of the rich fared best. There, more than elsewhere, most who had riches and other advantages looked to hold on to them. They donated money to right-wing political parties and helped them become powerful again. They donated because they were afraid of greater equality; not because they believed that most people would benefit from their actions by becoming more equal, but because they thought that the greater good would be achieved by promoting inequality. By behaving in this way they began to sponsor a renewed elitism.

One effect of right-wing parties winning power was that they attacked trade unions. And as unions declined in strength, left-wing parties were forced to look for other sources of finance. Having seen the power of funding politics, the affluent could then be cajoled to begin to sponsor formerly left-wing and middle-of-the-road political parties and to influence them, not least to give more consideration to the interests of the rich, and because they knew right-wing parties could not carry on winning throughout the 1990s. The rich spent their money in these ways, with their donations becoming ever more effective from the early 1960s onwards.[39] In hindsight it is not hard to see how the Democrats in the US and later New Labour in Britain began similarly to rely so completely on the sponsorship of a few rich individuals and businesses. Once it became common for the affluent to seek to influence politicians with money, and occasionally to receive political honours from them as a result, there was no need to limit financial sponsorship to just the right wing. In those few very unequal affluent countries where the self-serving mantra of 'because you're worth it' was repeated most often, part of what it meant to be in the elite came more and more from the 1970s onwards to be seen as someone who gave money to 'good' causes, charities to help animals or the poor, to political parties who do the same 'good' works, while not altering the status quo, not reducing inequality. Inequality can be made politically popular.

An equality worth fighting for

In the southern states of the US the ending of slavery brought the fear of equality. Initially this was translated politically into votes for the Democratic Party and the suppression of civil rights there through to at least the 1960s, including the right for children to go to the same school as their neighbours. In South Africa in the late 1940s apartheid was introduced with popular political support from poorer whites who felt threatened as other former African colonies were beginning to claim their freedom from white rule.[40] Again, segregation began at school. When Nelson Mandela was put on trial in 1963, and facing a possible death sentence, in his concluding court statement he defined, as an equality worth fighting for, the right of children to be treated equally in education and for them to be taught that Africans and Europeans were equal and merited equal attention. At that time the South African government spent 12 times as much on educating each European child as on each African child. Nelson

Mandela was released from prison in 1990. In that year children in inner-city schools in the US, such as those in Chicago, were having half as much spent on their state secondary education as children in the more affluent suburbs to the north, and 12 times less than was spent on the most elite private school education. By 2003 almost nine out of ten of those inner-city children were black or Hispanic, and inequalities in state school spending in America had risen four-fold. Inequalities rose even further if private schools are also considered, and were still growing by 2006 as private school fees rose quickly (at the extreme exponentially) while the numbers of private school places increased much more slowly.[41]

Admissions to private schools rose slowly and steadily in countries like the US and the UK from the 1970s onwards. They rose slowly because few could afford the ever-rising fees and because some held out against segregating their children. They rose steadily because despite the cost and inconvenience of having to drive children past the schools to which they could have gone, parents' fears rose at a greater rate. Rising inequalities in incomes between families from the 1970s onwards have tended to accompany increased use of private educational provision in those countries where income inequalities have increased. Rising income inequalities also increase fear for children's futures as it is easier to be seen as failing in a country where more are paid less. It is much harder to appear to succeed where only a few are paid more.

Just as anti-colonialism and the abolition of slavery fostered unforeseen new injustices, the success of civil rights for black children in the US and working-class children in Europe in the 1960s fostered the rise of new injustices of elitism, increased educational apartheid and the creation of different kinds of schools for children seen increasingly as different, who might otherwise have been taught together. By 2002 in many inner-city state schools in the US a new militaristic curriculum was being introduced, a curriculum of fear, according to a leading magazine of the affluent, *Harpers*. Not a single noise is tolerated in these schools; Nazi-style salutes are used to greet teachers; specific children are specified as 'best workers' and, according to a headmaster administering the 'rote-and-drill curricula' in one Chicago school, the aim is to turn these children

—

into tax-paying automata who will 'never burglarize your home ...'.[42] In 2009 President Barack Obama promoted Arne Duncan, the man who had been responsible for education policy in Chicago at this time, to be put in charge of education policy for the nation. He may have learned from what are now widely regarded as mistakes, or he may propagate them across the country, transforming 'schools from a public investment to a private good, answerable not to the demands and values of a democratic society but to the imperatives of the market place'.[43]

In Britain children placed towards the bottom of the increasingly elitist education hierarchy are not 'rote-and-drill' conditioned so explicitly but are instead now 'garaged', kept quiet in classes that do not stretch them by teachers who understandably have little hope for them. These children and young adults are made to retake examinations at ages 16–19 to keep them in the system and in education, but they are not being educated. The elitist beliefs that have been spread are that if just a few children are gifted, but most are destined for a banal future, then providing the majority with education in art, music, languages, history, even athletics, can be viewed as profligate, while such things are presented as essential for the able minority.

It is not that progress was reversed in the 1970s but that, as has so often happened before, with every two steps taken forward towards greater justice, one step is taken backwards. Ending formal slavery in the southern US saw formal segregation established, an injustice far more minor than slavery, but one that came to be seen as equally great. As the end of direct colonial rule was achieved across Africa, apartheid was established in the south, once again more minor, but colonialism at home, within a country. As segregation of children between state secondary schools in Britain was abolished during the 1970s, in the South East there was a boom in the private sector, in newly segregated 'independent' schooling. Thus as each great injustice was overcome, a more minor injustice was erected in its place, to be overcome again in turn as was segregation after slavery, as was apartheid after colonialism, as elitism probably will be after the latest British school reorganisation (based on renewed IQist beliefs) is abolished. In every case what had been considered normal behaviour

—

came to be considered abhorrent: slave holding, suggesting Africans were not capable of self-rule, proposing separate but far from equal lives. Separate lives are hard to justify, from the black woman forced to sit at the back of the bus to the children who are told that the only place for them is in a sink school. Separation is not very palatable once carefully considered,.

By 2007, in some parts of the UK there were hopeful signs of a move away from seeing children as units of production to be repeatedly tested, but the English school system had become a market system where schools competed for money and children. The introduction of 57 varieties of state school saw to that, as did the expanding of private schools, which saw their intake rise to 7% while the children in these schools took one quarter of all advanced level examinations and gained over half the places in the 'top' universities.[44] Almost all the rest of elite places in these universities go to children in the better funded of the 57 varieties of state school, or those who had some other advantage at home. Elitist systems claim to be meritocracies, but in such systems almost no one gets to where they are placed on merit, not when we are all so inherently equal. In more equitable societies numerous '… studies reveal the overwhelming educational and socializing value of integrated schooling for children of all backgrounds'.[45]

3.4 Putting on a pedestal: superhuman myths

Every injustice can be paired with a human failing. The failing that pairs best with elitism, given its 1950s' apogee, is chauvinism. This is typically a prejudiced belief in the inherent superiority of men, in particular a small selected group of men. To see chauvinism in action when it comes to elitism, all you need do is look to the top, and at the top in the field of education is the Nobel prize (although not all Nobel prizes concern education, most do). Out of almost 800 people awarded Nobel laureates by the end of 2008, only 35 of them were women, a staggeringly low 4%! Overall, more were given for work in medicine to men and women jointly than for work in any other single subject. In medicine, teamwork often involving subordination is more common, thus a significant handful of women were included among the medical laureates. Physics has lower but similar numbers of prize winners compared with medicine, but only two women have ever been awarded the Nobel prize for physics. While chemistry is fractionally more welcoming, literature is much more female-friendly, with women being awarded almost a tenth of all the prizes handed out. But given how many women are authors today, is there really only one great woman author for every 10 men? Peace is similarly seen as more of a female domain – women were possibly even in the majority as members of some of the 20 organisations awarded the peace prize over the years. But they were in a small minority of actual named winners. Prizes are very much a macho domain, as Figure 4 shows.

We know most people in the world are labelled as in some way 'stupid' or 'backward', 'limited' or having only 'simple' ability

Figure 4: Male and female Nobel (and economics) laureates, by subject, 1901–2008 (+ 2009)

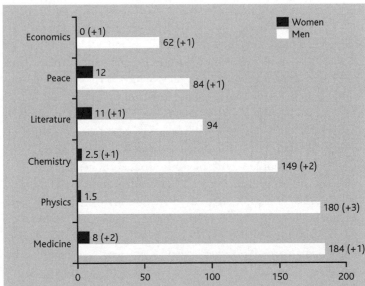

Notes: Marie Curie is split between physics and chemistry; John Bardeen and Fred Sanger are counted only once. The five prizes awarded to women and the eight to men in 2009 are shown in parentheses. The economics prize included here is the special prize awarded by the Sveriges Riksbank (see page 69).

Source: http://nobelprize.org/index.html

when tested by international examination (see 'world' histogram in Figure 2, page 47 above). What is less well known is that those not labelled 'stupid' have to live out lies which increase in magnitude the more elevated their status. At the top are placed mythical supermen, those of such genius, talent or potential as to require special nurturing, an education set aside. Within this set they are arranged into another pyramid, and so on, up until only a few handfuls are identified and lauded. Until the most recent generation this elite education has almost always been set aside for men. In the rare cases that women were recognised as having contributed, they were often initially written out of the story, as in the now notorious case of Rosalind Franklin who contributed to discovering the shape of the double helix within which genes are carried. Rosalind was not recognised when the Nobel prize was awarded to James Watson and Francis Crick.[46]

'People who have to deal with black employees'

Nobel prizes in science are the ultimate way of putting people on pedestals and provide wonderful examples of inherent *equality* when it comes to our universal predisposition to be stupid. In his later years James Watson provided the press with a series of astounding examples of this, for instance saying, it is claimed, that he had hoped everyone was equal but that '… people who have to deal with black employees find this not true'.[47] This is no one-off case of prejudice among prize winners. Around the time that Watson was being given his laureate for double helix identification, a physics laureate of a few years earlier, William Shockley, was advocating injecting girls with a sterilising capsule that could later be activated if they were subsequently deemed to be substandard in intelligence, in order to prevent reproduction.[48] Francis Crick's own controversial support for the oddly named 'positive eugenics' was also well recorded by 2003, if not so widely known and reported in the popular press.[49]

James Watson's work was mainly undertaken at the University of Cambridge and William Shockley ended up working at Stanford University in California. Perhaps we should not be surprised that men with backgrounds in the sciences who were educated and closeted in

—

such places as Cambridge or Stanford should come to hold the view that so many not like them are inferior. Why should someone who examines things down microscopes or who studies x-rays know much about people? Surely, you might think, those who *might* have been awarded a Nobel prize in social sciences, the arts or the humanities might be a little more enlightened, and so the academics in these areas often appear to be, but perhaps only because in these fields there are no such prizes and so no such prize holders to be put on pedestals from which to confidently pontificate.[50]

Telling someone that they are very able at one thing, such as passing a test or winning a prize, can easily make them think they are more likely to be right about other things, such as the morality of sterilising women. Fortunately, at least in order for this experiment in putting people on pedestals to continue, one social science was later treated differently and the results were telling. In 1969 the Sveriges Riksbank, Sweden's central bank, created a special prize in economics. Over the subsequent 40 years up to 2008 all the 60-odd prizes, some joint, were, *without exception*, given to men (although in 2009 one was awarded to the first woman, Elinor Ostrøm; see page 88).

Maybe only men are able to be good economists, and maybe there is such a thing as a good economist, one especially able to understand the monetary workings of society, to uncover the truth as to how there is some underlying logic to resource allocation by individual decision making other than the obvious. Maybe just a chosen few are able to glimpse these truths and reveal them to the small minority of the most able of the rest of us, the masses who are barely able to understand. Alternatively, maybe we have had here a group of men awarding each other prizes if they *fitted in*. Evidence that the latter is the case, and that these men are no more able or less stupid than other people, abounds.[51] Table 3 shows the subjects in which, up to 2008, a few women had been welcome and those in which almost none, or none at all (in the case of economics), were recognised as achieving greatness.

It is not just through the statements of a few on issues of how they deal with their black employees that we know that prize winners are so flawed. When you begin to search you find that top economists are often involved in what from a distance appear as childish spats

Table 3: Pearson goodness-of-fit test of Nobel prize by sex and subject, 1901–2008

		Medicine	Physics	Chemistry	Literature	Peace	Economics	Total
Observed	Men	184	180	149	94	84	62	753
	Women	8	1.5	2.5	11	12	0	35
	Total	192	181.5	151.5	105	96	62	788
Expected	Men	183.5	173.4	144.8	100.3	91.7	59.2	753
	Women	8.5	8.1	6.7	4.7	4.3	2.8	35
	Total	192	181.5	151.5	105	96	62	788
(O-E)	Men	0.5	6.6	4.2	–6.3	–7.7	2.8	0.0
	Women	–0.5	–6.6	–4.2	6.3	7.7	–2.8	0.0
	Total	0.0	0.0	0.0	0.0	0.0	0.0	0.0
$(O-E)^2/E$	Men	0.0015	0.2482	0.1235	0.4001	0.6524	0.1280	1.55
	Women	0.0327	5.3407	2.6579	8.6087	14.0354	2.7538	33.43
	Total	0.03	5.59	2.78	9.01	14.69	2.88	34.98

Notes: The prizes awarded in 2009 were so very unusual in distribution that they are not included here. For source of data and the 2009 distribution see Figure 4. Strictly speaking in statistical strictures too few women have been awarded the prize over the course of the last century for this simple goodness-of-fit test to be applied, as in three categories fewer than five women would be expected to have been awarded a prize. The sum of the squared differences each divided by that expected number is 34.98. The numbers of degrees of freedom are sexes less 1 multiplied by subjects less 1, or (2–1)*(6–1)=5. On five degrees of freedom a value of 20.515 is statistically significant at p=0.001. This is an approximate test as cell sizes are small. Nevertheless it would appear that sex and subject are far from independent (literature and peace above the average, physics, chemistry and economics below, while medicine awards prizes at the average rate). For an exact test see note 59.

with one another.[52] Given the passing of a few years their theories often do not look very clever, do not appear to apply well to today's world, or they appear to be simply the next logical step in a line of thinking that is, as a whole, too complex to be the work of just one mind, no matter how beautiful.

Examination upon examination

Some of the worst consequences of elitism in education are seen in what happens to those deemed to be the elite. In New York City, one of the twin hearts of the world financial system, live some of the richest people on earth. By 2008 the most affluent paid around US$25,000 a year per child for a pre-school place in an exclusive nursery.[53] Such pre-schooling is thought to lead to what looks like exam success in each year that follows. The children sent to nurseries like this are far more likely than any other children to end up as college students in the Ivy League universities, those universities that pay the highest salaries, partly to be able to employ the most Nobel laureates. Does this mean that these children will also exhibit great intellectual abilities? (George Bush the Second attended both Yale and Harvard.) Or will they appear a little more like especially spoilt (but cajoled) American adolescents who have been given little choice over their upbringing, who suffer from being repeatedly told how gifted they are, and from believing the people who tell them this?

Examination upon examination, exclusive school after exclusive school and then exclusive university, all the time being told you are special. And the only way out is down. Given this type of an education it is hard not to come to believe you are special, hard not to start to look down on the 'little people', hard to understand that you are not so clever. That initial US$25,000 down-payment may be followed by up to a million dollars' worth of 'investment' in each child of the super-rich as their way is paid through school and exclusive college. Fees, designer clothes, exclusive cars and the cash and credit cards needed to stay on the social circuit all increase in cost far faster than average commodities. An elite education tends to be a very expensive education.

Rising inequalities in income and wealth within the US were followed closely by increases in inequalities in educational outcome over the course of the last quarter-century.[54] Rich children appeared to be doing much better, a large part of that rise in educational inequality being their apparent advancement rather than increased illiteracy among the poor. However, what the affluent were becoming better at was passing examinations, not necessarily learning. Similarly, in Britain, it has only been from about the start of the last quarter-century that the most exclusive private boarding schools took conditioning their young ladies and gentlemen to pass examinations seriously. Before then, if they did not become scholars, access through old boys' networks to jobs in the City of London, or to high-ranking positions in the armed forces was still common, and the girls simply had to marry well. As the poor were being given access to comprehensive secondary education, and a chance, as compared with the no-chance future of being sent to a secondary modern, that led to the very richest of all being forced to 'swot'. They did not become wiser or cleverer as a result, just more able to pass a particular examination on a particular day, aided by a little more help each year from their tutors with the coursework.

People who have taught the children of the higher classes at the universities they go to see the result of the growth in elitism. These children have been educationally force-fed enough facts to obtain strings of A grades, but they are no more genii than anyone else. There is a tragedy in making young people pretend to superhuman mental abilities which neither they nor anyone else possess. To justify their situation they have to swallow and repeat the lie being told more and more often that only a few are especially able and that those few are disproportionately found among these high social classes. The pill is sweetened by living in a context where much of the assumption and perception of social status is taken for granted. High private school fees are paid as much to ensure this context as to secure high grades and a place in a prestigious university. The most prestigious universities of all, with their ivy and towers, also provide a comfortable sheltered context to continue to believe that you are especially able. Why else would you be there, you might ask.

The 'IQ gene'

In recent years, in the more unequal of affluent countries like Britain and the US, it has become a little more common for the elite to suggest among themselves that children born to working-class or black parents simply have less natural ability than those born to higher-class or white parents.[55] The people who tend to say this are not being particularly original; they are just a little more boldly and openly echoing claims made commonly, if discreetly, by the class they were born into or (in a few cases) have joined. They often go on to quietly suggest that children of different class backgrounds tend to do better or worse in school on account of some '... complex interplay of sociocultural and genetic factors'.[56] It may sound subtle to include the words 'complex' and 'sociocultural', but once 'genetic factors' are brought into the equation all subtlety is lost. 'Genetic factors' could be used to defend arguments that women are inherently less able than men, black people in essence less able than white. Slip 'genetic factors' into your argument and you cross a line.

The best evidence we have that genetic factors influence school results is that there is more chance of your star sign or month of birth influencing your mental abilities than there is of your genes so doing.[57] In contrast, it is the country and century you are born into, how you are raised and how much is spent on your schooling which all actually matter. Star signs matter slightly in that they indicate when in the year you were born and hence how physically developed you were when you first entered school. It does not matter whether you were born on a Monday; it matters only a little whether you are a Capricorn; and 'the IQ gene' does not exist. Sadly, it is belief in things like the IQ gene or equivalent that results in teachers being asked around the rich world to *identify* children who may become especially 'gifted and talented'.[58] We may well be born with varying 'idiosyncrasies', blue eyes or brown eyes, distinct chins or no chins, but these no more imply that the upper classes have superior genes than that Sunday's children are more likely to be born 'bonny and blithe, and good and gay'.

Putting people on pedestals is not always dangerous as long as those placed there are greatly embarrassed by the process. Researchers have found that different children can grow up to be differently able in ways other than through the fiction of inherent intelligence. Some children grow up to be adults who appear far more able to help others in a crisis, the most celebrated of these adults in recent European history being those very few who helped rescue and shelter Jewish people in occupied Europe. It is worth repeating that when the rescuers' backgrounds were looked into it was commonly found that their parents had set high standards for them as children, high standards as to how they should view others, and their parents did not treat them as if there were limits to their abilities, nor did they tell them that others were limited. If you see others as inherently inferior then inequality will always be with you. Childhood upbringings akin to those of the rescuers are now much more common than they were in the 1920s and 1930s. Far fewer young adults would blithely obey orders and fight for their countries now than agreed to then. However, it is still just as possible to train people to follow orders now. There is no inevitability to progress. But it is harder to cajole those who have been taught, while young, that others are equal and deserving of respect to behave in a way they find abhorrent. And it is just as hard to convince those brought up to think of themselves as superior that there is no natural unlevel playing field of inherent ability.

3.5 The 1950s: from ignorance to arrogance

The way in which women currently are and previously have been treated provides clear testament to the arbitrary nature of discrimination based on presumption of inherent difference. The development of gender roles also highlights how progress is far from inevitable. Figure 5 suggests that had you been observing the Nobel prizes tally in 1950 you might have felt (optimistically) that by the end of the century a quarter of prizes would have been won by women, or even half if you hoped for a little acceleration reflecting the rapid promotion of women into secondary education, universities and beyond. However, by the end of the 1950s you would have been shocked to find that *not a single prize* had been awarded to a woman that decade. Had you lived to September 2009, you would be perhaps saddened to find that the 1940s tally of 8% had never been matched again – even though 35 women were awarded Nobel prizes by the start of 2009, this was still less than 5% overall.

The awarding of no Nobel prizes to women in the 1950s did not occur by chance; it is too unlikely an event for that.[59] It also did not occur from conspiracy; it is too glaring an outcome for that. Conspiracy between the committees would have ensured at least

Figure 5: Female Nobel laureates (%), by decade, worldwide, 1901–2008

Source: http://nobelprize.org/index.html; note that since the 1950s almost all the prizes for women have been in literature or peace, and only a few in medicine. Note that 2009 and 2010 have not been included. See page 88 for the remarkable story of 2009.

one single woman selected during this decade, as a token gesture. Women had been given prizes in every previous decade so it did not occur because of how few women had been in 'top jobs'. It occurred because those who awarded the prizes and made the initial nominations were reflecting the times they were living through. The prizes had begun to matter greatly, not for their cash value, but for the prestige that they carried and the message that their awarding gave. Women were still nominated during the 1950s, of course. For the peace prize, nominations included educationalist Maria Montessori in 1951, birth control campaigner Margaret Sanger in both 1953 and 1955, and Helen Keller in 1954 for her work on disability and ability. As I write, only nominations for the peace prize up to 1955 can easily be accessed online, and these show that although a few women were nominated, such as those three, increasingly it was men, especially anti-communists, who were pushed forward, nominations flooding in on their behalf from groups of various members of parliament (MPs) who appeared to lobby the peace prize awarding committees most effectively. Other committees appear to have been even more strongly influenced by their times: Winston Churchill was awarded

—

the prize for literature in 1953, Ernest Hemingway in 1954, and Boris Pasternak in 1958.

We easily forget that as soon as the Second World War ended, a new cold war started. In affluent countries this became a war on enemies imagined to be within, on communists and their sympathisers. We similarly easily forget that with the great steps taken forward to secure basic social security, education, housing, employment and healthcare for most in the 1940s and early 1950s came the counter-force of a renewed interest in being elitist. The two were connected. It was, after all, communists who most loudly proclaimed the virtues of various equalities. That no woman was awarded any of the highest of international prizes between 1947 and 1966 was because of the social changes at that time, not due to any lack of achievement.

Fear of communism was first seriously fuelled when the 1917 revolution in Russia could not be overcome by foreign invasion and did not collapse in on itself, nor transform quickly enough back to market competition. Before it became clear that other ways of organising societies were possible, there appeared to be less at stake, no obvious route through which greater equality might quickly come and no need to defend unequal societies by claiming that those at the top were of greater ability. Although arguments that inequality was natural began in the gilded age, the alternative of communism in practice added a great impetus to those who would argue that different people were destined for different futures because they were of differing ability. In 1922 it was said (by Walter Lippmann, an oft-quoted early advocate of testing) that if it became thought that these 'ability' tests measured anything like intelligence, and revealed predestined ability, then it would be a thousand times better if both the testers and their tests were 'sunk at sea and lost without trace'.[60] The opposite transpired; the tests did come to be seen as revealing predestined ability. Testing became all-pervasive in education in affluent countries.

Testing became all-pervasive partly as a defence of privilege in response to greater equality being won by the poor in affluent nations, and partly because of the perceived threat from poorer nations, from communism and from former colonies winning independence. It is clear today that latent inequalities in individual talent did not and do not exist and thus that categorising some children as innately talented discriminates on an essentially racist basis.[61] But to understand the fear that leads to such renewed and expansive racism requires an understanding of the erosion of status position which was felt by those who had been placed at the peaks of society following the Second World War.

From IQism to league tables

After the Second World War the worldwide testing industry took off with a vengeance. There was no great legacy of mass testing and labelling of children around ages 11 or 15 before then. Only since the war have most children still been in school at 15, and then only in affluent countries. Mass testing of children is a symptom of affluence. It is an unintended by-product of riches, where to be seen as insufficiently clever, insufficiently scientific, is to err. Today's children's parents were taught to try to ensure they were not innumerate, their grandparents were taught to ensure they were not illiterate. Future children and grandchildren will in turn face different hurdles, but will not necessarily be strung up along a bell curve as today's children are by our current obsession to test.

As described earlier, the bell curve of supposed ability came to be used most perniciously in countries like Britain as a model immediately after the Second World War. Children were tested at age 11 and had their future roles, through future 'choice' of schools, allocated on the basis of that test result. The tests had taken 40 years to develop from their French origins at the start of the century. It took a further 40 years for the tests to be removed from the lives of most young children, so that by the early 1980s most were going to the same schools as others in their neighbourhood and had not had their futures predetermined by one test. For most this was the ending of a kind of racism in education, of institutionalised ignorance. A few still went to selective schools, including private schools, but until the late 1980s that proportion was dropping.

The tide turned back towards elitism during the 1980s. To continue with the British example, in the very early 1980s in England the number of selective secondary (grammar) schools was cut to its

—

minimum of just under 200 by 1982,[62] but the Conservative government that made that final cut had plans for new educational apartheids. These plans were far more subtle than the 1940s plan for each large town to have one selective grammar school for those deemed able, and several secondary moderns for those deemed less able. The new plans were to create a market in education, an economic curve, a continuum of supply differentiated by quality to cater for an imagined distribution of demand for education, from those whose needs were seen as least to those who, it was claimed, merited most attention. Every child was now to be educated,[63] but some educated in very different ways from others. Most crass were the assisted places introduced to subsidise the private school fees of children with especially pushy parents but with fewer financial resources. Much more subtle was the introduction of school league tables.

It took until the early 1990s for league tables to be introduced across Britain and in similar countries. These tables created a market for state school places with parents paying through their house price to access more selective state schools. Before owner-occupation had reached its early 1980s peak a spatial market in education could not easily operate in this way. Then, as higher and higher proportions of young adult incomes were spent on housing, a spiral of spatial educational discrimination set in. The same occurred in the US, but with even more emphasis on private provision in universities. The result there was that, from 1980 to the turn of the millennium, '... public expenditure on prisons increased six times as fast as public expenditure on education, and a number of states have now reached a point where they are spending as much public money on prisons as on higher education'.[64] This change in provision resulted in more prisoners than college students coming from many residential areas in states such as California. Americans put up with this because they had been taught to be optimistic. Very few people look at their new-born baby boy and say that he'll probably have been in prison at least once by the time he is 30. Many people look and hope he'll go to college. If few go to college from the area where they live, then they hope, they dream, he'll be the one, their baby will be the exception. A watered-down version of these dreams led parents in many of the few parts of England where the couple of hundred overtly selective state schools remain to vote in recent years to keep selective state schooling, a majority locally believing that their children were in the top fifth of some ability range consisting of all state-educated children who lived nearby.

To believe that your children are in the top fifth requires first to believe that there is a top fifth. At any one time you can subject a group of children to testing and a fifth can be singled out as doing best. That fifth will be slightly more likely than their peers to rank in the top fifth in any other related test, but that does not mean that there is an actual top fifth that is waiting to be identified. The higher the correlations between different tests, the more the same children come to be selected in that top fifth under different test regimes. The more this happens, the more they will have been coached to perform well, the more likely they will be to live in a society that takes the idea of such testing seriously, a society, from government to classroom, that implicitly accepts the idea of inherent differences in ability. It is the smallest of steps from that position to accept that what you think is inherent is inherited. From putting prize winners on pedestals to putting whole populations in prisons, how we treat each other reveals how we see each other. We no longer view it as acceptable to make black people sit together at the back of the bus, but we still think it acceptable to sit 'slow' children together at the back of the class. IQism has become the current dominant unquestioned underlying belief of most educational policy makers in the more unequal of affluent nations.[65] Thinking that you and your children are special and are likely to climb to the top is a very dangerous way to think. The steeper the slope to the top, the fewer the places on the pinnacle, the more likely your dreams are to be dashed. The result of taking such thinking to an extreme means that in a majority of schools in the US where a minority of pupils are white, armed police are now permanently stationed in the school. Schools in poorer areas of the US now routinely identify and exclude students they see as being on the 'criminal justice track'[66] (meaning on the way to prison). By doing this they cause these children to start along a route that makes such predictions a near certainty.

—

From prison to privilege

Britain and similar countries follow in North America's wake in penal and education policy, and are not as far behind as you might think. Over the course of a decade, around the start of this century, the rate of imprisoning children in Britain increased ten-fold, despite no significant increase in criminality.[67] Increased permanent exclusion from ever more competitive schools contributed. Most adults imprisoned are barely out of childhood; their biggest mistake is not their crime, but having been born at the wrong time, to the wrong family, in the wrong place, in the wrong country. There is nothing inherently evil within North Americans that means they are much more likely to commit crimes than any other group of people in the world. The overall US incarceration rate has become so high that worldwide it is on a par only with the imprisonment that followed the criminal actions of Rwandans during the genocide there.[68] The US imprisons more of its own people than any other country because of what it has become. Because of the extent of the elitism that has taken hold in the US, people are finally waking up to realise that the American dream is only a dream, a dream of a memory. That elitism now raises a few dozen young celebrities to stardom, a few hundred young entrepreneurs to riches, and projects a few thousand young people sent to Ivy League colleges to totter high on unstable pedestals while condemning millions of other children to criminal alternatives.

In education what was previously seen as fair, or at least fair enough for each generation, becomes unjust, from slavery being justified, to denying votes to the poor, preventing equal rights for women, discriminating over disability – all become unpalatable. But the extension of freedoms also triggers counteractions. On a small scale at first and only at the very pinnacles of power, the witch hunts for communists and the macho politics of the 1950s reflected the fact that more powerful people were feeling a little more out of control. By the 1960s across Europe and especially in North America that feeling was spreading. In the 1970s people who generally thought of themselves as affluent became yet more frightened of what they saw as threats from within. They did not have quite enough of the advantages which they thought were due to them, and to their children. Poor countries appeared to be gaining more power as oil and all other prices rose; poor people were being given more and more. There was a reaction. In the subsequent decades the affluent ensured indirectly through their political gains that almost every additional university place, especially in the more prestigious institutions, was offered first to their offspring. They did this not through conspiracy but by individually working to secure advantages that they had taken for granted in the past, securing their children college places in a way that might not have been necessary in earlier years. But, once all the university places were filled, once all their children went to college, what next? Do you begin to think of paying for postgraduate education for your children? Perhaps buying them PhDs? Or is it easier to talk about maintaining standards and voting for and funding political parties who support those universities that want to charge more and exclude more from entering their hallowed halls? You can even begin to see how your child's position of relative advantage can be maintained if you argue for more prisons to house other people's children once they grow up, rather than seeing other people's children as like yours. But great problems can arise from placing offspring on pedestals. This occurs most frequently when they fail to perform as expected.

Throughout the 1980s and 1990s the rich did not talk about those of their children who did not succeed on their terms, as that might be embarrassing. A misinformed few might even have thought that such talk would reflect badly on their genes. Instead they voted for and funded politicians who had an agenda that implicitly included limiting additional access to universities to exclude the poor, minimising subsidised access to 'elite' universities, cutting affirmative action (also called 'positive discrimination'). This was no conspiracy. It was simply referred to as 'practical politics'. Governments claimed that their policies were slightly widening access, even as it actually narrowed. They may even have thought that access *was* widening, as the overall numbers going to university increased and the numbers from poorer areas also rose. However, initially almost all the extra places taken up in universities in countries like Britain were taken up by more affluent children, especially, and more enduringly, in the more elite universities.[69] More obtusely, the affluent tended to be opposed to those who would raise their taxes to fund educational changes to lower the barriers to others' children. Did their own children thank them for this? Occasionally in those years you might have heard a young adult say how grateful they were for the 'sacrifices' their parents had made in sending them to a fee-paying school, but you heard such stories less and less over time as it became more obvious that being able to afford to make such a 'sacrifice' was hardly a state of privation. It also became more and more obvious that, as the establishment you got to began again to depend more on how rich your parents were, or how unethically they were willing to behave ('entrepreneurially', making as much money as they could), such 'a privilege' was becoming less of a thing to boast about.

From competition to capabilities

In the more unequal affluent nations educational discrimination rose during the 1980s and 1990s, but just as the rich children of the 1960s had not appeared particularly grateful to their parents or respectful of their views, so again privileged children did not necessarily embrace the elitism that their parents had fostered. The age of elitism did not produce a particularly happy nor knowledgeable generation of affluent young people despite all the money spent on their learning. Being taught that for most of your life you will have to compete to keep your place, that beneath you is a seething mass of competitors a little less deserving than you but just waiting to take your place, is hardly comforting. Being taught that if you fall at any point it is your fault, and that it will reflect badly on your family, does not provide a good environment in which to learn. *Being taught that you learn in order to secure your social position is no education.* The affluent could no longer learn more by studying further under such conditions, but became obliged to 'swot', to appear to study, to send their children to study, to justify their even more exalted future positions. They were no longer becoming more content as a result of greater wealth because they already had enough for their needs. Nor were they becoming more engaged in their work, but were working to maintain and increase their wealth. As they lived ever longer lives they lived into extreme frailty at rates that had been rare before. They were not made happier by additional material possessions, because you can only drive one car at a time, sleep in one bed, wear one set of clothes.

There comes a time when enough is enough, when you no longer feel driven to maintain your comparative advantage by holding others down, by denying others education, inclusion, respect, health and happiness. Injustice begins with education, its denial, its mutation, its mutilation. *Good, fair, just education is not provided in societies where the accepted belief is that different children have different capacities, where it is presumed that most people are always destined to struggle, and that each has a low limit to what they can be expected to achieve.* At times such assumptions are made explicit, such as in the official proposals to change English education law in 2005 in which it was claimed that 'we must make sure that every pupil – gifted and talented, struggling or just average – reaches the *limits* of their capability'.[70] In England the idea that different children have different limits has for so long been part of the social landscape that, despite the best efforts and advice, it still underlies key thinking.

English policy makers were often brought up on childhood stories written by authors during the dying days of the empire where a hierarchy of characters was presented to the minds of young readers, often with subservient ones being depicted as animals. The stoats and the weasels in the book *Wind in the Willows* had limits and needed to be kept in their places; so, too, with the great ordering of creatures in the *Narnia Chronicles*; and it was the unruly subservient class getting above its station in life that threatened to wreck 'the Shire' and the natural order of a fictitious world (looking remarkably like Europe) in *Lord of the Rings*. Thus in the most fictional of children's fantasy tales in hierarchical societies, hierarchy is defended, suggested as being under threat and in need of reinforcement. The same can be said of old stories of trains and tank engines with 'bolshie' buses and pliant (female) trucks, or of cabals of privileged 'famous fives', or 'secret sevens' rounding up criminals from the lower orders. But these are old stories. The new stories are different.

Children's stories and the stories we tell our children are changing. They might still contain fantastic animals that speak, and echoes of the society in which they are written, but less and less do they so

—

overtly defend hierarchy. For younger children the typical plot of illustrated stories now concerns such issues as how sharing makes you happier (*Rainbow Fish*). Underdogs are increasingly being portrayed as eventual victors (*Harry Potter*); hierarchy and authority as bad (*His Dark Materials*). The villain in children's stories became by 2007 the banker figure of '… a businessman in a grey suit who never smiled and told lies all the time'.[71] The settings might still be gothic boarding schools, Oxford colleges or imaginary lands, but the tales within those settings are no longer the same. With imaginations differently fired, and underlying assumptions not so strongly set, tomorrow's policy makers are likely to think quite differently.

From dissent to hope

Already in the US there are the beginnings of a 'detracking movement', advocating not grouping children into classes and sets by 'ability', not sitting the 'slow' ones together in class. There are subversive cartoons undermining what have been only recently promoted as traditional US values of selfishness. Even the pre-school children's book *Rainbow Fish* has been turned into a 26-episode series which has been shown on the Home Box Office television channel since the year 2000 (causing many cries of socialist subversion!). As the counter-culture grows there is also more formal rebellion. In Britain calls not to set children into school classes grouped by ability are becoming clearer, not to have gifted and talented ghettos which in turn simply end up being reflected by a more distinct set of bottom sets in schools for those destined for criminality.[72] In 2006 official but concealed education statistics were leaked to the press revealing that, on average, a black school child in Britain was five times less likely to be officially registered as either 'gifted' or 'talented' compared with a white school child.[73] The labelling was a stupid idea, but often stupid ideas have had to have been played out for the stupidity to be fully recognised. If children in Britain were not so badly educated, and those categorised as 'the top' did not so often grow up to become such elitist adults, then ideas such as the official targeting of the so-called gifted would be laughed off long before becoming policy.

—

In the US the 'no child left behind' policy of testing children repeatedly, including those who speak Spanish as a first language being tested (and humiliated) in English, is increasingly drawing criticism for its inherent racism. The results of such testing demoralise the majority and stoke up arrogance in a minority, while everyday interactions at home and school can reinforce these unfortunate outcomes. We also have only very recently come to learn that there are alternative strategies which could have fortunate outcomes as long as children are able to feel confident that they can succeed:

> We learn best in stimulating environments when we feel sure we can succeed. When we feel happy or confident our brains benefit from the release of dopamine, the reward chemical, which also helps with memory, attention and problem solving. We also benefit from serotonin which improves mood, and from adrenaline which helps us to perform at our best. When we feel threatened, helpless and stressed, our bodies are flooded by the hormone cortisol which inhibits our thinking and memory. So inequalities, in society and in our schools, have a direct effect on our brains, on our learning and educational achievement.[74]

Aspects of this kind of thinking are slowly creeping into policy, but only just getting in through the cracks not policed by those who favour inequality, or, as it is more often called, *competition*. Just two years after the Education Act that talked of children having limits, in the British government's *Children's Plan* of 2007 a recommendation appeared that group setting of children be abolished (hidden on page 69 of the plan). Everywhere there are signs of dissent. The higher up the hierarchy you travel the more such dissent is hidden, but it is there.

A key government adviser in Britain, Jonathan Adair Turner, was recently asked to tackle the issues of either drugs or pensions. He said that his belief was that drugs should be decriminalised – so he was given the pensions remit, and then the problem of climate change to solve![75] His background was in banking, as was that of most key advisers to British governments recently. Banking had become the most celebrated occupation and so it was thought he could understand anything, such as drugs, or pensions, or climate. But, as Adair demonstrates, even with bankers it is becoming harder to identify people to give these posts to who can be guaranteed to sing sweetly from a set-belief hymn sheet.

Elitism is partly sustained because people are unlikely to seek high office, or feel able to remain there, if they do not have a high view of themselves and of their abilities. But it is also sustained because we tolerate such arrogance, and accept so readily the idea of there being just a few great minds, of there being just a few who should aspire to great positions of power, who are able to advise, lead and lecture. We rarely question why we have so few positions of great power, so few judges, ministers and other leaders. But, if you took every top post and created two jobs, each on half the salary, you would do a great deal to reduce privilege. It is harder to lord it over others when your pay is made more similar to theirs.

The social evil of ignorance was the old injustice of too few receiving even the most basic education in affluent countries. The injustice of widespread elitism is revealed through the production today of a surfeit, an excess, of many more apparent qualifications bestowed on those who already have most. This leads to others' abilities being often now labelled as inadequate to excuse growing inequality in many aspects of life.

But there is hope. In 2005 Larry Summers, economist and then president of Harvard University, stated that part of the gender gap in academic appointments could well be due to differences in innate aptitude, with women simply being less able than men.[76] Within a year he was forced to resign. Those at the very top of our elite hierarchies are now more likely to be taken to task for their failings than has ever before been the case. All that is required to overcome elitism in education is not to believe in the myths of superhuman ability, not to be in awe of those who are placed on pedestals. All that is required is to argue that we all deserve a little more education and we should not concentrate resources on just a few. It was difficult initially to suggest that all children had a right to education, and then that all should have that right extended through to their late teenage years. Both of these propositions were said to be impossible to achieve and unwarranted, until the point at which they were achieved.

If we are to stop such elitism we need universal tertiary education. Universities in rich countries must be more comprehensive in their outlook and behaviour, must teach across the board, not concentrating on a few antiquated subjects, and teach at the ages when people want to learn. We could start to argue for slow learning in place of the fast 'get-qualification-quick' education marketplace of today: more rights to learn again later in life, and no special credit given for chalking up qualifications in ever greater numbers, ever more quickly.

From babies to battles

One day, in the near future, most likely when all children and young adults in affluent countries are given the right by law to be educated up to the age of 21, a declaration will be made. It will be announced that for the first time in human history, not as a result of pandemic, famine or plague, but simply because of what we have become and how we now behave, the number of human beings on the planet has fallen. On that day people will still squabble about what kind of education they are to receive and who receives most, but we will no longer consign six out of every seven children to categories of failure, and consign six out of every seven who are seen to be good to positions where they play purely supporting roles to their 'genius' betters. It is unlikely we will again allow so few to stand so high above the rest, as we did in the 20th century.

Outside the rich world, children will become more precious simply because their numbers are declining. Almost all children will routinely complete their secondary school education. The world will be a little more equal, partly because it cannot get much more unequal, but also because the vast majority of those who lose out from growing inequality can no longer be presumed to be ignorant, and be ignored. But the 21st century will be no utopia. There will still be Nobel prizes and women will be awarded far less than half of them; there will be sexism and racism, prejudice, bigotry and pomposity, but a little less of each, and all a little less tolerated. Change can occur suddenly and unexpectedly. From 1900 to 2008 only 12 women had ever

—

been awarded a Nobel prize in science. But, as I was correcting the proofs of this text, in 2009 three women, one based in Hong Kong, were awarded science prizes, along with a male scientist of Indian origin; a woman writer from Germany won the literature prize and, least remarkably of all in this changing context, Barack Obama was awarded the peace prize for deeds yet to be done. In just one week in October 2009 the prize-giving committees upturned a century of predictability. The change to Figure 5 (page 75) takes the first decade of the 21st century from being mediocre to off-the-scale: 9% of prize winners in the decade being female once that week in 2009 is included, the highest ever proportion, with women receiving a third of all the prizes in that one year. Then, on Monday, 12 October 2009, as if to confirm that the times really were changing, the economics committee awarded one of their prizes, for the first time ever, to a woman, Elinor Ostrøm.

All manner of other trinkets and tokens will be awarded in future, and there is nothing wrong in that. It is not hard to stamp more medals, to print more certificates. Many primary school children in rich countries already receive hundreds of prizes a year telling them 'well done' for all forms of achievements. It is not hard to imagine our schools changing to encourage children more and test them less. And when will these things come about? Although they make no claims about school-leaving age, success, failure, prizes or inequality, those who come together in the UN do prophesy one part of this story with growing certainty. The year in which the day will dawn with one less human being than the day before will be some time around 2052.[77] This will be simply because we have learnt to have fewer babies, not due to the public actions of an elite, but through billions of private and very personal decisions, made mainly by the group which has been treated as stupid for longest: women. Human population growth has been curtailed by the billions of decisions of mostly poor and only very cheaply educated women, not by any elite group. These women learnt that they held the power among themselves. Even in China fertility was falling rapidly before the state introduced compulsion.[78]

We become more able through learning, and we learn collectively. That is how we have come to control our numbers. It is through learning together that we will come to understand that if performing at a uniform level in tests of a particular kind of logic were an important trait for humans to possess then we would almost all possess it, just as we almost all have binocular vision and an opposable thumb.[79] There is so much more that is vital to being human, to working together, than being good at tests that simply involve manipulating numbers. There are no important genetic differences in ability which elitists can use to justify their elitism. The sun did not shine differently or the soil vary from place to place in a way that made it imperative that some groups of humans became better suited to later solving Sudoku puzzles than others. We are all human, but no one is superhuman. We work and live better if we are together rather than divided by caste, class or classroom. All this we are still learning.

All children have ability, not potential, capacity or capability. We can learn without limits, given the right to a good education based on access rather than segregation. The coming battle in affluent countries will concern access to universal comprehensive tertiary education. The coming battle worldwide will focus on the right to be seen as equally able. These battles will be fought against elitism.

4

'Exclusion is necessary': excluding people from society

Just as the post–Second World War surfeit of resources in affluent nations was initially directed at targets such as eliminating ignorance, but came through time to be focused more on education spending in support of elitism, so the old social evil of want, of poverty, of having too little, was initially the direct target of spending in many postwar states. Additional resources for extra personal expenditure, social security benefits, were initially aimed at the elimination of want, but then, when the worst of want was seen to have been eliminated, public monies, redistribution and state attention moved elsewhere in a way that supported growing exclusion. Tax rates were reduced for the rich, benefit levels tagged to inflation (or less) for the poorest. The income of the rich moved away from that of average earners, who in turn saw their incomes increase faster than those on welfare benefits. The initial compressing (reducing the spread) of income distributions that came with the introduction of social security in many affluent nations, and the taxation needed to fund it, was removed most quickly in those countries which began to choose to become most unequal. High social security spending was not essential for high levels of social inclusion, but low levels of income inequality were. Thus relatively few people would describe themselves as poor and needing to take out loans just to get by in countries as diverse as Japan and the Netherlands, whereas in Britain and the US relative rates of poverty have grown greatly in recent decades, simply because inequality has grown.[1]

Poverty that mostly results from inequality comes in the form of a new kind of exclusion: exclusion from the lives, the understanding and the caring of others. This is now not through having to live in abject poverty, but through social norms becoming stretched out along such a wide continuum, as most additional income becomes awarded to the most affluent, more of that left to the next most affluent and so on. The elimination of the worst of early 20th-century poverty, coupled with the tales of elitists who believed that those who were poorer were inferior, reduced the power of argument of groups that had previously succeeded in bringing down inequalities in resources between families and classes within many affluent societies. It is slowly becoming clear that growing financial inequality results in large and slowly growing numbers of people being excluded from the norms of society, and creates an expanding and increasingly differentiated social class suffering a new kind of poverty: the new poor, the indebted, the excluded.

The new poor (by various means of counting) now constitute at least a sixth of households in countries like Britain. However, these are very different kinds of households from those who lived through immediate postwar poverty. What the poor mostly had in common by the end of the 20th century were debts they could not easily handle, debts that they could not avoid acquiring and debts that were almost impossible to escape from. Just a short step above the poor in the status hierarchy, fewer and fewer were living average 'normal' lives. The numbers of those who had a little wealth had also increased. Above the just-wealthy the numbers who were so well off they could afford to exclude themselves from social norms were hardly growing, although their wealth was growing greatly. This wealth was ultimately derived from such practices as indirectly lending money to the poor at rates of interest many of the poor could never afford to fully repay.

4.1 Indebted: those most harmed by exclusion, a sixth of all people

There are many ways of defining a person or household as poor in a rich society. All sensible ways relate to social norms and expectations, but because the expectations as to what it is reasonable to possess have diverged under rising inequality, poverty definitions have become increasingly contentious over time. In the most unequal of large affluent nations, the US, it is very hard to define people as poor as so many have been taught to define 'the poor' as those who do not try hard enough not to be poor.[2] Similarly, growing elitism has increased support for arguments that blame the poor for their poverty due to their apparent inadequacies, and there has been growing support for turning the definition of the poor into being 'that group which is unable or unwilling to try hard enough'.

The suggestion that at least a sixth of people live in poverty in some affluent nations results from arguments made in cross-country comparisons which suggest that a robust way of defining people as poor is to say that they are poor if they appear poor on at least two out of three different measures.[3] These three measures are: first, do the people concerned (subjectively) describe themselves as poor? Second, do they lack what is needed (necessities) to be included in society as generally understood by people in their country? Third, are they income-poor as commonly understood (low income)? It is currently solely through low income that poverty is officially defined, in Europe in relative terms and within the US in absolute terms. A household can have a low income but not be otherwise poor, as in the case of pensioners who have accrued savings that they can draw on. Similarly a household can have an income over the poverty threshold but be unable to afford to pay for the things seen as essential by most people, such as a holiday for themselves and their children once a year, or Christmas presents or a birthday party, the kind of presents and party that will not show them up. A family that cannot afford such things is likely to be expenditure- (or necessities-)poor and very likely to feel subjectively poor even if just above the official income poverty line.

In Britain around 5.6% of households appear poor on all three measures (subjectively, by expenditure and by income), some 16.3% on all three or any two (see Figure 6). It should be clear that any household, person or family which is poor on at least two of these criteria is likely to be excluded from the norms of society in some significant way, hence a sixth is a safe lower band to quote when asked how many people are truly poor. Figure 6 shows how that sixth was constituted in Britain at the turn of the millennium.

In other similarly unequal affluent countries that proportion would be higher or lower and made up of differing combinations of the three constituent groups, but it would not be dissimilar. It changes year on year in all countries and varies for different groups in the

Figure 6: Proportion of households poor by different measures (%), Britain, 1999

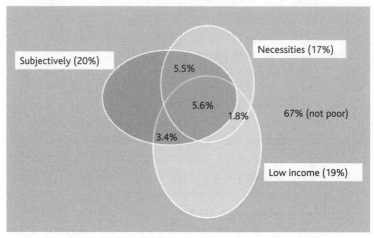

Note: The sixth who are poor on at least two criteria are shown in the areas with percentages labelled in them (5.5%+3.4%+1.8%+5.6%=16.3%, and 67%=100%−16%−6%−4%−7%).

Source: Drawn from figures given in table 6 of the original study: Bradshaw, J. and Finch, N. (2003) 'Overlaps in dimensions of poverty', *Journal of Social Policy*, vol 32, no 4, pp 513-25.

population, reducing a little for families with children in Britain in the early years of the 21st century through tax credits, but then increasing greatly for all groups as the economic crash is met with policies resulting in widening differentials, felt (subjectively) in what people can get (necessities becoming harder to acquire), and in what they are given (lower real income).

Necessities, worries and strife

In Britain, by the start of the 21st century almost as many households were poor because they lacked the necessities required to be socially included and because their constituent members knew they were poor (5.5%), as were poor because they fell into all three poverty categories (5.6%). When the population was surveyed as to what items were necessities and what were luxuries, the two key essential expenditures that the current poverty line pivoted on were, first, an ability to make small savings each month (£10 in the case of Britain);

and, second, to be able have an annual holiday away from home and the wider family. These were the two items that a majority of people in Britain thought others should, as a minimum, be able to afford and which the largest numbers could not afford.[4]

The injustice of social exclusion had, by the 21st century, debt at its heart in place of the joblessness, destitution and old age that were the key drivers of 'want' when today's pensioners were born. It is now debt that prevents most poor people from being able to afford necessities – you cannot save each month if you have debts to pay off and holidays are affordable to almost anyone except those with too much unsecured debt. As debt grew in importance over time, the link between low income and low expenditure on necessities weakened slightly, with the smallest overlap in Figure 6 being between those two poverty measures. This is because low income does not initially prevent the purchase of necessities if there is access to debt.

In countries where inequality is higher, debts are accrued to pay for holidays, and to allow the newly income-poor, those who lose their jobs, divorce or see their spouse die, to be (for a little while at least) less expenditure-poor. The effect in Britain of the increased necessity of falling back on debt and of keeping up appearances, in what has become one of the most unequal countries in Western Europe, was that half of the mountain of all credit card debt in all of Western Europe was held solely by British citizens by 2006.[5] A not insignificant proportion of that debt had been amassed to finance going on holiday. People were taking holidays more than ever before, because in Britain being able to take a holiday had become the marker of social acceptability, just as being able to wear a suit to church had been in a previous era, and just as being able to afford to run a car if you had children became a social norm not long after that. In the US another significant purchase, a second car for a family of four or more, serves the same purpose of establishing yourself as someone currently coping rather than not. It is not the object itself, but what it signifies and makes possible that matters. The US built suburbs without pavements. The UK built up the idea that those who worked hard would be rewarded with holidays. Tony Blair used to take his very publicly, alongside (Sir) Cliff Richard, the man who made millions singing about holidays in 1963 at a time when most people could neither afford an annual holiday nor choose to borrow to take one.[6]

Holidays matter now in most rich countries because they have become such a clear marker separating those who are just getting by from those who are doing all right from those who are doing well or very well. 'Where did you go on holiday?' is now an extremely intimate question to ask of another adult; the answers divide parents picking up children from school into groups; they divide work colleagues into camps; they divide pensioners by their employment history as it is that history that determines their pensions and hence their holidays.

Rest days and Sabbath days, festive seasons and taboos on working at certain times have all been built into human cultures to ensure that we take holidays. Relaxation is vital, but today's holidays are often not greatly satisfying, family holidays having the most minor of net effects on reported subjective happiness compared with almost anything else that occurs of significance in people's lives.[7] Perhaps it was always thus, but it is hard to believe that those who first won the right to an annual holiday did not usually greatly enjoy that time off.

In an age where holidays are common people mostly take holidays because other people take holidays. It has become an expectation, and as a result holiday making in affluent countries is remarkably similar within each country as compared to between countries. Most people in Japan take only a few days' holiday a year, but household working weeks and working lives are not excessively long. In contrast, the two-week 'summer holiday' and one-week 'winter break' have become standard in parts of Europe. In contrast again, only minimal holidays are common in the US where holiday pay is still rare. Everyone needs a rest, but whether that rest comes in the form of an annual holiday depends on when and where you are. Holidays became the marker of social inclusion in affluent European societies by the start of the current century because they were the marginal item in virtual shopping baskets, that commodity which could be afforded if there was money to spare, but which had to be forgone in hard times.

Safeguarding social standing

In any society with even the slightest surplus there is always a marginal commodity. It has been through observing behaviour historically in relation to those marginal commodities that the unwritten rules of societies were initially unravelled. The necessity of having furniture, televisions, cars and holidays came long after it was observed that workers needed good quality shirts and shoes (recognised in 1759), that in order to have self-respect they should not to have to live in a 'hovel' (observed by 1847), and that it was not unreasonable to ask to be able to afford a postage stamp (at least by 1901).[8] Mill-loom woven shirts, brick-built terraced houses, postage stamps, all became necessities less than a lifetime after the mass production of looms and large-scale brick making and the introduction of the Penny Post in Britain and equivalents in many similar countries. Within just one more lifetime, the mechanisation of looms, automation of brick making and (partly) of letter sorting had made shirts, brick-built homes and postage stamps parts of life that all could enjoy, no longer marginal items that the poor had to go without. Slowly a pattern was emerging.

Towards the end of the Second World War it was becoming clear to those studying (male-dominated) society that the '... outstanding discovery of recent historical and anthropological research is that man's economy, as a rule, is submerged in his social relationships. He does not act so as to safeguard his individual interest in the possession of material goods; he acts so as to safeguard his social standing, his social claims, his social assets'.[9] However, what was far from clear in 1944 was in what ways, as men's (and then women's) individual interests in material goods, their basic needs, were better met, would people need to act differently to maintain their social standing. Pecking orders and rank do not simply disappear in an abundance of goods. For men, social standing had largely been secured through earning enough to safeguard their family, enough to be able to afford to put a good shirt on their own back, enough to feel they were not living in a hovel. Occasionally a man might have spent the excess on trinkets such as a postage stamp for a letter to a lover, and much more often beer, the poorest of men and women drinking themselves to death on gin. However, from the 1960s onwards those times began to fade in memory, as mass consumption followed mass production.

Mass consumption often consists of what appear to be trinkets and trivia, of more clothes than people possibly need, no longer one good linen shirt, or of more shoes than can easily be stored, no longer just one good pair, of houses with more rooms than can easily be kept clean, and in place of that postage stamp, junk mail. However, trinkets, trivia and fecklessness only appear as such to those not over-purchasing or over-consuming. From the trading of shells in ancient Polynesian societies, to curvier cars in 1950s America, we have long purchased with our social status foremost in mind.

Trinkets have always held great social importance and mechanisation did not decrease this. Mass-produced trinkets, such as jewellery in place of shells, and production-line cars, and their purchasing, wearing and driving, soon came to no longer signify high standing; that requires scarcity. Mass-produced goods soon become necessities, and after that are simply taken for granted. In Europe in 1950 to be without a car was normal; 50 years later it is a marker of poverty. In Europe in 1950 most people did not take a holiday; 50 years later not taking a holiday has become a marker of poverty (and holidays can now easily cost more than second-hand cars).

Most of the increase in debt that has occurred since the 1950s has been accrued by people in work. Of those debts not secured on property (mortgages), most have been accrued by people in low-paid work. Work alone no longer confers enough status and respect, not if it is poorly paid. People working on poverty wages (in Europe three fifths of national median wages) tend to be most commonly employed in the private sector, then in the voluntary sector, and most rarely in the state sector.[10] The private sector pays higher (on arithmetical but not median average) because those in charge of themselves with little accountability to others tend to pay themselves very well, and by doing so reinforce the idea that the more valuable a person you are the more money you should have. The state sector pays its managers less because there is a little more self-control levied when accountability is greater. In the absence of accountability people in the state sector are just as capable of transgressing, as state-employed members of the UK Parliament illustrated when many of their actions were revealed in the expenses scandal of 2008/09. What they bought with those expenses illustrated what they had come to see as acceptable purchases in an age of high and rising inequality. The voluntary sector is a mix of these two extremes. God or the charity commissioners might be omnipresent in theory, but in practice he/she/they are not spending government money. In all sectors if you find yourself at the bottom of each pyramid, and the pyramids are being elongated upwards (to slowly look more like upside-down parsnips than ancient tombs), to then value your intrinsic self when others are so materialistic requires either great and unusual tenacity, or borrowing just a little extra money to supplement your pay. You borrow it to buy things which others like you have because 'you're worth it', and you want to believe you are like them, not inferior to them.

Mortification and empathy

If you have been led to believe that a valuable person is a well-paid person then it becomes especially important to accrue debt when your income is falling in order to maintain your self-esteem, to avert what even hard-nosed economists from Adam Smith onwards have identified as the mortifying effect of social downgrading.[11] People spend and get into debt to maintain their social position, not out of envy of the rich, but out of the necessity to maintain self-respect.[12] Social downgrading has a physical effect on human bodies, akin to the feeling of being sick to the depths of your stomach as you make a fool of yourself in public. Humans are conditioned, and have almost certainly evolved, to fit in, to be social animals, to feel pain, concern and anxiety which prevents them from acting in ways likely to lead to their being ostracised by their small social group. We have recently come to realise that it is not just our own social pain that we feel, but through possessing 'mirror neurons' we physically feel the pain of others as our empathetic brain appears to be '… automatic and embedded'.[13]

We now know some of the physical reasons why most of us react instantly to others' hurt, social hurt as well as physical. If you see someone hit on the head you wince. If you see someone shamed, you too feel their shame physically. If social standing is linked to financial reward it becomes necessary to accrue and to spend more and more in order to stay still. The alternative, of not seeing financial reward as reflecting social standing, is a modern-day heresy. It is possible to be a heretic, to not play the game, to not consume so much, to not be so concerned with material goods, but it is not easy. If it were easy to be a heretic there would be far more heretics; they would form a new religion and we would no longer recognise them as heretics. To reject contemporary materialism you would have to give others (including children) presents only in the quantities that your grandparents were given, own as many clothes as they did, quantities which were adequate when two could share one wardrobe; you are no heretic if you simply consume a little less than others currently around you and recycle a little more. It is partly because we consume so much more than our grandparents that we get in such debt.

For some, the alternative to getting into debt is not to take a holiday. At the height of the worldwide economic boom in 2001, in one of the richest cities on the planet, one child in every five in London had no annual holiday because their parents could not afford one.[14] Very few of the parents of those children will have chosen for their child not to have had a holiday that year because they saw package holidays as a con, or hiring a caravan for a week as an unnecessary luxury. Of the children being looked after by a single parent in London the same survey of recreational norms showed that *most* had no annual holiday, and that 44% of those single parent-headed families could not afford other things commonly assumed to be essentials, such as household insurance. If holidays are now seen as essential, household insurance is hardly an extravagance. Nationally only 8% of households are uninsured.[15] Insurance makes it possible to replace the material goods amassed over a lifetime, goods you could mostly live without physically, but not socially. It is the families of the poorest of children who are most likely to suffer from theft and the aftermath of theft, or fire or flooding because they more often live where burglary is more common, where house fires are more likely, and where homes are cheaper because they are built lower down the hill where they are at greater risk of flooding. So, for them, avoiding paying insurance is not a sensible saving.

While a few people get very rich running the firms that sell insurance, that does not mean it is sensible to avoid insurance altogether. The less you have to start with the more you may need what you do have. If you are not insured then the only way to cope with insurable events may be to get further into debt. It is often shocks such as these that plunge families into long-lasting debt, but rising debt is a product of rising lending. And all this is as true internationally as it is in the homes of the London poor.

Corruption and usury

Just as there is money to be made out of the poor who live in the shadows of Canary Wharf and Manhattan by those working in finance, as long as many are ripped off just a little, so too, but on a far greater scale, is there money to be made from the poor abroad. Commentators from rich countries, especially national leaders, often boast about various aspects of the roughly US$100 billion a year which their countries donate as aid (or spend on debt write-offs) for people in poor countries. They rarely comment on how, for every one of those dollars another 10 flow in the opposite direction, siphoned out of poor countries, mainly by traders who buy cheap and sell dear. The estimates that have been made[16] suggest that major corporations are responsible for the majority of the trillion-dollar-a-year flow of illicit funds to rich nations using webs of financial trusts, nominee bank accounts, numerous methods to avoid tax and simple mispricing. The firms most prominently featuring in many accounts are oil, commodity and mining firms. Traditional bribery and corruption within poor countries accounts for only 3% of this sum. Despite this, when corruption is considered it is almost always that kind of corruption and not the other 97%, the corruption of very rich Western bankers and businessmen (and a handful of businesswomen) that is being thought of. This corruption is orchestrated from places such as those gleaming financial towers of London's banking centre, from New York, and from a plethora of well-connected tax havens.

Between 1981 and 2001 only 1.3% of worldwide growth in income was in some way directed towards reducing the dollar-a-day poverty that the poorest billion live with. In contrast, a majority of all the global growth in income during the 1990s was secured by the richest 10% of the planet's population.[17] Most of that growth in income was growth in the value of the stocks and shares which were traded by people like those immoral bankers. However, for the richest in the world the returns from these were not enough, and they invested millions at a time in hedge funds run by yet more private bankers who worked in less obvious edifices than skyscrapers. It is the monies that these people hold which have come to give them a right, they say, to 'earn' more money. Ultimately those extra monies have to come from somewhere and so are conjured up from others as debt 'interest' (as more is lent). The richer the rich become, the greater the debt of others, both worldwide and in the shadows of the bankers' own homes. In Chapter 6, Table 6 (page 231) documents the many trillions of dollars of debt amassed in the US from 1977 to 2008, but to concentrate on it here takes this story on a little too far.

Before looking at where we are now, and to try to find a way out, it is always helpful to look at how we got here. To be rich is to be able to call on the labour and goods of others, and to be able to pass on those rights to your children, in theory in perpetuity. The justification of such a bizarre arrangement requires equally bizarre theories. Traditionally, rich monarchs, abbots of monasteries and Medici-type bankers (and merchants) believed it was God's will that they should have wealth and others be poor. As monarchies crumbled and monasteries were razed, it became clear that many more families could become mini Medicis. That they all did so as the will of God became a less convincing theory, although we did create Protestantism, partly to justify the making of riches on earth. More effectively, instead of transforming religions that preached piety in order to celebrate greed, those who felt the need to justify inequality turned to science (once seen as heresy, science is often now described as the new religion of our times). More specifically, those searching to find new stories to justify inequality turned to the new political and economic science of the Enlightenment,[18] then to emerging natural sciences, in particular to biology, and finally to new forms of mathematics itself.

4.2 Geneticism: the theories that exacerbate social exclusion

If most people in affluent nations believed that all human beings were alike, then it would not be possible under affluent conditions to justify the exclusion of so many from so many social norms. The majority would find it abhorrent that a large minority should be allowed to live in poverty if they saw that minority as the same sort of people as themselves. And the majority would be appalled that above them a much smaller minority should be allowed to exclude themselves through their wealth. It is only because the majority of people in many affluent societies have come to be taught (and to believe) that a few are especially able, and others particularly undeserving, that current inequalities can be maintained. Inequalities cannot be reduced while enough people (falsely) believe that inequalities are natural, and a few even that inequalities are beneficial.

It was only in the course of the last century that theories of inherent differences among the whole population became widespread. Before then it was largely believed that the gods ordained only the chosen few to be inherently different, those who should be favoured, the monarchs and the priests. In those times there were simply not enough resources for the vast majority to live anything other than a life of frequent want. It was only when more widespread inequalities in income and wealth began to grow under 19th-century industrialisation that theories (stories) attempting to justify these new inequalities as natural were widely propagated. Out of evolutionary theory came the idea that there were a few great families which passed on superior abilities to their offspring and, in contrast, a residuum of inferior but similarly interbreeding humans who were much greater in number.[19] Often these people, the residuum, came to rely on various poor laws for their survival and were labelled 'paupers'. Between these two extremes was the mass of humanity in the newly industrialising countries, people labelled as capable of hard working but incapable of great thinking.

Inequality as 'variation'

Scientific diagrams were produced to support these early geneticist beliefs. One, redrawn here as Figure 7, purports to show that the 1891 geographical distribution of recorded paupers in England and Wales followed a natural pattern, a result, it was presumed, of breeding. These paupers were people recorded as receiving what was called 'outdoor relief', the most basic of poverty relief which did not force the recipient to enter a workhouse. Such relief ranged in prevalence between geographical areas from about 0.5% of the population, to highs of around 8.5% (not at all unlike the variation in the rates of people claiming unemployment benefits in those two countries a century later). The figure also shows two statistical curves plotted on the original diagram by its original author, Karl Pearson, to try to fit the data best. These were the point binomial and normal (bell curve) distributions. The reason the curves were fitted was to further the attempt to imply that variation in numbers of paupers between areas followed some kind of 'natural' distribution. The normal distribution was around this time first being assumed to describe the distribution of intelligence. Hereditary thinking would have it that some areas had more paupers because more genetically inferior people had come to cluster there and had interbred; other areas were spared such pauperisation presumably due to the inherent superiority of the local populace, through the driving away of paupers or through their 'extinction' via the workhouse or starvation. The close fit of the two curves to the actual data was implicitly being put forward as proof that there was an underlying natural process determining the numbers identified as being in this separate (implicitly sub-human) group. This was apparently revealed to be so when all the subjects were separated into some 632 poor law union areas and the paupers' proportions calculated. The graph was published in 1895.

Figure 7 is important because it is a reproduction of one of the first attempts to use a graph to apply a statistical description to groups of people and to demonstrate to others that the outcome, what is observed, reflects a process that cannot be seen without that graph but which must be happening to result in such a distribution. Millions of similar bell curves have been drawn since of supposed

Figure 7: Geographical distribution of paupers, England and Wales, 1891

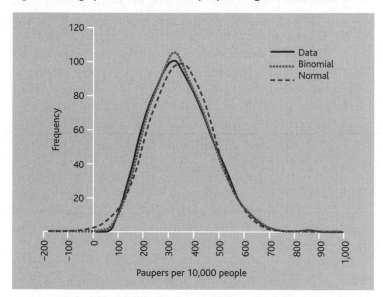

Note: Y-axis: frequency of unions reporting each rate, or modelled rates predicted under the binomial or normal distributions.

Source: Data reproduced in Table 4, page 108 below. Figure redrawn from the original (Pearson, K (1895) 'Contributions to the mathematical theory of evolution – II. Skew variation in homogeneous material', *Philosophical transactions of the Royal Society of London, Series A, Mathematical*, vol 186, pp 343-414, Figure 17, plate 13)

human variation in ability. The apparent smoothness of the data curve and closeness of the fit is the key to the implication and strength of the claim that some natural law is being uncovered. At the time the distribution in Figure 7 was drawn, the Gaussian (or Laplacian) statistical distribution being applied to a probability was well known among scientists, but the idea of it being seen as biologically normal was less than a couple of decades old.[20] It was very shortly after this that the Gaussian/Laplacian (bell-shaped) distribution came to be described as somehow 'natural', as 'normal'. Just at the time, in fact, that it came to be used to describe people.

When it comes to categorising human ability, the process by which a distribution comes to take on the appearance of a bell-shaped curve is far more likely to reflect the forces acting on those who count than those who are counted. Nowadays people who enjoy setting tests are taught to set them in such a way that the distribution of marks that students receive tends to form just such a shape.[21] It is always possible to set tests that form very different shapes, such as for quiz shows where the prize money doubles with each correct answer and the questions become progressively much harder, but if you want to suggest that your students are distributed by ability along a normal curve then you can easily set a test that shows this curve, or any other curve you fancy. For instance, if you want to suggest that almost none of your students are lazy, almost all are especially able, then you do not subdivide second degree classes in your university. It is also important to remember that random social processes, such as noting in which areas more winning lottery tickets are sold, having taken into account the numbers sold, will reflect a normal distribution if there are enough winners. Thus, if the marking of university degrees was largely a random process, we would expect a normal distribution to emerge. What is interesting is the occasion when the data fit so closely to such a distribution that it is unlikely that such a good fit would have happened by chance. This is what Figure 7 suggests.

Fixing the figures

In 1891 there was great pressure on poor law unions not to give too much 'relief'. Unemployment, a new term of the time, had hit different areas with different effects. Different places had had bad harvests; different industries had been differently hurt by the recession of the late 1880s; poor law union officials did not want to look out of line and tried to curtail their spending, so no surprising outliers were found; almost every district had a workhouse and some monies for outdoor relief (not requiring institutionalisation) so that a small number would always be provided for. Almost the very last people to have an individual impact on the shape of the distribution were the paupers themselves, but just as it is not the unemployed today who choose to be unemployed, or who carry some inherited propensity to unemployment, the paupers of yesterday had little say over what was said about them or whether they became paupers.

Today we largely recognise that in rich countries unemployment is mostly the product of being born at the wrong time in the wrong place and can strike us all, although with greatly varying probabilities depending on our precise circumstances,[22] but we live in danger of forgetting this and of reverting to the late 19th-century thinking of eugenics, the 'science' of drawing (what are either explicitly or implicitly claimed as) ability distributions from outcome events, of which Figure 7 is the world's first ever geographical example.

Like today's unemployed, the paupers of 1891 did have a small role to play in their distribution as many moved around the country. With little support people tend not to stay for long in a place with no work if they can help it, and so move towards jobs. Outdoor relief was supposed to be available only to local people, in order to reduce such migrations, but if there was a single process whereby the actions of individuals were helping to form the shape of the curve it was through their get-up-and-go, not their recidivism. However, it was recidivism for which the drawer of the curves was looking.

It would prove very little were the statistical curves in Figure 7 found to be good fits to the data. But it is an interesting exercise to test the degree to which the data and the two statistical curves are similar. There are many ways of testing the likelihood of data following a particular statistical distribution. One of the oldest is called Pearson's goodness-of-fit test.[23] It is named after the same man, Karl Pearson, who drew the graph and so it is appropriate to use his own test in order to test the assertion he was implicitly making in drawing these curves. The data behind the curves and the details of the working out of the probabilities are all given in Table 4. What is revealed is intriguing.

The normal curve as drawn by Karl Pearson appears to fit the data very closely. It departs from the data most obviously as it suggests that a few areas should have pauperisation rates of less than 0% and consequently its peak is a little lower than that of the other fitted distribution, or of the data. Normal curves stretch from minus infinity to infinity, suggesting (if intelligence really was distributed according to such curves) that among us all is both one supremely intelligent being and once supremely stupid individual with a negative IQ. Negative intelligence is as silly an idea as a negative pauper rate so it is odd that Pearson drew that line on his graph. However, it is not the slight practical problems of fitting the data to that supposedly normal

Table 4: Pearson goodness-of-fit test of Karl Pearson's pauper data, 1891

Paupers (P)	Normal (N)	Binomial (B)	Data (D)	B–D	(B–D)²	(B–D)²/B
−200	0	0	0			
−150	0	0	0			
−100	0	0	0			
−50	2	0	0			
0	4	1	0	1		
50	10	4	2			
100	19	18	20	1	1	0.043
150	37	44	47	−3	9	0.205
200	63	73	73	0	0	0.000
250	83	90	90	0	0	0.000
300	97	105	100	5	25	0.238
350	97	92	90	2	4	0.043
400	83	75	75	0	0	0.000
450	63	55	55	0	0	0.000
500	37	36	40	−4	16	0.444
550	21	20	21	−1	1	0.050
600	10	12	11	1	1	0.083
650	4	5	5		1	0.143
700	2	1	1			
750	0	1	1	−1		
800	0	0	0			
850	0	0	1			
900	0	0	0			
950	0	0	0			
1,000	0	0	0			
Total	632	632	632			1.25

Notes: For source of data see Figure 7. Both data and fitted curves were read off the original graph.

Columns: D is the number of poor law union areas recording a given number of paupers per 10,000 people (P). The Normal (N) and Binomial (B) are the two possible expected distributions as drawn on Karl Pearson's original diagram along with the data. Cells are amalgamated (*) with expected values of 5 or less (marked by two curly brackets) resulting in 12 categories. The difference between expected and observed (B–D) is calculated, squared, divided by expected (B) and summed. The sum (1.25) is less than the 0.995 probability value (1.735) on a chi-squared distribution with 9 degrees of freedom (12–2 estimated parameters and less another 1 degree given a fixed *n* of 632 union areas). The probability that the data were drawn at random from the binomial distribution is less than 0.5%; the fit using Pearson's own test is probably (with a more than 99.5% probability) too good to be true.

distribution that is intriguing. What is intriguing is just how well the binomial distribution fits the data. The fit is not just close; it is almost unbelievably close. In the language of probabilities it is sensible to never say never, but the chances that the pauper data distribution as drawn in Figure 7 did derive from a process that follows a binomial distribution is quite unlikely. Why? Because the fit is too close, too good, far too good to be true.

Pearson's goodness-of-fit test is usually used to test whether a set of data points are distributed closely enough to an expected distribution, a statistical distribution, for it to be plausible to be able to claim that they were drawn from just such a distribution. An early example of its use was in the discovery of genetics in determining the outcome of crossing different strains of peas. It was posited that the interbreeding of certain peas would produce a certain ratio of peas resulting in one example of one strain to every three of another strain, this just resulting from the crossing of two strains. Each pairing produced a strain by chance, but over time those particular pairings asymptotically resulted in that 1:3 ratio of outcome. It took a long time to arrange for pairs of peas to pair correctly (about the same time as with rabbits), and so a test was needed to be able to say with some confidence that, having recorded several dozen or hundred pairings, the pea offspring were following that 1:3 outcome distribution. This is a 'goodness-of-fit' test.

The goodness-of-fit test provides an estimate of the chances that a particular outcome could result if the underlying distribution were, say, 1:3, but as it can be (what is called) a two-tailed test, it can thus also provide an estimate that the fit is too good to be true. If a geneticist told you that they had crossed 1,000 pairs of peas, and those crosses had resulted in exactly 750 peas of one strain and 250 peas of another strain, the chances are more likely that they are lying about their data than that they actually conducted such an experiment and this was the result. To determine the probability that they were lying, the Pearson goodness-of-fit test, when two-tailed, in effect provides a test of that honesty.

The binomial distribution fits the data shown in Figure 7 so well that the probability that a fit at random would be this good if another set of data were derived from the distribution is less than 0.5%. The usual cut-off used to begin to doubt the plausibility of a fit is 2.5%. This is because, in a two-tailed test, a 95% chance that the data could have arisen from the distribution has been deemed a good level to use, again since around the time of Karl Pearson. In the notes to Table 4 (above) more details are given of applying Pearson's test to his data, and it is of course entirely possible (although unlikely) that results as close fitting as this could have been drawn from the binomial distribution.[24]

A new religion

Am I boring you? It may well be good news if I am. A propensity to find statistics and mathematical probabilities fascinating is not necessarily a sign of a well-rounded individual (see Section 3.2 above), although it is possible to be a well-rounded individual and have a fascination with numbers and sequences that goes beyond normal bounds. It is possible, but an unusually high number of those who find pattern spotting in abstract spaces not to be very difficult have generally found understanding people to be extremely tricky. When reading others' accounts of him it does cross your mind that one of these people might have been Karl Pearson.[25] It is possible that Pearson's thoughts about people led him, perhaps unconsciously, to draw those two curves, the data to the distribution, so closely together on that graph paper so many years ago. It is possible that the fit is true and the commissioners of the poor law unions arranged for the relief to be distributed geographically according to the binomial distribution. But even if most poor law authorities were following the herd in the amount of relief they offered, a few were more generous than most and a few more constrained; the fit should not, if there is also an element of random variation, be that close to the binomial curve. Either they, or Pearson, or both, could have been labouring under the belief popular at the time: that the poor were a curse and were in danger of over-breeding. It is when such beliefs become articles of faith that graphs are drawn with curves that fit as closely and as improbably as Figure 7 suggests. It is when people become convinced that they know a great truth, the underpinnings

—

of what might soon almost become a new religion, that the normal questioning and conventions are abandoned.

Just seven years after drawing his curves of the geography of paupers, Karl Pearson, who came to be seen as one of the founders of the science of eugenics, proclaimed (in 1902) that his belief would prevail and become widespread 'twenty years hence'.[26] He was right in that at least. Eugenics had become almost a religion by the 1920s, it being an article of faith that some were more able than others and that those differences were strongly influenced by some form of inherited acumen. It was not just among the earlier lovers of the new science of statistics that this religion took hold. These ideas were particularly attractive to male mathematicians, natural scientists and, among social scientists, to economists[27] (see Section 6.2 for how orthodox economics and eugenics are so closely related). It really was almost as if there was an innate predisposition to be attracted to eugenists' ideas among those men who found numbers easy but empathising with others a little more difficult. The chance of men being likely to find such communication difficult is four to five times higher than that of women,[28] although there were several key women in the early eugenics movement, when it was still not clear what folly it was. However, the dominance of men among those few who still argue for eugenics today is intriguing. Is it their nature, or their nurture, that leads men more often to such folly?

Women who knew him wrote that Pearson found women tricky. He was far from alone among Victorian men in either this or in believing in eugenics, but there were a few prominent people who offered different views who were not so much products of their time. For instance, although not all early feminists spoke with one voice, the fledging women's movement did argue against eugenicist ideas and specifically Karl Pearson's suggestion that women's primary function was reproduction of the 'race', and that women who resisted his arguments were asexual, in search of an equality with men that was not possible, and that such women were '... a temporary aberration in the race'.[29]

In the years prior to the First World War the myth was first spread that progress for the specific 'races' (mythical races such as the British race, the Aryan or the Nordic race) relied on the identification and empowering of men '… of exceptional talent from the mass … the mass is, almost invariably, feminized'.[30] If geneticist thinking saw races as fundamentally different, sexes were even more riven apart by biological determinist theories of gender difference.[31]

It was partly the immediate reaction of horror to the genocide of the Second World War, but also the experience of working together as a nation in that war, and the later realisation that generation and environment mattered so much more than all else over how well children performed in tests that led to eugenics later being shunned. Hitler's preference for eugenics helped in this. Ideas such as universal health services being made available on an equal basis to all arose as practical possibilities because of this[32] and arose out of that wartime experience which had the unforeseen result of a much wider acceptance of the idea that all people in one country at least were of equal value. It would appear that even mild eugenicists, such as William Beveridge in Britain, exorcised their policy recommendations of eugenicist thinking as they became aware of the genocide being perpetrated early on during the war. And so, in the aftermath of genocide, at the heights of postwar anti-communism, eugenics floundered. Its means and ends were too illiberal. As a result, eugenics as denial of freedom became linked then with fascism and that kept its popularity down.

Crypto-eugenics

By the time of the Soviet invasion of Hungary in 1956, eugenics had to be practised in secret as it had become associated with the totalitarianism of communists as well as fascists. At that time the idea's dwindling supporters used the term 'crypto-eugenics'[33] among themselves largely in secret. By the mid-1970s it was acknowledged that not a single reputable scientific study had been undertaken that suggested with any authority that inheritable intelligence existed.[34] By the early 1980s those few eugenists still out in the open were easy targets for ridicule.[35] And, while taught how to use his tests, university undergraduates studying statistics were taught nothing of Pearson's past and the murky origins of his subject of study. That eugenic past was being forgotten.

In the latter half of the 20th century, partly in reaction to the achievement of greater equalities, and as the passing of time resulted in forgetting the social miseries of 1920s inequality, the economic despair of 1930s depression, the moral outrage of 1940s atrocity and 1950s social contracts to counter communism, growing inequalities were again foisted on populations, and attempts at trying to justify social inequalities crept out of the shadows. At the forefront of the resurgence of the 'eugenic-like' argument was the oft-criticised, simultaneously both dreary and revolting literature on supposedly innate racial differences, literature which so clearly '... compound[s] folly with malice'.[36] But in the background was more subtle writing, driven by a little less overt malice, by men put in positions of power trying to justify the pedestals they stood on. A few examples follow. In those justifications they reached back to that early mixing of genetic theory and human social distribution. And so the too-good-to-be-true fit of two curves drawn by hand and reproduced in the few surviving copies of a dusty old journal of 1895 still matter. The first curves matter because the documents they appear in betray the follies in the founding tenets of geneticism. They matter because the greatest danger is to forget.

Contemporary work on epigenetics explicitly steers away from saying genetic make-up determines the social destiny of humans along an ability continuum.[37] In contrast, geneticism is the current version of the belief that not only do people differ in their inherent abilities, but that our 'ability' (and other psychological differences) is to a large part inherited from our parents. This belief is now again widely held among many of those who advise some of the most powerful governments of the world in the early years of the current century. Eugenism has arisen again 110 years after Figure 7 was drawn, but now goes by a different name and appears in a new form. It is now hiding behind a vastly more complex biological cloak. For example, David Miller, one University of Oxford-based educator among the advisers of the notionally left-wing New Labour government in Britain, suggested (in a book supposed to be concerned with 'fairness') that '... there is a significant correlation between the measured intelligence of parents and their children....

Equality of opportunity does not aim to defeat biology, but to ensure equal chances for those with similar ability and motivation'.[38]

Intelligence is not like wealth. Wealth is mostly passed on rather than amassed. Wealth is inherited. Intelligence, in contrast, is held in common. Intelligence, the capacity to acquire and apply knowledge, is not an individual attribute that people are born with, but rather it is built through learning. No single individual has the capacity to read more than a miniscule fraction of the books in a modern library, and no single individual has the capacity to acquire and apply much more than a tiny fraction of what humans have collectively come to understand. We act and behave as if there are a few great men with encyclopaedic minds able to comprehend the cosmos; we assume that most of us are of lower intelligence and we presume that many humans are of much lower ability than us.

In truth the great men are just as fallible as the lower orders; there are no discernible innate differences in people's capacity to learn. Learning for all is far from easy, which is why it is so easy for some educators to confuse a high correlation between test results of parents and their offspring with evidence of inherited biological limits. It is as wrong to confuse that as it was wrong to believe that there was some special meaning to the fact that the geographical pattern in pauper statistics of 1891 appeared to form a curve when computed in a particular way, ignoring the probable enthusiasm that resulted in a too-good-to-be-true depiction. Human beings cannot be divided into groups with similar inherent abilities and motivations; there is no biological distinction between those destined to be paupers and those set to rule them.[39]

There is a correlation between the geography of those today who make hereditarian claims and their propensity to reveal their beliefs. Today's hereditarians appear to come disproportionately from elite institutions. In Britain the elite university for the humanities is located in Oxford. To give a second example, a former head of Britain's Economic and Social Research Council, Gordon Marshall, and his colleagues suggested that there was the possibility '… that children born to working-class parents simply have less natural ability than those born to higher-class parents'.[40] In saying that the possibility of an inherited 'natural ability' process was at work these academics were only parroting what is commonly believed in such places, oft repeated by colleagues from the same college as the lead author. For instance, here is a third example, from yet another University of Oxford professor, John Goldthorpe, who claims that: 'children of different class backgrounds tend to do better or worse in school – on account, one may suppose, of a complex interplay of sociocultural and genetic factors'.[41] It would be a dreary exercise to trawl through the works of many more contemporary academics at the very pinnacles of the career ladders in countries like Britain and in places like Oxford to draw yet more examples of what 'one may suppose'. While these are only examples drawn from a small group, all three of the professors quoted had access to the ears of government ministers and even prime ministers. Tony Blair, the British Prime Minister during the time they were writing, had clearly come to believe in a geneticism of the kind they promoted, as revealed in his speeches.[42] He is unlikely to have formed such beliefs as a child. Whether he came to his views while he was studying at university as an undergraduate, or later through the influence of advisers, who were in turn influenced by academics (similar to these three), is unclear. What is clear is that by the 1990s geneticism was being widely discussed in circles of power. Should you wish to search for further examples there is now a literature that suggests we should link theories on behavioural genetics with public policy.[43] Rather than search further, however, it is often better to try to understand how particular groups and clusters of people came to hold such views.

We should recognise the disadvantages of working in a place like the University of Oxford when it comes to studying human societies. It is there and in similar places (Harvard and Heidelberg are usually cited) that misconceptions about the nature of society and of other humans can so easily form. This is due to the staggering and strange social, geographical and economic separation of the supposed crème de la crème of society into such enclaves. The elite universities in Paris could be added to a roll call of centres of delusion. They were not in the original listing of a few towns because it was in Paris that the man making that initial list, Pierre Bourdieu, ended up working.[44] And there is much more to Paris than its universities, but that is also true of Oxford, Boston and Heidelberg.

———

4.3 Segregation: of community from community

It is easier to grow up in Boston or Oxford and know nothing of life
on the other side of your city than is the case in Paris or Heidelberg.
This is because social inequality in the US and the UK is greater than
in France or Germany. Maintaining high levels of inequality within
a country results in rising social exclusion. This occurs even without
increases in income inequality. Simply by holding inequalities at a
sufficiently high level the sense of failure of most is maintained long
enough to force people to spend highly and get into further debt
just to maintain their social position. And one effect of living in an
affluent society under conditions of high inequality is that social
polarisation increases between areas. Geographically, with each year
that passes, where you live becomes more important than it was
last year. As the repercussions of rising social exclusion grow, the
differences between the educational outcomes of children going to
different schools become ever more apparent; buying property with
mortgage debt in more expensive areas appears to become a better
long-term 'investment' opportunity, and thus in so many ways, as the
difficulties of living in poverty under inequality increase, living away
from the poorer people becomes ever more attractive, and for most
people, ever more unobtainable.

When social inequalities become extremely high the poor are no
longer considered similar people to the rich (and even to the average
person), and issues such as poverty can become little investigated
because they are seen not to matter. Because of this, and because it
is hard to ask general questions about poverty and living standards in
the most unequal of rich countries (that is, the US, based on income
inequalities) it is necessary to look at slightly more equitable places,
such as Britain, to understand how poverty can rise even when
(unlike in the US) the real incomes of the poor are rising slightly.
Britain is among those nations in which rates of poverty resulting
from inequalities have been very carefully monitored, and so it is
worth considering as a general example of (and a warning about)
the way poverty can grow under conditions of affluence, even of
economic boom, given enough inequality. In the decade before the
2008 economic crash hit and poverty by any definition increased

sharply once again, Britain provided an abject lesson in how social exclusion could grow sharply. It grew simply because the rich took so much more of what growth there had been than the poor.

Poverty surveys

The social experiment of holding inequality levels in Britain high during the economic boom, which coincided with Tony Blair's 1997–2007 premiership, has allowed the effects of such policies to be monitored by comparing surveys of poverty undertaken at around the start of the period with those undertaken towards the end.[45] Among British adults during the Blair years the proportion unable to make regular savings rose from 25% to 27%; the number unable to afford an annual holiday away from home rose from 18% to 24%; and the national proportion who could not afford to insure the contents of their home climbed a percentage point, from 8% to 9%. However, these national proportions conceal the way in which the rising exclusion has hit particular groups especially hard, not least a group that the Blair government had said it would help above all others: children living in poverty.

The comparison of poverty surveys taken towards the start and end of Tony Blair's time in office found that, of all children, the proportion living in a family that could not afford to take a holiday away from home and family relations rose between 1999 and 2005, from 25% to 32%. This occurred even as the real incomes of most of the poorest rose; they just rose more for the affluent. In consequence, as housing became more unequally distributed, the number of children of school age who had to share their bedroom with an adult or sibling over the age of 10 and of the opposite sex rose from 8% to 15% nationally. It was in London that such overcrowding became most acute and where sharing rooms rose most quickly. Keeping up appearances for the poor in London was much harder than in Britain as a whole,[46] not simply because London had less space, but because within London other children were so often very wealthy. Even among children going to the same school the incomes of their parents had diverged and consequently standards of living and expectations of the norm did too. Who do you have round for tea from school when you are

ashamed of your home because (as a teenage girl) you do not want
to admit to sharing a bedroom with your older brother? Nationally,
the proportion who said their parent(s) could not afford to let them
have friends round for tea doubled, from 4% to 8%. The proportion
of children who could not afford to pursue a hobby or other leisure
activity also rose, from 5% to 7%, and the proportion who could not
afford to go on a school trip at least once a term doubled, from 3%
to 6%. For children aged below five, the proportion whose parents
could not afford to take them to playgroup each week also doubled
under the Blair government, from 3% to 6%.

For those who do not have to cope with debts it becomes easier
to imagine why you might go further into debt when that debt
allows you, for example, to have the money to pay a pound to attend
a playgroup rather than sit another day at home with your toddler.
Taking out a little more debt helps pay another couple of pounds so
that your school-age child can go on a school trip and not have to
pretend to be ill that day. Concealing poverty becomes ever more
difficult in an age of consumption. When you are asked at school
where you went on holiday, or what you got for Christmas, a very
active imagination helps in making up a plausible lie. Living in a
consumerist society means living with the underlying message that
you do not get to go on holiday or get presents like other children
because you have not been good enough, because your family are
not good enough. The second most expensive of all consumption
items are housing costs – the rent or mortgage – and these have also
diverged as income inequalities have increased. Having to move to a
poorer area, or being unable to move out of one, is the geographical
reality of social exclusion. People get into further debt to avoid
this. But usually debt simply delays the day you have to move and
makes even deeper the depth of the hole you move into. The most
expensive consumer item is a car (cars have been more costly than
home buying in aggregate). This is why so many people buy cars
through hire purchase, or 'on tick' as it used to be called in Britain,
or 'with finance' as the euphemism now is. The combined expense
and necessity of car ownership is the reason why not having a car
is for many a contemporary mark of social failure. It is also closely
connected to why so many car firms were badly hit so early on in

the crash of 2008, as they were selling debt as much as selling cars (see Section 6.1).

Poverty cycles

Snap-shots of figures from comparative social surveys reveal the direction of social change, but underplay the extent to which poverty is experienced over time because many more families and individuals experience poverty than are poor at any one time. The figures on the growth of social exclusion under the New Labour government often surprise people in Britain because they are told repeatedly how much that government was doing to try to help the poor, and there were a lot of policies.[47] What these policies did achieve was to put a floor under how bad things could get for most, but not all, people, by introducing a low minimum wage, and a higher minimum income for families with children through complex tax credits plus a huge range of benefits-in-kind 'delivered' through various programmes. However, the minimums were not enough to enable many families to live in a 'respectable' way. They were not designed to do this, but to act as a launching pad from which people tried to work harder and onto which they fell during the bad times. Like a trampoline at the bottom of a vertical obstacle course where different parts of the climbing wall are labelled exclusion and inclusion, New Labour policy helped cycle people around various 'opportunities' in life, including bouncing a few very high, given the government's parallel policies up until 2008 of being seriously relaxed about financial regulation, and also about the wealth of the super-rich.[48] More benevolent social policies might have put a slightly higher limit on how far down it was possible to fall if you had children, but they did nothing to narrow the range of inequalities in incomes and wealth overall, nothing to reduce the number of people who ended up falling down into a cycle of deprivation or the amount of money which ended up trickling into the pockets of a few.

Figure 8 illustrates the cycle of exclusion and inclusion in societies like Britain. Each circle in the figure represents the economic position of a household at one fixed instance; the arrows show the prevailing direction in which most households move socially, and the boxes

Figure 8: Circling from exclusion to inclusion and back again (model)

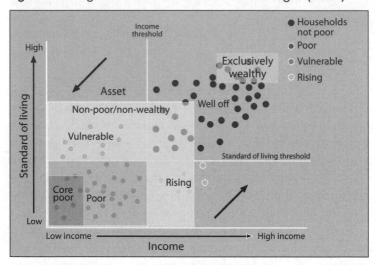

Source: Adapted from David Gordon's original and much replicated drawing.[50] See publication details of various of the works (where earlier versions appear) at the Townsend Centre for International Poverty Research, University of Bristol (www.bris.ac.uk/poverty/).

show how these households can be categorised at any point in time.[49] Starting bottom right, as a household's income rises when a job is gained or a partnership is formed, expenditure and standard of living also rise, but a little later. It is that expenditure that allows the household to become better socially included, to afford a little saving, to have an annual holiday. A few households, usually dual earner, see their incomes rise even further, experience no financial knocks, no redundancies, little illness, no divorce, and begin to be able to save more, take a few more holidays a year, move to a 'better' area, send their children to a private school. If all still goes well they typically take out private health insurance and move into the top right box where they are excluded from the norms of society by being above them. This group grew slightly in size under Margaret Thatcher's government in the 1980s and again since 1997 as the incomes of those already paid most were allowed to rise most quickly. However, most people whose incomes rose in countries such as the US and Britain did not receive enough extra to be able to enter this box, and many who did fell out, again through divorce, downgrading at work or simply through falling ill.

When a financial knock comes households are hardly ever in a position to immediately decrease their outgoings in line with their decreased income. Instead they move across the diagram in Figure 8, from right to left, from being exclusively wealthy to being normal; from being normal to being vulnerable, exhausting savings and getting into debt to avoid having to reduce expenditure as rapidly as their incomings are falling. They do this to avoid having to take no holidays at all, after they have become used to having several a year. They think they are being frugal, but they are spending more than is coming in because, as the width and the height of the cycle becomes larger with growing inequality, it becomes harder to learn how to live like others live. Households cut back, but rarely in direct proportion to the cuts in their income, largely because they feel they have to maintain their dignity and social standing. In the same way, they rarely increase expenditure directly in line with any windfall; given a lot of money, most people do not know what to do with it at first. It is because of our commitments and burdens that socially we spiral anti-clockwise around Figure 8, often in small circles in just part of the realm of possibilities, not too near the bottom if we are lucky, spinning round over larger cycles, or trapped in the bottom left-hand corner if less fortunate. After misfortune, those lucky enough to find another partner with a good income quickly following divorce, lucky enough to quickly get another job or to quickly recover from the illness that had led to their troubles, can cycle round again, but many are not so lucky and drop down the left-hand side of the cycle, down to poverty and social exclusion of various degrees of acuteness, and most stay there for considerable lengths of time.

Poverty choices

As expenditure is (over the long term) clearly constrained by income, the higher the income inequalities a society tolerates, the greater inequalities in standards of living and expenditure its people will experience, and the wider and higher will be both axes of possibility shown in Figure 8. Very few households cycle from the extremes of

---

top right to bottom left. Instead there are many separate eddies and currents within those extremes. The rich live in fear of being 'normal' and in hope of being ever more rich, but have little concept of what poverty really is. The richer they get the more they rely on interest 'earned' from their savings to fund their expenditure. Much of that income is derived from their banks lending those savings to the poor. Sub-prime mortgages were especially fashionable because they were aimed at the poor from whom greatest profit is usually made by lenders through the highest interest rates being charged. Without the poor paying interest on debt, and the average paying instalments on mortgages, the rich could not have so many holidays, could not spiral around in their own worlds as easily. Each rich saver requires the additional charges on debt payment of many dozens of average and poor people to generate the interest payments that their much larger savings accrue (or did before interest rates were slashed worldwide over the course of 2008). Thus there are only a few households that can ever get to the top right-hand corner of Figure 8; the rich can only ever be a small and very expensive minority.

For each affluent country in the world, in each different decade, a different version of Figure 8 can be drawn. In some countries the range along the bottom is much shorter than in others and as a consequence the range of expenditures along the side is shorter; far fewer families fall down into poverty, and slightly fewer families (but with much less money) move up into the box marked 'exclusively wealthy'. This was true of Britain and the US half a century ago; it is true of Japan and France today. We choose the shape that Figure 8 takes, or we allow others to choose to shape it, to stretch it, to make the eddies small and smooth or larger and more violent. Insecurity rises when it becomes easier to spin around, or reduces when we reduce inequalities or when we stultify the mixing such as when rank and race are made more permanent attributes and the cycle is a picture of many small eddies. In different countries different social battles have different outcomes; different decisions have been taken by, or were taken for, the people there.

Those countries on the losing side of the Second World War, including Germany, Japan and Italy, had in some cases great equality thrust on them through the eradication of the remaining wealth of their old aristocracies by occupying forces, and by the introduction of land reform resulting in wealth becoming much more equally spread out by the 1950s and 1960s. That land reform occurred under postwar military occupation. American military intervention in Korea and also the establishing of a presence (at one time) in Iceland, ironically also partly contributed to the rise of equality in those countries. The redistribution of land was seen as one way to avert the rise of communism by US planners working overseas after the war.

Figure 8 is drawn to represent the extent of inequalities and the exclusion that results, as experienced in Britain by the early years of the current century. The simplest and most telling way in which that inequality can best be described is to understand that, by 2005, the poorest fifth of households in Britain had each to rely on just a seventh of the income of the best-off fifth of households. A fifth of people had to work for seven days, to receive what another fifth earned in one day. Imagine working Monday, Tuesday, Wednesday, Thursday, Friday and Monday and Tuesday again, to get what another receives for just one day of work, that single day's work almost always being less arduous, more fulfilling, more enjoyable, and of higher status, than your seven. Well-paid work is almost certainly a far more luxurious pastime than seven days spent surviving on the dole, or on a state pension. Well-paid work is almost always non-manual, undertaken in well-heated or air-conditioned premises, sitting in comfortable chairs, doing interesting things, meeting people, travelling. People gaining well-paid work acclimatise extremely quickly to their lot and rarely count their blessings. The affluent are not paid more because their work is more arduous, but because of the kind of society they live in. They are paid similarly to other affluent people living in the same country.

International comparisons of the quintile range of income inequality are some of the most telling comparisons that can be made between countries. The best current estimate of UK income inequality on this measure is that the best-off fifth received 7.2 times more income on average than the worst-off fifth each year by 2005.[51] According to the tables in the UN Development Programme's Annual Report, the most widely used source, that ratio has most recently been 6.1 to 1 in Ireland, in France it is 5.6 to 1, in Sweden it is 4.0

to 1 and in Japan it is 3.4 to 1. By contrast, in the US that same ratio of inequality is 8.5 to 1.

To reiterate, in a country like Japan where, if you are at the bottom of the heap, you need 'only' work Monday, Tuesday, Wednesday and Thursday morning, to gain what those at the top are awarded for working just on Monday, low-paid work is not so bad; although the figures are disputed, and although all is far from utopia in Japan, that extent of equality has actually been achieved. Want to find a country where people of different social strata live more often in similar neighbourhoods than they do in Europe? Visit Japan. In contrast, in the US you need to labour for the number of days the worst-off (day labourers) work in Japan and a whole additional five-day working week to achieve the same reward, the same money as the best-off fifth earn in a single day. If you want to find a country with far less mixed neighbourhoods than in Europe, visit the US.

4.4 Escapism: of the rich behind walls

The human failing most closely associated with exclusion is a particular kind of bigotry, an intolerance of those seen as beneath you, and the extent of such bigotry varies greatly between places. The structure of human relationships varies between different affluent countries most clearly according to how unequal each is. In affluent countries with great inequalities it is possible to hire armies of cleaners and to set them to work each night making office blocks appear immaculate in the morning. And it is not just the cleaners, but many more people who need to wake up in the early hours to undertake the long commute to work in those countries as compared with more equitable ones (commuting times are shorter, there is better public transport and even the trains run to time more often in more equal affluent countries). Many more try to hold down several jobs at once in unequal countries because they need the extra money. More are day labourers, regularly looking for new piecework, often spending many days without paid work hanging around where they might be picked up to do a cash-in-hand labouring job. Of those with a work contract in unequal countries, many more have to work long hours in paid employment; holiday, maternity and sickness pay is often worse than in most OECD countries, or non-existent.[52]

Inequality and personal relationships

Children are far more often put into day care in countries where wages and benefits are more unequal. More inequality also results in more nannies, day care for the children of the affluent. With greater inequality the cost of day care in general is less for the affluent as the wages of the carers are relatively lower and more 'affordable', but the need for two adults to earn in affluent families is greater in unequal countries as even affluent couples tend not to think they have enough coming in when wide inequalities are normal. Those who are affluent do not compare themselves and their lives with the lives of those who care for their children or who clean their workplaces. They compare themselves with other couples they see as like themselves, in particular other couples with just a little bit more. In more unequal affluent countries when couples split up, which they do more frequently, they become new smaller households with lower incomes and so often drop down the sharply differentiated social scale. It is not just because of the awkwardness of the split that they lose so many of their 'friends'. It is because friendship in more unequal countries is more often about mixing with the smaller group of people who are like you.

People live far more similar (and often simpler) lives in affluent countries where incomes, expenditures and expectations are more equal. For instance, what they eat at breakfast will be similar to what others eat, and they are all more likely to be eating breakfast, not having to skip that meal for the commute, or sending their children to school hungry to save a little money. In more equal countries children are much more likely to travel to the nearest school to learn; so the lengths of journeys to school are shorter and far fewer children need to be driven. They are more likely to eat with their parents before school and they are more likely to still have two parents at home. Their friends will more often be drawn from nearby, and from much more of a cross-section of society than in more unequal countries. And that wider cross-section will not vary as much by income, standard of living and expectations. In more unequal countries parents feel the need to be more careful in monitoring who their child's friends are (and even who their own friends are). If they are rich then more often they drive their children to visit friends past the homes of nearby children considered less suitable to be their offsprings' friends, driving from affluent enclave to affluent enclave. If very rich they even have another adult do that driving. But the most effective way for parents in an affluent unequal country to monitor who their offspring mixes with is through segregating them from others by where they choose to live. Parents do this not because they are callous, but because they are insecure, more afraid, more ignorant of others, less trustful, in more unequal countries. The evidence that levels of trust are higher in more equal countries was made widely available in 2009 by the Equality Trust (www.equalitytrust.org.uk/why/evidence).

Insecurity and mistrust

Insecurity and mistrust rise as inequality rises. Those with resources have to look a longer way down to see where they might end up should anything go seriously wrong in their lives. Depression, unemployment and divorce feature highly as personal failings to be feared; fears of pandemics and atrocities, worldwide recession and large-scale immigration are more widely held fears that can be more easily stoked the more unequal the world as a whole becomes. If you cannot trust others around you in normal times how do you think they might react if the flu is spreading throughout your neighbourhood, or following some other disaster? Will people help each other out if there is flooding? Or will the National Guard or Territorial Army be sent in with guns to (supposedly) prevent looting? As inequality rises people begin to treat others less and less as people, and begin to behave towards others more as if some are a different species.

The higher inequality is in an affluent country, the more the poor over-estimate the security that wealth provides,[53] the more striving to become rich becomes an end in itself. Social status becomes the measure that most determines how strangers interact when they meet in unequal societies. Eye contact is avoided more often the more inequality grows in a society. We look more towards the feet rather than the faces of those above us, having ascertained their superior status from clues of dress and behaviour (called status cues), the homes they live in, the cars they drive.[54] As social status rises as the measure of apparent worth, it becomes seen as more important to spend, and for the very rich to spend on schooling that leads to particular behaviour patterns, manners and values, status cues, including everything from wearing the right shoes, carrying the correct handbag, to appearing to be confident and self-assured.

We become used to living in unequal worlds, to avoiding eye contact and worrying about our appearances, even having our hair cut at far greater expense (and more often) than our parents or grandparents did. It is a great shock to suddenly be cast into a more equal society, to be viewed for what you might be, not for which level you might appear to be at. In 1936, while George Orwell was in Barcelona (during the Spanish civil war), he found that for the first time in his life waiters in cafes looked him in the eye. It was a shock. It was only when what had been normal was removed that he realised how strange normality had been, how odd it was not to look others in the eye, how servile and rude language had become, how much better people treated one another when there were no 'better people', when all the cars were taken away and all travelled alike.[55]

Experiments in living under widespread social equality in affluent countries have been rare. George Orwell's example was wiped out by fascists in Spain, with support from fascists abroad, just a few months after he wrote about Barcelona. Experiments in equality were transformed a little more slowly to terror elsewhere in the Soviet Union, then China, then across Latin America, partly because the pressure from abroad for most overt experiments in increased equality to fail was enormous, mainly because dictatorship is never benign. Just as attempts to promote equality were usually crushed from abroad, imposing and sustaining inequality was often supported from abroad; apartheid in South Africa, dictatorships in South America and totalitarianism all across much of the rest of Asia and even into southern Europe received tacit and sometimes explicit endorsement from many of the most affluent in the world's richest countries. The rich supported dictators in Greece and Chile, in

Vietnam, Iran and South Africa, because they were afraid of what they saw as the potentially evil outcomes of great equality in each country, because the affluent had come to justify themselves through attempts to justify inequality.

Valuing money multiplicatively

The world distribution of income inequality appears to have a bell-shaped curve when incomes are compared on a scale that depicts the difference between existing on US$1 dollar a day and on US$10 a day as being the same as the difference between living on US$100 and on UD$1,000 a day. Figure 9 shows that curve, and within it four more curves, all bell shaped again, but of four very different continental income distributions. These incomes have been adjusted so that they refer to amounts of money that can buy the same amount of goods,

Figure 9: Distribution of income inequality (US$), worldwide, 2000

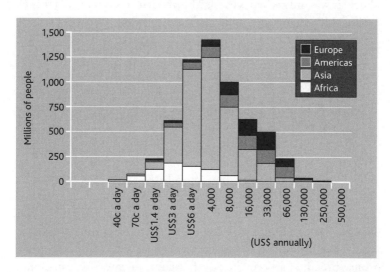

Notes: X-axis shows a continuous log scale of annual income in comparable dollars, Y-axis shows millions of people living in families supported by such incomes.

Source: Figures (in purchase power parity, US$) derived from estimates by Angus Maddison, from a version produced in spreadsheets given in www.worldmapper.org, based in turn on UNDP income inequality estimates for each country.

the same number of chickens or trousers or medicines regardless of whether they are cheaper in poor countries. Even adjusting for costs of living, annual modal family income in Africa around the year 2000 was still only equivalent to around US$4 a day (US$1,500 a year); in Europe modal annual family income was nearer US$30,000 (US$80 a day), but within both continents the spread either side of these vastly different averages was similar. Parts of both continents were becoming poorer and, as Figure 9 shows, a significant minority of Europeans were poorer than a significant minority of rich Africans. Within each continent, country by country, the same curves can be found again, a collection of curves that appear carefully chosen so as to sum to continental and then to global symmetry. But income distributions only appear vaguely symmetrical if you draw them on a log scale. Because of this an argument can be made that the symmetry suggests worldwide that the value of money is becoming multiplicative, rather than additive; what matters is how many more times others' income you receive.

Multiplicative beliefs in the value of money suggest that the actual value people have come to put on money only makes sense if you take into account expectations. Multiplicative beliefs become stronger in affluent and more unequal countries. Money is not valued for what it can buy, but for the status it confirms. Goods are not bought for what they can do, but more and more for the status they bestow on those who buy them. Clothes must look good rather than keep you warm. What matters about decoration, kitchenware, furniture, cars, homes, even holidays, is what you think others might think of you should they compare their possessions with yours, their incomes with your incomes, their lives with yours. Unions demand salary rises in terms of percentages of incomes; bonuses for bosses become even greater multiples of some measure; only the increases in the incomes of the poorest, state pensioners and others reliant on benefit or the minimum wage are described in pounds (although the increases are often in pence), dollars, euros or yen. Only for the poorest is money additive. Only for the poorest does one and one mean two; for others it means loose change, too little to give as a tip. For the very rich it means a sum not worth fishing down the back of the sofa for. In societies that have come to value money in multiplicative ways, conventional economic thinking makes absolutely no sense because the basic mathematical metric of reasoning has been transformed; it is not Cartesian. In a multiplicative-thinking country you cannot redistribute from a few rich people and make everyone better off because a majority dream of having riches, of having multiplicatively more, not just a little additional income.

For the majority in poor countries, money remains additive. An extra few cents means much the same to most people, an actual improvement in their standards of living, filling a hunger in their stomach, or a genuine material need, buying a pair of shoes that loosely fit a child's feet. It is only once consumption goes beyond genuine needs that money becomes multiplicative. A shilling in places like England used to mean the same thing to most people, which is why units of currency are mentioned in old novels. Today units of currency are rarely mentioned in books or films, not just due to the effects of inflation, but because there is far less of a common conception of what a reasonable amount of, say, pocket money might be for a child, of how much a pint of beer might cost in a pub or how much you might spend on a raincoat. People reading a novel in the mid-19th century, or watching television in the mid-20th century, were more similar to each other than audiences are today. In the 1980s in England there was even a game show on television where contestants had to guess the market value of goods. That show cannot be repeated now as the market value varies by consumer niche. In poorer countries there remains much of the uniformity of values that used to exist in affluent countries. At the bottom, so many are struggling to get by, the majority value things similarly but the market for films or novels for the poor is small and so prices are again not mentioned. In most of the world the poor really need the vast majority of what they purchase.

Dreaming of being normal

There are a few poor countries such as Cuba, and a few states within countries such as Kerala in India, which are more equitable than the global norm, but their impact on the global distribution is cancelled out by much greater than average inequality in places such as Brazil and South Africa. When there is a global pattern that is mirrored in local patterns it is usually the case that a common process is at work. This is how trees come to grow so similarly twisted, and how coastlines wiggle to the same extent whether viewed by eye or from space. This was why Karl Pearson wanted to show that paupers in Britain were strung along a bell curve by area. Income distribution curves tend to appear similar even when viewed for very different groups in different parts of the world. However, it is no natural process that results in the fractal nature of world income inequality, just a very human process that, by 2000, had become near universal: escapism.

Escapism is one way of describing the process whereby family incomes have become, over time, strung along a curve so skewed that it makes little sense to talk of social groups with different multiples of income, such as talking of those living on US$100, US$200, US$300, US$400, US$500, US$600 or US$700 a day, but instead different orders of magnitude are discussed: US$20, US$50, US$100, US$250, US$500, US$1,000, US$2,000 a day. Escapism becomes the dominant determinant of income distribution once the majority of income is no longer being used to satisfy basic needs, but is instead being used to signify social status.

There is no dignity in simply satisfying basic needs; just getting by is very little to be proud of in a place where that is no longer the norm. There was a great loss of dignity in not being able to buy a postage stamp to write a letter in York in 1900, just as there was loss of dignity in not being able to afford a computer to connect to the internet in New York in 2000. That computer is now the equivalent of the stamp when it comes to the means we use to communicate. Dignity is about having what others have, what is considered normal. The importance of dignity is so strongly felt that we quickly confuse what we want with what we need, because we feel strongly that we need these things to protect our dignity.

When basic needs cannot be met, where hunger remains, everyone is extremely thankful for an extra dollar a day, whether they are living on just one dollar a day, or two, or ten. However, offer that extra dollar a day to a person on an annual salary of US$30,000 and they may well be insulted by what is, in effect, a 1% pay rise. They might say that inflation is higher than 1% or, more likely, that other groups are receiving greater rises and an additional US$365 a year is an insult. It represents a drop in status if, on average, those receiving even more each year receive even greater annual multiplicative increases. It represents a demotion if some from below are receiving bigger increases.

The poorest tenth of the world's population regularly go hungry. The richest tenth cannot remember a time of hunger in their family's history. The poorest tenth can only rarely secure the most basic education for their children; the richest tenth are concerned to pay sufficient school fees to ensure that their children need only mix with their so-called 'equals' and 'betters' and because they have come to fear their children mixing with other children. The poorest tenth almost all live in places where there is no social security, no unemployment benefit. The richest tenth cannot imagine themselves ever having to try to live on those benefits. The poorest tenth can only secure day work in town, or are peasants in rural areas; the richest tenth cannot imagine not having a secure monthly salary. Above them, the top fraction of a percent, the very richest cannot imagine surviving on a salary rather than on the income coming from the interest that their wealth generates.

A wealthy man on television recently explained, in an attempt to show he was 'decent', that he would be happy for a daughter of his to become a nurse and would gladly pay her an annual income from her inheritance to make that possible (as living off a nurse's income was clearly not conceivable to him). He said he didn't want to spoil his children by just giving them his money; he only wanted to do that if they did something 'good'.[56] So taking a 'normal' job becomes 'doing good'. That attitude, out of place still in Britain, is not unusual in the most unequal large rich country in the world, where the poorest tenth have no access to healthcare, and the richest tenth shun the healthcare provided to most in their country, usually opting to pay much more to secure what they are told is better treatment.

The gulfs between our worlds are so wide that comparisons are rarely made between the lives of the richest and poorest on the planet. Worldwide the poorest tenth will die having hardly left a scratch on the earth. The richest tenth will each individually consume more oil through travel, and minerals through gadgets, than dozens of previous generations of their own families ever did, at least six times more each than their already affluent parents, and in doing so they consume the vast majority of all those resources that are consumed worldwide.[57] People who are illiberal claim there are too many humans on earth with no recognition that almost all consumption and pollution is down to a tiny affluent minority. And those who want to appear liberal say they will sponsor their daughters to be nurses!

If an affluent family in a rich country were to behave as their parents behaved they would be labelled as deep-green environmentalists. This would involve cutting down to a single car, very rarely travelling by air, not heating their home so often, owning just a couple of pairs of shoes per person, a few changes of clothes, rarely going out to eat, not eating meat very often, taking just one holiday a year. It is precisely because it has become normal in affluent countries to consume, to want so much more than our parents had, especially if our parents were rich, that escapism has taken hold. The reality of worldwide inequalities, of injustice, is so great that the well-off try very hard not to think of it and of others too much; for this they need escapism to a fantasy world where there is injustice in how they see themselves treated. In this fantasy they are over-taxed, much maligned and misunderstood. *It is hard to remember to be satisfied with what you have when you cannot remember not having most of what you wanted, let alone ever not having what you needed.* The cravings to satisfy basic needs transformed into cravings to satisfy ever-growing wants soon after the needs were mostly met. Consumerism, particularly of cars, in the US in the 1950s is often identified as an early example of such cravings being created. (Section 6.3 of this volume is largely devoted to the car and to advertising because of this.)

But what do you do when you have all your televisions, cars and holidays, when your home is full of possessions that cost such huge amounts? The answer is: you begin to live in fear. You move to what you conceive of as safer and safer environments. Eventually you can end up with a home in a gated estate, a gilded cage for the new gilded age. Visitors have to check in with guards before they can get to your door. Your children are too afraid to go outside the gates to play. They watch television. Maybe they dream of being nurses.

4.5 The 1960s: the turning point from inclusion to exclusion

Only a minority of North Americans got to satisfy the newly stoked-up craving for the trappings of wealth in the 1950s, trappings such as fast big cars and large homes, but with ever-growing access to television and ever more cleverly constructed advertising, that minority became the majority in the US during the 1960s. Collective craving created consumerism, driving in turn demand for domestic production that also peaked during the 1960s within the US, production that mostly moved abroad in the decades following. Despite many remaining in poverty, and the need for a 'Great Society' programme to tackle that, these were years of relative equality in the US, but also the years in which the rich became sufficiently frightened for some of them to act and for others to become complacent and placated enough not to see what was coming. Consumerism rose in Europe later and in Japan a little later still. Figure 10 shows that 10-year growth in the economy of the US (and by association during those more equitable times, the median average growth for all the Americas), which peaked at 30% in the decade to 1968, fell, then stumbled back up a fraction higher to 31% by 1973 before crumbling down to below 20%, occasionally below 10%, equating to average annual growth rates of around 2% then 1%. This was nothing like the crashes of 1929 or 2008, but enough of a shock for those who also had to get used to being more like others within those countries.

When the rich countries of the world are combined, their average annual growth rates between 1965 and 1979 were 3.5%; these more than halved by 1998. For the poor countries of the world, the combined rates were 2.4% in the early period, falling to an average growth of zero by 1998.[58] Gross domestic product (GDP) estimates are some of the oddest social statistics that have ever been created. Although the word 'domestic' appears in their title, they are as much a measure of success in international trade as of any kind of ingenuity at home. They are an estimate of the value of goods and services that are produced. The great assumption in their calculation is that value can be calculated from the amount people have to pay for those goods and services. The short-cut route to calculating GDP is to sum national wages, salaries and profit, as it is stated (by the theory

Figure 10: Real growth per decade in GDP (%), per person, by continent, 1955–2001

Source: Figures (growth in the decade to year shown) derived from estimates by Angus Maddison, from versions provided in spreadsheets given in www.worldmapper.org

that underlies their construction) that those wages, salaries and profits reflect the value of the goods and services that people produce. The theory goes on to suggest that, over time, due to innovation, people produce more and more valuable goods, become individually more productive and so their combined product rises. If that is the case then the question Figure 10 poses is: why, following the 1960s, did production per person fall so consistently worldwide?

Unsustainable growth

From the decade to 1955, through to the end of the 1960s, production per person in the world was rising by between 2% and 4% a year, between 22% and 48% a decade (the scale shown in the graph in Figure 10 is decadal). This is on average a doubling of global living standards in just one generation: 1945–68. But the doubling of already high living standards across rich countries had very different effects as compared to the doubling of very low living standards in poor countries. It took a hugely greater proportion of global income to double the incomes of the rich as compared to doubling the living standards of the poor. At the continental extremes of comparing North America with Africa, ten times as many resources were needed to double living standards in the former as in the latter, despite Africa's much greater population. The continuation of that kind of growth following the 1960s was unsustainable. Growth from 1945 to 1968 could partly only be so great because postwar productivity was initially so low. It was impossible to repeat that growth from 1968 to 1991 (we would have run out of places just to store the rubbish created). Not enough goods could have been made quickly enough for consumers with all that new money in rich countries to consume. China and India could grow, but they were growing from decimated economic beginnings. Instead of further worldwide growth there were three global economic slumps in the 24 years after 1968, and inflation initially soared. Inflation need not have followed the initial late 1960s price rises; the prices only rose because enough people in rich countries still had the incomes to pay the higher prices. They still had high enough incomes because, when the choice had to be made, at the end of the 1960s and into the early 1970s, as to how to manage a fall in resources, those with more did not choose to limit their own consumption but to curtail the consumption of those with less.

The *curtailment of the rise in the living standards of the poor* was not the snappy phrase used to explain the choice that was made, and it was not how those making the choice saw the choice they had made. Instead they called it 'anti-communism'. Anti-communism peaked in bloodshed during the 1960s and early 1970s. This was seen in British military interventions in the Middle East in the mid-1960s, with the support of western right-wing governments for the Greek military coup of 1967, across to the 1968 peak of the US invasion of Vietnam, through to interventions across much of the rest of Asia, much of Africa and Latin America. The bloodshed was also genocidal within communist countries. Genocide rarely occurs without the cloak of secrecy that comes with war or the threat of war and invasion. That genocide bolstered anti-communism, but there is a coincidence in the timing of the peaks of anti-communist action and the slump in apparent productivity that gives a hint as to how thousands of small decisions, soon to become a doctrine gaining in strength, arguing for inequality, became one great decision. The most significant point in that coincidence was when Richard Nixon unilaterally cancelled the Bretton Woods agreement and ended the direct convertibility of the US dollar into gold in 1971. He did not want to do it but was forced to due to the costs of the Vietnam War, and it may well be coincidence that productivity fell from then on, and debt rose unchecked. The decision to behave in this way was not taken by Richard Nixon alone − it was a great collective decision that was taken by many people who each had a little bit of power and quite a lot of wealth. It was taken through the results of many thousands of individual decisions taken under the newly forming doctrine that inequality was good. Inequality, it was suggested, led to competition, to people working harder; there would be more for all in the long term; a tide would come and all the boats would rise (as Ronald Reagan used to misquote John Kennedy). Equality led (the right wing thought and still think) to complacency, to inefficient decisions being made, to a levelling down, eventually to communism, misery for all and the denial of liberty. If a country turned communist its resources would not so easily be made available for exploitation (called trade). Their corrupt leaders might choose to try to maximise the production that stayed within their country and 'free' trade would be limited. As it began to become harder to secure more resources in general, particularly with the oil price rises of 1973, the great decision was finalised that the greatest sacrifice should be made by the poor, in concert, but not as a conspiracy.

The sacrifice of the poor

The poorest of the poor lost out most in the post–1960s swing to market-dominated economies. Figure 10 shows how the entire average income growth of the African continent went into freefall in the 1970s and then became negative by the mid–1980s and throughout the 1990s. That little dotted curve at the bottom of Figure 10 is the simplest visual summary of abandonment of a continent in the name of the doctrine of inequality. However, although resources from African countries could be squandered throughout these decades (cheap oil extracted from Nigeria with kick-backs to dictators, diamonds extracted from the Congo while exploiting miners on starvation wages), the amount of income that could be saved globally by giving Africans an unfairly low return for their product was very small. This was because they had been given so little to begin with. It was from denying fair terms of trade to most countries in Asia and a few elsewhere that more monies came to be amassed in the rich countries. Above all, however, it was from denying the continued internal spreading out of those gains within affluent countries that the rich within some of the richest of countries managed to not only retain the growth in their living standards, as living standards worldwide stood still or fell, but to increase the rate of growth of their own wealth. And that is how they came later, as a group, in the 1980s, to see their living standards rise more rapidly than any other group anywhere in the world (described later in Section 6.5).

Although it was just after these times that a few more affluent people, especially affluent North Americans, came to fund a new spate of right-wing think-tanks which promoted inequality, it was not a great conspiracy but something far more dangerous and difficult to prevent which resulted in a turning point occurring in the 1960s. It is the fact that it took thousands of smaller decisions to cumulate in a result of such significance that should be of concern. It was the everyday politics of the envy and fear of those who had come to know a little luxury, who wanted much more as a result and who lived in constant uneasy fear of it being taken away. The turning point came in the 1960s not just because those who might have opposed it did not try hard enough, or because of effective arguments from a particularly influential economist or two. It had to come then; what had gone before, a rapidly growing but relatively (proportionately) equitable sharing out of more and more economic spoils, year on year on year, had to end. The postwar boom ended simply because it had run out of resources. With only one planet, the easy gains had been made, the easy oil drilled, the easiest mass distribution of pesticides accomplished, the easiest industrialisation undertaken. What was occurring globally was way beyond the comprehension of any individual. As the 1960s ended the US landed on the moon and found it to be no great resource substitute, no consolation for having only one planet. Savings had to be found elsewhere. Although the 1960s were the turning point, it took all of the 1970s before it became clear to most from where most of those savings would come.

The slowdown in the rise in incomes in affluent countries from the late 1970s onwards was handled very differently in different countries. In the US, when the population was sorted into five equal-sized quintile groups, annual incomes were found to have risen from poorest to richest between 1949 and 1979 by 2.6%, 2.3%, 2.5%, 2.6% and 2.3% respectively. Rather like the global trend over a similar period, all had benefited with a slight equalisation over time at the upper extreme. However, between 1979 and 2003, under Reagan, Clinton and the Bushes, the respective annual growth rates diverged, those five rates respectively from poorest to richest quintile being 0.2%, 0.6%, 0.9%, 1.4% and 2.7%.[59] In the later Bush years (the years of George Bush the Second) these inequalities grew even faster and the median group even saw their incomes fall by over US$1,000 a year.[60] At the extremes, in the US, even average incomes finally had to fall to finance the wealth grabs of the super-rich in what became the heights of excess of a new gilded age.

In Britain, by poorest to richest quintile of the population, annual increases in incomes from 1979 to 1990 to the nearest percentile were respectively 0.5%, 1%, 2%, 3% and 4%,[61] with the incomes of those who had most to begin with being allowed to continue to increase at historically rare rates, with all the sacrifice being made by those who had least to sacrifice. During 1979–90 Margaret Thatcher's Conservative Party was elected three times to government; she was finally deposed by her own party rather than the electorate. John Major replaced her as Prime Minister, and from 1990 to 1997 there was no further increase in inequality, rather a slight decrease as the richest quintile's income rose annually by only 0.5% while the poorest's rose at three times that rate, by 1.5%.[62] This showed a slight move away from inequality but hardly dented the effects of those earlier 11 years. Then, under Tony Blair's government, income inequalities were almost perfectly preserved from 1997 to at least 2007, with initially all quintiles seeing annual growth of 2.5%.[63] However, high and sustained income inequalities led to rising social exclusion and increasing inequalities in wealth. When, 18 years after

Mrs Thatcher was forced to resign by her own party, Tony Blair was forced out by his, the richest fifth still received 42% of all income in Britain, the same proportion in 2007 as in 1991.[64]

Inequalities almost stopped rising 40 years after the 1960s turning point, not because of any great conversion to a belief in the merits of equality by British or US governments, but because there was little left to squeeze from the poor, and average rises in national and global incomes were still slowing.

Profligacy and promiscuity

In Britain the 1960s turning point mirrored an earlier one just prior to the 1880s when the original gilded age began. Inequalities in incomes between the best-off tenth of skilled men in full-time manual employment in Britain and the worst-off slowly rose during the original gilded age, from the best-off tenth being paid 2.09 times as much as the worst-off tenth in 1886 to 2.36 times as much by 1906. It was not just an economic crash but political agitation that brought the discrepancy down to 2.07 by 1938, and slowly fractionally further down to 2.06 by 1960. But soon after that it rose quickly to 2.19 by 1970, fell again to 2.07 by 1976, but then rose rapidly, peaking at 2.37 in 1986 (above even 1906 inequalities), and then soared to 2.55 by 1996.[65] Since then, inequalities by these decile measures have held up around this British historical maximum, before peaking again just a fraction higher in 2008.[66]

The increasing concentration of income and wealth among a few within countries like Britain and the US from 1980 onwards was mirrored internationally by a growing reluctance to see monies flowing out of rich countries in any form other than investments designed to secure that yet more money would flow back in. In 1980 some half a percent of annual national income in Britain was spent on international aid. This was cut by a third in 1983, then by more in 1984, and overall was halved by 1994 to reach a low of just a quarter of a percent.[67] It has since risen slightly, but this illustrates how monies were being clawed in from all directions to keep up the share going to the very richest of people in the richest of countries.

In Conservative writing and talk, the 1960s have come to be seen as the era of great evils of a different kind. They are not seen as the time when all those little decisions arising from fear of the poor (and envy of the super-rich) among the rich resulted in the unconscious group-think decision being made to begin to penalise the poor, but as a time when the poor and the young were first allowed in large numbers to behave badly, as a time of new social evils of immorality. Chief among these supposed evils was more freedom over sexual behaviour due to the introduction of the contraceptive pill. The pill became blamed for all manner of social ills, for destroying the 'cultural norm'. According to one commentator from New Zealand, Alan Gibbs, it supposedly '... relaxed the pressures that mothers put on their daughters to hold this cultural norm together'.[68] The pressure being talked about here was the pressure not to have sex before marriage, for fear of becoming pregnant and because of the huge social stigma that the birth of an illegitimate child was then usually associated with. There was also the risk involved (childbirth still being the greatest killer of young women worldwide today), and there was a lack of legal access to abortion at the start of the 1960s in most rich countries. Motherhood following conception was enforced by law.

Those who complain of birth control creating immorality forget that it was initially promoted to control the reproduction of the poor by elitist eugenicists who also believed in the need for the rich to breed more in order to improve the 'stock' of humanity. They also forget that it was the introduction of the pill coupled with the winning of other basic educational rights for women around the world that is mainly responsible for the rapid slowdown in population growth since the early 1960s, so that today – and it is worth saying again and again – worldwide, the average family is made up of two adults and three children, and those children are projected to form families of just two children, *ending worldwide population growth within 42 years' time* for the first time since possibly as long ago as the Black Death, or perhaps for the first time since the spreading of old world diseases to the Americas.

The monsters our fears create

The expected end of net natural global population growth within current lifetimes is hardly ever celebrated as a great human achievement in self-control and collective decision making gone good. All those men, from Adam Smith to the Reverend Thomas Malthus, to modern-day orthodox economists (and even that man, Alan Gibbs, in New Zealand[69]) who were so concerned about lust and temptation being uncontrollable, need not have worried. The fact that world population growth is ending due to the actions of women demonstrates that there is no need for thousands (or in this case billions) of individual human decisions to end up with a bad result. It should also be seen as a reason why we should be less concerned about the global slowdown in estimated production per person; we are also slowly and steadily, but ever so surely, producing less of ourselves, fewer in need of being provided for.

A great deal of production prior to the 1960s was work being carried out to prepare for the large generation to come, the children of the generation born shortly after the war, who had their own baby-producing boom in affluent countries in the mid-1960s. Homes had to be built for all the additional families being formed, highways constructed to link the homes, industries forged to provide for growing demand. All those increases are ending, but we still lament the ending of the postwar period of great prosperity that mainly employed people in building and preparing for the age to come. And, sadly too, many still talk of the advent of that age as being the advent of new evils. Their forebears, such as Ronald Reagan, talked of 'welfare queens', of the poor as having become sexually promiscuous, irresponsible and dependent since those days. In talking in this old way modern Conservatives try to change the terms of the debate as to why so many are now excluded from society to imply that it is somehow the result of supposedly timeless forces of nature and biology. 'The poor will always be with us because of their genes' is the current manifestation of this theory, but its antecedents were seen in places like Britain much further back, from the introduction of the poor law[70] and before.

We remain haunted by old ghosts, prejudices and the monsters that our fears have created over the course of centuries. These fears have come in recent decades to dictate the way in which those with more have come to view those with less. These are the fears that support racism, which underpin the idea of social exclusion as acceptable; they are the fears behind elitism. They are the fears which underlie the argument which says that since it is natural biological forces which have resulted in different groups of human beings living in such widely varying circumstances around the globe, then as a result there must be something natural, almost biologically preordained, about the unequal situations in which people find themselves. This highly prejudiced view suggests that human beings are ordered into different castes, races, classes and groups with destinies which vary naturally and in line with their supposed talents, resulting not in unfair exclusion, but in segregation, both worldwide and local, that is natural and good. This leads to an acceptance of a world where the wheat is sorted from the chaff, the sheep from the goats, the leaders from the people who make up their markets; this view has many faces but no common name. It is akin to a widening of racism, but for now let us just call it: prejudice.

5

'Prejudice is natural': a wider racism

Why did racism become so strong again in affluent countries in the 1970s? Why was it that postwar racist killing in Western Europe was most common then?[1] Why, from then on, was 'race' such a crucial determinant of the shape of the US political map, with whites in the south switching at that time in huge numbers to the Republican Party, later ensuring Ronald's Reagan's victory in the presidential election of 1980?[2] Was it just a backlash reaction after the winning by blacks of a few, albeit important, civil rights in the 1960s? Why across Europe did far-right parties start to form and grow again, in the late 1970s?[3] Had it been a sufficiently long time after the war? Why were the 1970s the decade of the greatest visible growth in racist graffiti, with swastikas appearing in support of the far-right National Front in Britain?[4] Why at that time did skinhead thugs reappear across Europe? Was it discontent and racist votes that were enough to tip the balance and allow Margaret Thatcher not just victory but a large majority in Britain in 1979?[5] Was all this just backlash to recent increases in immigration, and to seeing a few more black and brown faces on the streets? Did the same re-stirrings of racism occur in Japan when, from the early 1970s onwards, a few Filipino migrants were allowed in to do the dirty, dangerous and difficult jobs that the Japanese would no longer do (in Japanese: *kitanai*, *kiken* and *kitsui*, the '3k' jobs[6])? For some reason, in almost all the richest countries (most of those which closely circle the North Pole) prejudice towards others began to grow strongly again at this time.

Racism has a long history in all affluent countries, although it became briefly less acceptable to express anti-Semitic racist opinion publicly following the Second World War. However, in all these countries, as governments also sought to minimise idleness and unemployment, that great evil of xenophobia, used so effectively by fascists before the war, shrank. Racism was still rife in everyday life, especially as it affected the Irish in Britain and black people in the US, but as we forgot fascism (and as rank began to matter more again), in place of xenophobia, crude race-hate, and old-fashioned jingoism a space was created for new forms of prejudice to grow.

It was not just in Japan that the young sought harder to avoid dirty, dangerous and difficult work, but across all rich nations. The mass unemployment of the 1930s had resulted in far fewer children being born in these countries at this time. The postwar baby boom was only a boom seen against the backdrop of rapidly declining fertility within rich nations. People were individually becoming more precious in both their attitudes and their rarity. By the 1960s, for the first time in human history, a majority could say no to low-paid work that they did not want to do. But that majority also began to demand new services that required the work of more other people than ever before: more health services, more public transport, more shops. The demand for labour grew rapidly. The demand that was not satisfied internally was partly then met by immigration, facilitated for example by the slight relaxing of incredibly strict immigration laws in Japan. In Europe the demand was not curtailed by the tightening of less strict laws. Many people came in because they knew the laws were being tightened and others stayed for fear of not later being allowed to return if they left.[7] Immigration was greatest in the US, where the winning of more civil rights by some black people partly led to the importing of new waves of non-white people to fill in the void that a little emancipation had created, to do the jobs black Americans no longer had to do. Immigration rates in the US '... began to pick up in the late 1960s, and soared after 1980'.[8]

Anxiety over the arrival of peoples seen as new, coupled with the growth in want and exclusion for so many who saw themselves as 'indigenous white', was stirred up by racist agitators to incite racist prejudice, particularly from the late 1970s onwards. That agitation is traced back to different times in different places. In Britain in the West Midlands Conservative MP Enoch Powell made a speech in 1968 in which he used the words 'rivers of blood' in relation to immigration. He said he could see rivers foaming with blood as the British nation heaped 'up its own funeral pyre' by allowing immigration. At the heart of this racism was a bizarre rationalisation of why others should labour in your place, but only just enough others labouring near you, in your country, to meet your needs. It was an extension of the old rationalisation used by aristocrats to justify their luxurious existence when almost everyone else had to toil. The difference now was that the justification was not just being applied by a few families, but entire social groups were behaving like aristocracy. These groups consisted of people who had been taught to think of themselves as being of an ethnicity, class, nationality, religion and culture which allowed them to feel superior to others. For instance, ideas such as those of Enoch Powell were more favoured by people who were white, upper-working class, Anglo Saxon, more often male, English, middle-aged and Protestant.

The rationalisation that had trickled down from old aristocratic ideals (last espoused by the new aristocracy of the first gilded age) as our common wealth once again began to be more selfishly corralled by the new wealthy elite was as follows: there are different types of people. Some are best motivated by being given higher salaries; they deserve good pensions and good health insurance, and their children need expensive education. The highest caste of all requires and deserves the very highest remuneration including the right to live in luxury in old age, instant attention when ill, the most exclusive schools for its offspring, who in turn are also destined for wonderful futures (Enoch Powell thought as a young man that he was destined to become Viceroy of India![9]). Lower castes, this warped logic would suggest, are best motivated by fear. It is essential they are threatened with poverty, or even with the threat of repatriation to poor 'homelands', to ensure that they work hard and do not complain. Such repatriation could occur if people were found guilty of a criminal offence, for instance (as happens now). How else, they argued, are we to get people to undertake dirty, dangerous or difficult work? Questions thus began to be asked about 'us' in relation to 'them' much more often in the 1970s than before. The claims that are made about 'them' are that these lower castes do not need the promise of pensions to make them work hard; instead they only respond to fear; and their children do not need good education because they are not destined for great things. They do not deserve good healthcare when ill, because they are dispensable.

The old social evil of idleness, of mass unemployment in the 1930s, had been used to incite prejudice in Europe earlier. This new injustice was being incited without such dire economic conditions, although unemployment rose again in the 1970s. Living standards for most were still rising, but rose more at the top than the bottom, so that social rank grew again in importance. In this way the overcoming of mass idleness partly precipitated the great postwar rise in prejudice. The most vocal expressions of that prejudice were dampened down after the 1970s. Racist violence, especially murder, was at its peak in the 1960s in the US, in the 1970s in Europe, but is less common now. High proportions of younger people unequivocally express revulsion at racism today. The older members of the population of affluent nations in general have been slower to change than the younger, but all are now changing their collective view from the time when prejudice peaked. In the US in 1978, 54% of people said they disapproved of marriages between blacks and whites, some 36% approved and 10% would not say or had no view. By 1991 some 48% approved; by 2002, 65%; by 2007, 77%.[10] Prejudice rises easily, like anger, but can be dampened down with time. The proportion of North Americans in future who will be found to disapprove of the kind of marriages that resulted in their current President being born will be a telling statistic. But prejudice today is changing; it is less about skin colour and more about suspicions and feelings that there are biological differences between groups, differences that are more than skin deep. Prejudice is now more about genes than pigment.

5.1 Indenture: labour for miserable reward, a fifth of all adults

How would you answer the following question that is occasionally asked in social surveys: 'Which of these phrases would you say comes closest to your feelings about your household's income these days? Living comfortably, coping, finding it difficult to manage, or finding it very difficult to manage on present income'? Excluding those who responded 'don't know' or who did not answer, Figure 11 shows the typical response to such a question as recorded over the course of about two decades. On average around a fifth of the population (21%) routinely find it either difficult or very difficult to get by on their incomes. This particular proportion is the figure for Britain; the proportion is almost certainly usually higher in the US and much lower in Japan. International statistics are hard to compare, however, as language and meaning varies so greatly. 'Finding it difficult to manage' is a very British euphemism for not managing. Among those doing better than this, almost half the population in Britain describe themselves as 'only just coping'!

Figure 11: Households' ability to get by on their income in Britain, 1984–2004

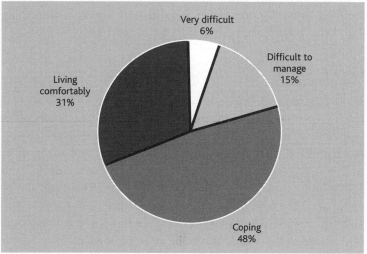

Source: Derived from ONS (2006) *Social Trends (No 36)*, London: Palgrave Macmillan, table 5.15, p 78, mean of 1984, 1994 and 2004 surveys.

In all affluent countries, governments do not like to admit how hard most households find it to 'get by'. Members of the governing party in Britain took great pride in pointing out how, just before the economic collapse, the share who appeared to be finding managing most difficult was falling, and the number of those who said they were living comfortably was rising.[11] These figures were published in 2006 in the official publication *Social Trends (No 36)*. The following year *Social Trends (No 37)* showed how those gains had been achieved by borrowing. Total lending in Britain had, we later found out, peaked in 2004 (Figure 6.13 in *Social Trends, No 37*). Personal insolvencies were rising exponentially by 2004 (Figure 6.14 in *Social Trends, No 37*). The next year *Social Trends (No 38)* revealed that even the wealthiest, those who had property they could borrow against, had managed to be comfortable mostly by borrowing yet more money against their property. This was then called 'equity withdrawal' and it was responsible for over 8% of all personal income in Britain by 2004 (according to Figure 6.14, *Social Trends, No 38*)! Again the peak had been in 2004, but it was not obvious until 2008 that even the wealthy had been increasing their borrowing to maintain their comfortable lifestyles. In hindsight even the minority who said they were living comfortably were often doing so partly by borrowing more.

No rest

Borrowing money to maintain a comfortable lifestyle is far from good, but it is not even imaginable for those who are finding it difficult or very difficult to get by, those who are doing worse than just coping. For the fifth that are not managing, debt is a necessity just in order to keep going, not as a means to maintain living in luxury. It is this fifth who have the fewest real choices in life in Britain and similar countries. They have few choices over what kind of work they do and take any job they can get. Having to do a job that you would not choose to do is as demoralising as being indentured to labour for a fixed term to pay off debts (although in the latter case at least the term of indenture tends to be known). In the past indentured labour was usually reserved for people thought of as being of a different racial group to those who employed them. Today we tolerate modern indenture, many people having no choice over labour and getting into debt, because enough of us still see others as sufficiently different, akin to racially different. In rich countries for a fifth of the population to be failing to manage is unjust. It is unnecessary to have nearly a majority who are only coping.

Being unable to manage in 21st-century Britain is considered being unable to 'rest', that is, being unable to have an annual holiday. Rest has meant different things at different times. From ancient times a day of rest has been called a Sabbath, where Abrahamic religions dominate, and it occurs every seven days. Outside that world, rest days and feast days have been just as plentiful if a little differently spaced out. For instance, the Chinese week was 10 days long.[12]

Weeks were invented when rest had to be scheduled in. Now, in much of the rich world, a fifth of households are unable to take a rest day. That is, they cannot take the modern-day Sabbath, a seventh day of rest. The modern-day Sabbath has very little to do with not working on Sundays, but has a lot to do with having a day off a week from worry, shopping, household maintenance and work-related stress. It is still essential to be able to rest, relax, not to be worried all the time about getting by. Those who cannot rest in their minds can be seen not just as the proportions who say they cannot manage, but as overlapping greatly with the fifth of people highlighted in Chapter 4 of this volume who have to toil and struggle, for seven days, to receive what another fifth are awarded for just a single day's labour. Given the contemporary cultural dominance worldwide of the seven-day week, it is now at the precise point where that seventh day has to be sacrificed, cannot be enjoyed and cannot be used for rest that basic common choices in life disappear most clearly.

From country to country the proportion of households that cannot afford a seventh day of rest varies (the international variation is described in Section 4.3 earlier). In Britain it is the worst-off fifth who must get by on only a seventh of the income of the best-off fifth. In the US even more of the population live such lives. In mainland Europe fewer people have to toil so long; in Japan even less. The overall rich world average can be assumed to be about a fifth being unable to mentally rest because they are finding it difficult or very difficult to get by. Invariably people in this fifth will be much more likely to be identified as members of those racial groups that are most discriminated against: more will be women; children are disproportionately born into households in this fifth; and adults more often fall into this fifth on having children. These become households whose time and labour are now, for all real purposes, indentured.

—

This indenture is not just of those able to sell their labour but also of those whose labour in caring for children or others is given no employment value, or those too old or sick to work whose labour is in looking after themselves but who still cannot manage to get by despite qualifying for a pension or an allowance.

False promises

In the past indentured debt might have been the cost of passage to the Americas, or the supposed cost of forcible deportation to Australia, in the case of convicts. The indentured are by definition not free to stop working, but also by definition their children will not be indentured, and so they differ from slaves in this respect. They themselves were told that after a number of years they would be free and usually they were freed on time. Today's indentured labourers are more fortunate in that the alternative to work is not starvation or the workhouse, but they are not so fortunate in other ways. They too are given a more vague promise of future emancipation for good behaviour. They are led to believe that they will be free eventually, and that if their life is lived with little in the way of choice or hope (on benefits or in low-paid work), the lives of their children will be more fortunate as a result of their pliant behaviour. This is turning out to have been a false promise.

Today's indentured labourers in affluent countries are not described as such and are not formally indentured; often they are not even in paid employment but indentured to benefits. They are, however, often in debt. What sets them apart is that their choices in life are so very limited. Those in work have not chosen their work but are compelled to work out of fear of poverty. Similarly, those reliant on social security do not, as is sometimes fictionally portrayed, choose such a life willingly. There is no great mass of feckless people who want to be living on the basics of social security in preference to having choices. No one rationally chooses to live on the miserliness of sickness benefits because they see it as a good living. Young mothers do not become pregnant because the social security benefits are so wonderful. Teenage pregnancies are highest in those affluent countries where benefit rates are lowest, where inequalities are greatest, where there is less money to 'be made' from having a baby.[13] Teenagers and other mothers, often young ones, are most likely to have to give their children up for adoption in those affluent countries where social benefits are worse.[14] Elsewhere teenagers and young adults simply choose, and are better placed to be able to choose, to have children less often. Teenage pregnancy rates are lowest in the most equal of rich nations, such as Japan, Sweden, the Netherlands, Denmark, Spain, Finland, Belgium, France, Norway, Germany and Austria (www.equalitytrust.org.uk/why/evidence/teenage-births).

What today's indentured have is a curtailment of all kinds of choices. The majority who work have little choice over the work they do, or whether to work. Within indentured households, most of those who do not work are children, sick, carers or pensioners. The indentured have very little choice over where they live, which city they inhabit, even the home they occupy. In countries with social housing they are allocated their place in a block; in countries without such housing the free market directs them towards 'skid row'. Their children then usually have no choices over their education. They have to go to school where others choose not to – choice for some reduces choice for others.

Contemporary indentured labourers in affluent societies owe their debts to car loans, clothes catalogues and other credit companies and to those to whom debts are sold on following initial defaulting. The indentured may be in arrears on their rent, on their mortgage, on paying their utility bills, on the taxes they owe local government, on loans arranged through banks that up until 2008 were more and more willing to give accounts and lend to most of the poor. These indentured are in default on hire purchase agreements, even on court orders to pay a fine for not having a licence to watch their television. They have all manner of ways in which they can be in debt, no longer owing to a single creditor, but usually owing to numerous faceless creditors. They owe because their incomes are insufficient to support their outgoings, outgoings needed to preserve basic dignity in the countries where they live, where it has become acceptable to string people out along a widening and ever more skewed curve of reward, creating many losers towards the bottom. Many losers are required to pay for (and service) every new winner high up at the top, and winners are expensive to support.

The indentured are treated like this because a powerful minority have come to believe that these are people who do not deserve more. Just as women were allowed to vote only when a majority of powerful enough people came to believe that they should vote, just as slavery was only formally abolished when the majority of the powerful minority deemed it right, just as children and older people were not required to work once such enforced labour was deemed wrong, so too modern indenture, people having to undertake work with no other option, will continue to be tolerated, even justified, until it is seen as intolerable. The various justifications begin by suggesting that if ending slavery, or introducing female emancipation, or reducing child labour, or introducing pensions, begins in one place, then that place will suffer economic loss. It simply isn't 'economic', such an argument begins, for there not to be slaves, for people not to be forced to undertake work they would otherwise choose not to do. When it is suggested that all could be paid a living wage in affluent countries, so that only those who freely chose to undertake undesirable work did so,[15] perhaps by being paid more to carry out unpopular work, the question of economic expense is raised to make such a prospect appear impossible, just as the idea of paying slaves was once an anathema.

Modern indenture requires more than just an appeal to strange notions of affordability to defend it. Something becomes easily more unaffordable when it does not apply to you personally. Slavery is defensible only when slaves can be painted as racially different:[16] Celts in Icelandic antiquity, blacks in recent American history, indigenous Indians in Brazil today, and women almost everywhere until very recently. The denial of women's liberties is only possible if you can persuade men that their mothers, sisters and daughters are less deserving than their fathers, brothers and sons. Child and old age labour requires us to forget our beginnings and not to try to imagine our dotage. Modern indenture requires us to see having no choice over work as being the fate of others in our affluent countries, those perhaps whom we imagine to have less ability.

The undeserving

A homogenising myth of our times is that people fall to the bottom because they are undeserving, that they probably did not have the inherent ability to ever do much better than they did. This myth is being questioned. People now know not to express such thoughts out loud in polite company, but they express them instead indirectly in ways that clearly betray their prejudice. The clues can be found in what they expect others to do for them that they would not do in return. This is the prejudice of believing that you and yours are so special that you deserve greatness, and that greatness will (by default) necessitate the indenture of others to provide the kinds of services and lifestyle that you and yours 'deserve'. The social security benefits of others have to be kept low to keep them in fear of not toiling, so as not to reward sloth, and because you and your family supposedly deserve so much and do not want to be taxed more.

It is always hard to draw the line at what is an unreasonable request to make of others, but everyone has a line in their mind. Few believe that even the heir to the throne should be dressed by royal butlers each morning. Such behaviour comes from a different era, but what about more common 'services'? The kinds of service those who are prejudiced may believe they deserve range from the making of the beds they sleep in, to having their children looked after by others, to having drinks made for them and served on a silver tray. Almost everyone is capable of making their own bed, childcare is done best when shared among the parents of children, and serving family and friends with drink is far more fun, than taking the glass from the tray of a waiter at some 'function'. In the past most children did the same work as their parents, but one of the very few occupations that children rarely followed their parents into was working in service. If former chambermaids, nannies and butlers impressed one thing on their own offspring, it was not to follow them into serving others in the same way (see table on the Injustice web pages at www.policypress.co.uk).

Spending time with children and with those in their dotage can be the best of times.[17] Instead it is usually made a trial by how we organise such spending. Care workers for older people are the largest least well-paid group in most affluent societies, because we don't value caring as a skill, and we don't generally like to be reminded of our own mortality. Carers are taught through their hours, wages and conditions of labour how little in turn we value older people. Most care workers do not choose to end up working in old age care homes; they simply cannot get any other work. When it was suggested that immigration controls in Britain be tightened after the economic crash so that care workers could only be imported if they were subsequently paid wages higher than the minimum, the care home owners lamented that they would never find enough willing staff locally at minimum wage, even under conditions of mass unemployment. Few people bring up their children in rich countries today to hope that one day they might grow up to be able to work in an old age care home.

In a grossly unequal society there are many jobs that most people would never believe their children will be lucky enough to hold. These are jobs which most people are told that their children are not capable of aspiring to. Remarkably these very same 'unachievable' jobs are, from even higher perches of privilege, seen as far too lowly to undertake. Thus the dream jobs of some are the nightmare drudgery of others. In Britain the former Prime Minister, Tony Blair, is said by Robin Cook to have sent his children to selective schools because he did not want them *merely* to become school headteachers or university professors, jobs he considered unworthy of his progeny.[18] These were the kinds of jobs secured by the offspring of another former Labour Prime Minister, Harold Wilson. Tony Blair thought his children were deserving of, capable of, entitled to, more. When people like Tony Blair think like this, and ensure that low wages remain low by not raising the minimum wage sufficiently, it is hardly surprising that the message percolates down that to work in a care home for older people is to have failed. Furthermore, in the most unequal and consumerist of rich societies instant gratification is encouraged and contemplation deterred.

Work harder!

Across the rich world, at the end of the last gilded age, aristocratic dynasties slowly crumbled in Europe following all the deaths of the First World War; robber-baron wealth in the US was decimated in the 1930s and began to be redistributed in the 1940s; aristocracy was dismantled in Japan following the Second World War; social rank and religious caste slowly and steadily fell in importance over the entire period from 1929 through to 1973. From 1950 to 1973 across all OECD nations, the average working week fell by half a day, so those at the bottom were allowed to toil less; their fears of poverty were reduced as social security was improved and it became possible to take more rest; all became more equal.[19] Then, with a little help from renewed prejudices, all those gains began to be reversed from around 1973,[20] and by 2007 people were again working longer hours than they had been working in 1950. However, they have not produced as much in those hours in recent years. Just as slavery and exploiting women, children and older people have been found to have been inefficient in the past as a means of creating a good life even for the few (for very long), so too is indenture inefficient today.

US productivity per worker hour fell by half between 1973 and the mid-1990s,[21] not because people were working fewer hours, but because more were working longer hours less effectively at more demeaning, dirty, sometimes dangerous and often difficult jobs for lower real wages than most of their parents had worked for; because they had become, in all but name, indentured. They could be indentured by the 1990s more often because they were (compared with the 1970s) newly looked down on, cast aside as inferior. The new prejudice had created vast new gross injustices. It grew slowly in the early 1970s. The early symptoms of rising prejudice can be seen in both the Adam Smith Institute in Britain and the Heritage Foundation in the US, both created in 1973 with donations from rich individuals and remits to promote policies which have, in hindsight, been seen to have fostered prejudice against the poor so effectively that it became normalised. Those rich donors only donated when they did because they thought we were then becoming too keen on ideals of equality, what they saw as market 'solutions' were being squeezed out, and they were fortunate that ideas of elitism and a new tolerance of exclusion had grown strong enough for what they proclaimed, what appeared at first to be unjustified, to quickly begin to be made to appear justifiable again.

The new injustices that result from a rise in prejudice do not fall solely on the poorest in rich societies. In the US the greatest increase in hours worked has been for those married couple households where both adults have a university degree.[22] Between 1968 and 2000 the average weekly number of hours spent in paid work by parents in households with children in the US rose from 53 to 64.[23] Similarly, in Britain, working hours have increased most for some of the more highly paid. All those in work laboured (on mean average) an additional 130 minutes a week by 2001 as compared with 1991.[24] There was an increase of some 7.6 weeks paid work a year in households where at least one adult was in employment comparing 1981 and 1998.[25] Some two to three months more a year is being spent in paid labour by adults in aggregate in households now in the US in the 2000s as compared with the 1960s. A large part of the increase is caused by more women being in paid work without any great reduction in the number of men in paid work.

When a fifth face modern indenture, many more than a fifth face a curtailing of their choices such as the choice to work fewer hours. They work harder to attempt to avoid indenture. Most people do not do this extra work out of choice. They are not indentured, they have some choices and crucially they are not finding it 'difficult or very difficult to get by' when asked, but they are less free. Most jobs remain mundane and boring. Most jobs held by people with university degrees now involve mostly drudgery. People work longer hours in rich countries because they feel they have to. The poor have to because the minimum wage in countries like the US fell in real terms so sharply from the end of the 1960s that they became indentured. The more affluent feel they have to work longer hours than their parents did because as the poor become indentured it becomes ever more important not to have to live like or live near the poor, and that costs money.

In the US, where the need to labour just to survive is greatest, over a quarter of the young elderly, people aged 65–69, have to undertake paid work simply to get by, as do a sixth of those aged 70–74. In the EU less than a tenth of the young elderly have to work, and almost none aged 70–74 work. Because opportunities for the poor to study are so curtailed and benefits so low (or non-existent) in many US states, less qualified people will take any job offered; almost half of young adults aged 15–24 are in paid employment in the US, as compared with less than a third of that group in the EU (even now when expanded to include most of Eastern Europe).[26] In Japan the proportions in work as young adults or when elderly are much lower again. Different groups of affluent countries have chosen different courses to take; within each, different prejudices have been allowed to rise while others have been curtailed.

5.2 Darwinism: thinking that different incentives are needed

When we compare with today the apparent freedom that people in rich countries had to work fewer hours in the 1960s, the freedom to 'tell their boss to shove it' (US) or 'pack their job in' (UK) if they did not like it and take another under conditions of near full employment, it is easy to see why modern indenture has increased. The choices of most have been reduced and the choices of a few constrained to almost no choice. This required a change in what we collectively came to believe was possible. We did not lose that world of choice overnight, and it was largely a world of choice only for men. But from almost all walks of life men could have a choice as to how they laboured in the 1960s in affluent countries. The main exceptions to this were the grandchildren of slaves in the US, where the legacy of slavery and the prejudice that legacy carried meant that more options were curtailed if you were black.

It is very simple to show that the choices of all but a tiny few have been curtailed, with that curtailment rising from the early 1970s onwards. Increasingly choice comes in a simple form, money; it tends to be coloured green if printed on paper, silver or gold if minted, but more and more frequently the ticket that allows choice is a small piece of plastic that, if affluent, you pass to the waiter at the end of your meal, the plastic which, for instance, you use to pay for your hotel room and the right to have others clean up after you, the plastic that pays for holidays, the new car, the new kitchen and for those weekends of shopping. As incomes and wealth have polarised, so too has choice. Increasing the affluence of rich people means more nights that can be spent away from home in a hotel, as more hotels are built. It is impossible to have more hotel beds without more bed makers, room cleaners, wine waiters. As the small group of very rich people becomes richer, each such affluent household buys more new cars. These have to be made, serviced and cleaned, and so more production line workers, mechanics and valets are required. If the affluent replace their kitchens more often they require more joiners, electricians and plasterers, and more rubbish collectors to take away the old kitchen. Huge numbers of extra shop assistants are required if more shopping is to be possible, more shelf stackers, shop security guards and so on. But it did not have to be quite this way and in most other affluent countries most people get to use their labour for a slightly greater good than do most in the US or the UK. There are fewer demeaning jobs and fewer low-paid workers in Japan, Norway, Germany, Denmark, Switzerland, the Netherlands and Canada. We know that simply by knowing that income inequalities are so much lower there (see end of Section 4.3 and Chapter 2, note 37, this volume).

The curtailing of choices that came with rising income and wealth inequalities also resulted in the revival of old ways of justifying such inequalities. When social inequalities were high in Victorian Britain Charles Darwin's novel ideas of evolution were drawn on to try to justify the enormous wealth gaps. The rich were painted as the 'fittest' who had survived most successfully, their pedigrees outlined on family trees which stretched back at least to the Plantagenets in the case of the few who owned the most land. These were those few families mostly descended (via the House of Angevin) from the Normans who seized land in England after 1066 and still held a tenth of all land in Britain by 2006. Many may have married into the new rich of Victorian industrial families to maintain their status, but it was not those sides of their families which were most celebrated when family trees of human 'pedigree' were being drawn up, documents showing how they came from 'good stock', royal blood or from some of the families which are more established and ancient than the royal family itself.

Opposing multiculturalism

Across Europe and the Americas and throughout Japan, from the 1970s onwards Darwinian racism rose again. When the rich once again became very rich, joined by a few newcomers, but mostly from the old families, the old ideas of survival, self-advancement and supremacy of the supposed fittest again rose to power, and rose most clearly in the way opposition to the growth of racism from those in power became muted in the 1970s. It was not just because Margaret Thatcher wanted to deny the National Front votes that she used the term 'swamping' in relation to immigrants on television in 1978; it is that she believed then what she said, that: '... we must hold out the clear prospect of an end to immigration ... [because] ... We are a British nation with British characteristics'.[27] That racism, and its new wider face of prejudice, fitted the revived Darwinian rhetoric too well to be too strongly opposed.

The racism that arose newly emboldened in the 1970s came with a nationalist twist, which was to see countries as natural units and to suggest that those which were supposedly home to a single racial group tended to be happy places to live where people got on with one another. Those portrayed as having had groups brought together, new groups brought in, tended more often to be places of strife, mistrust and inequality. It was suggested by opponents of multiculturalism that inequality was the natural consequence of trying to mix people together who do not easily mix. By this way of thinking the social problems of the US became the problems of dealing with black people. The US could never aim to be as equal as Europe, to have the kind of healthcare systems Europeans have, to have such widespread and respected state schooling as Europeans, because (so this misguided argument goes) the US is not a naturally homogeneous society – the US, by this prejudicial thinking, is said to lack 'ethnic homogeneity'. This way of thinking and of describing the world is now said to hardly deserve a response by people who look into others' psychological flaws.[28] But it is worth thinking about where this thinking came from, and what it leads to, especially as such thinking is at the core of much current racist ideology.

To be able to describe a country or a city as ethnically heterogeneous requires thinking of different residents of that place as belonging to a myriad of different ethnic/racial groups. It is possible to describe almost any place as being made up of a myriad of different racial groups. A university campus can often by typified in this way, but it isn't, because the students have more in common as students than they have differences due to ethnic background. You could describe the people of a major city in a country like Greece as coming from a huge variety of backgrounds because it is at the crossroads of continents, but national identity and a national orthodox religion are often stressed, rather than the huge variety of hair and skin tones of the population – these are usually simply not remarked on. A similar situation occurs in London where a majority of the mothers of newborn infants were themselves born abroad, but where this great mix of people also have a huge amount in common. When people have much in common, they are described using a common term, such as being all 'students', or all 'Greeks', or even all 'Londoners'. Where identity is less shared, lives less similar, opportunities and outcomes far more constrained by skin tone or family history, then the people in that place are more often called, for example, white, Hispanic, black or Asian, broken down into ethnic classifications.

A homogeneous ethnicity, the idea of a common identity, is created by how aspirations and beliefs are described. In 2004 one of the Swedish political parties wrote in its election material that '… everyone is fragile at some point in time. All Swedes need each other. All live their lives in the here and now, together with others, caught up in the midst of change. All will be richer if all of us are allowed to participate and nobody is left out. All will be stronger if there is security for everybody and not only for a few'.[29] Of course there is much racism in Sweden, where some people are not recognised as Swedes. Elsewhere in Scandinavia, in Denmark, in an argument that is as much about countering racism directed towards Muslims as it is about class, it is argued that the population cannot afford not to be egalitarian, not just out of idealism but because securing continuous improvement in human lives and ability is vital to the economy. Minimisation of poverty and insecurity is a precondition for effective social investment. A commitment to social citizenship, pooling risks collectively, is essential to successful 21st-century living.[30] A group of people comes to have a common ethnicity not just by having an identity thrust on them, but by creating one through working for a common identity. If those working for solidarity within Scandinavian countries win, then the homogeneous ethnic image of Scandinavia that is presented will change, become a little less white, more homogeneous. If they lose then it will be said that there are distinct different and separate ethnicities there, heterogeneity. However, whatever transpires, neither scenario will completely encapsulate the case.

Both ethnic heterogeneity and homogeneity are myths. Heterogeneity as a useful concept is a myth because we almost all live in heterogeneous communities; it is just that we often do not recognise that. Our communities are also not ethnically homogeneous because people are not more predisposed to mix better with others of similar skin tone or hairstyle. People are predisposed to mix better with those who society has made them most likely to mix with. Thus university students will mix on campus with other university students far more readily than they will tend to mix with poorer local young adults, even of their exact age and exact skin tone. Two people in a city in Greece will mix regardless of their skin tone and hair colour and even religion more easily if their families are of similar social status as, in Greece as elsewhere in the rich world, people tend to marry within social classes more even than within religious groups (Orthodox and Catholic, Christian and Muslim, Abrahamic and Dharmic). Where income, wealth and class differences are narrower, such as in Greece (when compared with, say, Portugal), people are a little freer to marry who they like, because more are of a similar social class. It is in countries of great income and wealth inequalities that there is more disapproval of certain groups within that country marrying: whites and blacks in the US, Christians and Muslims in the UK, Dalits and Brahmins in India. In countries with far lower inequalities, membership of an ethnic, religious, or caste group is much less of an issue, and also less likely. It is less likely because in more equitable countries there is more ethnic mixing, religion is less prescribed, and castes cannot mean so much.

Racial purity

Children will mix with other children who live nearby if allowed out of their homes to do so. They will live near a greater mix of children in those countries where people are less scared. In a country that is far more tolerant of what is seen as inter-racial mixing, there will be far more inter-racial mixing. This is far from obvious when, as often happens in such countries, almost everyone comes to be defined as a single race and most as of a single class (such as the Japanese middle class). In a very different country, like the US, where such mixing was until recent generations proclaimed as evil, in schools, in bed, even on the same seats on buses, there will be less mixing still.

Mixing of those seen as different occurs most where people have been given a huge variety of racial and ethnic labels and have been put in very close proximity to each other at relatively young ages, preferably in a place where housing is so expensive, and commuting so tricky, that people have to live in whatever home they can afford which is as near to their commuter routes as possible. Thus London is a good place for mixing. Londoners call themselves Londoners, often in preference to British (and certainly in preference to English), because no other word describes the mix. It is not solely because they live in London.[31] A Parisian is more likely to say they are French than identify first with Paris, and have you have heard what the word is for someone from Tokyo? But you know a New Yorker when you meet one (or you soon get to know they are from New York)! Thus a place defined as heterogeneous, like London or New York, is homogeneous.

Ethnic homogeneity is almost always a myth that is easily exposed. The supposedly homogeneous group can be found, after a little digging, to have a wide variety of origins, being made up of a collection of people with a far wider range of backgrounds than the myth would suggest. Scandinavian stories of the good of the many outweighing the selfish intent of the few can sometimes come also with the downside of invoking the myth of ethnic homogeneity and then suffering from the danger of excluding those seen as outsiders, those less Scandinavian than others. Iceland is a good example, a far flung island where the myth of the supposed purity of its Nordic race, the descendents of Vikings, gained credence over generations of morale-boosting storytelling in an otherwise very beautiful but very cold, desolate and, until recently, extremely poor place. Genetic testing of the ethnic origins of Icelanders reveals that the Viking past of their island resulted in a somewhat less pure Nordic bloodline than the stories suggest. The Vikings were generally successful at what they did. That is why they are remembered. A large part of what they did was to take slaves from places like Britain, mainly Celtic slaves. And, like all groups who take slaves, they mixed with their slaves, but this wasn't talked of in their stories. We know they mixed because the evidence is in their, as it turns out, very heterogeneous genes.[32]

A similar story to the Scandinavian homogeneity myths can be told anywhere where such claims are made other than for the most isolated of Amazonian tribes. The more preposterous claims are rarely entertained nowadays, such as the claim that the Greeks of today are largely the direct descendents of the Greeks of antiquity. A few Greeks will of course be descended from an Ancient Greek man who is still remembered today, but they will also be the descendents of many more former slaves than that one famous man (let's call him Aristotle), and most people in Greece are descended mostly from people who lived outside Greece.

In contrast to Greece, in places where people have been more physically isolated by oceans from others, it has been easier to sustain myths of racial homogeneity, as in the case of Iceland. Some claim that being a small population aids homogeneity, but large populations can also be presented as homogeneous. Population size is no barrier to myth making. For instance, the Japanese population is usually presented to itself as at least as ethnically homogeneous as the Icelandic population. Immigration from the Philippines, Korea, China and elsewhere, past and present, is seen as minor and to have somehow disappeared without effect. Internal identities such as those of the *Yanato*, *Ainu* and the *Uchinan-chu* (the islanders of Okinawa), or of those living within the enclaves of Tokyo, the differences you can see if you wish to imagine them in people's faces, are all rendered imaginary by the myth of the homogeneity of the Japanese. The reason why it is possible to promulgate myths of racial homogeneity on islands such as those of Japan and Iceland is that in both, income inequalities and hence social differences are among the lowest in the rich world. On each island the poorest fifth receive just under a third of what the richest fifth receive in income a year.[33] In contrast, on islands such as Singapore, New Zealand and Britain, where inequalities are much wider, ethnicity is seen to matter much more. You might say that the visual indicators of ethnicity are clearer on these other islands, but what constitutes a difference to your eye depends on what you see as a difference in your mind, and that depends on what you have been brought up to view as a significant visual difference. Do singer Björk Guðmundsdóttir and presenter Magnús Magnússon appear especially visually similar to you, or Prime Minister Junichirō Koizumi and artist Yoko Ono? I have not picked these pairs because they look so different. I have picked them because they are probably among the best known faces from the islands they were born in. Of course they look no more similar or dissimilar than do any pair of famous Malay or Chinese faces from Singapore, *Maori* or *Pakeha* from New Zealand.

Survival of the fittest

What is common to both homogeneity and heterogeneity myths are new forms of social Darwinism. Social Darwinism is the shady movement that grew strong about a century ago suggesting that in humans there is a survival of the individually fittest, that this is a good thing, and that it can be accelerated for the common good. The truth is that there is no such natural thing; there is an enhanced potential for survival of the most sociable in normal times of sociability, and of the most selfish only in times of extreme scarcity and anarchy. For humans, being ostracised by society is usually deadly. Humans survive and prosper best in groups. The awful situations where only the 'fittest', or to describe them more accurately, the 'fortunate', survive are massacres, famines, or genocide such as occurred with the mass transportation of slaves from Africa to the Americas.

Belief in social Darwinism and its precursors resulted in just these kinds of situations, not just in genocide, but also in the imposition of sterilisation on great numbers of people. You only sterilise people you see as not being like you, but looking at who has been sterilised in human history you can see where and when ideas of social Darwinism have taken hold most strongly. These are not old evils; most genocide and almost all mass sterilisation in human history has occurred within living memory. Between the 1930s and 1970s some 60,000 legal but coerced sterilisations were carried out in the US; over the same time span, 600,000 were carried out in Germany, mostly at the start of this period.[34] Poorer Indians were the target of the bulk of postwar sterilisation when millions were sterilised with bribes financed by monies coming mostly from the US and the UK;[35] sterilisation was also not uncommon in the postwar rich world. In Scandinavia and Japan in particular, both places suffering from the homogeneity myth, sterilisation was common right through to the 1970s. By then it was mainly being forced on those most considered 'undesirable', people suffering mental illness for instance. Elsewhere in the world the targeting was wider, and the purpose more overt. Even in the 1980s in Singapore, an island that had become newly rich, a sterilisation scheme was introduced where the poor, mostly identified with one ethnic group, were offered money to be sterilised while the rich from another group were offered tax breaks to have children.[35] (It is possible that this policy, coupled with poorer mothers having to have their babies outside of the island, has resulted in Singapore having one of the lowest recorded rates of infant mortality ever found in the world.) Worldwide rates of sterilisation did not peak until 1983, when 20 million people, mostly women, were sterilised in China. At the heart of sterilisation was the rise of new wider prejudices.

Geographer Ruthie Gilmore has suggested that any deliberate human act that ultimately results in the premature deaths of groups of others can be defined as racism.[36] Racism curtails the length of life by inflicting insults ranging from high chances of imprisonment, to lower chances of being treated with respect at school, through to almost any form of discrimination which has effects on health. All this is racist by Ruthie Gilmore's wider definition. But it is the racist actions that directly lead to death itself that are most shocking. In the 1990s two children were found dead in the undercarriage of an aeroplane that landed at Brussels. One carried a note which read 'Excellencies, gentlemen – members and those responsible in Europe, it is to your solidarity and generosity that we appeal for your help in Africa. If you see that we have sacrificed ourselves and lost our lives, it is because we suffer too much in Africa and need your help to struggle against poverty and wars.... Please excuse us very much for daring to write a letter'.[37] The children were aged 15 and 16. They were just two of thousands who died trying to enter Europe each year from the 1970s onwards, attempting to evade immigration controls: these were essentially controls of those not of the same 'stock'. Children seen as of the same 'stock' are welcomed in. The greatest concentration of immigrant children living in Britain is of those born in the US, resident, with their families, a seventh of all children found near the heart of London.[38]

Stoking fear

Almost no distinction is made between refugees and those who are labelled as immigrants (which excludes most immigrants and includes many people who are not immigrants, having been born in the country where they reside). Fears of immigration vary dramatically between countries and over time. Such fears can only be kept high by being constantly stoked. When asked in recent years whether it is immigration which most worries them, it was reported as the main concern of 8% of Germans, 11% of Swedes, 12% of the Dutch, 13% of the French, 21% of Australians, 28% of Italians, a third of the citizens of the US, and there are almost as many fearful Spaniards as there are fearful Brits, some 46% in 2007.[39] Although there are many Brits living in Spain, these rates bear no resemblance to the proportions of immigrants in each country or any effect these immigrants may have; they simply reflect how well those who want to cause fear and suffering are doing. It is said that people get the press they deserve but that press is also more thrust on them in unequal countries where a few rich men own much of the media. Note who controls much of the press in Australia, Italy, the US and Britain and look again at the list above. Fears and belief systems are built up and altered through many media, but the national press is vital in this. When the press criticises immigrants and bolsters celebrities as deserving of riches, it is clear which systems of belief it is promulgating.

The press does not promulgate prejudice simply because it sells more papers and gains more viewers in fearful times. The press also takes its lead from the actions of politicians. Causal direction is very hard to pin down but it is hard to argue that MPs were driven to be as cruel as they sometimes have been by either the electorate or the press. For example, in 2004 the British government passed an Asylum and Immigration Act, section 9 of which gave landlords, including local authorities, the power to evict from their homes families with children who refused to return voluntarily to their country of origin when not given a right to remain in Britain. These families with young children would thus be made homeless. At the time the legislation was described as 'one of the more overt aspects of cruelty within a system premised on cruelty'.[40] The political party system in Britain requires certain apparatchiks to be appointed as 'whips' to tell elected representatives how to vote on a 'party line'. Many MPs may simply not have been thinking, just following the 'whips', but enough appeared to not see these children as quite as human as their own, to not see these adults as people much like themselves, to be able to support this Act. This is what it takes for such racist legislation to become law.

The opposite of a celebrity is 'an unknown', the unknown hundred million who were never born due to the sterilisation of their potential parents; the mostly unknown 10 million a year who die before their fifth birthday due to poverty; the largely unknown million (as a minimum) who die each year as adults due to wars, massacres, or genocide; the single dead baby, name unknown, found in storage in a lorry travelling into Britain from France, smuggled in with parents in search of a better life. The unknown baby is, in this case, a fictional baby, invoked by an MP who asked (in the British Parliament) how a new law would work that would fine lorry drivers found to have smuggled people concealed in their vehicles. When queried whether the fine would still apply if the smuggled person was a baby the minister replied yes. When queried whether the fine would be applied if the baby was dead the minister said it would, but only if the baby had died on the British side of the channel. The minister did not appear to view the baby as all that human, just as a problem if it were still breathing.[41] The tale of the unknown dead baby in storage, not worth a fine, is where the story of how policies based on social Darwinism and the values it puts on human life ultimately ends – in deaths that need not have been premature.

As, according to Ruthie Gilmore, premature death caused by human harm including indifference provides evidence of the wider extent of racism in a society, and as racism is any act that ultimately results in the premature deaths of others, it is worth looking at trends in premature mortality as indicative of trends in racist behaviour when racism is more widely understood. Figure 12 shows how the rate of inequalities in premature mortality has changed in Britain over the period 1920–2006. Premature mortality rises when inequalities in mortality rise, as more people die before it is usual for them to die. The data used to draw Figure 12 are given in Table 5 (on page 176,

Figure 12: Inequalities in survival chances to age 65 by area in Britain, 1920–2006

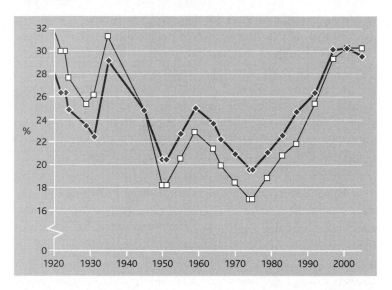

Note: The line marked by white squares shows how much lower the age–sex standardised under age 65 mortality rate of the best-off 10% by area is as compared with the average. The line marked by dark diamonds shows how much higher that of the worst-off 30% is than the average.

Source: Dorling , D. and Thomas, B. (2009) 'Geographical inequalities in health over the last century', in H. Graham (ed) *Health inequalities*, Oxford: Oxford University Press, pp 66-83, derived from Table 4.3, with interpolation between five-year rates in some circumstances.

following Figure 13). The graph shows that inequalities in mortality fell throughout the 1920s, but rose again in the Great Depression as lives again became cheap. You almost certainly do not think of this as resulting from a form of racism, but one class of people had to look a long way down on another class of people, living in different parts of the country, to allow this to happen in the 1930s. This dominant class lost power in the 1940s and the inequalities plummeted thereafter before rising slightly again following the remarkable equality achieved immediately after the Second World War, and probably during it too. The attitudes of the rich to the poor had been changed, although there was not always progress. Health inequalities between areas increased in the 1950s, but fell throughout the 1960s and early 1970s to reach a minimum around 1969–73 when the best-off 10% could 'only' expect about a one in six (16.6%) lower than average chance of dying before their 65th birthday any year, and the excess mortality of the worst-off 30% was 'just' a fifth (20%) higher than the average. After that time, as prejudice grew, so did inequalities in premature death. Today far more of the people living in the poorest of areas are not white than in average or better-off areas. At the start of the period shown in the graph more were Jewish or Irish. What mattered most at both times was that these groups were more likely to be seen as and treated as poor.

5.3 Polarisation: of the economic performance of regions

Prejudice, and the consequent rise in inequalities in income and wealth that accompanies its acceptance, does not just increasingly divide groups of people but also the places that they live in. Rising prejudices can encourage policies that increase the economic polarisation of regions, making it acceptable that certain areas and people are abandoned, while other places and groups are seen as vital and to be economically supported. At the micro-regional level, when it comes to choosing where to live, the rich are even more constrained in options than the poor. Entire towns and cities can lack almost any very rich people whereas almost no town or city lacks poor neighbourhoods. The super-rich are most constrained in their choice of residential location. There are simply not so many multi-million pound/dollar/euro and billion yen properties on the market. The super-rich could build a house almost anywhere, but they need more than a home – they need other super-rich people with whom to socialise, to identify with, to share their prejudices with, and they are very afraid of the poor. Because of all this they cluster in their enclaves, in particular regions, in particular cities in those regions, and in particular streets in those cities. When we talk of rising segregation it is often the segregation of ethnic or religious groups which is being imagined, but it is the rich who are most geographically segregated and have been becoming more so in more unequal countries.

Rising social prejudice is accompanied by growing social inequalities between neighbourhoods within cities, between cities within regions and between regions within countries. The super-rich tend to be surrounded (geographically as well as when out socially) by the slightly less rich. The place where these affluent households mostly settle becomes what is seen as the neighbourhood of choice. If a city has no such neighbourhoods it is shunned more widely. When inequalities are increasing, the city around and within which most of the rich settle becomes progressively richer and richer over time, even as it also attracts more and more poorer people to serve those affluent families. This is because each affluent family adds a great deal to the overall measure of wealth of the city, whereas each poor family adds only a small number to the overall population that such wealth is divided by. The wealth is less and less well divided in practice, but it is in theory divided ever so smoothly to calculate the *per capita* income rates through which cities and regions are ranked (and whereby GDP is estimated). A city with a high GDP, such as Luxembourg or New York, will tend not to be a place where most people are very well off, but a place that contains larger affluent enclaves than most similarly sized cities (or countries, in Luxembourg's case).

Within Europe, at least until recently, the London region was the richest when wealth was measured per person. This was despite London containing one of the greatest concentrations of poor people in Europe. London is one of those places where the super-rich of the world find they have to have a home if they are to fit into global super-rich social circles. One result has been that finding homes for the rest of Londoners who do not globetrot has been far from easy in recent years. For most of the previous 100 years London was declining in population and it was becoming easier to house families in the capital without them being grossly overcrowded as a result. The story in New York was similar; population decline in central New York City continued right through to the 1970s. Other financial centres also declined in population and then saw fresh people crowd in. Thus, from 1970 to 2000 the population of Luxembourg also rose dramatically (by over a third). A small part of that increase came because, from the 1970s onwards, the rich were settling in greater numbers in these places as their numbers declined elsewhere. In small town North America, in the outlying provinces of Britain and the more remote rural villages of Europe, in almost all of Japan except Tokyo, the children of the affluent did not return home from the cities they first moved to as young adults. In those societies that became more polarised, as social polarisation increased, the rich felt more and more at home surrounded by their own.

Not all countries saw such a concentration of the affluent in so few locations. In Japan, although particular districts of Tokyo did become synonymous with wealth and many more with youth, the dividing of areas between rich and poor did not occur nationally with anything like the speed with which such processes were seen to operate in the US. The young moved to Tokyo, but the wealthy and poor did not polarise as much. In Japan mixed neighbourhoods are the norm; houses are squeezed between apartment blocks; school children usually walk to school rather than being driven. Extreme geographical polarisation by wealth is the exception in affluent countries, not the rule. Similarly, in Europe, although Luxembourg became a pole of attraction for the rich, as did other small states with low taxes, across much of the rest of the continent there was no great abandonment of particular districts by the affluent and a squeezing of the majority of the rich into just a few districts by a process ironically called 'choice'. Wealthier people used to be more widely spread out across the country in countries like Britain. When polarisation occurred, all that began to matter when determining how well a city or region appeared to fare was how near it was to London. Train travel times from London provided the best guide to how well cities did in terms of seeing their residents' incomes rise, jobless rates fall, education levels increase, even health improve.[42]

Moving apart

Within countries, geographical, social and economic polarisation tends to take place slowly and steadily. You have to look at data over a long time period to see this clearly, partly because we come to accept the divides we currently live with. These forms of polarisation themselves cause beliefs to become more polarised. As polarisation rises more people come to believe that others living elsewhere are less deserving creatures than themselves. Within a country like Britain the changing extent of the divide is perhaps most simply illustrated politically by considering changes in how concentrated the votes have been by area for the main political party of government in the 20th century, the Conservative Party. Figure 13 shows how, beginning just after the First World War and continuing right through to the 1960s, Conservative voters became far less spatially concentrated. It depicts a measure of the minimum proportion of such voters who would have to be transferred between a fixed set of parliamentary constituencies if each constituency were to have the same national proportion of Conservative voters at each general election. By the time of the 1960s general elections, just moving some 6% of the national total of Conservative voters from some of the most Conservative seats to some of the least Conservative seats would have had the effect of making the share of the vote which the Conservatives secured in all seats the same. By 2005 that proportion had reached 16%, higher than at any time since just before the 1920s. This is not evidence of social polarisation, but of a geographical polarisation in underlying beliefs. In the 1960s, when the Conservatives were unpopular, their core vote was spread out. By the late 1990s, when again unpopular, their core vote had become geographically concentrated. A great deal had changed in between in the lives of people living in different places in Britain.

Figure 13 is reminiscent of Figure 12, of trends in health inequalities, and as is shown below, this also reflects the trends in wealth inequalities in Figure 14. When trends appear similar it can

---

Figure 13: Concentration of Conservative votes, British general elections, 1918–2005

Note: An average of the two 1974 figures is shown here; actual figures are graphed in the source and also used for the correlations reported here (they were 8.01% in the February election and 10.74% in the October election of that year, see Table 5).

Source: Drawn initially in Dorling, D. (2006) 'Class alignment', *Renewal: The Journal of Labour Politics*, vol 41, no 1, p 849, showing the spatial segregation index.

help to check the likelihood that such similarity might arise from chance. Such checks provide no proof of a causal link, but they are helpful in the search for looking for coincidences on which to speculate. For both simplicity and a little historical reparation this book uses only statistical tests associated with that great advocate of inequality, Karl Pearson. The Pearson product-moment correlation coefficient is named after him although often attributed to Charles Darwin's cousin Francis Galton, whom Pearson worked with and who was a far more unpleasant advocate of inequality (most who have compared the two suggest – see Chapter 4, note 29, page 339, this volume). Table 5 shows that the correlation coefficients are 0.72 and 0.75 between the trend shown above and the two trends shown in Figure 12. The conventional test results are also given in Table 5 and suggest that by one method of estimating probabilities there is

Table 5: Inequalities of health, privilege and wealth (%), Britain, 1918-2005

Year	Mortality inequality of decile groups by area		Geographical concentration of national Conservative vote by area[c]	National income share of the best-off 1%	
	Excess of worst-off 30%[a]	Advantage of best-off 10%[b]		Pre-tax[d]	Post-tax[e]
1918	29	35	19	19	17
1922	26	30	14	18	16
1923	26	30	12	19	17
1924	25	28	11	18	16
1929	23	25	9	17	15
1931	23	26	9	16	14
1935	29	31	10	14	13
1945	25	25	7	13	10
1950	20	18	7	12	7
1951	20	18	7	12	6
1955	23	21	7	9	6
1959	25	23	6	9	6
1964	24	21	7	9	6
1966	22	20	8	9	6
1970	21	18	8	7	5
1974 Feb	20	17	8	7	4
1974 Oct	20	17	11	6	4
1979	21	19	9	6	4
1983	23	21	11	7	5
1987	25	22	12	8	6
1992	26	25	12	10	8
1997	30	29	14	12	10
2001	30	30	15	13	10
2005	30	30	16	16	13
Pearson product-moment correlation coefficients of above (p<0.01 except * p=0.0105)					
	1[a]	2[b]	3[c]	4[d]	
1[a]					
2[b]	0.91				
3[c]	0.72	0.75			
4[d]	0.57	0.82	0.51*		
5[e]	0.60	0.86	0.58	0.97	

Notes: [a] Excess deaths under age 65 of those living in the worst-off 30% of areas by population compared with the national average rate.
[b] Reduction in under age 65 death rates of those 10% living in the best-off areas as compared with the national average.
[c] Minimum proportion of Conservative voters who would have to move parliamentary constituency if an identical proportion were to vote for that party in every constituency in the general election held that year (in Figure 13 an average of the two 1974 figures is graphed).
[d] Share of national income received by the best-off 1% of the population before tax.
[e] Share of that income enjoyed by the best-off 1% post-tax.

The Pearson product-moment correlation coefficients (r) shown above are calculated using the 'PEARSON' function in Excel. The p values are calculated by creating a z-score using the Excel function f='SQRT(n-3)*FISHER(r)' where n is 24, which is the number of observations above. The Excel function '2*NORMDIST(f,0,1,TRUE)' returns the p value. All this assumes, among many things, that the sample pairs are independently distributed, which coming from the same pair of years they are not, but the method remains a useful way of deciding whether to take a high correlation seriously. However, what you take seriously is ultimately up to you. Karl Pearson's friends measured skull attributes, attempting to correlate them with everything including penis length! See Gladwell, M. (2007) 'What IQ doesn't tell you about race', *New Yorker*, 17 December.

Sources: Columns 1 and 2, Figure 12; column 3, Figure 13; columns 4 and 5, Figure 14

less than a one in 10,000 chance that the distribution of voting is unrelated to the proportion of premature deaths occurring among the worst-off in society, and there is a less than a one in 100,000 chance that the concentration of voting is unrelated to the health advantage of the best-off 10% of society. This clearly does not mean that one causes the other, just that these two great falls and rises in inequality follow a similar periodicity. However, one pattern is not being measured on Mars and the other on Venus. Both almost certainly influence each other; they influenced and were influenced by much else and are part of a more general greater trend.

Figure 13 shows the fall and rise in the geographical concentration of right-wing voting in Britain, as represented by the Conservative Party. The Conservative Party throughout the 20th century was the party of old-fashioned views, often holding bigoted ideas, quietly accepting racism at whatever level it could be proclaimed in the polite society of the times, moving as slowly as possible towards, and often retreating from, a fairer future. Inequalities in health rose postwar when the Conservatives were in power in the 1950s, 1980s and 1990s, and only under Labour when it appeared to behave, in terms of statistical correlation with inequalities rising, as a Conservative Party, following the 1997 General Election. During the 20th century people who were persuaded to vote for representatives of the Conservative Party initially became both less in number and less spatially concentrated. This clearly occurred from 1918 onwards. There were still Conservatives everywhere, but there were fewer and fewer of them, and fewer self-reinforcing clusters of them. However, in hindsight, by the early 1970s it became clear that Conservative sympathies were about to begin to be newly created, concentrating spatially again and growing in number.

The tipping point

Although Figure 13 shows the slow rise beginning in 1966 and continuing through to 1974, the decisive point is probably 1974. Not shown on the graph, but noted under it, in the February General Election of that year (following the oil price shocks of 1973) voter segregation held steady at 8%. It was only in October that it rose, and rose abruptly. It was almost as if the country, to treat it like some individual, and the Conservative Party in particular, paused for a moment to decide which way to turn. It could choose between the collective path where all would take a hit together, accept that oil prices had risen, accept that standards of living could not be so high again, that the empire had gone and that the inequalities of the world should be reduced. Or it could turn the other way; a few people could try to make Britain supposedly 'great' again, concentrate on making money, exploit the rest of the world, abandon those parts of the country seen as unproductive, take away financial rules so that banks could make more and more profit out of individuals at home and overseas. By late 1974 the Conservative Party had still not converted fully to individualism, but it was the most right-wing alternative available. In October 1974 in the South of England there was a decisive swing in votes towards that selfish alternative, not enough votes to win the election for the Conservatives, but enough to give the signal to set the country steadily on a new route towards almost four decades of rising political, economic and social polarisation. A year later the grandees of the Conservative Party chose Margaret Thatcher to be their new leader. Less than four years after that, as their popular vote in the South East and the Midlands of England swelled, the Conservative Party reaped the benefit of having made that choice, and won a landslide victory.

The decision taken by so many voters in 1974 and 1979 and not reversed with sufficient enthusiasm thereafter meant that by 2004 Britain had become as socially divided as in 1934 in terms of differences between areas in life expectancy (as shown in Figure 12), in wealth (Figure 14), votes (Figure 13), housing (Chapter 6), education (Chapter 3), income (Chapter 4) and much more of the fabric of life than just these basics. Britain, however, was not leading those parts of the world that made this choice; it was following closely behind the world leader in the slide towards selfishness and rising prejudice, the world leader being the US.

Follow the leader

The US, for all its anti-communist rhetoric at home and wars overseas, was a remarkably equitable place in 1974. It had a minimum wage it was possible to live on, worth more than twice as much as the minimum wage in 2008 in real terms. Mean 'real' average wages were also higher than today (see Section 3.3 above). New civil and women's rights legislation was changing the face and feelings of North American society, and young people protested over war in a way their parents could not have even imagined themselves doing. All this and the slow and steady loss of their wealth, social position and power, angered many of those older white men with more money than most. As in Britain, where racism was used to bolster the 1979 Conservative vote, the Republican Party that these men supported used racist rhetoric. That rhetoric then helped create anger among poorer white people. Ronald Reagan's speeches about 'black welfare queens' helped him secure victory in 1980 with the support of unprecedented numbers of southern whites. The rally towards increased prejudice again began a little earlier in the US than the UK, but it is a larger country and it took right-wing North Americans a year longer to win their most important national election and to secure the presidency for Ronald Reagan in 1980. However, he was quicker to change rules, regulations and regimes to raise inequality. He may have left office in 1988 but his legacy and the legacy of those who supported him (or opposed him, but failed to reverse his impact) returned the US by 2005 not to inequalities last realised in the 1930s, but to levels not seen since the early 1920s.

In both the early 1920s and 2005 the highest income percentile of people living in the US received 17% of all income, and the highest 10% received some 44% of all income. All the years in between (1925–2005) were more equal. The trend followed that same U-shaped distribution which is seen in the graphs of Britain (Figures 12–14). It is also worth noting that inequalities became so unequal that most of the rich did not feel very rich in 1925 or 2005. The average household within the top 10th, but excluding the top 100th, was almost six times worse off than the average within that best-off percentile.[43] Income inequalities between the persons placed first in 100 and fifth in 100 were also as great as between those placed 10th and 90th in the US income parades of both 1925 and 2005.

Although the Conservatives in Britain in 1979 and the Republicans in the US in 1980 had secured the largest number of votes to put them in power (of those who could be persuaded to vote at all), they did not improve the living conditions of even most of those who voted for them, just those of the more affluent of their supporters. Thus in the US if people in most of the top tenth of society looked up they saw the top 1% flying away from them. When they looked down they looked in fear to see ghettos forming and neighbourhoods being abandoned, entire rust belt regions being consigned to the scrap heap. Because of this, for a long time they could be persuaded to continue to vote in support of the selfishness of the rich in what looked like protection from being abandoned themselves. This implicit threat was so powerful that it resulted in the Democrat and Labour parties mirroring right-wing policy to become electable. So when they came to power in the most unequal of rich countries these opposition parties made no discernible impact on the kind of graphs shown in this chapter. As with Ronald Reagan, the legacy of Margaret Thatcher and those who brought her to power continued long after she lost office. People living in areas that voted Conservative in 1997 in Britain saw greater improvements to their life expectancy and living standards over the course of the next 10 years than those experienced in Labour voting areas despite Labour being in power all that time, and similar trends occurred in the US under President

Clinton.[44] It is possible that without Labour and the Democrats the present would be far worse, that inequalities by 2008 would have surpassed that 1918 maximum. Alternatively inequalities might just have risen higher faster and the market failed a little earlier than 2008.

People do not happily polarise, but they will vote and act to polarise out of fear. When there appears to be no alternative to abandoning poorer areas and poorer people to keep average living standards stable, otherwise well-meaning people can be persuaded to act selfishly. They do this both in the ballot box, and in exercising what little choice they have over where they live. In the 1970s most white families in both the US and Britain were much freer to choose different residential locations than they are now. As private housing later became more expensive, freedom to choose where to live for those who could afford private housing declined even though the supply increased. The increased supply allowed a small group to buy several homes each. As the supply of social housing was reduced the small amount of freedom of choice that had existed there was also reduced. In both countries most families began to spend higher and higher proportions of their incomes to pay to live away from other people, often away from black and poor people, especially as prices rose in the mid-1980s and later 1990s. But hardly anyone ever said that they bought a home in the suburbs of Chicago or Birmingham (England) to get away from blacks or the poor. They talked about the schools, or the air, or the décor, but their actions betrayed their beliefs, their rising prejudice. The evidence was in higher and higher prices being paid for otherwise identical homes in posh areas as compared with average, as compared with poor; it was in the mantra that began in the 1970s and became a loud chant by the 1990s, that what mattered most in determining price was: 'location, location, location'.

Polarisation and cohesion

Once a process of economic polarisation begins it is very hard to turn it around. Attitudes harden, fear grows on fear; as people polarise geographically they begin to know less and less of each other and imagine more and more. Free market rhetoric stops being ridiculed as it was in the 1950s when economists described events in the late

1920s as free market madness.[45] It is only under rising prejudice that it becomes acceptable again to have many people looking for work all the time, as the workless become seen as part of the 'oil' that makes the whole machine work smoothly. It takes a long time again for people to realise that jobs being lost and gained around the world, or relocated, results in huge gross turnover of human lives for small net increases in apparent human productivity. The gross turnover is what affects individual lives: insecurity, feeling worthless, being made redundant, being made redundant again and again, having to take whatever work is on offer. The net increases in numbers of people in paid employment are what the government economist measures as success when selfishness has become the norm. We do not live in a zero-sum world where jobs have to be lost in rich countries for them to be gained in poor ones, where this will somehow make the world a more equitable place. If that were the case globally we would be so much more equal by now. Instead, areas are abandoned; other places become overcrowded and congested; the poorer people are the more they are exploited. But the aggregate economic statistics do not measure that; they just measure growth.

During the 1980s in Britain the motorway system was greatly extended to allow people to commute far further and more frequently by car than before. This aided the spatial polarisation between areas. You could live further away from the city centres in which you worked. Road building was part of a longer-term change in transportation when seen more widely. However, different affluent countries chose to undertake different levels of road and railway building. The road building and social polarisation in Britain led to so much more road use that the motorways became even more congested than before, despite so many more being built. The very richest people moved back to the city centres. Trams and urban railways had created the outer suburbs as residential possibilities. The car made commuter villages attractive. Now in many cities the rich have returned to the very core and the nearby initially affluent inner suburbs have recently been suffering decline. This is found in many European cities, across the US and in Australasia; recent changes in the larger cities, such as Sydney, typify this pattern.[46]

In different parts of the world, at different times, different parts of cities fare better than others. When in Europe and North America the poor became concentrated in the centres and the rich were spun out to the suburbs, the opposite pattern was found in poorer countries. There the rich were initially spun into the centre. In poorer countries local taxes tend to be low or non-existent. In rich countries the affluent often initially moved out of city centres to avoid being taxed at city rates (thus avoiding having to help support the poor within their city and avoiding having to live too near them). In richer countries they moved further out to create what has been called the often forgotten third ring of ex-urban sometime-commuters.[47] In the most unequal of all rich countries the most affluent ensure that local taxes are low and they have at least two homes, one in the city centre and one in the third ring, maybe in Chelsea and the Cotswolds, or in Manhattan and Maine.

Some of these people with homes in more than one community have the gall to complain of a lack of community cohesion. Both the Conservative leader David Cameron and the Republican presidential nominee John McCain were unsure when asked how many homes they owned.[48] It isn't possible to know all your neighbours when you own three, four, five, six or more homes. While community cohesion might be low where the most affluent live, these uncohesive areas tend not to experience many riots.

The phrase 'community cohesion' was not used before 2001. It is a strangely manufactured lament reflecting some old concerns associated with city living and migration, but perhaps also a new fear of the affluent who do not want to be blamed for causing others' woes by their own accumulation of riches. It is in the countries that have become more split apart by greed, in which the richest live as far away from the poor as they can, that you most often hear the lament that in poor areas people occasionally riot. Although the areas where the riots occur are always poor, reports on riots in recent years have not made the links between rioting and poverty that earlier reports made. Compare official reports on riots in places like Bradford in 2001 with reports in the 1980s, including the Scarman report on the Brixton riots in London, or the 1960s California gubernatorial commission's findings on the Watts riots in Los Angeles. It is now more common to hear that poverty is 'not an excuse', that the fact that those areas have been disinvested in should not have led to disturbance (as so much has somehow been 'invested' through 'regeneration'). But in these areas young people are given so little compared with most young people that they know they have little to lose. Instead of rioting, minor public order offences and what is called general anti-social behaviour are now more often blamed on supposed racial tension and on different groups of people labelled by skin colour and religion apparently not mixing much. Almost always these are groups that have mixed well in poor areas, as compared with the way the rich, despite flocking together, do not mix well with each other, let alone with the poor. The segregation and lack of community cohesion of the affluent is ignored, as is their lack of general community spirit, which harms the majority so much.

5.4 Inheritance: the mechanism of prejudice

Until recently in the US the myth that all could become rich was so strong that even a majority of the very poorest voters were in favour of abolishing inheritance tax, called 'estate tax'. This was despite the fact that less than 1% pay such taxes.[49] As US wealth falls with the economic crash it will become harder to sell the American dream as something to hang on to, and more and more vital to find sources of income to simply maintain the basic running of the US. Taxing the inheritance of the rich is the most obvious source of that income. However, the greatest obstacle to keeping, expanding and raising inheritance tax is racism. Inheritance tax is now seen as transferring money from white to black Americans, but it was not always so. Andrew Carnegie argued that inheritance tax was the only way to prevent a permanent aristocracy of the wealthy. This would have been prevented had the tax been maintained; instead North America got that aristocracy, the aristocracy of the descendants of robber-barons and bloated bankers.

The human failing most closely associated with the injustice of prejudice is racism. It is racist to believe that we are inherently different. The idea that mental ability and other 'gifts' are inherited and the concept of giving material and social advantage to your offspring, coupled with preventing them from apparently squandering their inheritances by urging them to marry from among a narrow range of partners, are the mechanisms through which prejudice is maintained over time. Where such behaviours over inheritance remain powerful, social inequalities remain high and social solidarity tends to be low. A belief in inheritance both creates and maintains the ideas of racial groups and racial difference.[50] What separates white and black people most in the US is wealth. When people are free to consort with whoever they wish in a society, that society quickly becomes seen as racially homogeneous. This occurred in Iceland as it came out of abject poverty and almost all were seen as alike, or in Japan following land reform that made all more equal and hence more alike. As a result most people in Japan and Iceland are viewed as being of the same race.

The creation of race

We have not always belonged, and do not always belong, to particular ethnic groups. When there are restrictions on mixing, either legally imposed or through the creation of a tradition, then races become created and begin to take on huge importance in connection with life chances. A race can be made in a flicker of time. One such flicker occurred only a few lifetimes ago, in 1770.

On 22 April 1770 there were no indigenous Australians, no natives, no black people in Australia, no Australia really; there were just a great many people who had lived in a very large land for a very long time. They belonged to many groupings, athough these were constantly reforming and far from all-encompassing. People were spread all across a continent. Not one of them was called aboriginal. In a flicker of time all that changed; all the nuances of grouping, kingdoms and respect went when James Cook, initially apprenticed by Quakers in the Yorkshire seaside village of Whitby, claimed Australia for the English Crown. If it hadn't been James Cook it would have quickly been another sea captain who would have, at a stroke, turned the oldest great collection of continuously surviving human civilisations in the world into what within a few years would become one of the poorest racial minorities on the planet. He did this simply by claiming that Australia was, from then on, part of the inheritance of the British.[51] The British themselves were a manufactured race who, only a few years earlier, had mostly been subjects of a Scottish monarchy. There were no British people in 1700; they were only 'made' to exist long after the successors of another James, King of Scotland from 1567, inherited the crowns of both Ireland and England in 1603.[52] These were times when the nationalities that people were given, their religions and the languages they were expected to speak, depended greatly on the whims of princes and kings.

Like nations, religions and ethnicities, races are created. They are manufactured from acts of royal marriage and infertility, exploration, discovery, colonialisation, imperialism and expropriation. And races can also be dissolved. They are dissolved by inter-marriage and when no one considers them any more as a race. Often religious groups are synonymous with racial groups, especially when persecuted, as in the cases of Jews, Huguenots and Rastafarians.

The Quakers were one such group that could once be seen as a race that was persecuted much as more accepted races were and that could easily have become a mainstream race. There was a time when Quakers mostly married other Quakers, gave birth to children who in turn became Quakers, and were seen in countries like Britain as a group apart. In England in 1753 the Marriage Act of Parliament contained an exception to allow Quakers and Jews to follow their own traditions. Just 17 years before James Cook landed on the Australian East coast, English law depicted Quakers on a par with Jews, and also as a 'race'/religion to be respected and tolerated. If respect and toleration last long enough, a race disappears. When respect and tolerance are absent, race is all-pervasive, and races are maintained through oppression and persecution. Oppression and persecution occur most frequently where there is great economic inequality.

Race was famously proposed as the reason '... for the absence of an American welfare state'.[53] The US does have a cut-down version of a welfare state, but properly functioning welfare states require a ?e of mutual trust and understanding greater than that common US. When trust is absent it is very hard to establish widespread for a system where those who have fallen on hard times will be supported through sickness or worklessness until they are better, or back in work, or both. You have to see your fellow humans as like you in order to support such a system. If you see them as a different kind of human being, following different kinds of motivation, perhaps as lazier than you, not as clever as you think you are, or as upright or as moral, then you may be less likely to back systems of mutual support. Seeing groups of others as generally lazy, immoral and stupid is usually social status-related; it is part of seeing them as beneath you. The great injustice of the lack of a well-functioning welfare state in the US is the direct result of the tolerance, maintenance and building up of great racism.

Racism is everywhere, but to differing degrees. In most of Western Europe racism has been kept subservient enough to permit the establishment of a series of welfare states. These welfare states were brought in most solidly after the Second World War, partly to curtail dissent among poor people over continued social inequalities, but also because social solidarity and equality were then high enough to make welfare possible. It was possible even earlier in New Zealand as the welfare state there was established in the 1930s. Not all people in Western European countries have been subject to the protection of welfare states – the reasons for excluding a group are usually racist. Guest workers, non-EU tourists, illegal immigrants, these are all groups who can be excluded from medical care and rights to social security which would protect them during times of worklessness. In Japan, for example, guest workers are encouraged to leave when they fall ill or out of employment.

Within Europe the right to move freely for those with citizenship is yet another example of races dissolving as Europeans come to be seen to have more in common with each other, to have common rights and expectations to be treated similarly, a common European inheritance. This is a constructed, not a natural, inheritance, as recent tensions over migration from Eastern Europe has illustrated. This common inheritance is also used, like the idea of US citizenship and Japanese nationality, as a reason to exclude others, others not fortunate enough to have inherited through accident of birthplace the right to a protected life.

If you are born in one of the three rich regions of the world you should never go really hungry, never expect to fall ill and die on the street without healthcare; your children will have a right to education; your basic dignity will be respected. These are all things you have inherited because they are your inheritance as a citizen, through the accident of your birth. However, rather than admit this, it can be easier to suggest that in the past people in these areas were specially endowed to become richer, and that superiority both existed and somehow justifies the current fortunes of their descendants, including almost everyone reading this book. Did the 'British race' come to rule an empire of many other 'races' that had its greatest extent in 1919 because 'the British' were especially able? This would be both a justification based on an identification of races and a racist argument.

It is hard to overplay the importance of how just being born in a wealthy country provides you with an inheritance that ends up marking you as different from others. This inheritance is not just of systems of social organisations that are efficient at keeping people healthy and well fed, occupied and educated. It is also of the physical infrastructure that makes all this possible, of roads and railways built decades ago from profits often made from trade – trade which was often imposed on others. Good health is maintained as much by the inheritance of sewer systems built at such times as it is partly the product of being born to parents who in their turn will have been better fed and cared for than most other people in the world. Being born in an affluent country also results in inheriting the right to have payments made indirectly to you in the form of interest on the loans your forefathers made to people in poorer countries. More generally, you inherit being at the right end of a mechanism that ensures that over time you pay less and less for what is made and grown elsewhere, while those in poorer countries pay more and more. By 2006 the UN Department of Economic and Social Affairs valued that transfer at US\$500 billion (net) moving from poor to rich countries annually.[54] All you need do to qualify for a share in these profits is simply ensure that you are born to the right parents in the right place at the right time. This is luck, not skill. Thus most of your pay packet, if you live and work in a rich country, reflects your luck in having been born there, not your skill at work.

Privilege and prejudice

Taxes, including inheritance tax, should be transfers of wealth from rich to poor. Protecting inheritance is all about maintaining unfairness. Inheritance preserves privilege and prejudice, and without it there would be precious little privilege or prejudice based simply on accruing power from accumulating money. No doubt new forms of privilege and prejudice would emerge, but they could not be based on looking down at others whose parents, for instance, could not afford to send their children to the same school as yours. When someone says they have been privileged to have had a good education they usually mean that they were lucky that others were not given their social advantages. No one in a country where state schools were as well equipped as private schools would say that they had been privileged to have been educated privately; they would say they had been duped if someone had made a charge for what was theirs of right. Rarely are those who mention privilege talking about an education where they were *actually* taught well, extensively or widely. It is fear of losing these inheritances that keeps people behaving in particular ways. Rights to pensions in old age, healthcare then and before, out-of-work and educational benefits, all help keep a population pliant and reduce the incentive for emigration. The recent experiences of people leaving Eastern Europe for Western Europe, or leaving Mexico for the US, or of Koreans moving to Japan, all show how easily places can lose their people when there appears less and less to inherit at home and more of a chance for a better life abroad.

Passports and border controls were only necessary once it began to be appreciated that inheritance was possible simply by being in a place. Emigration controls, having to apply for permission to leave in many countries in Western Europe (and other jurisdictions), only ended just over a century ago when enough reasons to stay had begun to be put in place. Unless you are seen as highly skilled, one of the few legal ways to move from the poor world to the rich world now, without relatives in the latter, is to gain rich relatives, to marry. Immigration though marriage is permitted partly because the unwritten rules on marriage are so well adhered to that it remains rare. If people married whoever they wished to marry, their choices not influenced by tradition or other social direction, the world would become a dramatically more equitable place within just a few generations. It is only through the most careful selection of who we marry that inequality is maintained over time and this careful selection is largely carried out unconsciously. Geographical proximity to potential partners is not just controlled by practical considerations of travel, but closely curtailed through monitoring by family and society over where young people travel and when. The extent of that control is reflected by the rates at which people marry those from families not like themselves, poorer or richer, black or white, not by what clothes young people are allowed to wear, for example; and it has been this way for some time. The question of who to marry, where and when became the staple of contemporary fiction in the English novel, dominating the market from shortly after James Cook returned to England and Jane Austen's writing gained favour, through to Catherine Cookson becoming the most widely read novelist in England by the time of her death in 1998.

'Assortative mating' is just one of the terms used to describe the myriad processes employed by varying human societies to ensure that like marry like. 'Homogamy' is another obscure word for the same thing. The fact that these terms are so obscure illustrates just how embedded the process is. It is not that some people practise assortative mating and others do not, or that a very sizeable majority follow homogamy; it is that these behaviours are so much the norm that these terms are not needed. When people married out of their economic class it used to be a great scandal. It was a scandal in 1960 when the prosecuting counsel in a well-known English obscenity trial asked the jury, 'Is it a book you would wish your wife or servants to read?'. Because the prosecuting counsel was a man from the upper classes who had married a woman from the upper classes, inherited property and employed servants, he assumed the jurors were in the same position and that they all had servants! Homogamy promotes and maintains such prejudices. The subject of that trial, *Lady Chatterley's Lover*, was written by D.H. Lawrence in 1928 about a woman who had sex with her servant. It was immediately banned from publication until the trial collapsed in 1960, which was indicative of how prejudice had been reduced between 1928 and 1960. The trial had been held in order to try to stop the publisher (Penguin) in its attempt to produce a cheap paperback copy. The particular timing, the talk of servants and of lovers, is all worth bearing in mind when considering Figure 14. Although banning books on subjects such as this became seen as absurdly old fashioned by 1960, marriage (if not so much sex) beneath one's station still carried great stigma; it still does, as evidenced by its continued rarity. That stigma may be rising in countries where social mobility is falling.

The richest percentile

Figure 14 charts the share in annual incomes received by the richest single percentile of Britons as recorded between 1918 and 2005, both pre- and post-tax. The richest percentile of people in Britain usually receive some of their income from earnings, but most from interest on wealth, dividends and shares, and returns on investments

Figure 14: Share of all income received by the richest 1% in Britain, 1918–2005

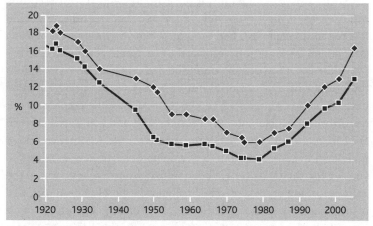

Note: Lower line is post-tax share.

Source: Atkinson, A.B. (2003) 'Top incomes in the United Kingdom over the twentieth century', Nuffield College Working Papers, Oxford (http://ideas.repec.org/p/nuf/esohwp/_043.html), figures 2 and 3; from 1922 to 1935 the 0.1% rate was used to estimate the 1% when the 1% rate was missing, and for 2005 the data source was Brewer, M., Sibieta, L. and Wren-Lewis, L. (2008) *Racing away? Income inequality and the evolution of high incomes*, London: Institute for Fiscal Studies, p 11; the final post-tax rate of 12.9% is derived from 8.6%+4.3%, the pre-tax rate scaled from 2001 (see Table 5, pp 176-7 above).

made in stocks. At the end of the First World War the richest one in every 100 people lived in total on about a sixth of the national income, 17 or 18 times more than the average family, 100 times more money than the poorest tenth saw in a year. The rich all had servants then, including gamekeepers like the one D.H. Lawrence wrote about in 1928. From 1918 through the 1920s, 1930s, 1940s, 1950s and 1960s their share of national income fell. Many of the heirs to great estates had died in the Great War, the government taxed the aristocratic families, but just as crucially, the 'great' families became a little more lax over who they slept with and subsequently married. There were far less groundsmen, gamekeepers or (paid) gardeners in the 1960s as a result.

The arithmetic of homogamy is simple. If you were a member of a family in the top percentile of income earners in 1918 you might expect to receive around £150,000 a year in today's money, 18 times the average individual income. If you were careful and ignored 99 potential life partners in every 100, you might in theory have met and only chosen from the one percentile like yourself. Because social networks were so limited it was not hard to avoid at least 90 of the other 99, or to meet them only as servants, but the other nine you had to tell yourself were beneath you when you did meet. Then as a couple, and later possibly as a family, you would remain in that top 1% of earners. However, if you found a young man or woman from the bottom of that top decile more attractive, or caring, or more understanding or interested, and you had successfully ignored 90 out of 100 other possible suitors, but not the 91st, and you paired up, then as a pair you would drop out of the top percentile. Another couple or individual would enter it but they would not have been as well-off as you (or else they would have been in that group already), and so the average income of the best-off falls. Figure 14 shows a combination of many things, but it also includes the effect of that equalising process at work, gaining in strength right through to the 1970s. Note that this is especially true for the very rich, as a large proportion of the income of the richest 1% is interest earnings from holding wealth, and high wealth is thus largely maintained over generations by marrying 'correctly'. In England debutantes (young aristocratic or upper-class girls) were presented at court at the start of each social season right up until 1958. They were presented to make it clear that they were available for marriage, into the correct families. After 1958 it became progressively harder to know so exactly who was most 'respectable'. The process carries on today, however, especially in the US at various huge 'charity' balls, but is less overtly state-sponsored than when the most suitable of young ladies were regularly presented to the Queen of England at court, just half a century ago.

A combination of high mortality among even the upper classes in the First World War, increased death duties and loss of wealth during the Depression and later redistribution by increases in income and inheritance taxation all helped to bring down inequalities in income and wealth from 1918 to the end of the 1970s. However, it is also not hard to see that as wealth became a little more equally spread, it became easier for people to choose who they might love, easier to tolerate a little less those they were expected to tolerate just to maintain the family silver. All this occurs with the aid of 'human nature being what it is',[55] but if that is so, then why should a large part of the story of Figure 14 be different? Why, from the late 1970s onwards, should we see individual earnings again concentrating within the best-off percentile? It was not just the progressive tax structure being dismantled after 1979. Earnings before tax (shown in the same figure) follow almost exactly the same trend. The rise is so quick that by 2005 the trend line suggests that we had returned to early 1930s levels of income inequality at the very top end.

The Pearson product-moment correlation coefficients between the pre-tax income share of the richest percentile and the excess mortality of the poorest 30%, the health advantage of the best-off tenth and the geographical concentration of Conservative votes over the 1918–2005 period are: 0.57, 0.82 and 0.51 respectively (see Table 5, page 176). Again, this is no evidence of a causal link – clearly the health advantages of the rich are most closely connected to their share of wealth. But these are also both in some way related to trends in inequalities in voting and to the fluctuations in the rates of premature mortality suffered by the poor. There is only a one in one hundred chance that even the lowest of these correlations occurred by chance. The correlations with the post-tax income trend shown above are even stronger: 0.60, 0.86 and 0.58 respectively, and they are both larger and even more statistically robust. When the rich take even more of the national income of a country, the health of the poor suffers and voting in general elections becomes more spatially polarised. Similar trends have been suggested in the US.[56]

Assortative mating

The story from the late 1970s onwards is again one of assortative mating becoming popular in times of rising inequality, but it is now no longer simply about the sharing of the family treasures, the counting up and weighing of the silver candlesticks before getting into bed. This assortative mating was a little more about marrying people with similar occupational incomes. From the early 1970s more and more women were permitted to hold jobs that did not pay a pittance, and to keep working after marriage. Looks and freedom began to matter less and less, even for the poorest; what mattered more and more was class.[57]

From the late 1970s onwards actual salaries at the top end began to diverge upwards rapidly. Warped morals also began to be countenanced again in countries like Britain, morals that suggested that competition was good, cooperation bad, just a few were truly talented and they should have their talents supposedly 'justly rewarded'. If you began to believe that, you became more careful who you slept with. It was not just that the lives of the rich became more separated from the poor, but that the implications of mixing became more daunting. Slowly at first, and then more quickly, the highest paid became even more highly paid. Dual-income higher-earner households moved away from all other household types most quickly. Income inequalities rose, and as they rose the idea of mixing socially with those a little less well-off became just a little less palatable with every year that passed; there was literally more, in terms of money, to lose by a 'bad marriage'. This reached such an extent in the US that by 2007 young people from affluent families were being told that on early dates they should be clear and say: 'There's something important I need to share with you. In my family we do prenups'.[58] It is difficult to think of a phrase, other than 'I have herpes, would you like to share?', as off-putting as 'in my family we do prenups'.[59]

Rates of mixing by marriage fell in the more unequal of countries from the 1970s onwards.

In the US those falls in social mixing resulted in a slowing down of the rise in the number of inter-racial marriages, although these were still rising as they had been since slavery. Until recently white and black couples were rarely shown on television in the US, and it is partly low rates of inter-racial marriages that maintain such high poverty levels among black Americans. In the US having great-great-grandparents who were in slavery is the legacy singlehandedly most likely to result in low financial inheritance, because of the legacy of slavery, and of laws and then traditions designed to prevent non-assortative mating between what were seen as separate races (miscegenation). This has resulted in both the huge extent of inequalities in wealth found in the US and the great reluctance of even those who own just a little wealth to work cooperatively and to sociably invest in the common good. There is a great misconception that affluent North Americans donate monies to charity to aid the common good, but, as a director of the Ford Foundation recently reported, only a tiny fraction of their charitable giving is for that.[60] The rich in the US are happy to take money from the poor, but do not like to 'give' to the poor either through charity or taxation. It is racism that begets a legacy that breeds the mistrust that maintains such miserliness. This mistrust is much greater than simply the self-interest of the rich, the majority of whom are ultimately rich directly as a legacy of inheritance and, in the not so distant past, of entrepreneurship such as slave owning. It is a mistrust that becomes endemic and spreads throughout almost the whole of societies where inheritance of wealth within very unequal families is so crucial to social security.

It is one of the cruellest ironies of inheritance that it results in the great-great-grandchildren of slaves in the US also being so likely to have their freedom denied, as they end up living in the one country in the world where imprisonment among blacks is so common. Incarceration in the US is predominantly applied to poor non-white Americans, whose inheritance is to be written out of that country's official picture because they have been born in a country where both their social position and skin colour make it very likely that they will find they are routed to live through the earnings of crime. It is the extreme end of more widespread prejudice that says so many black Americans are not part of the formal economy, not part of society, and once convicted of a felony, in over a dozen states no longer part of politics as they can no longer vote again under those states' laws.

Those in prison are not called unemployed, because it is said they are not looking for work. While it is true that they cannot look for work, it is disingenuous in the extreme to suggest, in effect by omitting them, that they would rather not have paid work. The unemployment rate in the US would be a percentage point higher if prisoners were included. The vast increase in the size of prison populations in those affluent nations which have chosen to build the most prisons has had the effect of dramatically increasing the range of the social scale in those countries, creating a lot more space at the very bottom, in cells. This great space in a way acts as a counter-weight to the great wealth of the few at the top. It is hard to find a country where the richest are so very wealthy, and where they do not also have many prisons. Racism is needed to maintain these differences, not just the inheritance of wealth but also the inheritance of disadvantage and prejudice. People would not tolerate mass incarnation in jails in Britain or the US if so many of the inmates were not labelled as a 'race apart' through the colour of their skins – jails in Japan and Scandinavia are few, and are individually much smaller and less punitive institutions.

The colour of our skin is one of the few things we clearly physically inherit. However, we only notice that inheritance because of the time and place we were born in. Had those who first sailed to the places that became called New England, the Caribbean, the Indies and Australasia differed most from the people they met there by height, or by the size of their noses, or the colour of their hair, then those characteristics would have become the physical features which would be used as a shorthand for social status. Because it was skin colour that most clearly and reliably differentiated Europeans from those they conquered, skin colour has the longest legacy, and is the great inheritance. As more and more extreme life events are considered, skin colour matters more in influencing life chances. The risk of suffering rises almost everywhere as skin colour darkens. Only deaths from melanoma are the exception. This prejudice born in Europe is now most blatantly expressed in those countries on the edge of rich world empires. Thus in Brazil nine out of ten of the suspects police shoot are black while five times fewer black civilians (2%) make it to college compared with whites (10%).[61] South Africa rivals Brazil, even after apartheid was formally abolished, in terms of income and wealth inequalities, and in India potential brides and bridegrooms are advertised in newspapers by the lightness of their skins to indicate a caste structure that was greatly reinforced through British rule. Countries which were not colonies tend to have far weaker such 'traditions'. All these evils are largely at source an inheritance, or an old prejudice preserved with European assistance, from thinking which dates from what Europeans still call their 'Enlightenment' period.

5.5 The 1970s: the new racism

On a visit to the US in the 1970s the Conservative politician and later Prime Minister, Margaret Thatcher, explained her thinking on equality: 'One of the reasons that we value individuals is not because they're all the same, but because they're all different.... I would say, let our children grow tall and some taller than others if they have the ability in them to do so. Because we must build a society in which each citizen can develop his full potential, both for his own benefit and for the community as a whole...'.[62] Her thoughts and occasionally her words were endlessly repeated by others. Eventually the assertion that different individuals have different 'ability' within them became normalised. Ability potential was to be treated like height. Apparently a child should be well fed upon showing potential to grow, and only well educated as a result of passing some test of their supposed inherent ability early on, or of their parents' high earnings.[63] And thus by the end of the century the strange notion that by acting selfishly people benefit others in some way became accepted.

The turning points in Figures 12–14 have all fallen in the 1970s. Whether we consider inequalities in health, in voting, or in wealth, in Britain people and places became less and less divided from the end of the First World War right through to the early 1970s. A similar story can be told of the US and of those other affluent nations that decided to go the way of the rich Anglophone giants (such as Singapore or Australia). The 1960s had been a decade of social achievement, not so much for what was achieved during those years as for their being the apogee of half a century of slow and steady social progress. This progress was partly won at the expense of the rest of the world, who took over much food production (freeing peasants in Europe), who began to mill textiles (freeing factory workers in Japan), and who dug coal (freeing many miners in the US from dirty dangerous work). The story told in these countries was that technology and mechanisation had made them rich, but that did not explain why, by the end of the 1960s, so much more of what they consumed came from abroad as compared with the 1920s.

While the 1960s might be portrayed as the progressive era within rich nations it was hardly so for other countries. Around the world people had to fight for their independence from colonialism. They were not released from those shackles willingly, although again this is not the story commonly now told. We easily forget that there was not long ago a point where it was only half-heartedly joked that the majority of the world's leaders had at one time or another seen the inside of a British-run prison. Today the majority of those leaders are more likely to have seen the inside of the London School of Economics and Political Science (LSE), or one of a few similar universities, as we now co-opt and attempt to convert future national leaders to our mythologies more often than incarcerating them.

The 1960s were also the time when talk of 'development' began to become commonplace. The story was that there was a path that could be followed, and that if poorer countries were to do what richer countries' mythologies said they had done, then the poor could be rich too. All that was needed was to mechanise, industrialise and democratise, then people of poor countries could be rich too. We still say this today. When this did not occur, the mutterings of racist reasoning began. Racists suggested that black and brown people were simply not capable of running countries, were inherently lazy, or corrupt, or both. They could not be trusted in countries like Vietnam to make their own choices; across Africa intervention was needed in terms of arms if not troops. Latin America was looked down on with concern from Washington from where strings began to be pulled in earnest, most obviously in Chile in 1973. The underlying rhetoric all the time was that these people needed 'help', that providing such 'help' was the continued 'white man's burden', that richer countries needed to indirectly rule those not so white, especially if they might turn to socialism or communism. As elitist thoughts were sustained in rich nations through the 1950s, and exclusion of the poor became tolerated again in the 1960s at home, in the 1970s the rich began again to see their destiny as to rule, but now through intervention, co-option and conversion rather than directly through colonial mandate. And they called this leadership.

Installing a sense of fear

Although tempting for the sake of simplicity, it would be wrong to claim everything fits neatly into decadal buckets. The antecedents of the rise of new racism in the 1970s abounded in the late 1960s but were then mainly found between the cracks of what were otherwise progressive politics. Briefly in 1969 rebellious students even took over running the LSE. Across the rich world students were becoming mistrustful of what they were being taught. But not all politics was moving to the left. It was perhaps the commissioning of the publication of the 1968 book *The population bomb* in the US which marked the beginnings of the 'new racism' most clearly. We now know that the book was commissioned by a group with the aim of using it to try to encourage the further restriction of immigration from poorer countries to rich countries. We also now know that similar groups and work spread to Europe very soon after.[64] The book was about attempting to protect the privileges of the rich and it was not produced with much concern for the rest of the population. It was written in the midst of mass sterilisation campaigns, mostly designed to prevent people in poorer countries who were not white from having their non-white babies.

In the US internally it was in the early 1970s that the political shift towards the right began. At first it was at grassroots level. In 1972 a young man called Karl Rove, who was later nicknamed George Bush the Second's 'brain', was elected chairman of the college Republican movement. People like Rove capitalised on the new fears of the rich of the time, fear of the levels that equality within their rich countries had reached, fear of unions, fear of women's groups, fear of blacks and civil rights, fear of homosexuals, of communists, of almost anyone who was not like how they liked to think they were, fear of the hordes they saw massing in the poor countries of the world, fear of all those black and brown babies, fear of an end to their status. The Republican message swung to the political right to address these fears and funding swung in from the scared rich to its campaigns. You could see repercussions both in votes, in Congress in 1976 and 1978, and in the nomination and election of growing numbers of far-right senators, doubling in number between 1975 and 1979, cumulating in the selection and victory of Ronald Reagan in 1980.[65]

Within the US, '... from the 1970s on, the state increasingly came to be conceived as a set of institutions supporting the undeserving.... Fear of a black state is linked to worries about a black planet, of alien invasion and alien*ation*, of a loss of the sort of local and global control and privilege long associated with whiteness'.[66] Thus it was a new racism itself that was at the heart of these political swings. Fear of 'oriental hordes' who could beat American troops in the 'Far East', fear of the grandsons and daughters of slaves who would march for and win their rights at home, fear that as economic growth in the US began its long and steady slowdown from 1973 onwards (see Figure 10 in Chapter 4), the empire of the US was beginning to see the end of its time. These were all fears held mostly by the elite in the late 1960s and early 1970s. By the end of that decade these fears had been projected into the consciousness of the public at large. Inflation rose, joblessness increased, and above all immigration was blamed and those so-called 'greedy Arabs' who were *all* becoming millionaires by making oil as expensive as gold (or so the myths went). Racism rose in the 1970s because the times were right and enough people thought they would benefit from promoting it. A long and steady progressive social trend was coming to an end, bringing uncertainty, and it is easy in uncertain times to breed fear. That new trend of uncertainty also concerned fertility and the demand for people.

Figure 15 shows the number of people who died or who are predicted to die in England and Wales as a proportion of the population who were born there (or will be born there) at their time of birth, from 1840 through to predictions made up to 2080. The trends it shows are similar to those found elsewhere in Europe, such as in Sweden, and the recent trends are also typical of the US. Of those born in the 1840s more people came to England and Wales to live (and die) than left. Famine in Ireland helped ensure that, but there was also great demand for labour in the 19th century, more than could be met simply by fertility at home and migration from the countryside. But as economic recession hit (towards the end of the century) demand for labour fell and emigration was the norm for those born in 1850 onwards, rising throughout the gilded age, peaking around the 1900 birth cohort for people who would try to enter the labour market in England and Wales during 1914–19 wartime or in the turbulent 1920s or the Great Depression of the 1930s. Emigration accounted for (as a net minimum at the very least) a tenth of those born in 1919 who left England and Wales and died elsewhere. But fertility also fell in the 1920s and 1930s; contraception became widespread; women slowly gained the power to say 'no' more often; and so by the time of the cohort of the late 1930s, those who were born and stayed in England and Wales were joined by at least an

Figure 15: England and Wales's net immigration by birth year, 1840–2080

Source: Dorling, D. (2009) *Migration: A long run perspective*, London: IPPR, Figure 8. The graph shows how many more people entered than left these countries, as a proportion of births, including official projections up to 2080.

extra 10% who were born overseas or in Scotland. They came in the late 1950s, 1960s and early 1970s. They came to replace the babies who were never born, and their arrival was used by many to reignite racism.

Immigration and colonisation

The peak in immigration to Britain in the 1960s and early 1970s of people born abroad in the late 1930s and early 1940s was clearly a response to demand for labour. It was seen as such then and in hindsight it is even more clearly apparent now. There was less demand in the 1980s, so the record in Figure 15 shows that later (net) immigration of people born in the late 1940s and 1950s fell rapidly as the baby boomers of 1946 onwards entered the job market and as the 1970s and 1980s recessions reduced demand. Figure 15 also shows how net immigration rates fell again until the cohort born in the 1970s began to arrive in large numbers into England and Wales in the late 1990s. Racism has recently again been rekindled, as reflected in votes for the British National Party in 2009.

People can easily be swayed into racist thought, and with a little more persuasion into racist action. On thought, opinion polls swing wildly. Ask the right question at the right time and you can suggest that uppermost in a majority of British, or American, or German or Japanese minds are fears of immigration. Say the right key words enough times, and never mention countervailing views, and you can pick up a great many votes from people who have been made to fear those not as white (or light-skinned) as themselves. It took right-wing parties in the US and the UK almost the whole of the 1970s to come to fully play the race card at the end of that decade. Richard Nixon played it a little, Ronald Reagan a lot; Edward Heath did not find space for Enoch Powell in his government, but Margaret Thatcher was careful to court racist voters. In Britain racist murders became much more common by the late 1970s, and it took all of the 1980s and most of the 1990s to bring levels of racism, violence, intolerance and fear back to what had been more normal in the 1960s. However, in both the US and Britain that new racism did not really lessen after the 1970s; rather it became transformed into a wider racism applied by those who felt superior not just to black people but to particular white people who they also saw as a group of humanity, as a race 'by common descent', as inferior to themselves. And once you see other human beings as a group as inferior when compared with your group, as different from you and yours, then your compulsion to behave well towards them is greatly reduced.

On acting out racism, the orchestrations of massacres in Vietnam, and those later made possible in Cambodia as a result, were the most well-known set of atrocities exposed in the years immediately before and during the 1970s. Connected with the Cold War, and undertaken in the fog of that war,[67] far more again were being killed in wars both in and on the borders of India, and in atrocities within China and Cambodia, but it was on Vietnam that the world's press first focused. One particular massacre, in the village of My Lai on 16 March 1968, drew particular ire once it was revealed that it had happened and that it had subsequently been covered up by the authorities in the early 1970s. Hundreds of civilians, almost all women, children or old men, were systematically murdered over the course of a day by just a handful of US soldiers. It was thought that the one soldier who blew the whistle on that massacre, Ron Ridenhour, turned out to have been one of the few hundred people tested in the famous psychological experiments conducted by Stanley Milgram in the early 1960s to find out how well people would follow orders if these were given by an authority figure. These were the experiments in which people were asked by a man in a white laboratory coat to turn a dial administering an electric shock to an unseen but screaming victim. Ron Ridenhour was one of the very few people undertaking Stanley Milgram's experiments who refused to turn the dial on the machine up high when ordered; it may not have been the same man, but another with the same name who refused to keep quiet over the My Lai massacre. However, if so, both of these men were unusual. Their attitudes were illustrative of the shape of things that could come.[68]

Just as there were a few individuals brought up well balanced enough to risk their lives saving people persecuted by the Nazis in occupied Europe, so when the US invaded Vietnam there were a few willing to act against their orders, and conscientious objection rose rapidly following news of the My Lai massacre. Never again could the US draft men to war; instead it had to coerce the poor to fight for money in its later wars. Men and women do not join armies by free will when the alternative is poverty, but many of the poor know how bad a deal this coercive 'offer' really is. By the 21st century the US had started bribing people from abroad with green cards to enter the country if they promised to join the army and fight in Iraq. The US military only met its 2008/09 recruitment targets because the economic crash had left so many young men jobless and desperate. Opposing a war, which was rare a century ago, became commonplace by the start of the new century, with the largest demonstrations of all time being the worldwide marches in protest of the US-orchestrated invasion of Iraq in 2003.

In the 1970s the protests were against the US, British and other affluent nations' governments' support for apartheid in South Africa. But most people did not understand what the protestors were protesting about. South Africa was a long way away and the people the protestors appeared to be concerned about were black. In the UK overt racism by the authorities was common in the 1970s. Young white policemen beat up young black men as a matter of routine. It has taken yet another generation for it to be widely accepted now just how abhorrent that was.[69]

The hardening of souls

In the past many individuals found it easier to follow orders. Childhoods across the rich world had been, in general, traumatic just a couple of generations ago, in an environment that fostered unthinking behaviour. Children were to be seen and not heard, often abandoned, regularly beaten and systematically terrorised to such an extent that the majority of children were what we would now consider abused.[70] Children who were abused can, in adulthood, make good, sometimes racist, bullies. Now in affluent countries far fewer children are brought up in these ways, but sadly many still suffer trauma, not just from abuse, but from events such as having the misfortune of experiencing the death of one of their parents early in their childhood, with insufficient care taken over their welfare subsequently. That can harden people. When the poor are hardened they teach their toddlers to fight, to harden them in turn, and often find ideas such as racism attractive.[71] When the powerful are hardened in these ways, they may be far less empathetic to the poor (or anyone else) later in life. And they may find it easier to behave in ways that are also racist. Upbringing of a particular type, regardless of wealth, is what later leads to racist beliefs.

Racism is the belief in the superiority of a particular race. A race is seen as a major division of humanity, a group of people connected by common descent. Traditionally racism has been targeted at a series of people who were seen to have their common descent revealed by the colour of their skin, facial features or language, but any group treated with disdain because they are seen as connected by common descent can become the subject of racism. As racism among many affluent people has evolved from its crude 1970s form to a more general detesting of the poor as inferior, so the nature of those who enact the changing racism, the treating of people as racially inferior, has changed.

Now the wider racism is much more enacted in boardrooms by businesspeople who consider their target groups of customers — as groups — as inferior, the kind of people (they say) you need to know in order to exploit, but who you would not want to live near or mix with. One estate agent specialising in 'executive property' in London in 2007 even took out newspaper advertisements suggesting that while you needed to understand 'the customer' to do well in business, there was no need to live near 'them'. It is worth comparing the renewal of racism in the 1970s and the rise of business thinking then, to the great racism of business behaviour now and the people who organise what can be most clearly thought of as racist ways of 'segmenting' markets of consumers. Why might they do this?

It is too much of a coincidence that successful but ruthless businesspeople have generally had traumatic early childhoods.[72] We also know from recent scientific research that people with psychopathic tendencies tend to do well in business[73] and that the 'business ethic' requires people to behave in ways that are seen as immoral in personal life. As a counter-culture grows, as their own children ask them why they are working to try to produce more and more when the world needs fewer goods, increasingly a few more people working towards the top of private businesses come to know within their hearts that what they are doing and how they are acting is wrong. The evidence comes when people drop out and say how much they hated themselves for what they were doing; it can be seen through attempts to 'greenwash' companies, and to try to suggest they are ethical, corporately responsible, in some ways. If businesspeople were happy with their image they would not engage in such puffery. There are a few who say they won't, and proclaim that they believe wholeheartedly in unfettered free markets. These are the kind who charge extra for a wheelchair on their airline's aeroplane. Such individuals exist, but most free-marketeers are less fundamentalist. Like all of us, businesspeople try to legitimise their lives and to find ways to defend why they do what they do, but it was becoming clear that this was becoming harder and harder to achieve before the financial crisis of 2008. People are now trying to run businesses knowing that they are increasingly despised for how they act, how they pollute, how they hire and fire at will, how they profit from misery.[74] Although a few more than before are learning, most still do not know that what they do is wrong. More and more of the general public are becoming aware that bankers are not often compassionate well-meaning people, but few realise that corporate law requires businesses to act in ways psychiatrists would diagnose as psychopathic in an individual. However, more are coming to know this because it is being said in increasing numbers of books aimed at the public rather than just within arcane tomes.[75]

Defending the indefensible

Trauma in the childhood or young adulthood of men in particular leads them to be more likely to later act in anti-social ways. This is undisputed as concerns criminality, but it is just as true for anti-social activity that is currently legal. For instance, to be able to take orders and kill as a sniper in the army it helps to have psychopathic tendencies: how else could you line the sights up slowly on another human being's head and then, when you are ready, gently pull the trigger? You need to be able to imagine that the target is not human. During the Second World War it would have been treasonable to say that of soldiers on your side of the war. Today it is common sense, but once you see sniping as psychopathic you begin to question war more widely. In England school children are given books by George Orwell as set texts for understanding literature. In one, Orwell wrote: 'In our time political speech and writing are largely the defence of the indefensible…. Political language … is designed to make lies sound truthful and murder respectable'.[76] We now collectively both know and can say so much that could until recently only be said in private. Similarly to what it takes to make killing in war appear respectable, we now recognise that those who tend to rise to the top in business and politics are more likely than their fellows (and it is normally fellows) to have what is called a '… ruthless readiness to disown the obligations of regard',[77] to be willing to tread on the necks of others on the way up, make promises but not honour them, take gifts but not give something back, be self-assured to the point of megalomania. In universities these more selfish people are more often found among '… the kind of people we find in business schools and economics departments'.[78]

What we think of as racism changes over time. It has only been since the 1930s that we began to widely recognise racism as it is currently thought of, and only since the 1960s that the word 'racism' has appeared in dictionaries (including the word 'racialism'[79] and the even more recent 'racist'). Just as with poverty, exclusion and elitism, racism has not always been with us as it appears now, and, as with poverty, only recently have very large numbers of people become committed to its eradication. The currently propagated mass prejudice, that the poor are somehow inherently inferior, will come to pass too. But its passing must be aided, and we must be vigilant for what spite will next be promoted by those who fear a world in which they and theirs are no longer supreme. Human beings are easily prone to prejudice, to fall under the spell of a single charismatic individual. We have seen this often enough to learn from our collective experiences. Those with less are not a 'race apart' that you should fear living near, mixing with, or your children marrying. It is as simple (and for some as hard to understand) as that.

6

'Greed is good': consumption and waste

Because 'the great and the good' know that suggesting in public that greed is good is seen as a little immoral, many of those who write the stories of our lives, who are in positions to tell us what we ought to believe, are nowadays very careful not to be too explicit, too often, about their beliefs. The majority of those who favour inequality use phrases such as preferring to be 'independent', or 'neutral', or wishing to be seen as 'considered', 'balanced' or 'reasonable' in what they say. Successful politicians want to win as many votes as they can from those holding as wide a range of opinions as possible, so those who believe that most citizens are feeble and destined to be ruled by the few like them do not say 'you need a firm hand' to 'their' public. Similarly, some leading journalists do not want to give their readers, listeners and viewers the impression that they look down on them, so they tend not to say what they really think of most people when on air or in print. Their real views are not displayed prominently. We know this from what they say in their more obscure publications, and sometimes from their affiliations. You have to look carefully for direct evidence that they believe in propositions such as that, ultimately, 'greed is good'. Similarly, academics in public life who believe that most people are not as able as they are usually polite enough not to say so in so few words because even egoists can predict the medium-term consequences of saying what they think about others.

Public figures often wish to appear to be concerned about the environment, inequality, even elitism, when speaking openly. On the printed page they are occasionally more direct, especially if that printed page is an obscure pamphlet, in an elite publication, or more than 300 pages through a book they have written. Take, for example, what in 2008 the British Broadcasting Corporation's (BBC's) business editor meant when (buried deep in his book) he suggested that: 'It may not be pretty but, on the whole, greed is good'.[1] The man who said this, Robert Peston, was subsequently the most viewed face to be seen on British television news describing the anatomy of the economic crash of that year, the same year in which his book made clear that he believed greed is good, not because of what he had seen and was seeing, but because of what he was taught to believe as a student of economics. His father was an economist and after university, before taking up journalism, Robert had become a stockbroker.[2]

The man who wrote the archetypal film of stockbrokers, 'Wall Street', who coined the phrase 'greed, for lack of a better word, is good', was talking on the radio one Saturday morning on a show to which Robert Peston frequently contributed.[3] When asked if he could write the film today he told the presenter that, whereas in the 1980s greed had been individual, in the early years of the current century it had become institutional. The BBC itself is an example of an institution that, for all its 'balance', subtly promotes greed as good through the style of its economic coverage. It would be harder to create a character like Gordon Gekko from 'Wall Street' today and make him plausible. Gekko was an unusual loner, out for himself, but convinced that his selfishness was for the common good. Now this thinking has entered the mainstream. Anyone with a private or occupational pension (they are in practice the same thing) now acts like Gordon Gekko by proxy. Their fund managers believe 'greed is good' and have acted on those beliefs. Laws have been passed which say they must do this; they must act to maximise the return on their clients' investments regardless of the consequences, and so they have done this on a global scale, acting solely on behalf of the most affluent section of society in just a few rich countries of the world. These bankers acted a little bit more diligently to maximise returns for themselves, it must also be said. Thanks to greed, fund managers tend to be better off than most people, even people with occupational pensions. Through greed, people on occupational pensions are now also much better off, as compared with those reliant solely on state pensions. This widening can be seen most clearly when the early 2000s with compared with the early 1980s, when we were again taught a lesson we last heard in the 1920s, a lesson about the apparent goodness of greed.

At the very top of the pile of fund managers were those managing the amalgamated private funds of just a few extremely rich individuals. These were the young bankers who, until recently, were often pictured in newspapers partying in Manhattan and Mayfair, metaphorically dripping with cash. At the dizzy temporal and spatial apex of the boom, in that Mayfair heart of London in 2007, you could spend £35,000 on a single drink. Three days after this fact was reported in a national newspaper, *The Guardian*, that same paper revealed how the British Labour government's budget decisions had resulted in a huge future transfer of wealth to the rich due to changes to the law on inheritance tax. A leading columnist wrote that the '... juxtaposition was cruel: poor children got another 48p a week, while the middle-aged middle class, whose parents leave a house worth, say, £400,000, gained another £40,000'.[4] That tax break for the rich, following even greater tax breaks occurring across the Atlantic (in the years up to and including 2007), was seen together with the bankers' most extreme excesses as evidence that we were back in the last years of a 'gilded age'. At the heart of all this was greed.

The £35,000 drink contained a diamond, so its true unrecoverable cost will have been much lower, but not very low, as diamond prices collapsed with the economic crash of 2008 so, unless the drinker sold his diamond quickly, the cost to him of that drink may have been around US$10,000. That is almost the exact equivalent of smoking a cigarette rolled in a US$100 note in the 1920s, which was a popular activity in parties of the North American super-rich held over a century ago right up to the eve of the great crash of 1929.[5] As the figures in Chapter 4 made clear, it was in the early decades a century ago that wealth inequalities were last as unequal as in 2007, when greed was last seen as being as great, when people were last so profligate, when consumption by those with money was last so vaunted as valuable. This chapter describes how we have come again to see greed as good and have erected a new great squalor of excess so quickly after having largely demolished the old squalor of the most unfit homes in the most affluent of countries. The injustice of greed has replaced the old social evil of squalor as surely as elitism has overtaken ignorance, exclusion has eclipsed want and prejudice has transcended idleness.

6.1 Not part of the programme: just getting by, a quarter of all households

Squalor in the 1940s was life in crowded damp accommodation with inadequate hygiene, no hot running water, often no inside toilet. By the late 1970s in most rich countries most such dwellings had been converted or demolished, but a new form of squalor then arose. The rich began to take a greater and greater share of all that there was to be taken that they valued, of the bricks to build houses even. Local life in poor areas became downgraded despite the new homes. Local shops closed, which meant people needed a car to do the weekly shopping if they also had children to look after or if they found walking difficult, especially in the US (a country largely bereft of pavements). In contrast, in urban Japan public transport is so good that it is not necessary to drive and many people who could afford a car choose not to own one. In Britain the latest statistics on car ownership are released through surveys of wealth. The surveys released in 2008[6] showed that almost two in every five households had goods and furniture in their home worth more than £30,000, often worth much more, while many others could not afford simple things that had become necessities, such as access to a car for those looking after young children. The survey revealed, through showing who did not have these goods, that in Britain it was people most likely to need goods like cars who did not have them.

In 2007 a quarter of households in Britain had no access to a car (26%). Among that quarter were almost half (48%) of all lone parents whose children were dependent on them for care. In contrast half (51%) of married couples with dependent children owned at least two cars, and more than two thirds (69%) of married couples whose children were no longer dependent on them (or who had no children) also had at least two cars. We allocate goods like cars almost directly in reverse proportion to need. Amazingly some 7% of all people who live on their own also have two or more cars! Clearly families with young children have more need for cars, in order not to have to carry shopping and push buggies simultaneously for instance. It would make sense also to bring shops back nearer to the people, and improve public transport.

In countries like Britain, where inequalities have been allowed to rise, households cope with this collectively by getting into debt; some 35% have unsecured debts, some of many kinds; 3% have store card debt; 6% mail order debt; 9% hire purchase debt; 13% have other unsecured loans; and 20% have credit card debt. The rates are higher for people in employment, who are more likely to be given and offered loans. The debt rates are highest for women aged 25–34, most of whom have unsecured debt they are trying to repay, and this is all before including student loans that are being deferred, or mortgages. All these numbers come from the 'Wealth and Assets' Survey. It was press released in an attempt at a triumphant January 2008 'good news' story with the headline that 'Seven in ten adults have savings or investments'.[7] They may well have done, but about a quarter were also in one kind of serious financial difficulty or another, and the assets of the rest were slowly (and in some cases rapidly) crumbling, not least as the British government was 'lending' unprecedented amounts of money it did not have to those same banks in which those seven in ten adults had investments (to keep them afloat, in theory). But most households with substantial savings were not suffering. To see who literally had least you need to look at the distribution of simple goods that have become essential and at who is unable to have those essentials.

Figure 16 shows how, by 2007, there were more households with two, three, four or even more cars than there were households with no car in Britain. These figures are again taken from data collected for the first survey of wealth, assets and debt to be carried out in Britain for many years. The previous survey was carried out in the 1970s by a Royal Commission after which successive British governments did not appear to believe that the distribution of wealth mattered enough to try to measure it properly. The recent survey showed clearly that there were more than enough assets to go round in the country, enough wealth and money for all to be well off, and cars provide just the simplest example of this. There are clearly enough cars for every household that needs a car to have a car. It is worth repeating that many cars are owned by single adults, who cannot physically drive more than one at a time. The majority of households without cars are also single-adult households. One in seven of all households

Figure 16: Households by number of cars and those with no cars in Britain, 2006/07

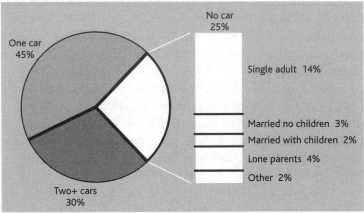

Source: ONS (2008) *Wealth and assets survey: Initial reports,* London: ONS, Table 3

are single adults without a car (the 14% shown in Figure 16, or just over half of all non-car-owning households). Clearly there are many households, especially single-adult households and households with no dependent children living in cities, that can get by relatively easily without a car. This makes it even more obvious that for those who need a car and do not have one, or for the households with families where their only car is failing, there are enough other largely unused (or unnecessarily used) cars to go round to meet their needs. Britain need not make or import a single extra car to meet its need for cars for some time to come. That will not happen, but there is no reason other than our collective inability to see clearly (and so distribute income and wealth more fairly) for cars not to be slightly more fairly shared out, year after year, rather than being progressively less fairly distributed as time passes. Exactly the same can be said of housing, where a slightly fairer system of allocation, with tax curbs on the buying of second and subsequent homes, would help house all far more efficiently than forever planning to build more homes in the south of England.

So far we have not considered the implication of this greed from the point of view of children. Figure 16 shows that two thirds of all children living in households without a car are living in lone-parent households.[8] Many people can travel, do their shopping and get to work or school without the need for their household to own a car. A lone parent struggling to carry shopping while looking after two young children is one of the clearest examples of someone in need, but there are many similarly worthy situations of others who find walking difficult. Many of those households who need a car could get that car now, but to do so they would have to go into further debt, not only just to buy it, but to insure it, fill it with petrol, park it, repair it, service it and tax it. Many of the households that do have a car cannot really afford to run it, but it is a necessity, and so they go into debt. Individualised transport solutions are presented as some kind of panacea, giving the freedom of the road to the masses; but in reality car manufacturers and car dealers make most of their profit out of the debt many of their customers get into to buy their product.

Calamity was coming

In 1951 one dollar of income for every seven earned in the US was spent repaying personal debts; by 1963 that ratio had risen to one dollar in every five earned.[9] The idea that it was normal to live life with debt began in 1950s America; it was exported around the rich world with credit cards and supposedly cheap home, car and consumer loans. By the start of the 21st century, with mortgages, extra home equity loans, credit loans, student loans, car, sofa, washing machine (and dryer) loans, to live by loans became what it meant to live normally in the US and in the most ardent of its imitators, the UK.

North American personal debts rose and rose through the 1960s and 1970s, but most rapidly in the 1980s. By 1999 the average US family held about US$5,000 of credit card debt at any one time, paying about a fifth of that total a year in interest, but not paying off the balance. This debt rose dramatically as people were told they were living through boom years and, by 2002, it stood at nearly US$9,000 per US family.[10] Although the near doubling of recent years may shock, it was in the 1980s that most adults received their first credit card and then in those same brief 10 years that personal credit card debt rose fastest. Personal bankruptcies became six times more common in the US between 1980 and 2002 as a result of all these changes,[11] and bankruptcy rates continue to rise in 2010.

In Britain by 2005 annual counts of statutory personal insolvency had risen to the record level of 70,000 individuals, double the number recorded just five years earlier. Overall amounts of debt also doubled in Britain between 2000 and 2005, rising to £1.15 trillion on mortgages, other loans and credit card debt by 2005. This was debt rising at about an extra £1 million every four minutes, and the trend was accelerating. All these figures were reported by the accountants PricewaterhouseCoopers, who, through their analysis and reports, advised the finance industry that calamity was coming.[12] A couple of years later the Citizens Advice Bureau reported that in Britain, between 2005 and 2008, the rate at which people's homes were being repossessed for failing to make mortgage payments had doubled.[13] Thus credit card debt doubled, then overall debt doubled, then home repossessions doubled. During 2009 the BBC reported that personal insolvencies were expected to double again, to 140,000, and company insolvencies were also expected to continue to rise.[14]

Apart from the very richest fraction of a percentile, the rich in North America also tend to borrow. Those who investigate their behaviour find that they borrow to try to keep up with those above them, to maintain what they see as basic standards, to 'invest' in multiple house purchases, to cope with what they hope are short-term stock market falls, or their diamonds declining in value. The debt of the very richest 1% of North Americans more than tripled between 1989 and 2004, growing twice as fast as their wealth grew. This is partly because the wealth of some grew more slowly on paper as they normally received interest from the debt of others and others were beginning to default. By 2007 the richest 5% of North Americans accounted for 20% of gross debt in the US. By 2004 the very richest percentile of North Americans owed US$383 billion more than they had borrowed in 1995.[15] Apart from a few at the very top, by the late 1980s significant proportions of almost every group were borrowing more to try to keep up with those they saw as just above them. So debt is no longer just for the poor – it affects even the richest and has also become normal for the middle classes.

A few years ago documenting these figures was seen as revelatory. Today it is just the history of the long build-up to the economic crash.

In Britain around 1990 only a quarter of university students took out loans. Students tend disproportionately to be the children of the rich but, of those who were not, many could not rely on their parents to help them out, and these poorer students took out the most loans. In 1990 that poorer quarter borrowed some £70 million. Ten years later, after the abolition of maintenance grants, almost three quarters of university students had to take out loans. Their annual debt was raised twenty-five fold in just one decade, to £1.8 billion (still a miniscule sum compared with the debt of the richest single percentage of North Americans, but a great deal of money as far as the students are concerned). Debt was spreading up the social scales and escalating in quantities to amounts never before recorded.[16] People also began to have to borrow more often just to tide themselves over for shorter and shorter periods of time.

In Britain the number of people taking out so-called 'payday loans' to get them through to the end of the month more than doubled between August 2007 and May 2008; these loans charged interest rates which, when annualised, could be as high as 2,000%.[17] 'Payday loans' may be a term new to Britain, but it is now part of the common language in the US, where there are more than 22,000 payday loan shops, including some 133 cheque-cashing outfits in central Los Angeles alone (one per 3,000 people). Roughly US$25 billion is thought to be loaned annually at far greater repayment cost in the US each year, and all this is just to tide people over to payday. Some 12 million North Americans additionally take out annual loans in anticipation that they will receive a tax refund later in the year. On top of that, by 2006 more than a third of a million extremely high interest rate sub-prime mortgages were also being sold in the US each year at an annual servicing cost of US$300 billion.[18] Lending at these rates in these conditions turned out not to be sustainable for more than 12 months longer. The 2008 crash was the end result of 30 years of debt being racked up and up and up; it was not simply a short-term event.

Money crowds out virtue

The increase in debt was planned. In both 1978 and 1996 usury laws in the US were relaxed by Supreme Court rulings. These were rulings that allowed far more monies to be lent far more freely than before to increase the short-term profits of the money lenders at a disservice to borrowers, increasing the medium-term risk to all.[19] These laws were relaxed because enough right-wing judges had been appointed by various presidents to the Supreme Court by this time to overcome the reservations of their older (wiser) colleagues, many of whom remembered the last crash. Similarly, in Britain usury laws were relaxed in 1986 by the Conservative government's 'big bang' for the City of London. Over-lending and negative equity (unsecured housing debt) followed in 1989; it fell, and then rose again in the early years of the current century, resulting in negative equity spiralling up by 2009.[20]

Usury laws are ancient religious laws banning profiteering from interest payments on debts. All human societies have found money lending for profit to lead to great injustice. In Venice prototype investment bankers had to claim it was at the discretion of their customers whether they paid interest in order to avoid the wrath of the church. Islamic teaching still bans simple interest payments. When people are valued by how much money they can amass, rather than by what they can contribute, disaster results. 'A great deal of evidence (both experimental and historical) has accumulated to show that money crowds out virtue. When the incentives of peer approbation are replaced by cash, the quality and quantity of performances suffer'.[21]

It is not just in Britain that one quarter of households cannot cope, have insufficient savings and often have to resort to debt. In the US the poorest quarter of households in theory survive on about US$50 a day, but many do not even see that. By 2001 over a quarter (27%) of these poorest of households in the US were in severe difficulties. These were the households that were trying to live on US$20,000 or less as their annual income. Severe difficulties meant having to spend at least 40% if not more of that income simply on debt service payments, not even on repaying the debt. This 27% were in effect trying to live on US$10,000 or less a year, US$20 dollars a day, in some cases just US$10 dollars a day, to pay for food, rent and clothes, and all this in the US at the start of the 21st century. Unsurprisingly some 13% of this quarter were 60 days or more late in paying their bills. One adult in every 28 in the poorest quarters in the US was on the edge of defaulting on their debts during Christmas 2000, the time when most people on the North American continent celebrated the 2,000th birthday of the man who had thrown the money lenders out of the temple.[22]

The contrast between rich and poor by the millennium in the US became so great that the small minority who had previously made money out of the poor, who were so much smaller in number than the poor, could no longer even begin to try to understand their problems. Even the merely quite affluent, people with incomes of US$90,000–US$100,000 a year (around US$250 a day), found it difficult to comprehend life on so much less. They had mostly become rich either directly from working in the financial services industry or indirectly, through, say, teaching in universities or working in private hospitals where the fees or bills were paid by these very rich people, or they had high income through sources such as investments. *One rich man's investment income is many poor women's payday loans.* The same source as used above (an Economic Policy Institute report on *The state of working America: 2004/05* – see note 22) records that, although the rich also had debt, only some 2% of them were having to make debt repayments of 40% or more of their income in 2001. Most were not living at great risk. The rich sometimes like to suggest they are highly rewarded for astute high risk taking, but the risks they have to take are not so high. Only 1.3% of those high earners *in debt* were 60 days (or more) late paying their bills – only one for every 4,000 in that pay bracket.

It was during the 1980s that societies such as those in Britain and the US changed from being relatively cohesive to becoming places where inequalities rose so greatly that it became near impossible for one group to comprehend the fears, concerns and wishes of another. By 1999 university students were being taught through their textbooks that: 'Debt for basic necessities is one of the severest manifestations of deprivation and mental anguish. Not being able to see a way out must cause constant strain and anxiety, particularly to mothers in lone parent families, as well as feelings of guilt and shame in a society where being financially independent is highly valued'.[23] By 2009, just a decade later, the next cohort of textbook-reading university students were facing a job market with fewer prospects and less support from parents (themselves now far more severely stretched than before); as a result, it has become less of a necessity to say things such as 'must cause constant strain and anxiety'. It has become easier to empathise. The stress has also trickled upwards – the children of the affluent have become a little more sensitised again: both a little more sensitised to others' lives and to the hypocrisy of many of their parents' beliefs.

The squalor of riches

When worldwide inequalities rose to their most recently measured pinnacle, in 2007, it began to be noted how: 'Wealth affects people's perceptions and sentiments, makes them much less sensitive to the indignities of poverty and much more likely to misperceive their own wealth as being richly deserved and in the national interest'.[24] However, it is not just between continents that empathy is hard; just as much insensitivity can be found within a single town in an affluent country where the rich talk of the laziness, laxness, fecklessness and general uselessness of the poor in contrast to their perceptions of themselves as great risk takers and great labourers, as highly efficient, intelligent and sensitive people. What they really have is a very highly developed sense of personal self-worth. It is difficult not to think like this if you are affluent, and it is how most affluent people think; if you are rich and admit to being only human too, well, how do you excuse your riches?[25]

It is necessary to get a long way above the heights of those with annual incomes of US$100,000 to see the true extent of the rekindled squalor of riches. In practice you have to get high up into the very top ranks of the exclusively rich before luxury really sets in; you have to look through the keyholes of the fine, great and old country houses (which the gilded age of the 1920s was fabled for) to see a past way of life which a few have recreated today. Today an income of two or three million dollars a year might mean you are expected to employ a staff of around six live-in servants, including a cleaner, a nanny, a cook and a couple of gardeners, but your 'household manager' will have to check with you the bills of the additional 200 tradespeople who will 'regularly come to the house.... It turns out you can't just call A1 plumbing to fix an Etoile faucet',[26] you are told (a broken Etoile faucet is a dripping tap of a particularly expensive make). Being very rich is not really very easy or free of care. And, if you are this rich, do you trust your 'household manager'? Do you trust those accounts? Are your investments safe? Who are these strange people coming to fit that dripping tap with their ridiculous bill? Why is your wife spending so long with the gardener? Why didn't you sign a prenup when you married? And when did you last talk with your children? Are your children as interested in you as they are in your money? All this might sound very personal, but a fantasy world of effortless happiness is presented alongside the idea of holding great wealth. Real life for the wealthy is often not quite as wonderful. Most wealthy people in a very unequal society would lead happier lives with far less wealth in a more equal society (see www.onesociety.org.uk).

Between 1987 and 2005 national average personal wealth in the UK rose from about four times the national average annual income to about six times that income.[27] Shared out equally that meant that everyone in the country could have taken a four-year holiday, taken 1987–90 off, before the money ran out, and just 18 years later they could have taken an additional two years to make six in all (a national 2005–10 holiday). In practice the money was very poorly shared out and became even more badly distributed over time, and if everyone were to take those holidays they would have to do so abroad because the country would almost immediately become uninhabitable. What these increases in wealth really meant was that British bankers and accountants had made, enough money out of people, mostly overseas, convincing enough to send money to Britain and to receive less in effect back, that, relative to the rest of the world, people in Britain could claim more riches and more leisure time. In practice it was just a very few people who had these riches, but they could take entire lifetimes' worth of holidays by 2005 given their apparent 'savings'. For most of these super-rich their household managers had not stolen their ill-gotten gains, and for a small cut (called a fee), their accountants had warned them as the economic crash played out, and they moved many assets to safer ground. Most of their money will (probably) still be relatively safe by the end of 2010; they can still holiday for the rest of their lives, if they choose to.

The lives of the extremely wealthy take on new forms. Most tend not to holiday forever as holidays are not such a fulfilling activity once they become normal life. Although the wealthy still take far more holidays than anyone else, they also find other ways to feel good, ways of being valued, being seen to give money to charity for example, or getting into expensive activities with a sense of exclusivity such as horse riding, polo or grouse shooting. Animals feature highly in the lives of the rich – they kill them, sit on them (ride), cuddle them. For instance, pets increasingly substitute for children in the richer parts of the globe where the once exclusive behaviour of the rich in pampering their pets is now becoming more mainstream.[28] A pet is not really such a gratifying acquaintance; the conversation is not great, but a pet is a substitute for human relationships so when your offspring come to distrust you and they and your spouse have eyes mostly for the money, at least you know the pooch doesn't have a bank account. It is remarkable how frequently the super-rich are found with their appreciative little animals: think of Elizabeth Windsor's corgis, Michael Jackson's chimp, Paris Hilton's chihuahua. The lives of the rich are not really enviable when you think carefully about them.

No claim is being made here that there is some intrinsic worth in poverty, or that it is better to be average than to be rich in an unequal society. What is being suggested is that even the rich, including many of the extremely rich, do not fare well under inequality. It is obvious that the poor suffer and fairly clear that those on average incomes do not do well under inequality, but it is far less well understood that even the very rich in unequal affluent countries, despite having so much more money, suffer as a result of inequality. Greater equality is in almost everyone's interest. The majority of the richest groups remain to be convinced.

An age of excess

Expect to see fewer celebrity animals in future because the age of excess is coming to an end. In 1915 and 1916, and again briefly in the late 1920s, the very wealthiest 1% of 1% of the population (0.01%) in the US received more than 5% of all national income. By 2008 inequalities had risen enough for that to happen again. The 15,000 US families getting by on around US$9.5 million a year or more were as pampered in relative terms as their gilded age forebears.[29] There are great problems managing when you 'earn' over US$9.5 million a year; your household expands far beyond six employees; and there are the other homes, the plane and the yachts to consider. You fear the stock market falling, you fear your girlfriend discovering the extent of your second wife's alimony, and you fear yacht-docking fees escalating. These are not even vaguely related to the kind of fears that those earning much less than US$9.5 dollars an hour have to worry about. They are quite different fears again from most of those worries which the very affluent people who live on US$950,000 a year might face, people who again are living in a different sphere from the merely rich, who are earning a tenth of that, on US$95,000 a year; in turn they mostly cannot comprehend the lives of the poor of North America, people earning ten times less again a year (US$9,500). What do those at the top say about their own lives and their own fears? What most frightens them? When asked, they say: ' … don't publish my name: if you publish things like that my children's lives get endangered … gun to his head … kidnappers … I'm not speculating; it does happen'.[30]

It is hard to admit that great wealth is not a great asset, but that it simply protects you from poverty, which is worse. Wealth does not bring wonderful benefits to your life; to suggest it does is to sustain the greatest myth of our times. If you are wealthy enough you can see the evidence from the air. Around the world, where it is warm enough, in rich enclaves many swimming pools were built in back gardens at huge expense during the 1980s and 1990s. Most of the world's swimming pools are for the exclusive use of the rich and most are just a decade or two old. And there is almost never anyone swimming in them. A swimming pool in the garden, or a hot tub, a

---

tennis court, or a spare car (or three), all sound like great things to have. In practice it is more convenient, safer and more fun to use the same pools that other people use; by definition it is far less of a lonely pursuit to use sports facilities that are communal. Parking and the upkeep of all those cars becomes a bit of a drag; it's just hard to admit it. You can't admit it openly, but in private you often say life would be a lot easier with less; you are just afraid of having less. But what do you do with those cars if you decide not to keep them all for yourself? It takes a newly developed and finely honed lack of imagination not to be able to see the answer. Unfortunately this is the lack of imagination that gave us the idea that inequality is efficient, the warped thoughts which grew out of the modern incarnation of the academic discipline of economics, the thoughts which provide just enough justification for the rich to hold onto their riches because they are told to view them as some kind of reward.

6.2 Economics: the discipline with so much to answer for

The most serious and in the long term most deadly outcome of rising inequality is that as inequalities rise, those who argue that inequality is good become politically stronger and their arguments gain ground. When inequality is rising, if there is recession, market forces are allowed to operate unfettered and the poor are the first to be laid off. The ranks of the unemployed are not swelled by too many managers. They sack themselves last. When inequality is rising, if there is an economic boom, it is the highest paid who tend to win the highest pay rises, and inequality rises even further as a result. There are times when inequalities are allowed to rise and there are times when inequalities are engineered to fall, and these times are independent of boom or bust. There are people advocating rises in inequality and people arguing for falls. The former have won the debate for most of the last 40 years in those rich countries that have become most socially unequal as a result. Social inequalities do not rise by unforeseen accident.

Those advocating rises in inequality see inequality as good. They see it as the quantitative expression of how they view human nature. A great many people need to be fooled by a few especially able people (they think) to ensure that the majority go on buying things they mostly do not need, and to ensure that demand for new goods remains high. Not all the advocates of inequality argue that people are rational. Those who argue for inequality most effectively foresee problems if most people acted rationally. If most in future were to buy what they need, rather than purchase so often on impulse and go shopping simply for recreation, then the economy that has been built up on social pressures and obligations (made reality by inequality) would slump very badly.

The strict orthodox side of the academic discipline of economics rose to the fore of the social sciences in the 1980s and 1990s in terms of how it was perceived outside universities, how much funding it received from government and private business within universities, how it spread into bright new shiny schools of management there, how its acolytes preached on efficiency outside academia to the private sector, and how a degree in economics became almost essential to becoming a policy adviser over the course of those decades in certain countries. Orthodox economics is opposed by a wide and growing range of heterodox economists, but it is the orthodox economists that are still in almost all the positions of real power. By 2005, however, the revolt among those just below the most powerful economists was spreading. Even a few economists based in business schools began to explain, apologetically, that their subject had veered so far from having an interest in human beings, and that it had become '... so obscure that even orthodox economists are bemoaning its intellectual poverty'.[31] However, modern-day orthodox economists continue to produce asinine academic papers, such as the now famous paper from the *Journal of Economic Perspectives*, which argued that eating junk food was beneficial because of the amount of time people saved given how much more quickly they could eat.[32]

Orthodox economists have always had a lurid interest in junk, in desire and temptation. Academic papers that suggest junk food is good for you because it saves time are no worse than the argument put forward in the first ever essay to be written by a paid economist, Thomas Malthus's treatise on population of 1798. That essay led others to assume that to create wealth it was '... necessary to bring the urges of sexual attraction under control'.[33] Thomas in turn was following the concerns over sexual temptation expressed by Adam Smith in 1776, concerns that 'wealth gave rise to temptation, temptation to indulgence, and indulgence ate up the wealth'.[34] Over the course of the 19th and 20th centuries many economists moved away from these old orthodox obsessions. However, by the early 1980s, a group had arisen again in large numbers who saw the poor as monsters driven by '... growling stomachs, clenched fists and insatiable genitalia'.[35] On pages 69 and 332 of this volume the conceptualising problems of some leading economists have been noted, including the creation on the heterodox side of that discipline of a 'post-autistic economics' movement. While unfair to autistic people (who cannot help being autistic, whereas most orthodox economists did have a choice to make), the movement does hint at difficulties with social thinking among many modern-day orthodox economists. As a group they appear to find it harder to think of other people as human as compared with most social groups. Future studies may well find that certain types of people with particular traits and idiosyncrasies were more attracted to becoming the new orthodox economists than others.[36]

Just as Adam Smith (1723–90) influenced Thomas Malthus (1766–1834), Thomas Malthus influenced Francis Galton (1822–1911), Francis Galton influenced Karl Pearson (1857–1936), Karl Pearson influenced Joseph Schumpeter (1883–1950) and Joseph Schumpeter influenced Milton Friedman (1912–2006). The full web is more complex but not incomprehensible. In hindsight it is not surprising to find that economics, biology and statistics all borrowed from each other for those parts of the tales their advocates told, which most often turned out to be wrong. Even when what is now seen as part of heterodox economics, that form dominant immediately following the Second World War, was the norm, the old social Darwinism was being kept alive by men who would later be labelled as members of the new neoclassical, or the new orthodox, varieties. In 1947 economist Joseph Schumpeter, for instance, claimed that what was crucial to economic success was enough '... men of superior energy and intelligence'.[37] Joseph Schumpeter was far from the worst. At least he tried to think of the economy as if it contained people, not just as an abstract mathematical model. However, more careful historical analysis has revealed that such superiority and vigour were not so essential to becoming rich, but an advanced degree of unscrupulousness was useful.

Brains to master difficult skills?

As a discipline, almost as a whole, economics turned towards the orthodox, towards worshipping selfishness in the 1960s and 1970s as typified by the writing of Milton Friedman. It attracted young acolytes who would later come to see and describe themselves as being the modern embodiment of Schumpeter's energetic super-able individuals. It is not hard to find many quotations from such contemporary economists in which they claim that either they or their students possess special brains, the kind able to master difficult skills, the implication being that others simply do not make the cut. There are even orthodox economists who continue the temptation–obsession theme by writing popular books that imply that women are attracted to them because of their economic intellect. In one, in a chapter entitled 'High heels and school uniforms', under a picture of two large male moose locking horns, a popular contemporary economist (Robert H. Frank) writes that: 'Some traits, such as intelligence, not only contribute to individual reproductive success but also serve the broader interests of the species'.[38] His book was subtitled *Why economics explains almost everything*. It is surprising that economists have not reintroduced polygamous marriages to maximise their imagined utility and reproduce much more quickly the armies of little orthodox economists that they clearly feel the world would benefit from. There remains only a small but highly astute minority who still realise that '… there is not usually a queue to jump into bed with economists'.[39]

Orthodox economists are not monstrous or demonic individuals (although a few are remarkable fantasists). When it comes to considering the alternatives most simply suffer from a 'total absence of thinking … the refusal to read, to think critically or deeply, the rejection of all but one or one kind of book'.[40] Although this description applies well to followers of the faith of economic orthodoxy it was not written of economists. It was written about an unremarkable man, Adolf Eichmann, who efficiently timetabled the railways in Germany to ensure that as many Jews (and others deemed undesirable) could be routed to the gas chambers as possible. He was technically accomplished, very good at what he did, but as Hannah Arendt carefully explained, he just did not stop to think much about what it was he was doing and the effect of what he was doing. He believed the words of the one rulebook he had been taught, the one faith. Orthodox economists suffer from the same banal refusal to open their eyes.

Modern-day orthodox economists describe how they are spat at by officials in airports in Africa when they reveal that they work for bodies such as the World Bank and argue for policies such as 'Economic theory does give us the right answer, but it is not very attractive. The government needs to create a convincing signal of its intentions, and to do this it has to adopt reforms that are so painful that a bogus reformer is simply not prepared to adopt them. It thereby reveals its true type, to use the language of economics'.[41] These men are just beginning to realise how many people hold them largely responsible for evils such as 'structural adjustment' and the idea that governments in poor countries should behave so callously towards their populations as to give 'the free market' the clear 'signal' that no bogus economic reformer could give. The signal that the market apparently wants to see is that officials are prepared to watch and stand aside as their citizens die, due, for instance, to lack of clean water as the supply is privatised by a Western contractor. Given this it is no wonder that popular books now describe how orthodox economists behave like members of a cult, as if in '… part of their training, their brains get … reprogrammed … everything they were taught when they were young as being right and true is removed and replaced by a new understanding of the laws of the universe'.[42] Now that great economic misfortune is hitting rich countries so hard, many orthodox economists are trying to appear reformed characters, moving towards the side of the heterodox, but it is not clear whether they are bogus reformers; it is through their actions that we should look for the 'signal' that they now doubt the god of the market. Just as crypto-eugenists kept eugenics alive in the 1950s, someone will still be holding a torch for the wonders of the market's fictional ability to achieve equilibrium in a few years to come.

The orthodox faith

Orthodox economists are blamed for allowing the debt mountain to build in the richest of countries and, especially in the US, they are blamed for having the belief that if you leave the market alone it somehow naturally corrects itself. By 2005 members of an average household in the US owed 127.2% of their annual income in outstanding debt, more than twice the debt level of 1975 (see Figure 17). Although that debt ratio had risen every five years from 1975 onwards, before 2000 it had risen fastest, by 15%, in the period 1985–90. This was not a period of recession; it was not a period when households were borrowing more for their material needs; it was the period in which people were told for the first time since the 1920s that greed is good.

Figure 17: Outstanding consumer debt as a proportion of disposable income, US, 1975–2005

Note: The bars show the ratio of debt to annual disposable income on the axis to the right. The line shows the percentage change in that ratio over the coming five years on the axis to the left (31% = [127.2–96.8]/96.8).

Source: Foster, J.B. (2006) 'The household debt bubble', *Monthly Review*, vol 58, no 1 (www. monthlyreview.org/0506jbf.htm), Table 1: disposable income is the income after paying taxes. Derived from: Board of Governors of the Federal Reserve System, Flows of Funds Accounts of the United States, Historical Series and Annual Flows and Outstandings, Fourth Quarter 2005, 9 March 2006, available at www.federalreserve.gov/releases/Z1/Current/, table 2 (p 8 of 'complete file').

The rate of household debt growth was curtailed a little in the 1990s, as Figure 17 demonstrates, before accelerating beyond all previously known or recorded levels of growth in the years 2000 to 2005; in those five years alone average US consumer debt rose by some 31%. Then came the crash.

Levels of annual debt growth in billions of dollars a year across all domestic and financial sectors of the US are given in Table 6 for the period 1977–2008, drawn from the same source as Figure 17 above. Table 6 shows that mortgage debt and other consumer debts rose both quickly (and at other times more slowly) in tandem, rising most quickly when an additional US$1.041 trillion of mortgage debt was incurred in 2005 alone. This trillion was a figure that turned negative within three years, with borrowers repaying more than they borrowed for the first time since at least 1977, and probably since 1929, in 2008. However, they repaid just US$46 billion more, around 4% of that extra trillion dollar debt amassed in 2005 alone. The correlations reported at the end of Table 6 also show that there was no evidence of a relationship between federal government debt growth and household mortgage debt growth, and a negative correlation between consumer debt changes and federal debt trends. In short, when the federal government borrowed less to spend less, households borrowed more on their credit cards. That had to change with the economic crash. As households borrowed a trillion less additional income to buy homes or otherwise spend in 2008 as compared with 2005, the federal government borrowed an additional trillion just between the two years 2007 and 2008 in an attempt to keep the market-based banking system running. The footnotes to Table 6 reveal how even more drastic action was required in the first three quarters of 2009. Summing the final two columns in Table 6 reveals that the financial sector in the US itself had borrowed an additional 18 trillion dollars over the 1977–2008 period, all on the advice of their orthodox economist high priests. They were being greedy. But discovering that is hardly surprising given that they had only recently been taught, and come fully to believe, how good greed supposedly was.

Table 6: Additional debt added annually by sector (US$ billion), US, 1977–2008

Date	Household debt		All debt							
	Home mortgage	Consumer credit	Total debt	Household total	Business total	State and local government	Federal government	Financial sectors	
								Domestic	Foreign
1977	86	36	388	128	117	20	56	54	14
1978	106	46	489	160	139	39	53	75	24
1979	117	43	498	170	159	27	36	91	15
1980	90	3	440	108	135	22	77	73	24
1981	67	20	538	106	190	28	86	105	24
1982	47	19	549	84	153	42	161	93	16
1983	105	48	695	176	165	47	185	104	17
1984	127	82	958	219	323	53	197	158	8
1985	182	84	1,164	314	256	164	226	204	1
1986	199	56	1,185	261	295	74	216	329	10
1987	222	32	1,016	264	221	90	144	291	6
1988	216	47	1,042	272	307	50	155	250	7
1989	225	47	920	283	208	47	146	225	10
1990	199	15	892	232	131	47	247	211	24
1991	174	–9	641	184	–84	91	278	156	15
1992	171	9	775	199	–7	17	304	239	24
1993	157	61	923	238	10	58	256	292	70
1994	167	135	1,029	323	145	–46	156	462	–11
1995	154	147	1,197	310	285	–61	144	440	78

cont .../

Date	Household debt		Total debt	All debt					Financial sectors	
	Home mortgage	Consumer credit		Household total	Business total	State and local government	Federal government		Domestic	Foreign
1996	206	106	1,336	336	273	-21	145		514	88
1997	216	70	1,458	301	439	51	23		574	70
1998	302	97	2,071	426	567	67	-53		1,027	37
1999	380	112	2,090	495	582	37	-71		1,027	19
2000	386	177	1,735	584	560	17	-296		807	63
2001	507	151	2,016	672	381	106	-6		874	-11
2002	706	108	2,385	831	180	144	258		879	93
2003	860	104	2,786	984	177	120	396		1,067	42
2004	938	115	3,126	1,061	455	115	362		978	155
2005	1041	95	3,553	1,171	677	172	307		1,114	113
2006	964	104	4,025	1,169	889	151	183		1,301	331
2007	652	134	4,395	849	1,228	186	237		1,771	124
2008	-46	44	2,728	51	507	48	1,239		1,040	-158
	Pearson product-moment correlation coefficients with annual federal government borrowing									
	0.01	-0.24	0.29	-0.01	0.01	0.20			0.19	-0.29

Notes: The first two columns of data make up most of domestic household borrowing in normal years (data column 4). 2008 was not a normal year. Data column 3 is the sum of columns 4-9. Statistical tests can be applied as described under Table 5. They show that each of the coefficients in the last row of this table could be reporting random variations, in other words, with true correlation of zero, with a probability of 10% or much more (thus not unlikely).

As of February 2010 third quarter mortgage debt flow was −370 US$ billion, consumer credit −82 US$ billion, and total debt increase had fallen under a trillion dollars for the first time since 2000 excluding the financial sectors. Including these sectors, total US debt fell to the third quarter by US$276 billion. It has never fallen in this series before, and has fallen in every quarter of 2009 so far reported. Business total debt fell for the first time since 1992, but by much more than it did then: some US$284 billion by the third quarter of 2009. Only local, state and federal governments kept up borrowing levels in their various attempts to deal with the crisis.

Note also that revised figures will have been released by the Federal Reserve on 11 March 2010, including for the fourth quarter of 2009.

Source: US Federal Reserve: Debt growth, borrowing and debt outstanding tables (www.federalreserve.gov/releases/Z1/Current/), figures above as first released, March 2009

High priests of gold

The danger of selfishness and greed in business and finance has been recognised since trading began. Warnings have been copied from religious book to religious book: 'Business turns human producers into commodities. Nor does it spare their employers – "For what shall it profit a man, if he shall gain the whole world, and lose his own soul?"'.[43] However, words and thoughts such as those are not our religion now. Too many of us began to worship money; we created a new religion of science and, within that religion, high priests of gold: economists. Thus, according to a contemporary philosopher of social justice, while '... economists present themselves as disinterested scientists, they function today more typically as ideologists for our political and economic "elites" – much as theologians did in an earlier age'.[44]

In the orthodox church of economics, profiteering (termed 'arbitrage') is seen as price stabilising, as a public service! It is now becoming commonly accepted that this is not what happens, most people do not think or behave like calculating little cogs and the world does not balance out and reach some *equilibrium* like this. Arbitrage resulting in price stability has been termed the 'dead parrot' of utility theory. The idea that 'greed is good' no longer has any validity outside orthodox economics; it has ceased to be a concept to be treated as rational. And yet, in the self-justifying minds of too many men of money, they still tell themselves that they are of some great value; they find a way of justifying their actions and existence as good, or, much more worryingly, do not care much about what others care for. However, the orthodox are far from immune from being hurt, and it is mainly to preserve their sense of identity that they continue to hold onto their faith. As the economic crash of 2008 hit, suicides among bankers rose and one observer of the rise noted that: 'The identity of these people is so tied into their career that when it's gone they don't know who they are anymore'.[45]

Returning to a world of frugality from a world of greed will be hard to comprehend for those whose lives have revolved around amassing money. There is growing evidence that orthodox economists have been finding it hard to understand altruism and the fact that people have developed not to be naturally anti-social. A small group of such economists are even engaged in an endless debate about lighthouses and why we build them, arguing that the private sector could do it for profit![46] Some have even extended their models to try to build in a degree of wider social motivation and to find some kind of communal rationality in the selfish actions of the few which limit freedom of real choice for so many. Others, however, are looking back at the history of an older economics to find that rational choice theory was only developed by an economist (Vilfredo Pareto) to explain that very narrow slice of human conduct where individual preferences were possibly best satisfied through such emotion-free 'rational' behaviour. Vilfredo (1848–1923) never meant it as a general theory.[47] If people were naturally selfish why did they pull over to let ambulances overtake them? It is not because they don't want their cars damaged as ambulances try to get past them. All but sociopaths understand why we pull over when an ambulance has its lights flashing.

It is calculated, even by orthodox economists, that at least half of the US economy is devoted purely to transactional purposes. These purposes involve monitoring who does what, accounting, logging the shipping of goods and selling of goods (including point of sale work at tills). One economist, in an attempt to justify this, said it was '… in a sense, a tribute to the productivity of the market economy that it can bear costs of this magnitude and yet provide high standards of living. The cost of counting beans is repaid many times by the extra beans which result from careful counting'.[48] It is a tragedy that otherwise able human beings, once drawn into the culture of orthodox economic thinking, become compelled to defend the indefensible and have to say there is an intrinsic value in so much stock taking and barcode scanning. These are both so clearly modern inventions which we could largely dispense with in a society where consumers and producers work much closer to (and more closely with) each other. It is hard not to imagine when an orthodox economist begins to talk of tribute economies in this manner, that like some priest who has begun to doubt the existence of a particularly fearsome and vengeful god, they too are beginning to doubt the proclaimed truth of the wonders of free markets. Unfortunately, like the priests of old, so much of their own status is invested in their religion that they usually see no alternative. They dare not voice their doubt in public, and they redouble their belief in and preaching about the orthodox. In early 2009 one anonymous member of the British government's Cabinet with apparently a little economic savvy was reported to announce: 'The banks are fucked, we're fucked, the country's fucked'.[49] They say such things in private to journalists but are not willing yet to have their names put on the record.

In praise of the counting of beans!

The same group of economists who say that huge transaction costs, the inefficiency of the market, are in fact a tribute to its productivity, also claim that it is only orthodox economists who can truly understand these things, others having not been sufficiently trained in the way and the light of their scriptures. They attack any attempt to uncover the illogical nature of their arguments as amateur do-it-yourself economics.[50] They talk of other people as being only 'normally intelligent', by implication mere mortals not trained in their orthodoxies, people who are unable to comprehend the arcane truths of the market. Orthodox economists unsurprisingly react very angrily on reading even the politest of books that carefully explain how they have become so misguided.[51] Having your beliefs questioned is upsetting. Having your beliefs publicly questioned when you too are beginning to have doubts but are having to put a brave face on things must be infuriating. Orthodox economics will not simply disappear; it has to be argued out of court. It has to give the market of public opinion the proper 'signals' that it is changing. It has to stop praising the counting of beans.

When it is suggested that a tribute economy in which most people count beans can maintain high standards of living for a long period, it is worth asking for how long such economies have successfully operated in this way before. For whom in the US are such high living standards being maintained? Does the median North American, the woman in the middle, experience a good life compared with the median citizen of other affluent nations? And it is worth asking from whom in the rest of the world is the physical tribute mostly extracted, and with what effect? The example quoted above (of how the price of counting beans is supposedly repaid many times over) is continued by its protagonist to suggest that people in the US receive better 'medicine' by having more accountants in hospitals. The people making these kinds of claims do not concern themselves over whether healthcare is *actually* better in the US, where life expectancy is lower than across all of Western Europe and Japan, for example.

For the very few who can afford to sign up to concierge doctor schemes, those private doctors who serve only a few rich families, health appears to be good and on average they live long, if far from unmedicated, lives. But the health of most people in the US is worse than that of many citizens in countries that are poorer. For the very rich too, the interests of their private physicians are not in maximising their patients' health but in maximising the cost of their health treatments, and when a doctor wants to maximise his or her income that is not necessarily good news for the patient. These realities and life expectancy figures are inconvenient truths that orthodox economists prefer to ignore, along with ignoring the millions who go hungry and sleep rough in the US, despite (or when you think about it, more likely because of) the 'efficient' accountant culture there.

The effects of living in a country where orthodox economics has been allowed to run wild have been closely studied as a natural, if unethical, mass experiment. It has been found that households in the middle of the income distribution in the US have been forced to spend higher and higher proportions of their income over time on things such as housing to maintain their social positions. This includes the housing costs that enable them to send their children to the median-quality publicly funded schools. As inequalities in education rise, mirroring inequalities in income, schools become more and more differentiated in terms not just of average pupil exam success, but also over whether or not armed police are stationed in the school to deal with gun crime. In the childhoods of parents in the US the stationing of armed police in school was much farther from the norm than it is now. The effect is to make geographic location ever so much more important and this in turn raises house prices in all areas not seen to be at the very bottom, raising them fastest the further from the bottom they are. The middle-income family struggles to pay its mortgage. At the top the rich see the value of their assets rise dramatically even while a few of their number borrow greatly to keep up appearances. Simultaneously, in Britain, the proportion of young families unable even to afford the lowest of regular payments on a mortgage to become first-time buyers rose from half to two thirds between the mid-1980s and 2001; four fifths of all such households in London could no longer afford to get on the bottom of a very long ladder by the turn of the millennium.[52] Of the *shrinking minority* who could afford a mortgage across Britain by 2001, some 20% relied on inheritance or premature inheritance from their parents to help pay the deposit. This rose to 40% of first-time buyers needing such help by 2005,[53] a huge rise in a very short time, and in hindsight one of many portents of doom.

For most of the 20th century, however, homes have not been the greatest personal expense of families in affluent nations; that has been cars.

6.3 Gulfs: between our lives and our worlds

The automobile and its recent history provides the pre-eminent example of how the growth of greed out of the eradication of squalor has created a new and very different kind of squalor. The old squalor was that of damp homes with earthen floors, of dirty water and of roads covered in horse manure. It was of people tramping to work, undertaking journeys that were repetitive, arduous and often (especially in poor weather) miserable. The advent of mass motorised travel offered an apparent end to such misery. It appeared to herald a brave new world of short efficient journeys, clean streets and happy upright people, not stooped as in Lowry landscapes, not tired out as they arrived at their destination.

Largely unforeseeable when cars were first sold was the congestion of streets and motorways that filled up with thousands of cars, the choking of lungs with millions of tiny particles. The need to fight wars for oil to keep people moving was also then unforeseen. Perhaps hardest to foresee would be the psychological attachment people would form with their cars, especially many men in their middle age. Cars became status symbols of rank. People began to pretend that they liked the particular clunk of how the door closed on an expensive model, and that that clunk alone was itself worth many thousands of pounds, maybe even the average annual salary of a typical worker! This was behaviour not dissimilar to house buyers explaining that they had taken out such a high mortgage because they liked the décor, rather than admitting they were paying for the area they wanted to live in, for the kinds of neighbours they wanted. Lovers of the clunk of an expensive car door shutting had fallen in love with what they thought owning that car said about them, how it showed they were adequate men, even depicted them as highly successful if the clunk was right. The squalor of greed is a vice to be pitied. It is hard not to conclude that the rich spent so much of their money on such expensive cars because so very much more began to be missing from their lives as their riches rose.

From the beginnings of mass motoring cars began to take on a value way beyond their functional utility. In 1940s rural small town North America, where it was easier to see their practical value, people began to buy their first car before they purchased their first bathtub. If an early example were needed of how the old squalor of grime began to be overtaken by the new squalor of greed, then the purchase of the near relations of the Model T Ford before bathtubs would be a good one. Even earlier, in 1929, as the economic crash hit, social commentators could be found stating that 'People give up everything in the world but their car'.[54] Much the same was being said 70 years later when attempts to persuade people to become more 'green' saw them agreeing to recycle, avoiding flying, turning off lights and insulating their homes, but not giving up their car or even one of their many cars. It is not simply the convenience of having a car that encourages people to hold on to them so dearly, it is the psychological attachment that forms – it is cheaper to use taxis in most cases than to buy, to service and to park your own car.

The new squalor

From the 1960s onwards at least two thirds of the rise in the cost of cars every year was due to the cost of changing how cars looked, not due to their improving functionality.[55] This was called 'styling'. From the mid-1950s onwards cars would be restyled, later called having a 'face lift', every single year, so that new models could constantly be offered. All this styling and the marketing that went with it was aimed at getting inside potential drivers' minds and persuading them that to be complete, to be seen as adequate for their social standing, they needed a new motor. By the end of the century the sports utility vehicles (SUVs) that were being sold to North American men had become enormous, and were being given militaristic names such as 'The Raider', 'Trooper', 'Liberty', 'Commander' and 'Patriot'. In Britain it was along the medieval street layouts of London, not on some off-road prairie, that the majority of men and a few women who had budgets large enough to waste on huge motor cars lived. They still live there today, but often have a little less cash now and are a little more circumspect about their purchases. However, these cars were not sold in increasing numbers simply to bolster egos; they also made their occupants feel safer, driving higher in their 'Chelsea tractor' above the road. But, as deaths mounted, it became apparent by 2007 that when these huge cars collided with smaller, less statement-making cars, the occupants of the smaller cars were *ten times* more likely to die as a result of the collision, not to mention pedestrians and cyclists.[56] This is the new squalor. Cars are now the main killers of people aged under 35 in countries like Britain. In the past, the main killers were diseases spread through the old squalor of untreated sewage. This is what we got by buying cars before bathtubs.

By 2006, even though the price of housing in countries like Britain had sky-rocketed, the average Briton was spending some £5,500 per family per year simply on buying and running their cars (as compared with roughly £5,000 spent annually on their home).[57] These sums of money were enough to buy and run an old second-hand car every year for every family in Britain; many people, however, want nearly new cars. Those with the most money almost all want new cars and those with most of all want the most prestigious new cars; cars of very particular makes.

The sums of money being mentioned here are so high because they are what are called mean, or arithmetic-average, prices. They are the total spent on cars by all people divided by the number of families in a country. Just a few people spending inordinate amounts on cars have pulled those averages up sharply, and it takes many families to spend nothing on cars to counter-balance the effect of a single expensive purchase by a single individual. For example, in the US in 2007, it was suggested that rich men became embarrassed to be seen by their friends, enemies and acquaintances as being miserly for only spending around US$55,000 on a car as a present for their girlfriend. In one case the car was a Mercedes SLK, and the report continued by saying that a year later, when this particular man spent US$110,000 on a Bentley for his girlfriend, he thought he had escaped the sniggers. However, these brand-name cars, including BMWs and Jaguars, had come to be seen as '... almost common'[58] among the glitterati of the super-rich during those pre-crash early years of the current century. The arithmetic averages are thus being brought up so sharply because a few men are worried about impressing their girlfriends, their so-called friends, and especially people who do not know them (but look just at their car). Great wealth is no predictor of great ability or of any sense of proportion. If it were, there would be no luxury car market.

Eyeing up the talent

The super-rich have also been bamboozled by the cult of orthodox economics. When US economists try to write popular books on economics, they tell their (presumed to be male) readers that: '... one can make a crude guess about how talented a person is by looking at the kind of clothing he wears or the kind of car he drives'.[59] It is true that the super-rich do differ in one significant way from the rest of us – they are much more likely to feel a little more insecure, perhaps even a little incredulous as to the position they appear to have reached. A few step back and say, well, they were handing out all these top jobs and someone had to get one. Many say to themselves that they were specially able and deserving of their fortunes, but it is hard to keep telling yourself that if you know in your heart of hearts that you are not superhuman.

If you dress up in expensive suits, put a watch worth thousands of dollars on your wrist, step into a car worth hundreds of thousands of dollars from a home worth millions in the morning, it can be easier to tell yourself you are worth it, that you *are* a big man. There are subtle psychological reasons why so many very well-paid men spend so much of their income on cars, leading to more being spent on cars than on homes nationwide. It remains '... the nature of status symbols that people are rarely aware of their motivations for acquiring them. No man buys a sports car thinking of it as a penis substitute'.[60] But it is better to think you brought your car to make up for the inadequacies of your penis than for your lack of super-sized all-round talent.

Even those who have only one small car, or no car at all, cannot indulge in smugness. In the US it was found some time ago that college-educated men often bought slightly smaller cars because they gained their sense of superiority in other ways, or felt they did. Rarely, however, would they live in poorer neighbourhoods or dress cheaply and scruffily. Much of our normal behaviour is about keeping up appearances. We do not think of how we dress, drive and live as statements we make about ourselves. It is also worth noting that modes of transport change more quickly than the rate at which we learn not to show off. The (now) billionaire founders of the company Google are reported to have bought cheap environmentally friendly hybrid cars to show their commitment to a better world while at the same time purchasing a 224-seat wide-bodied aeroplane (and refitting it to take only 50 very large seats) so that they could get '... to places like Africa ... that can [apparently] only be good for the world'.[61] Other millionaires and billionaires reported to the same source how depressed they felt in their private jets when forced to queue to take off at airports, backed up among their kind, with so many 'important guys' all just sitting on the tarmac behind their pilots in their private jets looking out at each other. And from this deep well of rich people's tales comes also the apocryphal story of the daughter of a billionaire who asked if she could have a 'normal' air ticket for her birthday so that she could see the inside of an airport, a pleasure the children of the super-rich are denied when their chauffeurs deliver them to the doors of their jets.

Looking up to the heavens

Mass air travel is another example of the new squalor of our times. Although the super-rich might fly most often with the least care about their actions, many more of us in affluent countries now fly. We might fly to avoid a long train or road journey, to get to where it is sunnier because we think a holiday there will be more relaxing, or we might fly simply for a weekend 'city break' to see a place we have not been to before. We also, of course, may choose to fly because sometimes it is cheaper than taking trains or buses, and sometimes it is the only way we get to see family abroad. But we mainly now fly so much because we can, and because we think we will lose out if we do not, because we think we might be missing out on something that others who fly so much are gaining.

Every year more and more people are born who will never fly and a greater proportion of the world's population will look up at the heavens rather than down from the clouds. Also, every year, more and more people live lives in the world that are not centred on the petrol-driven motor car. Most extra cars are consumed by families that already have one and most of the extra families being formed in the world will never get to own a car. For those who have cars, roads become ever more clogged and dangerous to walk near (and across) as more and more cars squeeze through them. Flight lanes are also becoming congested; airports are becoming even more anti-social places, with fewer seats to sit on, more shops to walk through. The increased pollution and travel of a minority not only increases the squalor of lives in the rich world, but raises the sense of failure and pollutes the air and feelings of all those who have never got (or hardly ever get) to travel in these ways. Cheap air travel to where you might want to travel is not as cheap as the adverts suggest. If it were the poor would fly much more – more than three quarters of air passengers in the UK are middle class, and while the number of flights being taken was growing in number between 2000 and 2004, the number taken by the poorest fifth of society simultaneously fell.[62]

Great gulfs are created by the new squalor between our social worlds. Those looking out from a poor city neighbourhood in Britain (or the US) at the cars passing their bedroom windows on the dual carriageway (or freeway) nearby look at the faces of those who fear them, who have paid so much not to live near them. These people drive to offices in town to receive salaries which they can spend on the suits they are required to wear, the car they need to get to that office and to feel good enough about themselves. When they look out from their car windows they see why they paid their mortgage, so that their children did not have to go to the schools they drive past. They do not worry that in driving past poor estates (or blocks) they will fill other people's children's young lungs full of far more particles than their children will ever have to breathe in, nor do they think for a moment of the irony that other people's children have to breathe all these pollutants and risk crossing busy roads despite their own families not having a car. The greatest risk to children in a country like Britain (or the US) is of being killed by a car. That risk is seven times greater in poor areas as compared with affluent ones. Part of the reason for this is that the rich drive by and through poor inner-city areas on their way to and from to work.[63] Given all this, isn't it bizarre that the rich fear the poor?

Squalor was much more widely felt in the past. It was harder to avoid tuberculosis or cholera simply because you were affluent. To some extent affluence did help; for example the rich lived higher up the hills where both the air and water were cleaner; on the other hand, smog across towns harmed almost everyone. A century ago even the most affluent of families saw one in ten of their children die before their first birthday, mostly as a result of infectious diseases, a rate only 2.5 times lower than that experienced by the very poorest of families. That gap is far *wider* today as affluent families have seen the environmental conditions under which their children are brought into the world improve materially so much that they are now as much as one hundred times more likely to survive to their first birthday than were their great-grandparents. *In countries like Britain, and even more so in the US, the improvement experienced by poorer families in the environments into which they have to bring up their children has not been so great.* Although those environments are much better than they were, the improvements to their lives and areas have come more slowly, so that poorer infants are now many more times more likely to die young than infants from affluent families.[64]

———

Ingesting the dirt of others

In the rich world in these times of unparallelled affluence, common goods such as air are much more unevenly distributed geographically in terms of quality. In affluent countries now it is emissions from car exhausts that do most harm to air quality, not coal fires or factory chimneys. Figure 18 shows how those people living in the fifth of wards in Britain where air quality is worst are much more likely to be poor on average, with poverty rates in these areas ranging from 20% up to 40% of local residents. The graph tilts up towards the right and front because those areas where the poverty rates reach 40% of families, and where pollution is highest, are also in the fifth of areas where local residents are responsible for producing the *least* emissions, where fewest people own and run cars. *The very poorest neighbourhoods in Britain pollute the least but suffer from the most pollution.* The tallest

Figure 18: Poverty, car exhaust emissions and pollution inhaled in Britain, by area, 1999

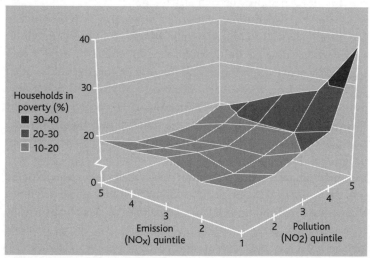

Note: Low emitting and polluting quintiles are labelled 1, the highest are labelled 5. The proportion living in poverty is derived from breadline surveys. The areas used are local government wards, amalgamated by emission and inhalation rates and defined on the boundaries of those existing in 1981.

Source: Mitchell, G. and Dorling, D. (2003) 'An environmental justice analysis of British air quality', *Environment and Planning A*, vol 35, pp 909-29, Figure 9: Poverty rate by NO_x emission and ambient air quality for 10,444 British wards in 1999.

spike in Figure 18 represents those inner-city neighbourhoods that the rich have to drive by in their polluting cars to get to their offices.

Figure 18 shows the local distribution of the injustice of new squalor in Britain. It is in microcosm a reflection of the worldwide pattern whereby those who pollute most currently suffer least from the results of their actions. It is not just that they do not suffer, physically, but they also pollute the minds of others with the ideas they have come to believe. A very small but ever so significant group of them who own newspapers, television channels or political parties employ others to promote their views. Our greatest polluters are often lauded as examples to be followed. It is repeatedly suggested that people should aspire to run businesses and have their own private jets; if not Boeing 767 aeroplanes capable of flying them and 49 of their friends to Africa, then just a 'small' jet, or to be able to fly first class, or business class, or even 'just' being able to fly.

We are taught to aspire to car ownership, particularly of large cars. We are taught to aspire to travel around the planet. The way in which we are taught to do this most frequently is through the actions of celebrities and how they are portrayed. Just as no one sat down two centuries ago at the start of the industrial revolution and planned to create enormous slums of squalor, so no secret committee met in the early 1980s under an agenda headed 'How can we persuade the masses that they should always aspire to have so much more?'. There were no 'break-out' meetings to determine how best to try to explain to people that true happiness was not possible without high exhaust emissions. There were just people trying to sell things, lots of things. And there were people whose faces and images sold things, who sold movies, who won in sport, people who could be portrayed as special, as inspirational, as worthy of emulating. Celebrity became part of the new squalor, the part that helps best to explain just what is going on.[65]

6.4 Celebrity: celebrated as a model of success

What is the most you can spend? There are limits, and it is at those limits that true global celebrity is found. Those at the very top often keep a lower profile than the popular celebrities of television and magazines who are still trying to work their way up. True celebrities do not sell their wedding photographs for a few million – a few million is too little to bother with.

Have you ever wondered how much money would be 'enough'? The most it was possible to spend on underwear by 2007 was US$5 million on a diamond-studded bra, about seven times more than the most expensive watch on the market at that time.[66] You can get more diamonds on a bra. However, a bra studded with diamonds works less well than one you can buy for just US$12. Similarly, a watch you buy for hundreds of thousand of dollars is likely to be of less use to you in telling the time accurately than a cheap digital watch because very expensive watches have mechanical, not digital, workings. Furthermore you won't wear the expensive timepiece as frequently for fear of losing it or breaking it, or for fear of someone robbing you for it.

The cult of celebrity and of watching the super-rich is part of a wider trend that has been incorporated into and has transformed the lives of almost all people in affluent countries. Chauvinism, bigotry and racism were the human failings associated most closely with the injustices of elitism, exclusion and prejudice. With greed the failing is a new kind of financial narcissism born out of insecurity, spending money on ourselves and our possessions because *such spending temporarily, fleetingly, boosts how well we value ourselves in societies where we feel less valued in general.* In the early years of the current century it was reported that homeowners in Britain alone spent £150 billion on (what a magazine said were) tasteless home improvements that had actually reduced the values of their homes but which clearly they must have felt at the moment of purchase were worthwhile. At about £7,500 per homeowner this was a huge national outlay to achieve a series of very short-lived 'warm' feelings.[67] All that money was just the average cost over recent years of those decorations and fittings deemed to have lowered the market value of properties (putting in a jacuzzi and losing a bedroom as a consequence is an extreme but sadly not uncommon example). Homeowners were persuaded to part with their money by the 'home improvement' industry, an industry that offered to provide that instant feeling of gratification that comes by adding yet another fixture, fitting or inappropriate carpet.

We can now spend many hundreds if not thousands of pounds on refrigerators which have designer labels on them but which in essence do not do a better job than one many times cheaper. We are enticed to purchase expensive televisions with screens so flat and so wide that our sitting rooms do not let us sit back far enough to view them properly. When the television breaks down, we rush out immediately to buy another because the cost of repairing it is even greater, or it is not possible to make a repair, and even a few days without television is hard to contemplate for the 99% of us who regularly watch it. Just as we can buy cars that are ever shinier and more stylish, kitchen work surfaces are now sold which, if you are affluent enough, enable you to see your reflection in highly polished granite. This can be granite shipped out of war-torn Angola if you are willing to pay or borrow enough for the privilege of being able to say that your worktop was made of chic 'Ooba Tuba' stone. It is worth pausing for a few seconds to count up the hypocrisies involved in shipping a ton of granite (that in the past was only used to be cut up for gravestones) half way round the world to put your fair trade coffee cups on. Low trade is better even than fair trade; consuming less reduces both exploitation and pollution. For every mile travelled, shipping burns more oil than flying because there is more friction when travelling through water than through air. However, the hypocrisy of kitchen worktops made from African granite is minimal when you consider that entire kitchens are now sold that cost more than mid-priced and comfortable terraced homes, or that some very affluent people are being encouraged to redecorate most of their home every two years or less because style changes so quickly. When people begin to view the way they themselves chose to have their homes decorated two years ago as tasteless enough to warrant redecorating, it is fair to say that we live in a society that is suffering deeply from the afflictions of affluence.

The afflictions of affluence

The greed for ever more designer goods, sleek cars, flash kitchens, bathrooms that would not look out of place in a five star hotel, anything that mirrors celebrity, went way beyond people's means to pay for those goods at the heights of profligacy, heights that were reached in the early years of the 21st century. It was in the most unequal of rich countries that debt rose fastest and became highest as a result. Average credit card debt in the US soared to raise consumer 'credit' in total by US$104 billion in 2006, and then a further US$134 billion was borrowed in 2007 (the rise fell to 'just' US$44 billion more than the year before in 2008; see Table 6 on pp 231-2). Across in Britain consumers held more than half of all Western European credit card debt by 2006 (see Section 4.1 of this volume on how social inequalities had fuelled that borrowing). Proportionately Britons also held twice as many of their mortgages under rates that could be varied at the will of their lenders as were held by residents of any other European country by 2007. The most similar country, with half as many variable mortgage holders, then, was Italy.[68] The US and the UK, and to a lesser extent Singapore, New Zealand, Australia and Canada, were following more closely than most other rich countries a model that had led to doom before and was about to do so again. It is possible that exposure to the worldwide cult of celebrity has its worst effects on those who speak the language in which most movies are released, right-wing papers printed and contributing satellite television broadcasts made. Although it is debatable, speaking English may not be as particularly advantageous in the age of greed and high volume global trade as is often suggested.

Times of great inequality are typified by great excesses. The world's largest home (George Vanderbilt the Second's 255-room Biltmore Mansion) was first envisaged in 1895 and built when the very richest had even more wealth than the richest have today. It has yet to be replicated in opulence or arrogance, but larger and larger 'homes' were, until very recently, being built once again in the US. The largest equivalent built today is only a third of the size of Vanderbilt's and is marketed at 'just' US$135 million. It is in Aspen and is owned by Prince Bandar bin Sultan of the Al Saud Royal Family (nicknamed Bandar Bush for his close working relationship with former President George Bush the Second). It is a typical example of the extreme end of the housing market, a market in which, until very recently, both larger and larger properties were being built out of town, and former enormous townhouses were being converted back from flats to single homes, most commonly along some of the more pricey streets of the world's richest cities, such as London.[69] The effect of all this greed was to end up housing fewer people in these larger properties, forcing those progressively further and further down the social scale to occupy relatively smaller and smaller homes.

Across cities like London overcrowding rates have risen rapidly in recent years as the rich and super-rich have begun to occupy yet more and more square feet per person. Outside London in the nearby English countryside a trend in building country mansions began at a similar time, so that, as the housing shortage has risen, a small group at the top has never before had as much space, as many rooms, home gyms, home cinemas and swimming pools. Similar mansions were documented as being built, again until very recently, in and around New York. These were built to provide for celebrity lives that were last depicted as so crudely greedy during the era of the Great Gatsby (the summer of 1922).

About 100 English council-built family maisonettes could be fitted within the floor space of Bandar Bush's modern US mansion. The space ratio calculations are less dramatic within cities, but it is certainly not the poor or poor immigrants who take up most space. There is no overall lack of space to house people well in the rich world, but a huge lack of willingness. Among the relatively quite rich in the US (as even for many MPs in Britain by 2009), second home owning is now passé; the trend is to maintain four homes, flying into your fourth home, a mountain retreat in, say, Montana, for just a few days of the year.[70]

How did we end up accepting the afflictions of affluenza? Once it became normal at a certain income bracket to own a second home and inequalities continued to rise, it was only a matter of time before it became normal for a growing minority to own a third, then a fourth home. In those countries where inequalities in income and wealth were rising most quickly these could be: the family home, the city pad, the bach by the sea in New Zealand (a holiday home to escape from the northern winter for a few sunny weeks), and that house kept in London as an 'investment'. The bach could be rented out occasionally, and the London home might house tenants intermittently, but a couple (or one of those bachelors which gave those homes their name) could much more happily retire to a bach by the sea, a family could grow up in the London home (not in fear that it might be sold from under them), a city pad could be the permanent home of someone who both works and lives in the city. People could commute, or retire, and instead rent a property when they went on holiday or stay in bed and breakfast accommodation. However, rising inequalities, lax taxes and easy tax evasion made all these purchases appear to be good investments, until the economic crash came. People felt they deserved all those properties; they had 'worked hard' for them. If pressed, they thought, well, there are just too many people in the world, we can't house them all so why start with my 'homes'? Once you start to think like that, why worry about others, why pay taxes? It becomes what the British call 'a mug's game' to do what the Americans call 'the right thing'.

Limits to people or growth?

If you had a chance to avoid paying a little tax you might well take it; after all, what miniscule difference could your contribution make? It is thinking more and more like this that has contributed to make it acceptable from the 1980s onwards that authorities increasingly prosecute the poor when they are found to cheat social security systems but not others for the far greater sums stolen when people do not pay their taxes. Figure 19 shows just how clear the trends are. Data from Australia are used here but all of the more unequal affluent countries would show similar trends.

The idea that there is not enough space to house people and that there are too many to feed is an old one. The world's first salaried economist, the Reverend Thomas Malthus, was just one of many to dream up the idea that there were limits to how many people there could be, rather than limits to what people in total could consume. Shortly after the 1922 peak of global excess among the super-rich, but before the last crash, it was declared (in 1927) that, on reaching 104 million people, the US had surpassed its 'optimum'. This was according to some ornate and in hindsight clearly misguided mathematics credited to one Henry Pratt Fairchild. Then again shortly afterwards, just some seven years later but on the other side of the

Figure 19: Social security and taxation prosecutions, Australia, 1989–2003

Source: Redrawn from figures given in McMahon, W. (2008), Centre for Crime and Justice Studies, 'Graph of the month, London, personal communication, originally appearing as a graph in the *Journal of Social Policy*, and in a presentation on 'Welfare fraud, welfare fiction' by Greg Marston, Social Policy Unit, University of Queensland (www.bsl.org.au/pdfs/Greg_Marston_Welfare_ fraud&fiction_29Nov07_.pdf)

world, Sir John Megaw said that the population of India, which had expanded despite the famines that came with colonialism, had in 1934 reached its 'optimum' limit. Sir John became Director-General of Medical Services in India in 1930, and illustrated clearly how humans could be viewed as animals when he declared that the Indian population 'multiply like rabbits and die like flies'.[71] Sir John retired in 1939 and died 10 years after India secured independence. He is remembered for advocating air conditioning to be used across India.[72]

Places rarely suffer from having too many people, but frequently suffer from a few people taking far too much. By early 2008 it became evident that preceding the economic crash, the acquisition of most of the world's remaining available land was occurring at rates never seen before. Huge swathes were being bought up by a tiny number of the super-rich. Pop stars, celebrities and former presidents had bought up almost all the large ranches in places like Santa Barbara (California), forcing the rest of the population to live at the highest of densities ever seen there. Around London, up until at least February 2008, land prices in the South East were soaring for similar speculative reasons. Far away it was principally US money that was being used to buy great tracts of land in places like New Zealand, and according to at least one newspaper report, some 45% of the land area of Cambodia was 'seized' by property speculators in 2008 alone, along with two thirds of the British Virgin Islands.[73]

Celebrities do not just want land; they want the most valuable and rarest land. Riverside and shoreline, including a space to moor yachts, come at the highest premium. *The world with its billions does not have too many people, but it does have too many in their thousands who think that they are worth a million others.* Individually these people take up the space that used to house hundreds; they consume fossil fuels and other resources far less sustainably than thousands of others collectively consume, and they demand the time and labour and subservience of tens of thousands of others in mining for their needs, manufacturing for them and servicing them in a way that deprives millions more of the potential benefits of that labour. Just think of all the human work required to create the materials and technology needed to furnish a grand mansion, to kit out a large yacht or construct a private plane, and then you can begin to comprehend how just one of the world's many hundreds of billionaires, someone who can spend a couple of million dollars a day on leisure time outgoings, harms millions of other human beings *who in total* get by on less than that for *all* they need. Billionaires and multi-millionaires live in a state of luxury that could only be sustained, and can certainly only be justified, if they were a separate species. However, at the same time, the average reader of this book – who may be living what they think of as a modest life in comparison – is living the life of a king compared with most people in the world. When you read of the excesses of celebrity it is worth considering which aspects of your more ordinary life may appear just as excessive to most other people alive today. There is a continuum of insularity.

For the most affluent of celebrities even cupboards and closets can become pricey items requiring home alteration. Readers of popular accounts of the lives of the 21st-century super-rich can marvel at how some have come to require drycleaning factory-style conveyor belts to help organise their 400ft^2 walk-in closets.[74] Before dismissing such excess and greed as simply the acts of a few with far more money than sense, consider how numbers of self-storage facilities have shot up so frequently in recent years in towns across rich countries so that when moving home people can put their furniture and other possessions in storage. Or perhaps people can do this when they simply have a little too much, or inherit some stuff, or just want a little more space. Look at your own clothes and consider how often you are likely to wear any item before you throw it away. You may think it is many times; it is most likely to be on average just a dozen or so washes before, after languishing in your stuffed cupboards unloved for a few years, the garment is binned. If we wore our clothes until they began to wear out, then the global garment industry as currently arranged would collapse, only shortly after the demise of the fashion industry.

Clothing has mattered for a long time. We have not suddenly become fashion conscious, but many of us have suddenly been able to satisfy our desire for quantities of apparel that could only be dreamt of before. Adam Smith talked of the need for men to have good quality shoes and linen shirts to be able to hold their heads up high. Clothing was also a constant theme in the accounts of the century that followed his pronouncements. It was used to demarcate style and respectability; dress had to be correct. There was extensive theft of clothing as a result to preserve respectability and a '... large and sophisticated trade in second-hand clothing, the development of fashion styles in adornment and ornamentation'[75] across 18th-century Europe which, by the 20th century, became called 'accessorising'. But there were no 400ft^2 walk-in wardrobes even for Marie Antoinette, no purchasing and abandoning of garments so freely, no consumption that was quite so conspicuous as was seen in the last years of our most recent gilded age.

Purchasing new cars, clothes, homes and home decorations are not the most conspicuous acts of consumption of all. That label has been reserved for the purchasing of new looks for ourselves, new faces, breasts, noses.... By the start of the current century the British were reshaping themselves at only a tenth of the rate they were reshaping their homes, but still undergoing 2.5 million acts of cosmetic surgery a year out of a population of about 50 million adults in Britain, at a cost of about £5,000 a face lift.[76] Many more were having bits chopped off or sucked out and stuck together again in the US. The great increase in stomach stapling as obesity increased coincided with increases in starvation and hunger elsewhere as food prices also rose. The leading private plastic surgery company in Britain now follows a model from the US and offers its customers loyalty cards whereby they receive discounts on later operations (if they have enough procedures carried out in a specified period).[77] Liposuction and stomach stapling, taking laxatives and all manner of other tortures are now used to shrink our bodies when the search for instant gratification settles on food and then settles on looks, before we head off shopping again to make ourselves feel good ... before the money runs out.

The fear of not being recognised

Why do we idolise celebrity? Do we fear not being rewarded? Or fear not even being recognised as human? Above all else celebrities are recognised, not just literally, but financially. Their faces adorn hundreds of magazines in just one corner shop. They are the staple ingredient of the most watched television shows. Surveys in unequal affluent countries routinely report that '... ten-year-olds think the very best thing in the world is having money and being rich, followed by being famous'.[78] When one school teacher asked her primary school children what they wanted they too said, "to be famous"; when asked famous for what, they typically replied: "Dunno, I just want to be famous".[79] Another primary school teacher with a similar tale to tell said of her pupils and of their ambitions: "These kids don't know they're working class; they won't know that until they leave school and realise that the dreams they've nurtured through childhood can't come true".[80] Those most damaged by living through our times of greed have yet to grow old enough to experience all the repercussions. Already in North America one in seven adolescent girls report enough signs of serious depression for it to be clear that an upward trend in an epidemic of anxiety is occurring at the point, past primary school, when most young people suddenly realise that they will not be famous (see Figure 21, Chapter 7, page 276, this volume).

In a world in which celebrities are lauded, where the super-rich are so visible, where fat cat salaries are discussed as rational and lives of luxury presented as normal, it is easy to feel undervalued. When our labour is sold cheaply we rightly fear '... falling victim to the denial of human dignity which went together with such a sale...'.[81] Human dignity falls to its lowest under such circumstances where labour has no price on it at all, no worth. Housework is put in that category, as is much childrearing and care for the sick within families, but at least most families recognise their relatives as human.

In 2007, and again where greed has progressed furthest, in the US, researchers reported that they had scanned the brains of a sample of university students while simultaneously showing them photographs of people, including the homeless, to ascertain the degree to which the key part of their prefrontal cortex, the part which is normally active when empathy is felt, reacted at the point when each photograph was shown. The researchers were subsequently shocked to find that when the university students viewed photographs of people such as the homeless and drug addicts this stimulated no activity in the region associated with empathy at all. The suggestion was that typical US university students had come to consider this group of their fellow citizens to be less than human. This was a coping mechanism on behalf of the students that allowed them to carry on with their lives without having to think further and deeper. Fortunately, the researchers also reported finding that if a question was asked about the homeless people in the photographs being shown, such as 'what food do you think this beggar might prefer?', then the emotional part of the cortex began to become active again on the scanner.[82] The damage that had been done to these students was thus not irreversible.

Some young children, adolescents and students can be more damaged than others. We know now from empirical studies that people who in recent times have chosen to try to become economics students have tended (when assessed at the time they made that choice) to be both less cooperative than most and to be more self-interested individuals, according to psychological tests.[83] Other studies have found that on average those who take degrees in economics go on to express an even greater preference for selfish beliefs at the end of their courses than they did at the beginning; they become more self-interested.[84] It is quite likely that those who were most willing to believe what they were taught were more likely to get the higher grades, the starter jobs, to become policy advisers, to rise high in business or government and to accelerate the process. And a few did become famous. Where this takeover by the newly indoctrinated occurred, it did so with most vengeance in the 1980s, and the scars can be seen in the statistical record on inequalities in income and wealth, and the terrible outcomes later seen for mental health.

6.5 The 1980s: changing the rules of trade

When it comes to the distribution of wealth, it was in the early 1980s that the tide turned, and it turned in those countries where the rich won the debate over whether to increase inequality or not. In Britain inequality in wealth fell from the late 1920s through to 1981 when the richest 10% of people held an all-time low for their group of 'only' half of all the marketable wealth in that country.[85] The trend was similar in the US with wealth slowly becoming more evenly distributed, if still grossly unfairly awarded, year by year right through to the very early 1980s. Earlier, redistribution from rich to poor had come about because of progressive income taxation and effective inheritance tax, but also because wages for poorer people (including the US minimum wage) were higher in the past in real terms; unions were successful in fighting for workers' rights, rights which in the long term reduced wealth inequalities. The famous super-rich families of the gilded age saw their riches slowly whittled away, taxed away, wasted by their offspring and in a few cases given away. Crucially they were not immediately replaced by a new aristocracy of wealth. This did not occur until governments in Britain and the US changed in 1979 and 1980, and changed the very meaning of being fair. They followed the teachings of economists such as Milton Friedman associated with the University of Chicago, teachings first tested in Chile, New Zealand and Britain before being enacted in the US, with remarkable effect.

Two thirds of the wealth increases in the US in the 1980s and 1990s were in assets held by the richest single percentile of the population. By 2000 the wealthiest 1% of US citizens owned 40% of the wealth and the poorest 40% owned 1% of their country's wealth, that 1% shared out very thinly between them all. Thus those in the wealthiest single percentile of the population were each individually 1,600 times better off, on average, than two out of every five people walking on the streets that they were chauffeured past or which their private planes flew over.[86]

Holding on to your place on the hill

In 1980, average households in the US spent 11% of their disposable income simply on servicing two parts of their debts: the interest on their mortgage and the interest on their credit card debts. This does not include money spent actually paying those debts off, paying off and servicing other debts, or costs such as rent which can be seen as a debt for borrowing property. Once lease payments for cars were added, rental payments on tenant-occupied property, homeowners' insurance and property tax payments, most things that simply had to be paid (and which mostly did not pay off debts), the debt service ratio rose to almost 16% of annual disposable income. It is that ratio, called the overall financial obligations ratio (FOR), which shows by how much more North Americans became indebted in the mid- to late 1980s and mid-1990s onwards, and which is plotted in Figure 20.

For renters the FOR in 1980 was nearer a quarter of their annual income; for mortgage holders it was more like a seventh. It fell from 1980 through to the first quarter of 1984 as people spent less on things that might put them into further debt. But as the US and most of the rest of the rich world began to exit the mass unemployment legacy of the early 1980s recession, the ratio began to rise again, rose quickly and peaked at almost 18% in 1987. The housing market then slowed again and there was another, smaller, recession, but the debt servicing ratio never fell back below 16%. Debt servicing rose again from 1994, passed 18% in 2000, 19% in 2006, peaked at almost a fifth of average incomes being spent solely on interest and rent payments in 2007, and then began to fall back again in 2008 as the economic crash rapidly curtailed spending coupled with, at first, interest rates falling. The world is now awash with debt, and those debts increased most quickly, as Figure 20 shows, in the mid-1980s because it was

Figure 20: Debt payments as a percentage of disposable income, US, 1980–2008

Source: Derived from data provided by the Federal Reserve Board on required debt payments on mortgage and consumer debt, car lease payments, rental payments, insurance and property tax payments (www.federalreserve.gov/releases/housedebt/). For a series of just mortgage and consumer debt see Chart 1 in Foster, J.B. (2006) 'The household debt bubble', *Monthly Review*, vol 58, no 1 (www.monthlyreview.org/0506jbf.htm), or Table 6, pp 231-2, this volume.

then that we were told most often, most clearly and consistently, and with the least understanding of the implications, that 'greed is good'.

As the debts rose again in the late 1990s as a result of both 1980s deregulation and the 'greed is good' mantra spreading, something had to give. Poorer households became forced by other people's spending to have to spend more themselves just to maintain their social standing. Once others decided to rent a 'pad' in the city to reduce weekday commuting, the supply of rental property was reduced and its price increased. Once others decided to try with just a little more urgency to spend more to buy a house slightly higher up the hill, all house prices were shifted upwards. Again, a few more deciding that they 'needed' two or three or four homes more than before was crucial in ensuring that space was not opened up at the bottom due to aspiration rising so quickly at the top. Richer university students having homes bought for them by their parents, and not living at the kinds of densities students used to live at, also added to the squeeze, as did the influx from abroad of affluent bankers and other financial and service people into buzzing world cities like London. The largest single immigrant group in the centre of London consisted of people born in the US who lived in greatest concentration in some of the most expensive areas. In the most expensive of places in London, such as around Hyde Park, one seventh of all children living there were US-born, according to the 2001 Census.[87]

All this increased the cost of living further. It is affluent immigrants who take up space at the top. Poor immigrants squeeze into the cheapest of rented property at the bottom of any housing market and have many times less effect on prices and space than a single rich banking family does on its arrival in London from the US. All these pressures led to increasing and ever more insecure debt being amassed in affluent countries where inequalities had been allowed to rise rapidly. By 2008 it was reported that almost one in ten households in Britain had a mortgage for which they had agreed only to repay the interest. These households also had no other savings set up or being put away to repay the capital sum. Some 6% of married couples with dependent children had this kind of mortgage by 2007.[88] These mortgage holders were not and are not buying their homes; they are in effect renting with a fraction more security of tenure than renters usually enjoy. The situation in the US over mortgage lending is even worse than in Britain, and Figure 20 does not highlight this problem; it only shows interest payments and not the amounts required for debts to be run down. As debts increased in general and interest payments rose, less and less was actually being repaid. People were not simply being feckless in amassing this debt – many have had to amass it to be able to live in an average place, and even more were being constantly advised to get into debt.

Misselling, debt, exploitation and tribute

In Britain the Financial Services Authority (FSA) carried out mystery shopper surveys in 2005 and 2006 and found that *the majority* of financial advisers surveyed broke all eight of the basic rules laid down over misselling products such as those for 'equity release'.

Unsurprisingly (perhaps) the majority of financial advisers were simply interested in lining their own pockets and were happy to break every single one of the rules that they were expected to follow if they thought they would not be found out. Remarkably, when the Council of Mortgage Lenders reported these numbers they suggested that as few recipients knew how to complain or thought it was worth complaining about the awful service, then: 'It is important to put these negative views and images in perspective. Complaints to the Ombudsman about equity release products are limited'.[89] In other words the lenders admitted that misselling was taking place in most cases, but said it was not that bad as the customers did not appear to realise that they were being misled!

In the US writing about the predatory and unethical mortgage and loan industry is an academic staple. It provides many scholars with a livelihood. In looking for stories similar to those of misselling in Britain they find an abundance of '... evidence suggesting that subprime mortgage segmentation exacerbates rather than reduces traditional inequalities of denial–based exclusion'.[90] Thus being lent so much did not help the poor and did not get them out of ghettos, but for a short time it did make the rich much richer. During the 1980s in the US the top 1% more than doubled their share of national wealth while (when calculated in fixed 1995 dollars that adjust for inflation) the bottom 40% of households in the US, those who now have just one percentile of the total wealth to share among all of them, also saw their mean net wealth fall from US$4,000 on average in 1983 to US$900 by 1995.[91] They were robbed, and they were robbed first by being put into debt by the 1980s loan sharks who were presented as respectable bankers in suits helping them to enjoy a trickle down of wealth, then by increased material poverty in the 1980s recession, then through falling wages in real terms at the bottom. All this, coupled with rising inequality, led to it becoming necessary for those with even small savings to spend rather than save in the round. There was little point in having faith that the future would be better than the past and that meagre saving would be worthwhile; it wasn't. It turned out to be right to enjoy yourself when you could if you were not at the top. And not just for the poor in rich countries. The poor worldwide were being robbed too, just on a far grander scale

Internationally the poor countries of the world had to produce 40% more goods in 2006 as compared with 1977 to buy the same amount of similar goods from rich countries at each date. Simultaneously, between 1997 and 2006 the total debt of the domestic, business, government and finance sectors of the US rose by US$41.9 trillion (see Table 6 above). North Americans were not making more things to sell to afford what they purchased at ever greater discount abroad; instead they were borrowing more to afford it at those discounts. Given this it is hardly surprising that poor countries progressively received less back in return for what they sent in tribute. Increased global trade has increased inequalities not just between countries but also within poorer countries as well as within rich. Within 90% of Latin American countries (when measured between 1985 and 1995) it was the rich who benefited most from trade liberalisation.[92]

It was also during the 1980s that consumption in rich countries rose most steeply because the primary economic activity of some rich countries turned from 1970s manufacturing towards full-blooded 1990s finance. When a good is manufactured and sold at a profit, the ability to exploit others is limited in that the good has to physically exist, be physically transported to those who are to buy it, and it must work for at least a short period of time. This is if customers are to be enticed to produce yet more agricultural crops to buy the next offer. Clearly if the interest is in profit then what is sold should soon break down and have obsolescence inbuilt, or be designed to be destroyed (as in the case of the arms trade) in order for future sales to be guaranteed, but something actually has to be delivered. Financial services are not like this.

When financial services are provided people are given promises, often not even pieces of paper but electronically transferred pieces of a promise. These are promises to insure them and to pay up if there are great natural disasters, to satisfy the desire of others who feel a need to hedge their bets, insure their lives or livelihoods. You charge them far more than the risk for these things; you transfer funds electronically to pay for those misfortunes that do occur, it is true (unless you go bankrupt), but you transfer as grudgingly as you can if you really want to get rich very quickly, and you do not have to make a single actual widget. Nothing physical needs move from you to those you 'serve' for you to provide them with financial services. However, a huge amount needs to move physically in the opposite direction. Because you quickly make large profits when you convince others to buy your financial protection, to invest in your schemes, or simply just to deposit their little sums of wealth in your huge coffers, you quickly amass great sums of money to spend. To your offices in New York, London and Tokyo are sent all manner of tributes. These are not things that are usually needed, but you need to spend money.

Ensuring that the rains come

People gawped when the very first barrels of 'special' water arrived at the most prestigious of offices to be plugged into early 1980s water coolers, but soon every top office had one. It is only recently that people have criticised the water cooler as being environmentally lacking. What will some future archaeologist make of all those plastic water barrels that have ended up in 1980s and 1990s landfill sites? Will they assume that the public water system broke down? Will they ever find out that a few countries rigged the system in their favour by establishing reserve currencies,[93] and much else? The countries in which larger numbers of water coolers became affordable were those with reserve currencies.

Archaeology involves a great deal of head scratching. When the city at the centre of the ancient Chaco canyon civilisation of the southwestern US was being unearthed, the key question the diggers asked themselves was: what on earth had the city produced to justify its existence? It was placed in a canyon that provided insufficient space to produce food or goods to trade. There were no signs that advanced tools were manufactured in the city, or that it was a site for the exchange of goods to an extent that justified its size, opulent buildings and what appeared to have been a very large population. Eventually the archaeologists looked to ancient Rome and modern-day London to find the model that could explain its existence and persistence (until its environmental collapse in the 12th century). The city had existed on tribute. Food and goods had been sent to its inhabitants purely because of who they were, how they were venerated and presumably because of what powers they said they possessed.

Just as London bankers at the start of the 21st century said, 'send us your chattels and we will multiply them, trust us', priests of the 12th-century city of Chaco will have said, 'send us food and we will ensure the rains will come'. And the rains came. But the rains were eventually insufficient to grow everything demanded by those who ruled the temples at the heart of the city in the centre of the Chaco canyon. The Anasazi civilisation centred on Chaco is now only known from the signs left in the dirt and the stories told. 'Anasazi' literally means 'ancient people'.[94] The civilisation is thought to have ended because all tribute economies eventually result in environmental degradation too great to continue producing the tribute.

As the last of the Anasazi who had enjoyed that culture were dying of starvation, a third of the way around the world, in Lombard Street in London, the prototypes of the first international banks were being established with the help of immigrants from Lombardy. They were established to ease the trading of wool, just as the Medicis of Venice, the city in a swamp, grew rich first by facilitating the trading of textiles and only later through lending at supposedly discretionary interest rates (just as the Dutch did later). In low-lying London newly established bankers also grew rich from the debts of others. Much later, by 1740, these debts were being sold through 550 coffeehouses;[95] caffeine helped create an air of opulence and emboldened the spirit of the man about to borrow. Contemporaries such as Adam Smith (1723–90), seeing this, and with no knowledge of tales such as that of the Anasazi, wrote about how such debt-supported trade could only be for the good. It was the spirit of these times, and a forgetting of the lows, the bubbles and the crashes in between, that led in the 1980s to the rise in London and New York of a political new right who revelled in '… the rediscovery of the 18th century economics of Adam Smith'.[96] By 2006 the cost of even a modest home in the London banking borough of Westminster exceeded half a million pounds. It had taken just three decades from the rediscovery of Adam Smith and the re-veneration of banking, to its demands for tribute becoming unaffordable.

Entire countries have largely become tribute economies where people do very little of any real value but have to perform particularly intricate rituals to justify their existence while growing no crops, making nothing and helping no one. Being a tribute economy does not greatly benefit most citizens of these countries or most inhabitants of tribute cities (such as London and New York). The roads are not paved with gold as a result. It is only a tiny few at the top of these tribute systems who collect many more tithes than they can spend. Beneath them are lackeys who are mostly consigned to undertake work that is soul-destroying in its banality. This is the kind of work that economists label as 'transaction costs' (see the earlier discussion of the counting of beans at pages 234–7).

The taking up of so much of our money and time by transaction costs is not a new phenomenon. In 1970 almost half of US 'productivity' was transaction costs, most (55%) occurring between firms, while the proportion of sales workers in the US rose from 4% of all employees in 1900 to 12% of all by 2000.[97] If that rate of 'progress' were to carry on then a third of the US's great-grandchildren will be working in frontline 'sales' in future, another third will be counting the receipts, and the final third will be managing the others. This cannot possibly come to pass; *somebody somewhere has to do something of actual value.* What matters is not that it has to end, but how it unravels.

North Americans have yet to understand that most of what they think they own came about due to banking 'liberalisation' in the 1980s affecting what tribute they received from abroad. However, many are beginning to see that what is happening within their states is now unsustainable. Take for instance that rural green idyll, the one place that should be self-sufficient, Montana: '… half the income of Montana residents doesn't come from their work within Montana … Montana's own economy already falls far short of supporting Montana [which is] by and large dependent on the rest of the US'.[98] The half that this particular author refers to is made up partly of social security payments flowing in, but mainly of '… out-of-state pensions, earnings on real estate equity, and business income'. It is easy to see why it is now commonly understood that the entire country is in deficit if looked at in this way. The US does not support itself by its own labour or resources and could not possibly support its current rate of consumption and behaviour on its own; it *must* have 'free trade'. To those outside of the US this is trade which is often far from freely entered into and where much is not traded back from the free traders in return. In microcosm, Montana, despite its mountains, forests, mines and grasslands, could not support the average lifestyle of its population through what it could truly freely trade. This lack of sustainability is partly because of the lavish lifestyle of a minority of its most wealthy residents, but also because many other North Americans have come to think they can drive where they like and many think they can fly where they like, when they have already burnt almost all the oil under the land they live on. Those who currently consume most have most to give up. In such a situation it is easier to see how, like priests in the Chaco canyon, they try to cling on to their past beliefs to the last.

How it all unravels

Sustainable ways of living are likely to involve much greater social changes than a massive curtailment of air travel and the demise of the petrol engine. For instance it is only our current generation of human beings who do not as a worldwide majority live in villages, and it has been villages that have proved to be most sustainable as a form of settlement over time. Traditionally, village life means multigenerational living, in households that are home to several families. When people live in large households they each consume less on average, waste less, travel less and have less need to have recourse to the inefficiencies of the market to provide care for the young and old, or simply to find someone to fix things. When people help each other out, out of obligation and for regard rather than for purely financial reward, they are more likely not to do things which are not worth doing.

There can be much to be fearful about in returning to more village-like living, places where too many know your business, where women could be made subservient more easily, and communities in which strangers are more often feared rather than being the norm. Traditional villages are the very opposite of cosmopolitan living, yet despite this, a return in many ways to such social units, or larger village-like small eco-towns, is being repeatedly suggested by social activists as a valid proposal for a preferable '... social unit of the 21st century [as culture] has nothing to do with numbers'.[99] This is not so much a garden city movement, but one which sees cities as less of a necessity, since internet technology means that it is no longer essential to live in settlements of millions to be able to visit a theatre or to be able to read a specialist newspaper. The gross inefficiency of living in ones and twos in city apartments is now commonly calculated by mainstream scientists and reported on in the most respected of their journals.[100]

The 1980s saw the population revival of London and New York after decades of shrinking; people began to move into tiny apartments. Around the rich world the young flooded into the largest of cities again; city living and city jobs were lauded. Being single became normal for people of working age across all of London by 1991, then across much of the rest of Britain just a decade later. However, being single, living on your own, is expensive, and often lonely, but it became harder and harder not to live like this across the rich world. It has become the norm across all of Japan most recently. Only excessive tribute made such cell-like existences possible, because it is so economically inefficient to live alone. Monasteries with their monks in single cells also often survived on tribute, just as rich world cities do today. A monastic life can be a lonely life too. If we are to begin to move away from the 1980s trend towards isolation, we will have to start living together more.

In Britain, surveys undertaken in 2006 found that, when multiplied up, some nine million adults reported experiencing feeling lonely at weekends. Almost one in five people aged 55 and over admitted to regularly spending a full day without speaking to anyone. And although 'only' one in 50 people said they had no one to turn to in a personal crisis, the numbers of both single old and single young found to have died alone with no one claiming their bodies rose at this time.[101] The great cities we have created also happen to be places of great loneliness for many. Admitting you are lonely is only allowed in secret in columns entitled 'lonely hearts', or revealed in statistics on urban suicide,[102] but it is worth remembering loneliness when lauding cities.

Cities now cover just 2% of the earth's land surface, but house 50% of the population, who consume 75% of all resources and produce 75% of all human waste.[103] Because they are usually served by public transport they can appear environmentally friendly at first glance, but life within cities could simultaneously be so much less wasteful and more fulfilling. We commonly now *mistake our wants for our needs* and consider our way of living to be the only possible way, whereas the bricks and mortar of our homes would not disappear if we changed the rules of our lives. Suppose we moved away from a design for life based on amassing debt and then expecting others to finance our pensions through their debt payments. Suppose we introduced citizens' incomes, incomes where not just our pensions, but all our basic needs, for all of us, are met as a right from current expenditure, not from desperately hoped for future 'capital growth'.[104] How much of what we currently quietly despair of is simply supported by a mirage of inevitability? To what extent have:

> … we in the developed world … completely lost track of the connection between the practical need to have a home and what it communicates about our social significance to others[?] To a remarkable extent, the price we pay for our inflated borrowings is far greater than the monthly direct debit. Suppose for a moment that you had no mortgage, and no one else you know did…. You would be able to walk away from jobs or careers that had no intrinsic value to you. You would be liberated from the pressure to keep up with the Joneses by having a home in the right street, decorated in ways that will impress them…. The truth is that it is the rich who mainly benefit from so much of our capital and income being tide up in housing. They can afford to buy homes for their children and benefit far more than the rest of us from inflated property values … but they unite the size, number and grandeur of their homes with their fragile identities.[105]

Greed has benefited the rich materially, but it has not made a better world for them to live in. It has not led to their families being much happier as compared with previous generations, or to their children and partners trusting them any more than anyone else would trust a person who is so greedy. The most serious and long-term deadly outcome of rising inequality is that, as inequalities rise, the rich (who argue that inequality is good) become politically stronger and their arguments gain ground. Seeing inequality as a necessary evil is bad enough; seeing it as the solution is worse. Seeing inequality as unnecessary for human beings to live well requires a change in core beliefs as great as that which priests who begin to doubt their own religion usually cannot stomach. It is not the greedy we should fear – we can all be greedy – but those who carry on preaching that there is good in greed. They are likely to continue doing so long after they have stopped believing it themselves, because they can see no alternative.

7

'Despair is inevitable': health and well-being

Human beings are not mentally immune to the effects of rising elitism, exclusion, prejudice and greed. They react like rats in cages to having their social environments made progressively more unpleasant. It is because we can now measure how humans have reacted and where they have reacted most badly that many now claim with great conviction that all the injustices and inequalities which underlie most rich societies are having a 'dose-response' effect on the mental well-being of populations: the greater the dose of inequality the higher the response in terms of poor mental health.[1]

In this penultimate chapter, Section 7.1 brings together new evidence to show how there appears to have been an especially strong rise in depression among children living in the most unequal of affluent countries, as recorded from the mid-1980s and throughout the 1990s. This is yet another new finding which suggests that poor mental health among affluent nations is worst in the US and least common where social inequalities are lowest. It suggests strongly that it is being brought up (and living through life) in more unequal environments that increases recorded poor mental ill health most strikingly.

The mechanism behind the worldwide rise in diseases of despair is suggested, in Section 7.2, to be the anxiety caused by particular forms of competition. School children's mental health appears most damaged as they are given progressively more and more examinations to undertake. The effects of the advertising industry in making both adults and, especially, children feel inadequate (if they are not constantly competing to consume more) are also documented here and many of the latest calls from all quarters – from psychiatrists to psychologists to archbishops – to curtail that advertising are listed.

The powerful have little immunity from the effects of despair if they live in more unequal countries. The most detrimental damage to ill health is found near the geographical hearts of the problem – the widest health inequalities in rich countries are to be seen within the very centres of London and New York. Section 7.3 shows this and also illustrates the fractal geography that results from psychological damage and social inequality. Section 7.4 illustrates just what kind of 'bird-brained' thinking was required to get us into this situation and how such thinking has continued throughout the economic crash despite its credibility having come to an end. It is not just that the mental health of human beings is damaged as social injustices increase, but our collective capacity to think well and work well together to do the right thing is also clearly much harmed. Under high levels of inequality great untruths become presented as truths and much effort (that could otherwise have been spent for good) is either used for harmful purposes, is wasted outright or is exerted by many trying to explain that some particular rise in inequality is not some great achievement.

Finally, Section 7.5 documents the rise in mass medicating of populations that has resulted from this situation in the context of a very brief history of psychiatric prescribing practices. The pressure on pharmaceutical giants now to make a profit is so great that if a pill was discovered that would cure mental illness with one dose, it would almost certainly have to be destroyed. However, it is unlikely that such an effective 'happy pill' could exist. The human condition (drive, questioning, angst and concern) means that we cannot always be happy, but learning to live better with each other is beginning to be seen as the key to learning to live better within our own minds, to be happier or at least more at ease with ourselves. Not making children anxious, tearful, fearful and stressed in the first place is the best place to start. By looking to see in which places children are most anxious we can also begin to see what might underlie the problems of adults who grew up under different social regimes.

7.1 Anxiety: made ill through the way we live, a third of all families

There are dangers in all shapes and sizes; it is the little numbers you have to look out for. The danger of saying that a certain proportion of children or adults suffer a particular mental illness is that it sustains the fantasy that everyone else is fine. All but the psychopathic have an '... innate need for social connection and egalitarian community',[2] and it has been shown that psychosis (mental ill health) is a natural human reaction to being deprived of the sustenance of that need. Being deprived of feeling valued, connected together to others as equals, makes us mentally ill. Evidence is now emerging that psychosis is normal behaviour for the human social brain when living under social isolation. Psychiatrists now suggest that our brains have developed in a way that means we cannot cope when not treated as equals.[3] The effects on our psychological states of mind of living in some of the most unequal of times in the most unequal of places have recently been recorded as enormous, so great in fact that we have become normalised to mental ill health. In Britain: 'According to the respected Psychiatric Morbidity Survey, one in six of us would be diagnosed as having depression or chronic anxiety disorder, which means that one family in three is affected'.[4]

Mixed anxiety and depression is the most common mental disorder in Britain, with almost 9% of people meeting the criteria for diagnosis. Between 8% and 12% of the population in Britain experience depression in any year. Women are more likely to have been treated for a mental health problem than men (29% compared with 17%). A quarter of women will require treatment for depression at some time, compared with a tenth of men. Women are twice as likely to experience anxiety as men. Of people with phobias or obsessive compulsive disorders, about three fifths are female. One in ten children between the ages of 5 and 15 has a mental health disorder. And the figures for the US are worse.[5]

In Britain around a fifth of children have a mental health problem in any given year, and about a tenth at any one time. Rates of mental health problems among children increase as they reach adolescence. Disorders affect 10.4% of boys aged 5–10, rising to 12.8% of boys

INJUSTICE

aged 11–15, and 5.9% of girls aged 5–10, rising to 9.7% of girls aged 11–15. Not all mental disorders have their origins in the way we live, but the way we live greatly affects how we are able to live with people suffering all kinds of distress or confusion and whether we exacerbate or mitigate suffering. At the other end of the age range to children, as the number of older people increases, the total number of people with dementia in the UK is forecast to rise to over one million by 2051.[6]

Anxiety in adolescence

Studies undertaken since 1974 have found a rise in what are known as 'conduct problems' among British children aged 15 and 16, accelerating in the 1990s and providing '... evidence for a recent rise in emotional problems'[7] among these children. The conduct problems included in these studies were a propensity to be involved in fighting, bullying, and/or stealing, lying, disobedience, fidgeting, restlessness, inattention and fearfulness of new situations. This particular study found that for both boys and girls the increase in these problems had been substantial, with faster rises between 1986 and 1999 than those found in earlier years.

The proportion of British children with severe problems doubled over the period 1974–99. The increase in the number of children suffering emotional problems was even starker, with almost all the increase having occurred since 1986. An earlier study of children in Scotland found similar results, with rising levels of distress from 1987 to 1999 but concentrated among girls and most acutely felt among the *most affluent* of girls. Overall, by the start of the 21st century, a third of adolescent girls in Scotland were reporting symptoms of being depressed as compared with just over a sixth in 1987. The fact that these figures are so high is in all probability related to the part of Scotland where the study was undertaken, a part which also has one of the highest rates of anti-depressant prescription levels for those aged 15 and over. A tenth of the entire population of Greater Glasgow were being given an anti-depressant dose-a-day by 2006 (see Section 7.5). The researchers of this study of adolescents reported that a significant relationship was found between these children's distress and how near to school examinations they were when surveyed again, in 1999. The authors of the same study concluded that it was changes in society that had harmed the mental health of so many adolescents, not any increase in sensitivity.[8]

Recently contrasting research was reported which suggested that there was no epidemic of increased anxiety in adolescents. Here I use the same data from this research to suggest that there is. This research, published in 2006, reported on 26 studies producing some 45 data points (each point being a rate of mental illness reported for a particular group of children at a particular time). The conclusion of the authors of the study was that there was no long-term rise to be seen in the rates of depression being reported. However, the authors had taken studies from a wide range of countries.[9] The full set is shown in Table 7. If a subset of their studies is selected, just those studies undertaken on children living in North America, then a different trend results. In North America rates have more than doubled since 1984, one extra adolescent girl in ten suffered symptoms of depression by the start of the current century as compared with two decades earlier; 14% prevalence rates are projected for 2008 and are the highest recorded in Figure 21, as compared with rates of around 4% being reported in 1988. Thus one in seven adolescent girls in North America now suffer mental ill health, as compared with possibly as few as about one in 25 of their mothers' generation at their age.[10]

Figure 21 is constructed by taking those studies that reported depression rates for girls aged between 13 and 18 and which were undertaken in countries in North America. These studies were mainly undertaken in the US, but two were based in Canada and one in Puerto Rico. The average year in which the adolescents' state of mental health was being assessed is calculated as the average of the study group birth years plus their average ages at interview. The collection of 16 studies shown in Figure 21 suggests a rise in rates of depression as diagnosed among girls in their teenage years. The Pearson product-moment correlation coefficient of the strength of the rise with time is 0.56 ($p=0.024$). That 'p' value means that there is a 2.4% chance that there is no relationship over time, or to put it another way, a 97.6% chance the rates really are rising. The data are not sufficient to be sure with much precision how quickly rates are

Table 7: Studies of adolescent depression available for meta-analysis, 1973–2006

Study number	Place	Year of birth	Age at interview	Obs	Rates (%) Age<13	Rates aged 13-18 (%) Both	Girls	Boys
1	*Isle of Wight	1954-55	14-15	483		3.2		
2	USA	1965-74	10-20	776	2.5	3.7	7.6	1.6
3	USA	1965-74	10-20	776		3.1		
4	USA	1966-75	15-24	1,769		7	12.4	1.5
5	USA	1966-75	15-24	1,769		13	21.5	4.4
6	Canada	1966-79	6-16	2,852	0.6	1.8	2.3	1.2
7	Puerto Rico	1968-80	4-16	386				
8	*USA	1969-74	14-18	1,710		2.9	3.8	2
9	USA	1969-74	14-18	1,710		3.2	3.7	2.6
10	*USA	1971-72	13	792	1.8	2.1	2.2	2.1
11	New Zealand	1971-72	15	792		2.8	4.4	1.2
12	USA	1971	8	70	1.5			
13	USA	1976	12	70	1.5			
14	USA	1980	17	70		5.7		
15	USA	1973-77	7-11	300	0.8			
16	USA	1973-77	12-17	300		5.4		
17	USA	1973-81	9-17	336	3.4	6	5.6	6.4
18	USA	1973-81	9-17	542	0.7	2.1	3.4	0.8
19	USA	1974-82	9-17	1,285				
20	USA	1974-83	8-16	2,762	0.4		2.4	2.1
21	Netherlands	1975-80	13-18	780		3.6		
22	Canada	1975-82	12-19	1,847	2.6		12.5	6.2
23	New Zealand	1977	15	986		6.3	9.2	3.3
24	New Zealand	1977	18	1,011		18.2	26.5	9.7
25	Switzerland	1978-82	15-19	203	0.6	5.3	9.8	1.1
26	USA	1978-83	12-17	4,023			13.9	7.4
27	Switzerland	1978-87	7-16	1,964	0.3		2.4	0.0
28	Sweden	1979-81	16-17	231		1.4	2.2	0.6
29	*USA-Anglo	1979-82	12-15	558		4.3	4.5	4.0
30	*USA-African-American	1979-82	12-15	665		6.1	6.5	5.7
31	*USA-Mexican-American	1979-82	12-15	429		9.0	11.4	6.3
32	*Japan	1979-82	12-15	494		1.3	0.9	1.8
33	Germany	1980-83	14-16, 16-19	1,395		8.0	10.2	5.8
34	USA	1980-84	9-16	4,984	1.9	3.1	4.2	1.9
35	USA	1980-84	9-16	1,691	1.1	3.0	4.2	1.9
36	Finland	1981	8-9	278	3.2			
37	Finland	1981	8-9	278	5.9			
38	Finland	1981	8-9	255	7.8			
39	Finland	1981	8-9	180	4.7			
40	Australia	1981-92	6-17	3,597	2.3	4.0	4.7	3.4
41	Puerto Rico	1982-96	4-17	1,886	2.1	5.8	9.7	2.0
42	Great Britain	1984-94	5-15	10,438	0.3	2.5		
43	Brazil	1986-89	11-14	625	0.2	1.9		

Study number	Place	Year of birth	Age at interview	Obs	Rates (%) Age<13	Rates aged 13-18 (%) Both	Girls	Boys
44	Brazil	1990-93	7-10	625	0.2			
45	*USA	1990-93	11-12	508	3.0			

Notes: * Country of study not obvious from article title or journal. It is assumed that the final study was located in Seattle assuming the reference in the source is to: Vander Stoep, A. et al (2005) 'Universal emotional health screening at the middle school transition', *Journal of Emotional and Behavioural Disorders*, vol 13, no 4, pp 213-23. In the graph the two results from one study (4 and 5) are excluded because the figures reported in the original article are for 15- to 16-year-olds only, not 15-24-year-olds as reported above, and rely on 12-month recall under a diagnosis method which reports higher rates in general: composite international diagnostic interview (see Kessler, R.C. and Walters, E.E. [1998] 'Epidemiology of DSM-III-R major depression and minor depression among adolescents and young adults in the National Comorbidity Survey', *Depression and Anxiety*, vol 7, pp 3-14). If rates were not reported for girls or boys separately, or at all, in the original source they are also not shown here.

Source: Costello, E.J. et al (2006) 'Is there an epidemic of child or adolescent depression?', *Journal of Child Psychology and Psychiatry*, vol 47, no 12, pp 1263-71, Table 1.

rising. The rise of about 0.46 points per year (10 percentage points in 22 years) has an approximate confidence limit around it of plus or minus 0.37 per year. It is thus unlikely to be zero, but it could be much lower than 0.46, or it could be substantially higher. Furthermore, weighting by the number of observations in each study increases the strength of the estimated annual increase slightly, to 0.53 points per year. However, if we include studies from the US alone, the estimated chance that the rate is definitely rising falls to just below 95% given the slightly smaller number of studies. For boys there is only a 0.42 correlation coefficient ($p=0.108$) and thus 'only' an 89.2% chance that the rate is rising. Studies usually require a higher chance than this to be taken seriously. So let us just talk about the girls for now.

National context is key

The original meta-analysis of many studies that formed the basis for this repeat study came to the opposite conclusion to that shown here. Its authors suggested that there was no rise over time. They made this suggestion because they thought that it was fine to include all affluent countries as they assumed all such countries provided at similar times sufficiently comparable environments for children growing up. Countries outside North America mainly studied their children in later years, and so in the original study in later years the

Figure 21: Adolescent girls assessed as depressed (%), North America, 1984–2001

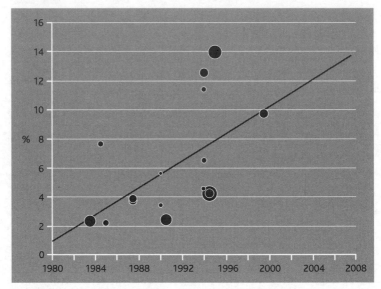

Note: Each circle represents a study; the area of the circle is drawn in proportion to study size. See Table 7 for the details of when and where each study took place.

Source: Re-analysis of Costello, E.J. et al (2006) 'Is there an epidemic of child or adolescent depression?', *Journal of Child Psychology and Psychiatry,* vol 47, no 12, pp 1263-71. The data shown above are for those studies where the children lived in the US, the US territory of Puerto Rico, or Canada (excluding one study that used different diagnosis methods from the other 16, see notes to Table 7). Those included are study numbers: 2, 6, 8, 9, 10, 17, 18, 20, 22, 26, 29, 30, 31, 34, 35 and 41.

authors included studies from Australia, Brazil, Finland, Germany, Japan, the Netherlands, New Zealand, Sweden and Switzerland where, in many cases, the rates reported for children in these age groups were lower than those found in North America. Apart from Brazil, all these countries are also more equitable than is almost all of North America. In earlier years most of the studies available to the original meta-analysis used samples of girls assessed in North America.

Given that we have only recently begun to understand how crucial differences in human geographical context are to social well-being it is not surprising that the authors of the original meta-analysis that Figure 21 is derived from assumed that they could pool studies from different countries. One study they included, itself reporting in 2001, found that the rates of adolescents suffering major depression without (and with) impairment were: in the US 9.6% (and 4.3%) for Anglo-American children aged 12–15, 13.4% (and 6.1%) for African-American children, 16.9% (and 9.0%) for Mexican-American children, and for children compared in the same way living in Japan: 5.6% (and 1.3%) respectively. That study suggested that these huge differences, with Mexican-American children living in the US being seven times more likely to suffer major depression with impairment than Japanese children living in Japan all '... disappeared after sociodemographic adjustments ... [concluding that] ethnicity does not have a significant impact on the risk of adolescent major depression after sociodemographic adjustments'.[11] The implication of this finding is not that it is fine to compare children living in different countries, but that the sociodemographic differences between the lives of children living in different countries are so great that those differences can account for such great inequalities between countries. The children living in Japan are excluded from the re-analysis above, as are all other children not living in North America.

Feeling safe and connected

The above re-analysis of data for this volume, suggesting that depression in adolescents is rising in unequal affluent countries, is itself taken from (and hence refutes) a study reporting no increase. It is backed up by many other studies. For adults it is well known that in the US those born after 1955, as compared with those born before 1915 (when tested at the same ages), are up to ten times more likely to found to be suffering major depression, and that similar, if less extreme, trends have been reported from studies undertaken within Sweden, New Zealand, Germany and Canada.[12] Given these rises it would be surprising if the rates for adolescents had not been rising, but the implications of the most recent rises are clearly that worse could be to come.

We know from other studies that the average North American child by the late 1980s was already more anxious about life than some 85% of North American children in the 1950s. In fact the *average* North American child has become more anxious than child psychiatric patients in the 1950s in the US. The reasons found for this have been the collapse of a safe society and an increase in environmental dangers as perceived by children. By 2000 it was said that economic factors had so far played only a little role in explaining these trends. The study that reported these findings concluded that: 'Until people feel both safe and connected to others, anxiety is likely to remain high'.[13] That was written eight years before the economic crash. All these studies either show that rates of anxiety and depression are rising in children in North America and in Britain, or in the one confounding case they once again show that same upwards trend when that one study is re-analysed to avoid mostly comparing rates in North America from earlier studies with rates from Europe and Japan found later.

What is driving the increase in adolescent despair, particularly in North America, but also in Britain? In Britain a remarkably similar proportion of around one in seven children reported in recent official government surveys that they often felt sad or tearful, were often anxious or stressed. Those receiving free school meals due to poverty were, unsurprisingly, slightly more likely to say this,[14] but not very much more likely than the rest. In recent years something has been making children feel worse in these particularly unequal of rich countries.

7.2 Competition: proposing insecurity as beneficial

Why should rates of depression be rising among children? What is it about their environments, especially in North America, which has caused not just more adults, but many more children, to become depressed? There is a mix of reasons, but it is worth looking first at those who have said that their actual aim is to make people anxious, especially to make children anxious. These groups are found in that part of commercial industry whose very purpose is to make children in rich countries insecure: advertising. An advertising agency president recently helpfully explained that: 'Advertising at its best is making people feel that without their product, you're a loser. Kids are very sensitive to that.... You open up emotional vulnerabilities, and it's very easy to do [that] with kids because they're the most emotionally vulnerable'.[15] This president is no lone voice; a year after her words were published another advertiser, in 2003, explained: 'In our business culture, children are viewed as economic resources to be exploited, just like bauxite or timber'.[16]

The fact that advertisers behave in ways that deliberately have detrimental effects on the mental health of children is not some secret knowledge of conspiracy theorists. In Britain in 2007 the BBC reported that: 'Children see some 10,000 TV adverts a year and recognize 400 brands by age 10, Children's Secretary Ed Balls says'.[17] The most recognised symbol is the twin arches of McDonald's, which 70% of British three-year-olds recognise. Less than half of these children know their own surname, but they know Mr Mc's.[18] The head of the established church in England in 2008 explained (in his own press release) that more and more research has found that advertising on television is harming children, making them harmfully competitive, and promoting what he called 'acquisitive individualism' to such an extent that: 'Evidence both from the US and from the UK suggests that those most influenced by commercial pressures also show higher rates of mental health problems'.[19] The situation is far worse in the US where exposure to the harmful effects of commercialisation has been so much greater that the young adult population can now be described as having been *marinated* in the mentally stultifying stuff of advertising.[20]

Fostering acquisitive individualism

Advertising grew first and grew most strongly in the US out of work undertaken to study how best to produce propaganda in wartime and later in public relations. Arguments for using propaganda to alter consciousness in peace-time can be traced to around the time of men like Walter Lippmann (1889–1974). Walter Lippmann was a colleague of Edward Bernays (1891–1995), the man credited with the creation of the industry of public relations. Lippmann worked for the US government helping to manufacture propaganda during the First World War. As a result of those experiences Lippmann came to believe that the 'manufacture of consent' must become a '… self-conscious art and regular organ of popular government. The whole process would be managed by a "specialized class" dedicated to the "common interests" of society … the key role of the new public relations industry was to keep society in the dark'.[21] Modern-day advertising aimed at children grew out of this and is no less sinister. The adverts never say 'this toy is no fun; you'll be bored with it in minutes, why not go play in the park'. There are very simple reasons why those who run businesses and favour competition see advertising as essential. People cannot be allowed to be too happy, as (in the most consumer-orientated societies) if they are satisfied with their lot, they might slow down their consumption. If people were '… allowed to follow old routines and stick to their habits, [it] would spell the death knell of the society of consumers, of the consumer industry, and of consumer markets…. Consumer society thrives as long as it manages to render the *non-satisfaction* of its members (and so, in its own terms, their unhappiness) *perpetual*. The explicit method of achieving such an effect is to denigrate and devalue consumer products shortly after they have been hyped into the universe of the consumers' desires'.[22] Today archbishops preach against advertising, psychologists proselytise for an advertising-free world, philosophers ponder on its harm in their writing, all while it remains the bread and butter of business, especially of public relations.

It is an open secret that it is the job of many people to make us and our children feel uncomfortable, to develop a feeling of failure, of lacking. What is less well known is that, while women record the highest rates of depression (both as girls and as adults), when the results are fatal it is men who are many times more affected. Figure 22 shows, calculated over a 140-year period, the chances of men dying as compared with women, by age and by their decade of birth. It is based on data taken from all the rich nations of the world and combined. These are all the nations rich enough to afford to have systems of recording mortality rates that were reliable at each point in time. What the figure shows is that right across the rich world, for the most recent cohort born in the 1970s, by the time they reached their twenties men had become three times more likely to die than women of the same ages.

Figure 22: Male:female mortality ratio by age in the rich world, 1850–1999

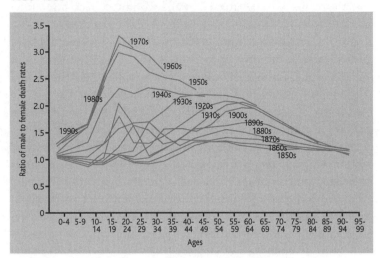

Note: Each line refers to the cohort born in the decade it is labelled by. The X-axis gives the age of cohort members. The Y-axis gives how many more times a man of that age born in that decade is likely to die in a year as compared with a woman living in the same set of countries born at the same time and of the same age.

Source: Original figure given in Rigby, J.E. and Dorling, D. (2007) 'Mortality in relation to sex in the affluent world', *Journal of Epidemiology and Community Health*, vol 61, no 2, pp 159-64, sample size one billion people.

The manufacture of consent

Figure 22 shows that at first the rises in mortality inequality between the sexes began in old age for men born in the 1890s as compared with those born in the 1880s (Bernays' generation as compared to Lippmann's), those later-born men being encouraged to take up smoking when mass-produced cigarettes became available in their twenties, and so more often dying a little earlier than women 40 years later. In this case it was because women were not usually permitted to smoke (at first) that a difference in mortality later emerged. Similar differences occurred at young ages for those born at times that meant they would be young adults in wartime. However, it was to be born in the 1940s and 1950s and especially later that had the greatest *relative* detrimental effect on men. This was long after the birth cohorts for whom childbirth had been made much safer.

281

Men born in the 1940s and more especially in the 1950s were particularly likely to be affected by the worldwide recession of the mid-1970s, and later generations by the recessions of the early 1980s and 1990s. The source from which this diagram is drawn looks in greater detail at the timings to confirm this. Being brought up in societies which increasingly labelled you as 'failing', and then being also seen to have failed in the labour market, a market that became ever more competitive, was sufficiently deadly for men to cause changes in mortality ratios greater than those seen either at the height of the smoking epidemic or during wars. There were many ways in which young men in rich countries began to die at greater rates than women: suicide, accidental overdoses, fights, road accidents, even cirrhosis. And the health and welfare services (which might have looked after those whose early deaths were more preventable) were also beginning to fail due to competition in recent years so that almost all adult men of almost all ages up to at least 70, in any given year, are now (across the rich world) twice as likely to die as are women of their age. Men react worse to competition. Men suffer far more than women from a prevailing belief that when they fail in competition no one will be there to help.[23] Competition is greatest in the US where health and social care is so often found to be the worst among affluent nations. Competition and care are in many ways opposite ways of behaving, with very different outcomes as a result.

Someone there to help?

Every year around 100,000 people die prematurely in the US simply because of a lack of basic medical care, not care they did not seek, but care they were denied. This is three times the numbers who died there of AIDS in the early years of the current century. Those who revealed these facts found it hard to cope with the lack of interest they received. They wrote: 'Any decent person should be outraged by this situation. How can we call the United States a civilised nation when it denies the basic human right of access to medical care in time of need? No other major capitalist country faces such a horrendous situation'.[24] But no other capitalist country believes so ardently in competition. Rising competition not only causes more deaths but also helps prevent the efficient treatment of diseases that, if not treated, lead to early death. *Competition is inefficient.*

Some types of competition are more inefficient that others. Private medicine is found to be inefficient by every decent study carried out on it. The UN Research Institute for Social Development (based in Geneva) confirmed recently that it was the spending of a significantly higher proportion of money on state healthcare, rather than private healthcare, which marked out countries where life expectancy was high and infant mortality low. Spending on private or even charitable health services was counter-productive.[25] It is even counter-productive for the rich.

Very wealthy people do not necessarily get good healthcare. When they are ill they become surrounded by people who have an interest in keeping them alive, but such an interest is not the same thing as providing good healthcare. The ideal patient from the point of view of private medicine is one who is very ill for a very long time, who requires constant treatment and the injection, inhalation and ingestion of very many expensive drugs. It makes sense for private physicians to scour the bodies of their most affluent patients particularly thoroughly in search of any malady that can be further investigated and treated, and then the side-effects of those treatments can also be treated. Ideal private patients are ones in a coma as they do not object to the way in which they are being used. As a result death is a very private thing in most of the US. In many states death records are not public, as they are in much of Europe, and the last years of the lives of the very rich are generally hidden from view, although they can be pieced together from their hospital receipts which detail every needle put in their carcass, every exploratory invasion of their bodies, every operation, even every meal they are sold.[26]

Private medicine may not improve the lives of the rich very much but it does deprive the poor from receiving some of the most basic of services from doctors because it diverts these doctors from doing their job. The wealthy in the US only receive the pampering that they mistake for a good health service because so many others there have no health service at all. Similarly, wealthy North Americans can only live in homes built and serviced by so many servants that they appear as palaces because so many other North Americans do not even have the right to have their rubbish collected by a government agency.[27] Being surrounded by people paid to be sycophantic, to crawl or to otherwise suck up, does not add greatly to the well-being of the rich, but it does deprive others of the potentially useful labour of all these people. Amazingly it is often suggested in Britain that ideas on introducing markets, even health markets, be brought over from the US!

Introducing a little competition and a market-based system into state healthcare is dangerous. More competition is being introduced into the NHS, especially its variant in England. In England between 2002 and 2005 the number of GPs rose by an extra one for every 25,000 people. However, in the poorest fifth of areas an extra GP was only provided for every 35,700 people, whereas in the least deprived areas an extra GP was made available for every 18,500 people. The poorest areas had the lowest number of doctors per head to begin with, and the least poor areas had the most. Somehow the NHS administrators managed to further widen the inequality, despite having more resources to share out in the shape of some 2,000 extra doctors to be deployed in just these three years. In 2008 England's Department of Health proudly published the graphs that these figures were derived from to show how well it was monitoring the situation as part of its evidence-based drive to reduce inequalities in health.[28]

7.3 Culture: the international gaps in societal well-being

Insecurity is not good. Being told you have to compete rather than work together is not good. Introducing private markets into state healthcare is not good. The 'notion that market price is the only measure of value [is] "crass, offensive and contrary to human beliefs and actions". Price based on scarcity does not reflect the value of a commodity to human life, as "the low valuation of water and the high valuation of diamonds" shows'.[29] However, even 'health and safety' inspectors are now being told by their political masters that they must see making money as something they should encourage. If some form of making money is detrimental to health and safety why encourage it? The 'economic progress' seen as paramount in the US has in recent years been inflicted ever more forcibly on people in the UK to the point whereby British health and safety and other regulators are now told by Her Majesty's Government that '… regulators should recognize that a key element of their activity will be to allow or even encourage economic progress'.[30]

Ultimately, if you want people to compete you have to keep them needy. Otherwise most people in rich countries come to realise that there is enough to go around. Over two centuries ago, among those with power who thought that there was too little to go around to cater for all, it was becoming widely recognised that: '[Slavery] … is attended with too much trouble, violence, and noise, … whereas hunger is not only a peaceable, silent, unremitted pressure, but as the most natural motive to industry, it calls forth the most powerful exertions…. Hunger will tame the fiercest animals, it will teach decency and civility, obedience and subjugation to the most brutish, the most obstinate, and the most perverse'.[31] Just over a century ago in London, those again in positions of power had refined what kind of a wage they saw as needed: 'The ideal wage, therefore, must be sufficient to persuade a man to offer his labour, but insufficient to allow him to withdraw it for more than a few days. Capitalism thus replaces the whip of the overseer with the lash of a more terrifying slave-driver — hunger'.[32] Today we have the advertising of fast food that makes people hungry, and the results are obesity and heart disease. It is time to stop making people hungry.

Mental despair and the imagined need to consume more and more to try to avert it are greatest where politics is rendered most meaningless, where it has been captured by those with the most power and money. That sense of meaninglessness is enhanced when the news media is almost totally controlled by a small number of men, such as very rich businessmen in the US, or a few communist party bosses in China. As in both the US and China, the more advertising and other propaganda people are exposed to, the more they are told that individually they need to be wealthy and collectively they need to support economic growth. The more that public opinion and debate is almost totally controlled by a small elite with a tiny number of carefully vetted people allowed to speak, those drawn from the 'top' couple of universities, from the dominant party or party-pair, the more 'positional competition and success are celebrated relentlessly',[33] then more and more the idea of being a loser will come to cross everyone's mind.

The poison of capitalism

Despite the recent heart attack striking their twin beating hearts, world finance continues to be utterly dominated by London and New York. The large majority of the world's hedge funds were organised from these two cities in 2007, although some four fifths were registered in tax havens like the Cayman Islands. The derivative markets in these two centres were worth US$7 trillion a day by 2007; two days' trading was the equivalent of the annual US GDP.[34] And almost all commentators agreed by then that these excesses were harmful, that the speculators were harming rich countries as well as poor. In 2005 the Deputy Chancellor of Germany said of the London and New York-based speculators: 'Some financial investors spare no thought for the people whose jobs they destroy. They remain anonymous, have no face, fall like a plague of locusts over our companies, devour everything, then fly on to the next one'.[35] These words appeared in a German newspaper and resulted in the response in the *Wall Street Journal* from a hedge-funded chief executive who claimed that at least the North Americans and British bankers were '… bringing a measure of capitalism to Germany'.[36] As a result of that particular little poisoned spoonful of capitalism, the GDP of Germany was reported to have fallen by 3.8% in just the first three months of 2009, the fastest collapse measured since modern records began.

The top one fifth of earners in Manhattan in 2000 earned 52 times more than the bottom quintile living there, a gap similar to that found only in countries as desperate as Namibia.[37] An infant born on the poor side of the tracks in New York (Morningside Heights in Harlem, for example) has a 2% chance of dying in his or her first year of life, 12 times greater than the chance for infants born in the nearby salubrious Upper East Side.[38] By 2004 unemployment rates for black men in Harlem were up to 50% worse than they had been even during the 1930s depression.[39] By the start of this century, by age 15, US teenagers had only a 75%, a *three in four*, chance of reaching age 65, one of the lowest rates in the rich world. The chance is partly not higher because black teenagers in the US have only a 33%, a *one in three*, chance of seeing their 65th birthday.[40]

In the heart of London in the borough of Westminster a woman who has made it to age 65 living in the Church Street estate can expect on average to live roughly another 12 years. In contrast, a woman of the same age living in the opulent Little Venice enclave in the same borough can expect to live another 26 years[41] (most thus living to at least age 91). On the streets outside their incredibly sumptuous and expensive homes are found more rough sleepers and more people who are officially counted as suffering serious mental illness and seeking housing than anywhere else in Britain. And just down the road are the women of Church Street who have had such different lives and whose prognosis beyond 65 is to live half as many more years as those in Little Venice.[42]

The lines that divide

The convergence of people labelled as mentally ill on Westminster and Manhattan was an unforeseen outcome of the successful movement to close down asylums from the 1970s onwards, the failure of medicalisation in 'the community', including wider 'care in the community' and some strange attraction among those labelled as 'mad' towards these financial centres (Westminster borders the City).[43] There was over-optimism in the 1970s that psychiatrists could cure mental illness with drugs. These drugs mostly suppressed symptoms rather than cured problems, so mentally ill patients usually never really felt better and were often reluctant to continue to take medication. Simultaneously, as banking hours became longer and longer the rumours that city traders could only keep going with artificial stimulants became more often the truth. It wasn't just those sleeping rough on the streets outside the trading houses who were taking drugs.

Geographical divides come with varying degrees of contortion. Just as those supposed to be taking their drugs to calm them down (but not doing so) stumbled so close to those financiers supposed not to be taking drugs (but nevertheless partaking), so too were the living quarters of the very poor and very rich in these centres closely intertwined. It is hard to find social statistics as extreme and environments as different but so close together as are found within the hearts of London and New York. The intertwining of rich and poor neighbourhoods is far greater in the centres of these two cities than anywhere else in the rich world. The line separating rich and poor in the centres of these cities is most twisted at their hearts and less and less contorted further out. The lines that divide inner from outer London and New Jersey from Long Island are less convoluted to draw. Further out still they become straighter, or more smoothly curved. An outlying affluent suburb can be seen to be surrounded by slightly less affluent suburbs, and then by average places and only then do they touch on poorer districts. In Britain at the far commuting boundary of London the smoothest divide is now found, that which separates the south of England from the rest of the UK.

Figure 23 shows my attempt to provide a description of where the North–South divide runs through England. To say that it does not exist because the Midlands has its own identity is to miss both how divided the Midlands are, and how the identity which they did have has been chiselled down with the repeated decimation of manufacturing employment decade after decade. The North–South divide in England, drawn in Figure 23, is really the outermost boundary of London. It can be seen in how people vote, how they die, in their wealth, but even in things as mundane as how the fittings of pumps in pubs are altered so that a different head forms on pints of beer on either side of the border. You don't really leave London until you've crossed this line; you can tell that you are still in the South not just from the cost of homes but from the taste of the drink. However, places both north and south are slowly losing their identities as what begins to matter more and more within the human geography of Britain is what the exact orbit of your locality is in relation to the capital. In other words, how well placed is your place to trade with, and in, that capital?

The origins of inequality

Divides are everywhere; they are the stuff of geography. They are found along country lanes in Lincolnshire, between regions in

Figure 23: The fractal nature of geographical divides, North–South/West–East, Britain, 2010

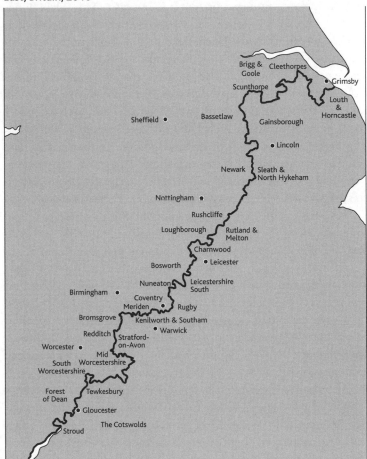

Note: This particular divide is the social, economic and political divide in England. Below the line people live about a year longer on average; identical houses cost much more; people in similar situations are more likely to vote Conservative below than above the line, and much more besides. For a more detailed description of the line and exactly where it is estimated to run see: www.sasi. group.shef.ac.uk/maps/nsdivide

Source: Drawn by the author with help from John Pritchard and derived from many sources.

Europe and between countries worldwide. Divides are not there because of lack of interaction, but because over the borders things move in particular directions. Today the best health in the world is enjoyed in countries like Japan, Belgium and Norway, the worst in the Congo. There is both an indirect and a direct connection. The indirect connection is trade. Belgium and Norway both need things that come from the Congo – industrial diamonds for machine tools, minerals that make mobile phones function – and both countries pay a pittance for these. If they did not there would be much less of a divide. We don't know exactly how these goods get from one place to another, but we know that they do, and that what matters more and more to how well you are likely to fare, is where you are to start off with, your orbit within the world trade system.

The direct connection that explains why the Congo is poor and other places are rich is less well known. From around 1885 Europeans and later people in North America and then people in Japan began '... to live longer partly *because* people in other parts of the world were suffering deprivation and dying young'.[44] The direct connection was that very soon after King Leopold the Second of Belgium took the Congo as his own private property in 1885, as well as instigating one of the first large-scale documented cases of genocide, his officers ensured that there was a rapid increase in the harvest of latex rubber, a proportion of which was exported to become condoms and diaphragms, resulting in smaller families in richer countries. Villagers who failed to meet their quota for producing rubber in a year could pay the remainder in baskets of severed hands cut from protesting fellow villagers, including children.[45] It comes as a shock when you first learn that baskets of severed hands became the symbol of the Congo 'Free' State under colonial rule. But we quickly become anaesthetised. You probably know that there is at present a worldwide death toll of about two million young children from diarrhoea every year. This is equivalent to 15 per 1,000, a rate that matches that found in many English towns around a century ago, and diarrhoea is just as preventable abroad as it is in England today.[46] You probably don't think every day of these deaths as shocking. That is because they occur far away, and while it is kept at a distance it is a shock to which we can easily become anaesthetised.

International divides make local divisions often appear paltry, but not caring about poverty within rich countries is a precursor for not caring more widely. On Sunday, 15 March 2009 the Health Select Committee of the House of Commons released its report on health inequalities within Britain. The report had been produced because the government was set to fail to achieve the target on health inequalities that it had set in 2003. The target was, by 2010, to reduce inequalities in health outcomes by 10% as measured by infant mortality and life expectancy at birth. Success in Britain is still counted in the live bodies of babies. The report described this as perhaps one of the 'toughest' health targets in the world. However, other affluent countries did not need such tough targets because, apart from the US, they tended not to have such great health inequalities, inequalities that have such an impact on the overall health of their citizens.

There was a precedent for all this 'tough' talk. In 1985, when she signed up to the World Health Organization inequality targets, Margaret Thatcher had agreed to a tougher target of a 25% reduction in health inequalities by 2000. Britain spectacularly failed then, with health inequalities increasing dramatically instead of reducing. They continued to increase under New Labour, and even the most recent statistics show little sign of the widening gap abating. In the US in 2008, long before a single case of swine flu occurred, and for completely different reasons: 'For the first time since the Spanish influenza of 1918, life expectancy is falling for a significant number of American women.... The phenomenon appears to be not only new but distinctly American'.[47] The phenomenon being discussed was absolute rises of poverty in the poorest of US counties. Two years later, in January 2010, the charity Save the Children reported absolute rises in the numbers of children living in the worst states of poverty in the poorest areas of the UK.

7.4 Bird-brained thinking: putting profit above caring

The cost in the US alone of the 2008 bail-out of banks was estimated to be greater in real terms, even in November 2008, than the combined sum of the costs of the Marshall Plan (US$155 billion), the Louisiana Purchase (US$217 billion), the Moon-shot

(US$237 billion), the Savings and Loan Crisis (US$256 billion), the Korean War (US$454 billion), the New Deal (US$500 billion), the Iraq War (US$597 billion),Vietnam (US$698 billion) *and* the all-time budget of NASA (US$851 billion).When combined, all these nine giant expenses, at US$3.9 trillion, are dwarfed by the US$4.6 trillion bail-out price tag. And that was just the price as first announced.[48]

Something changed in 2008; this was not business as usual, not even crisis management as usual. It was the result of the most spectacular example of bird-brained thinking ever to have occurred in human history. Bird-brained thinking is a particular trait that humans have for *not* being able to think well ahead and for flocking in their behaviour in ways that can bring about catastrophe. It was bird-brained thinking, by bankers, businessmen (and a few businesswomen), politicians and consumers that led to the crash of 2008. Figure 24 shows just one of what will become thousands of similar graphs to be drawn of the crash. This one could be drawn early because the crash was initially most acute in the US.

Even early on the economic crash looked very unlike an economic recession. By August 2009 a tenth of the world's merchant shipping was reported to be anchored up.[49] And electricity consumption in countries like Britain fell in a year by a similar amount, mainly as so many industries shut down operations.[50] A recession, such as that of the early 1980s, tends to see home borrowing fall as fewer houses are sold, but then borrowing increases again afterwards, as in the 122% rise in borrowing shown in Figure 24 that occurred in the US between 1983 and 1984. The recession in the early 1990s saw home borrowing slow down again, the rates of change go slightly negative, but then rise gently again in the late 1990s, then oscillate, then go higher, then peak at over a trillion dollars in 2005 and then come crashing down and down. Change in net lending did not just go negative, but exceeded (negative) 100% in 2007–08, when borrowing fell by US$698 billion, falling by 107% of what it had been in 2007. Recessions are not depicted by the plummeting figures seen in US mortgage lending. Recessions are slowdowns, not crash landings. It takes concerted bird-brained thinking to rise so high that the only way down is to crash.

Figure 24: The crash: US mortgage debt, 1977–2009 (% change and US$ billion)

Notes: Right-hand axis: net US$ billion additional borrowed in year shown by the bars in the graph. Left-hand axis: percentage change in that amount. Final percentage change unknown, but known to be based on a denominator of 'just' –46 US$ billion (the only negative bar). It is shown plummeting down off the scale. The 2009 mortgage debt to Quarter 3 was –370 US$ billion.

Figures for the fourth quarter of 2009 were not released at the time of going to press, but preliminary estimates suggest an even faster fall in 2009–10 than is shown in the graph above for 2008–09. There was no sign of a mortgage market recovery in spring 2010.

Source: Table 6, **p 231-2**, this volume, first column of data (household home mortgage debt change); see footnotes to Table 6 for 2009 data.

Snakes in suits

The small groups of people who run corporations in the most profit-hungry of countries act most often with a kind of bird-brained thinking that is called hyperbolic discounting. That is because *culturally* they have evolved in a way that is similar to the way birds evolve *biologically*, to behave in this way. Corporate bosses have not literally evolved to become bird-brained. Rather the modern corporation in unequal rich countries has evolved to favour promoting most often those individuals who demonstrate bird-brained behaviour.[51] Whichever organisation was at the top under such a situation was going to look bad when the problems that were the product of believing so much in markets unravelled during 2008. Graduates of the Harvard Business School began to admit in 2009 that 'There's a certain self-consciousness now that we may be part of the problem'.[52] The school's graduates have, far more often than others, been running banks that crashed, heading security exchanges that failed to spot massive fraud (such as Bernard Madoff's 'Ponzi' scheme), or have even been directly involved in fraud themselves. These stories were reported not in the obscure left-wing press, but on Bloomberg News, the television/internet channel of big business! But the greater fraud, not broadcast on Bloomberg, was the fraudulent message that the elevation of people with MBAs to such heights of reputation sent out. This was the message that bird-brained short-term thinking was somehow efficient.

Bird-brained thinking, of the kind corporate bosses recently engaged in (and still do so), was first recognised when it became clear through studying pigeons that an accounting method called 'hyperbolic discounting' could explain how birds choose to eat or store grain. Essentially, pigeons exhibit a huge appetite to consume now rather than save. Saving would allow them to be able to eat a little more evenly later. However, it is not that pigeons eat as much as they possibly can now, but they can be observed to discount the potential future value of grain according to a function that sees its value fall hyperbolically (very fast) with time.[53] Clearly behaving in this way helped pigeons survive in the past, or at least the few that evolved into those we get to study in experiments now. These are the kinds of experiments in which the pigeons get to tap on a lever and receive grain now, or on another lever and get twice as much grain in one minute's time. Which would you tap?

Currently it is still not legal to put business school MBA graduates into cages and to give them levers, one which gives them a treat now, and another that makes them wait, but get more later. What we can do instead is look to the past to see how their forebears behaved in these situations. The particular economics that people who take MBA courses are taught tells them that when a good becomes scarce its price rises, which both reduces consumption and increases the number of people trying to supply the good, so preserving its availability. This theory was, ironically, first tested on some cousins of those same pigeons whose behaviour taught us that hyperbolic discounting is natural, at least natural in birds.

Catching the pigeon

Soon after Europeans arrived in North America they observed staggering numbers of passenger pigeons, flocks said to be a mile wide and *300 miles long*. These were hunted to extinction, the last one dying in 1914. They were killed for their meat, the price of which did not rise one blip as their numbers fell and scarcity rose.[54] People simply ate other food, and ate pigeon when they could, to the very last bird. These hunters of passenger pigeons killed them at a rate explicable only if they were applying hyperbolic discounting to their value. A dead pigeon in the hand was worth so much more to a pigeon hunter in 1900 than two in the bush, even though two would breed more, more which he might be able to hunt in future.

Stories such as the passenger pigeons' fate led those with imagination not curtailed by undertaking an MBA to worry that there is no reason why conventional economics should preserve oil supplies. The price of oil need not rise sky-high as the last marketable drops are squeezed out of the last well or from the last sands. If substitutes for oil are found, such as electric cars, organic fertilisers, paper instead of plastic, then as long as they provide short-term alternatives the last drops of oil can be sold cheaply. Corporate thinking is short-term thinking. It does not portray itself as such, of course, but it says that there is no alternative to the market, and the market works by a kind of magic to result in the best of all possible worlds. In 2008, just as the great crash had begun, the World Bank published its central argument on market magic; it suggested that:

> Growth is not an end in itself. But it makes it possible to achieve other important objectives of individuals and societies. It can spare people en masse from poverty and drudgery. Nothing else ever has. It also creates the resources to support health care, education…. We do not know if limits to growth exist, or how generous those limits will be. The answer will depend on our ingenuity and technology,

on finding new ways to create goods and services that people value on a finite foundation of natural resources. This is likely to be the ultimate challenge of the coming century. Growth and poverty reduction in the future will depend on our ability to meet it....[55]

Technological innovation is the great trump card played in these arguments. In future we will be able to genetically engineer a new passenger pigeon, the MBA candidate may suggest at interview. But new technology causes as many problems as it solves. It is no great panacea. Being able to genetically engineer old species back into existence gives you the ability to create monsters. Being able to create new sources of power allows you to burn up even more of some other resource to carry out an activity that you perhaps do not need to undertake. Worldwide it has been the very opposite of growth that has spared people from poverty and drudgery. It has been through curtailing growth and greed that most people who have been spared from poverty have seen their parents brought out of it. Trade unions curtailed profiteering by bosses and argued wages up. Governments nationalised health services and freed their citizens from fear by curtailing the greed of private physicians. In Britain they told those physicians that if most wanted to work they would have to treat all those who were sick, not just the wealthy. Much earlier the French rebelled against the excesses of a king in a revolution partly inspired to reduce poverty; the North Americans had a revolution to overcome the greed of the English; the English reduced poverty in England by exploiting others but also partly by occasionally voting down the power of the aristocracy between 1906 and 1974 to distribute wealth better within England. The world bankers are unfortunately being selected for their bird brain-like attributes. They appear to remember little and either know or accept nothing of most of the history of actual human progress. Bird-brained economic thinking requires almost no memory.

Most mammals do not undertake hyperbolic discounting; many even store food excessively. Presumably there were at times some particularly severe winters in the past and those cautious few prudent savers prevailed. A few humans are not so prudent but have been found to behave in predatory reptilian ways towards others, sometimes due to being a little brain damaged. The evidence for this is found in abnormalities in the prefrontal cortex and the potentially criminal-like disregard of some psychopaths who have been well educated and have found agreeable work in business.[56] Fortunately, most humans behave in mammalian rather than reptilian or bird-brained ways; they save and store, including for others. We are not doomed to greed or vicious selfishness. However, humans did not collectively plan the world systems they came to live in: these systems came about because we did not plan. Like passenger pigeons flocking across the North American plains, we mostly follow our nearest neighbours, and do what they do. The nearest neighbours of world bankers are other economists, and especially elite MBA graduates.

Before asking why all the passenger pigeons were wiped out, ask first why there were so many. Passenger pigeons, it is thought in some quarters, expanded to such huge populations partly due to the decimation of competitors when Europeans first arrived and so altered the ecology of the North American continent. Just as we are not sure why there were so many pigeons, neither are we sure why there were suddenly so many extra humans available to come to the Americas. We do not have much of an idea as to why human populations rose rapidly when they did, to spread out around the world from Europe. What we do know is that the latest rise coincided with a new order of thinking, a new leniency over profiteering becoming permissible. The two are coincident. Something did enable population growth and it may well have been that population growth which spared us from drudgery, resulting (among much else) in those French and then American revolutions. Profiteering, however, is not a magic solution, but a monster: 'Capitalism is a machine programmed to do one thing – make profit. That is its great strength. There is no morality, no sentiment, just a never-ending quest to increase profits, locally, nationally and ultimately globally.... Enough is never enough. Capitalism always ends up eating itself. It's like a shark that has its stomach cut open and briefly feeds on itself'.[57]

Ending the feeding frenzy

For 64 years, between 1926, the end of the last gilded age, and 1990, the beginning of the end of our current gilded age of wealth, gross national product (GNP) in the US rose by an average of 3% a year. The return rate on the shares of all corporations trading on the New York Stock Exchange over the same period rose by some 8.6% a year on average. While it could be argued that technical growth and education may partly account for the GNP rise, the same argument cannot be used to account for the much higher share price increase. The researchers who highlighted this discrepancy favour the suggestion that shares rose faster in price through the increased exploitation over time of people and parts of people's lives which were not part of the market system in 1926, but which had been incorporated into it by 1990, not just within the US, but also from abroad.[58]

The rises in share prices relative to GNP were a measure of how much was being sucked out of the rest of humanity and out of the planet's resources. This blood sucking fell for a short time after 1926 and it is falling again now, but between economic crashes it was rife. Many argue that, in the 1930s and 1940s, economic recovery began because of the marketing of consumer goods and then services to people in poorer countries of the world. This eventually turned depression into growth. Today there is no new poor world to exploit. And it is because there isn't an extra planet waiting to have its surplus extracted that we have to start planning for a more frugal future now.[59] This frugality is required not because we consume so much more in rich countries than is consumed in poor countries, but because we consume so much more than even our parents did. We consume more mostly because we are offered so many more things that our parents never had, things that are made from materials that are not sustainable and, to a much lesser extent, because there are more of us. Those of us living in the rich world, the rich fifth of global society, consume on average *six times* more oil, minerals, water, food and energy than did our parents.[60] It is not that we literally eat six times as much as they did, but we waste so much food and eat so much meat. We do not drink six times as much water, but more water is used in the production of many of the extra things we now consume that our parents did not.

The way corporations create food today and the way in which we consume it is responsible for almost a third of carbon emissions from rich nations.[61] Far more food is created than we can healthily eat (and than we do eat), far more meat is produced to be eaten than is healthy, and is produced in ways that certainly are not healthy. We throw away a huge amount of food, but it is estimated that we throw away *five times* as much food packaging in weight each day as even the food we throw out. Of the food that we do eat, its nutritional value has been falling as its sugar and fat content has been increased to sell it more easily. The worldwide redistribution of fat and oil production over the course of the last third of a century, coincident with the industrialisation of food production, has been staggering, as the rich in the richer countries progressively consume healthier olive oils while most people in the poorer countries consume more of the least healthy of fats.[62] Food poisoning is becoming more common, especially as we eat out more, eating in restaurants whose core interest is not necessarily to serve good food, but to make profit. Our food system is essentially unhealthy, both globally and locally.

The idea that economic growth is essential is based on the belief that human beings cannot escape their bird-brained tendencies, the belief that we will always be greedy and stuff our faces given the opportunity. This is a counsel of despair that fails to recognise how simple it would be to eat more healthily. The first step is to eat less or no meat and much less fish. Meat is simply not very good for us and hugely expensive to rear, let alone dangerous in indirect ways, from promoting new strains of disease to making the industrial treatment of animals a norm that is easily transferred to people. The health benefits of eating fish have luckily recently been found to be over-rated. Medical reviews have found that evidence of reduction in cardiovascular events and mortality from eating fish is less conclusive than was recently thought.[63] This is lucky because fish stocks are now so depleted that we cannot substitute fish for meat.

Eating more healthily is not just good for individuals, but for social groups and the environment. Consuming both less and more healthily, and spending more time on pursuits that involve exercise rather than purchasing, also has far wider social and environmental benefits. Most of the rise in pollution from poorer countries such as China has been due to the generation of the power needed to run factories to make things for people in rich countries to buy. The levels of lead in the blood of people who live in cities in China are now recorded to be at twice what is considered a dangerous level and certain to harm the mental development of huge numbers of children in China.[64] Occasionally, high lead levels are found in the paint on toys made in China, but we rarely wonder why it is in the paint in the first place. People in China have had to live under a regime of having far fewer children than almost anywhere else in the world partly to allow their factories to be built so quickly and staffed so fully by adults not occupied in childrearing. The epidemic of lead poisoning among children in China is just one of many cruel and largely unforeseen consequences of those policies. More factories and power stations in China will not raise levels of health in China in future. It would be a bird-brained response to continue to add to that pollution, to produce goods for others overseas just in order to have growth at home.

7.5 The 1990s: birth of mass medicating

When you are no longer in control of your life you live in fear. The most extreme case of losing control is imprisonment. At the start of the 1990s it was reported that more sedatives, tranquillisers and other such drugs were being dispensed per inmate in British prisons than in its psychiatric institutions. The highest recorded 'doping' was of an average of 941 doses per woman per year in Holloway women's prison in London.[65] Worldwide, at the same time, a single company was making a billion US dollars a year just from selling *Valium*.[66] By the end of the 1990s some 11 million children in the US alone were being prescribed *Ritalin* to calm them down and 83 million adults were being prescribed *Prozac* or its equivalents.[67] It is being reported more and more often that to stabilise populations '... mass treatment options are not far off'.[68] These could include anything from over-the-counter sales of former prescription drugs, to more sinister suggestions which would begin with compulsory medicating in prisons.

In an attempt to prevent what may become seen as necessary mass treatment, governments are turning to behaviour therapies that involve talking more than 'doping'. In Britain alone an extra 3,500 cognitive behaviour therapists were recruited in 2008, trained to talk to people and to suggest ways in which their clients could become more optimistic; the patients do at least get someone to listen to them, a government-provided substitute for having a friend who is good at listening and who is upbeat. These therapists will be organised around 'happy centres' and it has not gone unnoticed that '... the idea of 250 happiness centres to promote rose-tinted bubbles of positive illusions is faintly sinister...'.[69] The problem is that in many cases the real reasons for people's mental distress are genuine and cannot be talked away that easily. This may partly be because an underlying reason for rising mental ill health is that much of the way we are living in the rich world is mentally unhealthy. To see what treatments for distress are now advocated and why, we need to take a short journey through the history of the medication revolution.

Treating the symptoms

Governments respond to rising distress by trying to treat the symptoms. The UK government has been employing health trainers for our bodies as well as more therapists for our minds. The Department of Health in England reported in 2008 on what its 1,200 new health trainers were doing. Its assessment was undertaken by recounting the anecdotal case of Tammy and Jane (using fictional names). In its report, the Department suggests it is doing well because its employees have found a 'service user' (a person) who is grateful for their help. 'Tammy' for instance, talking of her trainer 'Jane', says: 'Jane has supported me from the beginning of my referral programme. Without Jane's presence and guidance, I would have felt unable to attend to begin with because of my low self-esteem. With her help I feel able to reach my goals of improved health and fitness'.[70] Why was Tammy's esteem so low? How have human beings been able to be mentally healthy and physically fit for generations without personalised health trainers? What could Jane be doing more usefully in a society in which people like Tammy were not so crushed? Do people really talk with such near perfect English as this, or was the conversation as fictional as the names?

At least 'Tammy' can talk of her esteem being low and 'Jane' can talk of not giving Tammy a pill (as Jane isn't allowed to give pills). Tammy and Jane's grandparents lived in a world where mental ill health was less common but just as greatly feared (see discussion on page 273), and there was not much that could be done about it. Since then we have developed many drugs, and not all drugs are bad for us. Some work, especially for severe mental illness (psychosis) and severe depression. The first anti-psychotic drug, *Chlorpromazine*, was marketed in Europe as *Largactil* and in the US as *Thorazine*. It was synthesised in 1950 and began to be widely used to treat schizophrenia by 1954. *Chlorpromazine* belongs to a group of drugs called phenothiazines, and their use was a major factor in the halving of the population in old-fashioned lunatic asylums in Britain to stand at some 75,000 by 1975[71] (the majority by then being inpatients rather than imprisoned). Phenothiazines suppress hallucinations, delusions and violence and thereby allowed so many to be released, but many were reluctant to keep taking the pills.

The first effective anti-depressant drug was *Imipramine* (*Tofranil*), first licensed in 1956. It belongs to a class called tricyclic anti-depressants, the most effective probably being *Amitriptyline* (*Tryptizol*), licensed in 1961. These drugs changed a situation where seriously depressed patients were admitted to psychiatric hospitals often for six to twelve months before recovering well enough to cope, to a situation where many were getting better within a month. However, partly because of the danger of overdoses from taking too many of these tricyclic anti-depressants developed during the 1950s and 1960s, older drugs such as barbiturates continued to be used and other new drugs were introduced, many of which turned out to have other particularly harmful side effects.

Largactil, *Tofranil* and *Tryptizol* were breakthroughs that had their problems but worked well in particular situations. But both before and after them there have been other drugs that in retrospect it would have been better never to use in many of the situations for which they were prescribed. In Victorian times *Laudanum*, a solution of opium in alcohol, was used to help sleeping problems as well as to relieve pain. It was, of course, a very addictive drug. The first sleeping 'tablet' was not licensed until 1903, the barbiturate *Veronal* (which was initially used to put dogs to sleep). Ten year later, in 1913, another barbiturate, *Luminal*, was licensed, a sedative used to treat tension and anxiety. It was one of the first of many which were lethal in overdose and also contributed to depression. The First World War saw demand for this and other barbiturates explode. The Second World War saw a similar explosion in the demand for another set of the newly marketed drugs, amphetamines, which were first put in tablet form in 1937.

By 1970 barbiturates were rarely prescribed in Britain as sleeping tablets because of their dire side effects, and because a new set of drugs had been developed, the benzodiazepines. *Diazepam*, the form of *Valium* that made its owners over a billion US dollars a year by the 1990s, was licensed in 1963, *Mogadon* in 1965, then *Temazepam* (a later favourite of addicts). These drugs turned out to have numerous harmful side effects including depression. *Lithium* was given to manic depressives from the 1960s onwards, and reduced manic episodes, but also took the spice out of life. There were no magic pills, but given the profits that could be made through claiming to have found one, there was no slowdown in the search for that magic, nor any great profit to be made in looking for the underlying causes, rather than for potential treatments.[72]

Feeling better than ourselves?

In the 1970s, a new class of anti-depressant was developed, the selective serotonin re-uptake inhibitors (SSRIs). They were based on theories that depression was caused by a shortage of serotonin in the brain. There is still very little evidence that this is actually the case. The best known is *Fluoxetine* (*Prozac*), approved in 1988. It became very widely used and very widely criticised: 'Prozac is the emblematic anti-depressant, and the fact that is has become as common a household name as "aspirin" illustrates the extent of the phenomenon ... that allow[s] depressed subjects to work on their inner selves so as to "feel better", or even "better than themselves"

... [but] it is becoming difficult to tell which is the self and which is the artificially reworked self'.[73] *Prozac's* one great advantage is that overdose on SSRIs is rarely fatal and you can take it for months, or years and years and years. In contrast, for children there was also the development of the amphetamine derivative *Methylphenidate*, marketed as *Ritalin*, which, by 2008, turned out to be so harmful that it had a health warning put out against its continued use in Britain.[74]

SSRIs became the mass medication drugs of the 1990s. They had the effect of stopping people complaining, which caused speculation that this was a large part of the reason why so many GPs were willing to prescribe them so often. This was despite repeated stories such as that blazoned on the front page of *The Guardian* on 26 February 2008 that read: 'Prozac, used by 40 million people, does not work say scientists'. A year earlier, in 2007, the BBC had reported (as a national news story) the fact that in Scotland anti-depressant use had risen more than four-fold, 85 daily doses of anti-depressant drugs being prescribed by 2006 per 1,000 people in the general population as compared with 'just' 19 doses per 1,000 in 1992. The report itself showed that it was between the ages of 25 and 44 that use peaked. Across the whole of Greater Glasgow around 10% of people aged 15 or over were taking daily doses, the implication being that in poorer parts of Glasgow rates would be far higher. Mass medication had arrived; the targets (which the 2007 report announced) were simply to try to stop these high rates rising further.[75] Then came the economic crash of 2008 and the rise in mass joblessness across Britain, concentrated in places like Glasgow. Figure 25 shows just how rapid the rise in prescriptions across all of Scotland had been. It shows how policy, and possibly market saturation, was having the effect of a slight curtailment in that rise after 2004. But for that curtailment to continue would require a remarkable change in Scotland given the most recent rise in economic distress, and given so little curtailment of the underlying causes of mass despair; the underlying causes being that despair is often rational, given the life that so many people now find they have to live.[76]

Figure 25: The rate of prescribing anti-depressants by the NHS in Scotland, 1992–2006

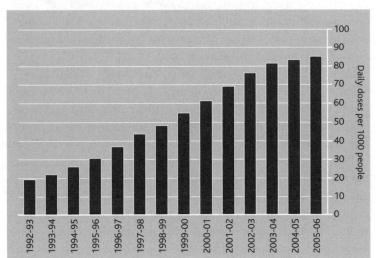

Notes: The NHS uses financial years when reporting on prescribing rates because costs are still mainly counted in terms of money rather than human misery. The measure shown is what is called standardised defined daily doses per 1,000 people aged 15+.

Source: NHS Quality Improvement Scotland (2007) *NHS quality improvement Scotland: Clinical indicators 2007*, Glasgow: NHS Quality Improvement Scotland, Table 1.1, p 12.

The ultimate reward

The adults (and children aged 15, 16 and 17) being prescribed anti-depressants, almost always now SSRIs, include the parents of the girls who had recorded such sharp increases in depression in the study undertaken around Glasgow with which this chapter began (when describing the rise in anxiety among children in unequal countries in Section 7.1). It will also include some of the girls themselves. There are many reasons for expecting to see despair and the treatment of its symptoms rising in years to come. Almost all the legalised medical drugs we have to treat despair with were inventions of the last century. We are only now beginning to fully discover the long-term detrimental side effects of many prescription drugs. This is because they are such recent inventions, because of the reluctance to accept that there is not a pill for every problem, and because of the manufacturers' wish to suppress any information that might have a bad effect on sales. There are also those drugs for which you do not need a prescription. We still turn to alcohol more than to any other drug to try to deal with our despair, with hugely detrimental results for both our physical and mental health.

Despair reaches across social classes. Rates were a little higher in Glasgow by 2006, at 10%, than in the least affected part of Scotland, Grampian, where the Royal Family goes on holiday, and where 'just' 7% of adults are currently taking anti-depressants daily. For children, rates of anxiety and depression are now found to be higher in higher social classes in Scotland. Wealth does not shelter you or those you love from despair. Should you be rich and live in a rich unequal country, your children are far more likely to suffer from mental illness than you were. Should they escape the worst effects, around them huge proportions of other people will be zoned out, behaving in placid ways, artificially 'enhanced' not to complain. Your children will grow up in a world where they will listen to others talk about their therapists, their anxieties, their pills, repeatedly, if current trends are allowed to continue. At the extreme, just prior to the 2008 presidential election, those suggesting new ways to imprison people more effectively in maximum security jails in the US were quietly implying that inducing a coma in inmates might be an option. Mass medication is no real cure. If any reason were needed as to why injustice is harmful it is the effects that we now know the resulting inequalities have on our general mental health. Material wealth offers no protection, when, after all and ultimately, '... all rewards are in the mind'.[77]

8

Conclusion, conspiracy, consensus

Chapters 3–7 each began with a statistic of injustice: a seventh of children being labelled today the equivalent of delinquents, a sixth of households excluded from social norms, a fifth of people finding it difficult or very difficult to get by in these times of prejudice; a quarter not having the essentials, when there is enough for all; a third now living in families where someone is suffering from mental ill health. The fraction that ends this series of statistics concerns people's ability to choose alternative ways of living and how limited those choices are: *half are disenfranchised*. In the US almost half of all those old enough to vote either choose not to vote or are barred from voting (see Table 1, Chapter 1, page 3). The greatest indictment of unequal affluent societies is for their people to be, in effect, disenfranchised, to think they can make no difference, to feel that they are powerless. Apathy has risen as we all become distracted by trying to make a living, lulled into a false comfort through consuming to maintain modern living. In the space of about 100 years we've gone from fighting for the right for women to vote, to a situation where half of the population in the most unequal of affluent countries are not exercising their right to vote.

Although there has been coordinated action, and many advocates of inequality, there has been no great, well-orchestrated conspiracy of the rich, just a few schools of free market thought, a few think-tanks preaching hate, but no secret all-powerful committees. Suppose there was, in fact, a conspiracy of the rich, a grand plan coordinated to preserve inequality. Conspiracy theories are often suggested as attractive explanations, as suddenly everything can be made to fit, and they are often revealed long after events. However, these are almost all relatively simple conspiracies, the assassination of a leader, the covering up of evidence, a plan to ensure a friend's election to be party leader through apparently legal but devious means. Grand conspiracies require a degree of organisation and secrecy that humans are not capable of.

There is no great conspiracy. This was first realised in the aftermath of the First World War, when it became clear that no one '… planned for this sort of an abattoir, for a mutual massacre four years long'.[1] The 'donkeys' in charge, the generals, planned for a short, sharp, war. Similarly, there is no orchestrated conspiracy to prolong injustice. That would be easier to identify and defeat. Instead unjust thoughts have seeped into everyday thinking out of the practices that make profit. Ideologies of inequality have trickled down. Once only a few argued that hunger should be used as a weapon against the poor. Now many grumble when inconvenienced by a strike, talk of those requiring benefits as scroungers, hope to inherit money or to become famous.[2]

As the nature of the beast has changed, as the nature of injustice has evolved from the former five giant evils to the new five modern evils of elitism, exclusion, prejudice, greed and despair, injustice begins to propagate itself more strongly. Because they do not recognise the transformed injustice for what it is, too many people favour arguments that actually bolster contemporary injustices in rich nations. But humans are far from being simply the pliant recipients of the seeds of social change they sow. Hardly any foresaw what they would reap as side effects of affluence, but great numbers are now working in concert to try to counteract those effects. Many people now recognise that the nature of injustice has changed; that in Britain and the US, 'Beveridge's Five Giants – Disease, Idleness, Ignorance, Squalor and Want – are different now …'.[3]

This conclusion is deliberately short. Often books of this kind struggle in their conclusion to make suggestions as to what should be done. Some will say that it is easy to criticise but hard to find solutions. The central argument of this book is that it is beliefs, the beliefs which enough of us still hold, that today underlie most injustice in the world. To ask what you do after you dispel enough of those beliefs to overcome injustice is rather like asking how you run plantations after abolishing slavery, or run society after giving women the vote, or run factories without child labour. The answers have tended to be: not very differently than before in most ways, but vitally different in others. However, dispelling the untruths that underlie the injustices we currently live with will not suddenly usher in utopia. A world where far more genuinely disapprove of elitism will still have much elitism and something else will surely arise in place of what we currently assume is normal. We cannot know what it will be, just as no one could have been expected in the 1910s to have predicted the world a century on. But what we currently view as normal will soon appear as crude old-fashioned snobbery, as has happened before. No one in an affluent country now so obviously bows and scrapes, or otherwise tugs their forelock in the presence of their 'betters'. What do you do today that will appear so quaint and yet so tragic in 2110?

The limits of humanity

Human beings are not superhuman. Elitism, exclusion, prejudice, greed and despair will not end just by being recognised more clearly as unjust, just as slavery did not end when formally abolished, women were not emancipated simply by being allowed to vote and the child abuse of dangerous labour did not end with the Factory Acts. It is, however, *in our minds* that injustice continues most strongly, in what we think is permissible, in how we think we exist, in whether we think we can use others in ways we would not wish to be used ourselves.

All the five faces of social inequality that currently contribute to injustice are clearly and closely linked. Elitism suggests that educational divisions are natural. Educational divisions are reflected both in those children who are excluded from life choices for being seen as not having enough qualifications, and in those able to exclude themselves, often by opting into private education. Elitism is the incubation chamber within which prejudice is fostered. Elitism provides a defence for greed. It increases anxiety and despair as endless examinations are taken, as people are ranked, ordered and sorted. It perpetuates an enforced and inefficient hierarchy in our societies.

Just as elitism is integral to all the other forms of injustice, so is exclusion. The exclusion that rises with elitism makes the poor appear different, exacerbates inequalities between ethnic groups and, literally, causes racial differences. Rising greed could not be satisfied without the exclusion of so many, and so many would not be excluded now were it not for greed. But the consequences spread up through even to those who appear most successfully greedy. Rates of despair might be highest for those who are most excluded but even the wealthy in rich countries are now showing many more signs of despair, as are their children. Growing despair has become symptomatic of our more unequal affluent societies as a whole. The prejudice that rises with exclusion allows the greedy to try to justify their greed and makes others think they deserve a little more than most. The ostracism that such prejudice engenders further raises depression and anxiety in those made to look different. And as elitism incubates exclusion, exclusion exacerbates prejudice, prejudice fosters greed and greed – because wealth is simultaneously no ultimate reward and makes many without wealth feel more worthless – causes despair. In turn, despair prevents us from effectively tackling injustice.

Removing one symptom of the disease of inequality is no cure, but recognising inequality as the disease behind injustice, and seeing how all the forms of injustice which it creates, and which continuously recreate it, are intertwined is the first step that is so often advocated in the search for a solution. Each route to that solution only differs in how the twine is wrapped around different descriptions of the object we are trying to describe. Think of injustice in these ways and you can begin to distinguish between suggestions that will increase it and those that will be more likely to promote fairness and equality. The status quo is not improved 'by introducing an inequality that renders one or more persons better off and no one [apparently] worse off'.[4] The awarding of more elite qualifications to an already well-titled minority reduces the social standing of the majority. Allowing those with more to have yet more raises social norms and reduces people on the margins of those norms to poverty through exclusion. To imagine that others are, apparently, no worse off when you introduce inequality requires a prejudicial view of others, to see them as 'not like you'. This argument legitimises greed.

In 2009 the US government introduced policies to tackle injustices, the first designed to be effective for 30 years. With some great changes taking places in the US, Britain may appear more clearly as a backwater of social progress; this is certainly the case where social security is concerned, and where human rights are rapidly being curtailed, but there are exceptions in other areas. For instance, the work to move away from elitism is under way. Even the 2007 *Children's Plan*, the British government's official guidance for schools in England (published before the economic crash made change so obviously imperative) suggested that schools should aim for children to understand others, value diversity, apply and defend human rights. It suggested that schools should help ensure that their staff were skilled in ensuring participation for all and should work towards the elimination of inequality. There should be '… no barriers to access and participation in learning and to wider activities, and no variation between *outcomes* for different groups; and … [children should] have real and positive relationships with people from different backgrounds, and feel part of a community, at a local, national and international level'.[5]

Less bound by elitism, the Welsh administration had earlier decreed that: 'For young children – when they play – it is their work'.[6] The Welsh government's advice to schools is that they should encourage more play, as learning is about play and imagination. In Wales it is now officially recognised that children can be stretched rather than being seen as having a fixed potential; the Welsh government says that if children play just within their capabilities, they then feel their capabilities extend as a result. In Scotland the educational curriculum is similarly being redesigned not to be based on learning for children to become factory fodder, or competition careerists, but learning to ensure the development of '… wisdom, justice, compassion and integrity'.[7] All this for Britain is very new, and for England much of it is yet to come, but it may be a tipping point in the long-term trend of what people are willing to tolerate for their children's futures. As one young father from Northern Ireland in 2008 commented, on living through troubled times, '… when you've got kids you don't want them to live what you've lived'.[8] Times can change abruptly, as often for the better as for the worse.

Our changing circumstances

The pendulum of public opinion was swinging in the US even before President Obama was elected. That was why he was elected. The US has historically been a place of remarkable bigotry and intolerance, which was partly why Barack Obama's selection as a candidate was initially such a shock. For instance, in 1987 a majority of adults in the US believed that schools should be able to sack teachers if it was discovered that they were homosexual, and more than two thirds agreed with (or did not strongly dispute) the idea that women should return to their traditional roles. By 2007 only a quarter still held the former view and a narrow majority completely disagreed with the latter.[9] However, public surveys also show how far US public opinion still has to go. There was a great swing back towards believing again that government should ensure that all were fed and also sheltered in 2007, but these are only the most basic of human rights. That same survey that revealed rapidly changing attitudes to women's roles reported as a great success the fact that growing numbers of people in the US knew that inequality was rising. This is slow progress but is welcome in a country where a Texan politician recently said: 'Where did this idea come from that everybody deserves free education? Free medical care? Free whatever? It comes from Moscow. From Russia. It comes straight out of the pit of hell'.[10]

It is not entirely the fault of the kind of Texans who talk of hell when they hear of equality that some still think in this way. Such thinking began long before Texas was overrun by European immigrants, immigrants with the profit motives of protestant ethics. The thinking got its first strong foothold around 400 years ago, on the other side of the Atlantic, in old Amsterdam. In 1631 a young man named René Descartes noticed that all around him people had stopped thinking about much more than earning money. He said: 'In this great city where I am living, with no man apart from myself not being involved in trade, everyone is so intent on his profits that I could spend my whole life without being seen by anyone'.[11] In the same year that Descartes died, 1650, a Dutch prince, William of Orange, was born, who, in 1688, invaded England. Despite the fact that he was then a king (not a revolutionary) and because he ended up on the side of history's victors, the event became recorded as a 'glorious revolution' rather than as the beginnings of a new mind-set of mercantile and militaristic misery. Within a dozen years he had increased the national debt of England from £1 million to £15 million and set in place the idea that a nation-state should permanently borrow in order to fight wars and expand trade. He ordered massacres of Catholics in Ireland where he is remembered as King Billy. And the killing cost: national debt rose and rose, to £78 million by 1750 and £244 million by 1790.'The trend was remarkable and indeed exceptional, by European standards....What did the government do with all the new resources, tax and loan money at its disposal? It conducted wars.'[12] These were wars with Spain, Austria, France and lastly with North America, which the British lost. As a result, the mantle of 'defender of the free world' began to move across the Atlantic. In 1791 Thomas Paine wrote that, for the English government,'... taxes were not raised to carry on wars, but ... wars were raised to carry on taxes'.[13] He could have added,'... and debts rose'. And he could have been writing about what his own country was to become.

The Texan politician's idea of fraternity and cooperation as hell was first fermented in the commercial imperatives that had swept Amsterdam by 1631, it was further brewed up in the militarist megalomania of England rampant in the eighteenth century, and the gilded greed of the US that was apparent to Mark Twain, who coined the phrase 'the gilded age' in the 1870s. All these in one way or another involved debt dressed up as wealth, debt dispensed in order to gain wealth. However, just as the definition of a language has become 'a dialect with an army and navy', a national debt is only 'a debt' if your military power is not sufficient for you to rename it as 'a deficit'. Depending on how you count money (and it is a slippery business), the US current account was in surplus until 1977, in deficit but balanced by overseas 'investments' until 2002, and after that the US became truly a debtor nation in any sense of accounting. In 2004 the writer, Richard Du Boff, who pointed this out, like many others at the time, warned that all this could result in a dollar rout, which '... could cause skittish investors to dump US stocks and bonds, sending Wall Street into a dive'.[14] In the event much more than a rout took place. And that Texan legislator's political party, the Republicans, were routed from office. What replaced them was a little different from the Democrats of old, not just because of the President's skin colour, or what that revealed about how people in the US could now vote.

President Obama's proposals for the 2010 federal budget were released in March 2009. The proposals appeared designed to reverse the growing levels of economic inequality in the US. This was seen as a significant development given that inequality had been rapidly increasing in the US for 30 years, mostly as a deliberate result of government policy. Commentators initially said it was difficult to predict exactly what the effect of the hundreds of proposed budget measures would be, but they included approximately US$100 billion a year in tax increases for the rich and US$50 billion a year in net tax cuts for those less wealthy. The *New York Times* predicted that these changes would result in an increase in the take-home pay of the median household of roughly US$800 a year and tax increases on the 'top 1%' of US$100,000 a year.[15] Some of the budget policy proposals which appeared to be aimed directly at helping the poor included: US$20 billion to increase food stamp benefits for desperate families, US$15 billion to increase pensions and benefits for nearly 60 million retired Americans and Americans with disabilities, the increasing of weekly unemployment benefits by US$25, and the expansion of the child tax credit programme.

The introduction to the 2009 US budget proposals was entitled 'Inheriting a legacy of misplaced priorities' and was widely welcomed as a remarkable document by recent historical standards. It stated that: 'By 2004, the wealthiest 10 percent of households held 70 percent of total wealth and the combined net worth of the top 1 percent of families was larger than that of the bottom 90 percent'.[16] Figures in the report also showed how the top 1% of earners had increased their share of the total income from 10% in 1980 to 22% by 2006, and how the cost of health insurance had increased by 58% since 2000, while average wages had only increased by 3%. By spring 2009 it had become clear to those in power that business as usual would no longer suffice.[17] By spring 2010 it was becoming clearer that curtailing business as usual, its lobbyists, the dissent and the protest at reform that its billions of spare dollars paid for, was going to be far from easy.

Contrast the US budget proposals of 2009 with the criticism made by more maverick (although as it turns out, largely correct) academics writing just seven years earlier on how global problems were being faced up to: 'All these and other problems of global or more local magnitude are ... the icebergs threatening the Titanic that contemporary world society has become. The icebergs are financial (currency speculation and over-valued stocks [over-valued until fairly recently]), nuclear, ecological (global warming), and social (billions of people with no prospects for gainful employment or decent living standards). There is no captain and the officers (the world's politicians) mill around disclaiming authority and denying responsibility'.[18] Responsibility is, of course, still denied, but what was impossible one year became possible the next as what was solid economic certainty in 2007 melted into the air of social reality of 2009 and recrystallised in a new political battle when the consequences for the rich became clear in 2010.

All that is solid melts

In the British budget of spring 2009 taxes were raised so the rich would, if they earned over a certain limit, again pay half their surplus gains as tax. The House of Lords proposed an amendment that all companies should, by law, publish the ratio of the wages of their highest paid director or executive to the wages of the lowest paid tenth of their workforce.[19] And a minister, Harriet Harman, introduced the new Equality Bill to Parliament, stating that it was now the British government's understanding that inequality hurt everyone (although she was not very clear over which kinds of inequality she meant[20]). In the spring of 2010, inequality, bankers' bonuses and greed all featured strongly in pre-election debate.

Greater equality is easily possible; we have had it so recently before, even in the US. In 1951 the communist-hating, soon-to-be consumer society, nuclear-powered US taxed the rich at 51.6% of their earnings. It has been estimated that returning to that tax rate for just the richest percentile of a percentile of North Americans would raise US$200 billion a year, three times all that the US government spent on education and the environment combined in 2008, or more than half of the (early) 2008 federal budget deficit.[21] However, that deficit is now hugely greater, having exploded in just 24 months, and the super-rich are not as opulent as they were. Their investment earnings have certainly suffered. Nevertheless, President Obama's tax proposals are to net roughly half that sum. It is well worth remembering that Barack Obama won the nomination of the Democratic Party in 2008 largely due to millions of small campaign donations from ordinary voters making him a credible candidate. Only after that did the corporate money also start rolling in to his campaign coffers.

Almost every time that there is a victory for humanity against greed it has been the result of millions of small actions mostly undertaken by people not in government. Examples include: votes for women, Indian independence, civil rights in America, or that earlier freedom won just to be able to say that the earth goes around the sun.[22] People can choose between falling into line, becoming both creatures and victims of markets, or they can resist and look back for other ways, other arguments, different thinking. When they have resisted in the past, resistance has always been most effective when exercised by those taught that they were the most powerless. But we quickly forget this. We need to be constantly reminded. It is often said that: 'The struggle of people against power is the struggle of memory against forgetting'.[23] Thinking that you have to do all the thinking anew and alone is the wrong place to start. To remember times before your times, times before you were born, you need stories, stories that tell you it need not be like this because it has not always been like this.

In 2008 adults in the US remembered that they had power in their vote, and were repeatedly reminded of this by a grassroots political campaign. As a result more (of those who were allowed to vote) exercised their vote than at any time since that pivotal 1968 election which Richard Nixon won, partly with George Wallace's help, and partly on a racist ticket. That was the last election that changed the trend but, like me, you probably don't remember it. In the US it is only necessary to go back to the early 1960s, before many civil rights were won, to see terrible inequality, of a kind that has been eradicated.

In countries such as Britain people last lived lives as unequal as today, as measured by wage inequality, in 1854, when Charles Dickens was writing *Hard Times*. Wage inequalities after those hard times fell, but then rose in the gilded age, peaking in 1906 before falling for 70 years, then rising in just 10 years to be as great again in 1986. They rose again to unprecedented levels by 1996.[24] By 2003 British researchers were writing in their careful prose that wage inequalities 'are higher than at any point since the Second World War and probably since representative statistics were first collected at the end of the nineteenth century...'.[25] People in Britain thought little of this in 2003; they were told it did not matter that great inequalities had become portrayed as natural. Key members of the government said they were 'seriously relaxed' about the situation; inequality was not an issue for them.[26] Religious leaders concerned themselves with the plight of the poor, not the size of the inequality gap. The British had forgotten that for most of their recent history they had not lived like this.

Despair grew, greed spiralled, prejudice seeped in, more were excluded, the elite preached that there was no alternative, and they preached that their experts were so very able, that the 'little people' were so safe in their hands, and that greed, greed of all things, really was good. Even when the economic crash came they said recovery would come soon and things would soon be back to normal. Many are still saying that as I type these words in the autumn of 2009 (and check them in the spring of 2010). In some ways we have been here before.

In 1929 the stock market rallied several times. In the early 1930s unemployment rates in the US exceeded 14 million before the statisticians who did the counting were sacked. In Britain there were real falls in prices, which occurred again in 2009. The government cut wages across the public sector by 10% in the 1930s. Although we began to become more equal in wealth during those years inequalities in health peaked as the poorest died young in greatest numbers in that same 1930s decade.[27] In many other newly rich countries, but especially Germany, it was far worse. W.H. Auden's poem '1 September 1939' ends:

> *I and the public know*
> *What all schoolchildren learn*
> *Those to whom evil is done*
> *Do evil in return.*

The most unequal of rich countries were those most willing to go to war abroad 64 years after 1939. More equitable nations more often find it easier to refuse to join, or make only paltry contributions to any supposed 'coalition of the willing'. It is when injustice is promoted at home to maintain inequality within a country that it also becomes easier to contemplate perpetrating wrongs abroad. At home they sought to plaster over the wounds caused by inequality by building more prisons, hiring more police and prescribing more drugs. But by 2007 it was becoming widely recognised that rich countries could not simply try to pay to ease the symptoms of extreme inequality, and that realisation was at a time when they thought they had the money to do this. Time and again articles were written explaining that: 'Extreme social inequality is associated with higher levels of mental ill health, drugs use, crime and family breakdown. Even high levels of public service investment, alone, cannot cope with the strain that places on our social fabric'.[28]

Overcoming the power of kings

The latest era of growing inequalities is coming to an end. It is something that cannot go on forever, so it won't. But it will not end without the millions of tiny acts required to no longer tolerate the greed, prejudice, exclusion and elitism that foster inequality and despair. Above all else these acts will require teaching and understanding, not forgetting once again what is fundamental about being human: 'The human condition is fundamentally social – every aspect of human function and behaviour is rooted in social life. The modern preoccupation with individuality – individual expression, individual achievement and individual freedom – is really just a fantasy, a form of self-delusion…'.[29] Accept this, behave differently, and even the most apocalyptic of writers will agree that every act of defiance, no matter how small, makes a difference, whatever '… we do or desist from doing *will* make a difference…'.[30] We can never know precisely what difference, and have no reason to expect our influence to be disproportionately large, nor should we expect it to be especially small. It is equally vital to recognise that none of us are superhuman; we cannot expect others to do great deeds and lead us to promised lands (at least not with any reliability). We are slowly, collectively, recognising this, learning not to forget that although we can learn without limits, our minds were not made to live as we now live: 'The world is indeed a strange and mysterious place, but not because of any hidden causal order or deeper purpose. The mystery is largely in the operations of the human mind, a strange organ capable of creating its own vision of reality with little regard to how the world really is'.[31]

In our minds we can despair or celebrate history. At some times we can see absolute immiseration as food prices soar and barbarism takes place in wars on terrorism that repeat older histories of persecution. At other times a celebratory story of human history can be told where injustices have been progressively defeated, the power of kings overcome, principles of equality in law secured, slavery abolished, voting franchises extended, free education introduced, health services or health insurance nationalised, minimum incomes guaranteed (for unemployment, sickness, old age or childcare). Legislation is won to:

> ... protect the rights of employees and tenants, and ... to prevent racial discrimination. It includes the decline of forms of class deference. The abolition of capital and corporal punishment is also part of it. So too is the growing agitation for greater equality of opportunity – regardless of race, class, gender, sexual orientation, and religion. We see it also in the increasing attention paid by lobby groups, social research and government statistical agencies to poverty and inequality over the last 50 years; and most recently we see it in the attempt to create a culture of mutual respect for each other.[32]

And we see it in a redistributive budget in the US that could not have been imagined a year earlier. We see it in the contempt in which many of those who have taken most are now held, but we can also see the danger of a return to business and misery as usual. 'The tradition of all dead generations weighs like a nightmare on the brains of the living.'[33] We see our history, our future, our nightmares and our dreams first in our fickle imaginations. That is where we first make our present. How we come to live is not predetermined.

Geographically all it takes is a little imagination, a little 'wishful thinking', to see that a collection of movements will achieve the change we wish to see in the world; these are movements that need only exist in our imaginations in order to work, to have faith. These are movements to '… make our own world from below [where we] are the people we have been waiting for'.[34] These are the opposite of movements towards world government: too many of those have been proposed '… in which the best stocks could rule the earth'.[35] These are, instead, movements where it is proclaimed that '… the future will be amazing, and after that the whole world will become a better place. If we cannot make that happen, then no one can'.[36] And these are movements about which people who advocate them repeatedly tell us that: 'It can happen – so long as everyone does not leave it for somebody else to do …'.[37]

All the endings have already been written, all the enthusiasm and eulogies have been penned, posies of men's and women's flowers have been offered, future students are exhorted to work with joy, humour or at least irony, and with an expansive love, to keep honest, humble, honourable, and '… on the side of the proverbial angels'.[38] And all these writers end in one way or another, similarly saying, although rarely with as much humility as this:

> Having come to the end of this book, the reader now knows what I know. It is up to the reader, then, to decide whether there is any validity and utility to what is presented here and then to decide what, if anything, to do about the developments and problems discussed. While I would like to see the reader choose a particular course of action, I do not think that other choices are indications that those making them are judgmental dopes.[39]

And slowly, collectively, with one step back for every two taken forward, we 'dopes' inch onwards to progress; we gradually undo the mistakes of the past and recognise new forms of injustice arising out of what we once thought were solutions. We collect together posies, all tied a little differently, and we realise that, although none of us is superhuman, neither are any of us without significance. Everything it takes to defeat injustice lies in the mind. So what matters most is how we think.

Notes and sources

Chapter 1

[1] The affluent or rich world consists of those countries where the best-off billion people live, that is, almost all of the countries in Europe and in North America, and Japan.

[2] Table 1, on page 3, gives an indication of how many people suffer most directly from each injustice in rich countries. On the categorisation of injustices see Wolff, J. and de-Shalit, A. (2007) *Disadvantage*, Oxford: Oxford University Press, pp 38, 39, 106 and 191, who in turn refer to Amartya Sen's listings; and for similar categorisations see Watts, B., Lloyd, C., Mowlam, A. and Creegan, C. (2008) *What are today's social evils? Summary*, York: Joseph Rowntree Foundation (www.jrf.org.uk/publications/what-are-today's-social-evils). Both of these tend to produce lists of around 10 modern evils, or sources of injustice and disadvantage, but many are easily paired and so are collapsible to five (as is shown in Chapter 2, Table 2, page 17).

[3] A mantra exposed very clearly and recently in Lawson, N. (2009) *All consuming*, London: Penguin.

[4] Health budgets are raided (top-sliced) to fund armies of counsellors to tell us that all is not so bad, family doctors spend most of their working hours dealing with people whose problems are not physical, and the World Health Organization (WHO) ranks mental ill health higher and higher with every assessment it makes of the leading causes of death and distress worldwide, and specifically shows that the rates of prevalence of mental ill health are almost perfectly correlated with income inequality in rich countries. See WHO comparable psychiatric surveys, as reported in Wilkinson, R.G. and Pickett, K. (2009) *The spirit level: Why more equal societies almost always do better*, London: Allen Lane, p 67.

[5] See Krugman, P. (2007) *The conscience of a liberal*, New York, NY: W.W. Norton, p 18. The height of excess in the last gilded age was seen in the 'Great Gatsby' summer of 1922. Money moved more slowly then and the financial crash came seven years later. The height of excess in the current gilded age was recorded in the autumn of 2007 as City bankers partied on their bonuses right up to Christmas. The hangover in 2008 was unparalleled: see Chakrabortty, A. (2007) 'If I had a little money ...', *The Guardian*, 8 December. For the origin of the term 'new gilded age' see also Bartels, L.M. (2008) *Unequal democracy: The political economy of the new gilded age*, Princeton, NJ: Princeton University Press.

[6] Pearson, K. (1895) 'Contributions to the mathematical theory of evolution – II. Skew variation in homogeneous material', *Philosophical Transactions of the Royal Society of London, Series A, Mathematical*, vol 186, pp 343-414: this paper may have contained the first histogram of human subjects by area.

[7] For the cycles to exist, enough people had to be given the opportunity to cycle up the social scales to then be available to fall back down in sufficient numbers, and that circumstance first occurred only in the 1960s, which is why the term 'cycle of deprivation' first came into widespread use in the 1970s. With the prejudice of those times it was more often, and erroneously, used to suggest 'family pathology' as a mechanism whereby poverty was passed down the generations. This was simply a rehashing of the old claim that paupers mainly bred more paupers. The phrase 'cycles of exclusion' here means those shown in Figure 8 (Chapter 4, page 120).

[8] The figure varies between times and countries. This particular fraction best fits Britain in 1999 as an estimate of the proportion of households found to be poor by at least two definitions. See Bradshaw, J. and Finch, N. (2003) 'Overlaps in dimensions of poverty', *Journal of Social Policy*, vol 32, no 4, pp 513-25.

[9] For the statistics see Dorling, D., Rigby, J., Wheeler, B., Ballas, D., Thomas, B., Fahmy, E., Gordon, D. and Lupton, R. (2007) *Poverty, wealth and place in Britain, 1968 to 2005*, Bristol: The Policy Press, and for the mechanism read Bauman, Z. (2006) *Liquid fear*, Cambridge: Polity Press, which provides a very succinct description of the process by which the social distancing between rich and poor occurs as inequalities rise.

[10] See Hayter, T. (2004) *Open borders: The case against immigration controls*, London: Pluto Press, p 151 for examples of what then results, ranging from the building of the Cutteslowe Wall between neighbourhoods within one city to the widespread toleration of an intolerance of international immigration.

[11] Bauman, Z. (2007) *Consuming life*, Cambridge: Polity Press, p 147, quoting Neil Lawson on consumption.

[12] See Section 6.1, in Chapter 6, this volume, and Offer, A. (2006) *The challenge of affluence: Self-control and well-being in the United States and Britain since 1950*, Oxford: Oxford University Press, pp 190-6.

[13] See Bauman, Z. (2008) *The art of life*, Cambridge: Polity Press, pp 57, 120, 132.

[14] See Figure 21 in Chapter 7, page 276, this volume. There are also data from Scotland showing similar results.

[15] CEPMHPG (Centre for Economic Performance's Mental Health Policy Group) (2006) *The depression report: A New Deal for depression and anxiety disorders*, London: CEPMHPG, London School of Economics and Political Science.

[16] Kay, J. (2004) *The truth about markets: Why some nations are rich but most remain poor* (2nd edn), London: Penguin, p 323.

[17] See Clarkson, T. (2001 [1785]) 'An essay on the impolicy of the African slave trade', in G. Davey Smith, D. Dorling and M. Shaw (eds) *Poverty, inequality and health in Britain: 1800–2000 – A reader*, Bristol: The Policy Press, pp 2-6.

[18] For an early example of the debunking of those who were supposedly especially great and good, see Strachey, L. (1918) *Eminent Victorians*, New York, NY: G.P. Putnam and Sons.

[19] We have traditions of telling fairy stories that do not state the mundane truth, that all inventions were of discoveries about to be made because it had just become possible to make them, and who exactly made them is largely inconsequential. We also rarely point out how constrained people are by their circumstances, and that '… the average newspaper boy in Pittsburgh knows more about the universe than did Galileo, Aristotle, Leonardo or any of those other guys who were so smart they only needed one name' (Gilbert, D. [2006] *Stumbling on happiness*, London: HarperCollins, p 213). You can argue that most of the now forgotten toilers who were just beaten to the winning post of invention were also equally exceptional people, but that argument fails to hold recursively, as for every one of them, there is another. Elvis Presley is a good example of the right (white) man being in the right place at the right time to become seen as so special later.

[20] According to www.geog.ubc.ca/~ewyly/acknowledgments.html, the home page of Elvin Wyly.

[21] According to John Bartlett (1820–1905) in his book of *Familiar quotations* (10th edn, published in 1919), quotation number 9327, this was attributed to Michel Eyquem de Montaigne (1533–92). It is attributed to *Of physiognomy* (book, 3, chapter 12) (see www.bartleby.com/100/731.58.html).

[22] See Cohen, G.A. (2008) *Rescuing justice and equality*, Cambridge, MA: Harvard University Press.

Chapter 2

[1] Miller, G. (2000) *On fairness and efficiency: The privatisation of the public income during the past millennium*, Bristol: The Policy Press; see pp 53-7 on rent.

[2] Irvin, G. (2008) *Super rich: The rise of inequality in Britain and the United States*, Cambridge: Polity Press; see pp 37-61 on 'Do we need fat cats?'.

[3] Shah, H. and Goss, S. (2007) *Democracy and the public realm: Compass Programme for Renewal*, London: Lawrence & Wishart, p 83.

[4] Kasser, T. (2002) *The high price of materialism*, Cambridge, MA: The MIT Press, pp 110-15.

[5] See the projections for the years 2050 and 2300 mapped in Dorling, D., Newman, M. and Barford, A. (2008) *Atlas of the real world: Mapping the way we live*, London: Thames and Hudson, maps 7 and 8.

[6] For a good example see Lawson, N. (2009) *All consuming*, London: Penguin.

[7] Diamond, J. (1992) *The rise and fall of the third chimpanzee* (2nd edn), London: Random House, p 168.

[8] Neolithic farming life appears now to have often been taken up out of necessity rather than choice as it began to develop around the world. We first farmed when we were forced to due to there being too many of us in one area simply to hunt and gather, or due to some change in the climate reducing the supply of what there was to hunt or gather. The story archaeologists tell is that we became a little shorter following our first forays into farming, at first because farming was not very efficient, and later, especially outside the North China plain, as farmers became peasants who became subject to taxes, tolls and population pressures that caused food to be often insufficient. See Davis, M. (2000) 'The origin of the third world', *Antipode*, vol 32, no 1, pp 48-89.

[9] Modern women remaining an inch shorter than their distant ancestors may be modern biology faithfully marking the cumulative effects of our remaining gender insults.

[10] Greek news report (translated by Dimitris Ballas in 2007) of 19 November 2004 (www.in.gr/news/article.asp?lngEntityID=581606).

[11] Dorling, D. (2006) 'Infant mortality and social progress in Britain, 1905–2005', in E. Garrett, C. Galley, N. Shelton and R. Woods (eds) *Infant mortality: A continuing social problem*, Aldershot: Ashgate, pp 213-28.

[12] The speed of the rise in internet access would suggest that majority access is possible in a lifetime when that rise is coupled with projections of how many fewer children there soon will be worldwide. The deciding factor is currently the date when the manufacturers of silicon wafers decide it is profitable for them to double the diameter of the discs they produce, discs from which the silicon chips are made. To decide that, they too look at the same rise in access, the spread of money worldwide and projections on population falls. Currently it is only global inequality in incomes that deters them (according to the author's personal communication with some who advise the manufacturers).

[13] At any one time there are now at least one hundred million university students in the world, with a narrow majority being female; see Dorling, D., Newman, M. and Barford, A. (2008) *Atlas of the real world: Mapping the way we live*, London:

Thames and Hudson, maps 221 and 228 on the growth in tertiary education, map 229 on youth literacy and maps 241 and 242 on changing internet access.

[14] The title headed *The Guardian* newspaper's report of the publication of Wilkinson, R.G. and Pickett, K. (2009) *The spirit level: Why more equal societies almost always do better*, London: Allen Lane.

[15] Smith, R. (2007) *Being human: Historical knowledge and the creation of human nature*, Manchester: Manchester University Press, p 89.

[16] Wolff, J. and de-Shalit, A. (2007) *Disadvantage*, Oxford: Oxford University Press, p 7.

[17] Watts, B. (2008) *What are today's social evils? The results of a web consultation*, York: Joseph Rowntree Foundation; see p 3 on reciprocity, empathy and compassion.

[18] Leech, K. (2005) *Race*, London: SPCK; and see Leech's pamphlet on Brick Lane referenced within.

[19] Gordon, D. (2009) 'Global inequality, death, and disease', *Environment and Planning A*, vol 41, no 6, pp 1271-2.

[20] Amin, S. (2004) 'World poverty, pauperization and capital accumulation', *Monthly Review*, vol 55, no 5.

[21] Kelsey, J. (1997) *The New Zealand experiment: A world model for structural adjustment?*, Auckland: Auckland University Press, p 256.

[22] Richard Tawney in his book *Equality* published in 1931 (p 57 of the 4th edn), quoted in George, V. and Wilding, P. (1999) *British society and social welfare: Towards a sustainable society*, London: Macmillan, p 130.

[23] Rose, S., Lewontin, R.C. and Kamin, L.J. (1990) *Not in our genes: Biology, ideology and human nature*, London: Penguin, p 145.

[24] Baggini, J. (2008) *Welcome to Everytown: A journey into the English mind* (2nd edn), London: Granta, p 195.

[25] Marmot, M. (2004) *Status syndrome: How your social standing directly affects your health and life expectancy*, London: Bloomsbury.

[26] Wilkinson, R.G. (2009) 'Rank', D. Dorling, York, personal communication.

[27] Or, put properly: 'Men make their own history, but they do not make it as they please; they do not make it under self-selected circumstances, but under circumstances existing already, given and transmitted from the past. The tradition of all dead generations weighs like a nightmare on the brains of the living' ('The Eighteenth Brumaire of Louis Bonaparte, Karl Marx, 1852', www.marxists. org/archive/marx/works/1852/18th-brumaire/ch01.htm).

[28] The mantra was first coined by Michael Douglas playing Gordon Gekko in the 1987 film 'Wall Street'.

[29] As the counter-mantra of a generation later relayed: 'Choose life. Choose a job. Choose a career. Choose a family. Choose a fucking big television, Choose washing machines, cars, compact disc players, and electrical tin openers. Choose good health, low cholesterol and dental insurance. Choose fixed-interest mortgage repayments. Choose a starter home. Choose your friends. Choose leisure wear and matching luggage. Choose a three-piece suite on hire purchase in a range of fucking fabrics. Choose DIY and wondering who you are on a Sunday morning. Choose sitting on that couch watching mind-numbing spirit-crushing game shows, stuffing fucking junk food into your mouth. Choose rotting away at the end of it all, pishing your last in a miserable home, nothing more than an embarrassment to the selfish, fucked-up brats you have spawned to replace yourself. Choose your future. Choose life ...', from the 1996 film of the book *Trainspotting* (www.generationterrorists.com/quotes/trainspotting.html).

[30] James, O. (2008) *The selfish capitalist: Origins of affluenza*, London: Vermilion, p 1.

[31] Dorling, D. (2007) 'Guest editorial: the real mental health bill', *Journal of Public Mental Health*, vol 6, no 3, pp 6-13.

[32] Dorling, D., Mitchell, R. and Pearce, J. (2008) 'The global impact of income inequality on health by age: an observational study', *British Medical Journal*, vol 335, pp 873-7.

[33] The labelling of a seventh as, in effect, modern-day delinquents, is true even in the more equitable of these affluent countries. By the same criteria a sixth of children in the UK and a quarter of all children in the US qualify as modern-day delinquents; see Figure 2 and Table 1 in this volume. These education statistics are derived from OECD publications and are discussed in Chapter 3. The statistics on poverty and exclusion mentioned in Chapter 2 are discussed further and sources are given in Chapter 4. The claims of current levels of debt and prejudice are given in detail in Chapter 5. Chapter 6 provides a breakdown of wealth, housing and automobile statistics. And Chapter 7 is concerned with statistics on rising mental ill health and general despair.

[34] Dorling, D., Rigby, J., Wheeler, B., Ballas, D., Thomas, B., Fahmy, E., Gordon, D. and Lupton, R. (2007) *Poverty, wealth and place in Britain, 1968 to 2005*, Bristol: The Policy Press.

[35] Those who labour hardest in the world have the least wealth. Those who have most wealth need to (and usually do) labour least. The most cursory observation of the lives of the poor in poor countries and comparison with the lives of the rich in affluent nations reveals this.

[36] Sabel, C., Dorling, D. and Hiscock, R. (2007) 'Sources of income, wealth and the length of life: an individual level study of mortality', *Critical Public Health*, vol 17, no 4, pp 293-310.

[37] Of all the 25 richest countries in the world, the US and the UK rank as second and fourth most unequal respectively when the annual income of the best-off tenth of their population is compared with that of the poorest tenth. In descending order of inequality the 10%:10% income ratios are: 17.7 Singapore, 15.9 US, 15 Portugal, 13.8 UK, 13.4 Israel, 12.5 Australia, 12.5 New Zealand, 11.6 Italy, 10.3 Spain, 10.2 Greece, 9.4 Canada, 9.4 Ireland, 9.2 Netherlands, 9.1 France, 9 Switzerland, 8.2 Belgium, 8.1 Denmark, 7.8 Korea (Republic of), 7.3 Slovenia, 6.9 Austria, 6.9 Germany, 6.2 Sweden, 6.1 Norway, 5.6 Finland, and 4.5 Japan. This is excluding very small states and is derived from the UN 2009 *Human Development Report*, Statistical Annex, Table M: http://hdr.undp.org/en/media/HDR_2009_EN_Indicators.pdf.

[38] For instance, in countries with less greed more people can spend more time doing more useful things than working to try to overcome the outcomes of greed.

[39] The questions begin: 'Been able to concentrate on whatever you are doing?' and end 'Been feeling reasonably happy, all things considered?'.

[40] Shaw, M., Dorling, D. and Mitchell, R. (2002) *Health, place and society*, Harlow: Pearson, p 59; this book is now available on creative commons general open-access copyright: http://sasi.group.shef.ac.uk/publications/healthplacesociety/index.html

[41] Dorling, D. and Barford, A. (2009) 'The inequality hypothesis: thesis, antithesis, and a synthesis?', *Health and Place*, vol 15, no 4, pp 1166-9.

Chapter 3

[1] For one of the clearest explanations of why so much is not so complex see the work of David Gordon on child poverty; for example: 'The absence of any useful economic theory of child poverty is not a result of the complex nature of this subject. In fact, the economics of child poverty are very simple and are entirely concerned with redistribution – where sufficient resources are redistributed from adults to children there is no child poverty; where insufficient resources are redistributed from adults to children child poverty is inevitable' (Gordon, D. [2008] 'Children, policy and social justice', in G. Craig, T. Burchardt and D. Gordon [eds] *Social justice and public policy: Seeking fairness in diverse societies*, Bristol: The Policy Press, pp 157-79, at p 166).

[2] OECD (Organisation for Economic Co-operation and Development) (2007) *The Programme for International Student Assessment (PISA), OECD's latest PISA study of learning skills among 15-year-olds*, Paris: OECD, p 20.

[3] Ibid; OECD (2009) *PISA 2006 technical report, OECD's technical report on the latest PISA study of learning skills among 15-year-olds*, Paris: OECD.

[4] For all of these phrases see OECD (2007) *PISA, OECD's latest PISA study of learning skills among 15-year-olds*, Paris: OECD, pp 14 and 7.

[5] As in Britain in 2009 when 10,000 'extra' places were made available in universities for science, technology, engineering and mathematics students, but in the small print universities were told that they could also provide more places in business studies and economics. This small print appears to have been kept from the public. Given the huge increase in demand for places that year, and a small increase in cohort size, these 'extra places' were, in practice, a cut in opportunity to study.

[6] Gerhardt, S. (2004) *Why love matters*, Hove: Brunner-Routledge, p 127.

[7] Glover, J. (2001) *Humanity: A moral history of the twentieth century*, London: Pimlico, p 382; referring in turn to the works of Samuel and Pearl Oliner and of Emilie Guth.

[8] Bauman, Z. (2008) *The art of life*, Cambridge: Polity Press, p 97.

[9] The way in which collaboration occurred in the Channel Island offshoots of Britain that were occupied by Germany during the Second World War is only just being acknowledged today. Similarly the fact that the high commands in Britain, the US and the Soviet Union were not overly concerned about genocide in Europe is a tale also only just beginning to be told.

[10] Goldberg, D.T. (2009) *The threat of race: Reflections on racial neoliberalism*, Oxford: Blackwell, p 155.

[11] Ball, S.J. (2008) *The education debate*, Bristol: The Policy Press, p 33; referring in turn to a description of the OECD posted on the web by others in May 2002. As a provider of data the OECD does have some uses, and it does of course have many supporters, but you have to be so careful in looking for the assumptions made in any data it 'models' that those uses are limited.

[12] OECD (2009) 'History of the OECD' (www.oecd.org/document/63/0,33 43,en_2649_201185_1876671_1_1_1_1,00.html).

[13] Such as: 'what are all the possible factors that could influence global temperature change apart from carbon dioxide emissions?'. The OECD testers give naming one of these as an example of the kind of 'harder questions' they set to be awarded a high score, but they do not give a list of what would be considered suitable answers, although they must have given such a list to their

markers (see OECD [2007] *PISA, OECD's latest PISA study of learning skills among 15-year-olds*, Paris: OECD, p 17).

[14] At least since a century ago: see Tuddenham, R.D. (1948) 'Soldier intelligence in World Wars I and II', *American Psychologist*, vol 3, pp 54-6; and the arguments of Flynn, J.R. (1984) 'The mean IQ of Americans: massive gains 1932 to 1978', *Psychological Bulletin*, vol 95, pp 29-51.

[15] Flynn, J.R. (1987) 'Massive IQ gains in 14 nations', *Psychological Bulletin*, vol 101, pp 171-91.

[16] Two standard deviations below the current mean according to the Psychological Corporation (2003, p 229), as reported in Flynn, J.R. (2007) *What is intelligence? Beyond the Flynn effect*, Cambridge: Cambridge University Press.

[17] Wilkinson, R.G. (2009) 'Intelligence', D. Dorling, York, personal communication.

[18] That country with the maximum of 4% of children at level 6 (genius status) being New Zealand (OECD [2007] *PISA, OECD's latest PISA study of learning skills among 15-year-olds*, Paris: OECD, p 20), the unsaid implication being that, given this international distribution, even in the best of all possible worlds we should not expect more than, say, 5% of children in rich countries to ever reach level 6. If it were possible for more to do so, then (the testers might argue) that should have occurred somewhere by now. It would not be hard to counter such an argument by pointing to how very high average test scores can easily be achieved for a large group of children simply through hot-housing them in the most expensive of private boarding schools. The outcome often produces children who can pass tests and who have also been led to believe that they should be leaders.

[19] Note that the technical report was released three years after the survey: OECD (2009) *PISA 2006 technical report, OECD's technical report on the latest PISA study of learning skills among 15-year-olds*, Paris: OECD, p 145.

[20] White, J. (2002) *The child's mind*, London: RoutledgeFalmer, p 76.

[21] You can search the internet and easily find such examples, but it is far more rewarding to be diverted by insights such as that it is: '... factors in modernized societies that have made music a specialty – individuality, competitiveness, compartmentalization, and institutionalization [are not found].... In small-scale pre-modern societies (and in any large modern sub-Saharan African city, as well as in children anywhere who are customarily exposed to frequent communal musical activity), everyone participates in music – regularly, spontaneously, and wholeheartedly' (Dissanayake, E. [2005] 'A review of *The singing Neanderthals: The origins of music, language, mind and body* by Steven Mithen', *Evolutionary Psychology*, vol 3, pp 375-80, at p 379).

[22] Jolly, R. (2007) 'Early childhood development: the global challenge', *The Lancet*, vol 369, no 9555, 6 January, pp 1-78, at p 8.

[23] The idea of innate intelligence is the idea that human brains are wired so that people who are good at some things are more often good at others and that correlation cannot be greatly influenced by society. James Flynn has recently explained (while discussing Clancy Blair's findings) that: 'The only thing that could prevent society from unraveling the correlational matrix would be brain physiology: a human brain so structured that no single cognitive ability could be enhanced without enhancing all of them. As Blair triumphantly shows, the brain is not like that' (Flynn, J.R. [2006] 'Towards a theory of intelligence beyond *g*', *Behavioral and Brain Sciences*, vol 29, no 2, pp 132-4, at p 132).

[24] Kamin, L.J. (1981) 'Some historical facts about IQ testing', in S. Raby (ed) *Intelligence: The battle for the mind*, London: Pan Books, pp 90-7.

[25] Howe, M.J.A., Davidson, J.W. and Sloboda, J.A. (1999) 'Innate talents: reality or myth?', in S.J. Ceci and W.M. Williams (eds) *The nature–nurture debate: The essential readings*, Oxford: Blackwell, pp 258-90, at p 279.

[26] Clark, L. (2009) 'Middle-class children have better genes, says former schools chief ... and we just have to accept it', *The Daily Mail*, 13 May.

[27] Wilkinson, R.G. and Pickett, K. (2009) *The spirit level: Why more equal societies almost always do better*, London: Allen Lane; see Chapter 8 on education and comments on ethnicity on pp 177-9.

[28] Some people suggest that it could be genetic similarities in the structure of the brains of identical twins that may cause them to behave slightly differently to other pupils in class and that difference could then be greatly magnified by environmental factors. There is, however, no evidence for this, whereas there is a great deal of evidence to suggest that teachers and other key individuals treat children slightly differently according to their appearance, and of course the one thing we know about identical twins is that they tend to look very much like each other. You might think this point is obvious but it is remarkable how well it has been ignored by those involved in twin studies. The idea that the similarities in the physical appearance of separated identical twins might matter so much is one of the very few ideas in this book that I think might be mine. I am almost certainly mistaken to imagine this! For one of the most insightful discussions, which does not discount the genetic possibilities, but which says they are so tiny that by implicit implication appearance could be as important, see the open-access copy of James Flynn's December 2006 lecture at Trinity College Cambridge: www.psychometrics.sps.cam.ac.uk/page/109/beyond-the-flynn-effect.htm; the full-length version of the argument is in Flynn, J.R. (2007) *What is intelligence? Beyond the Flynn effect*, Cambridge: Cambridge University Press.

[29] Gladwell, M. (2007) 'What IQ doesn't tell you about race', *The New Yorker*, 17 December.

[30] Goldberg, D.T. (2009) *The threat of race: Reflections on racial neoliberalism*, Oxford: Blackwell, p vi. The US prison population actually peaked in 1939 and fell then to a low in 1968 when incarceration rates were much less than 10 times below contemporary rates; see Vogel, R.D. (2004) 'Silencing the cells: mass incarceration and legal repression in US prisons', *Monthly Review*, vol 56, no 1.

[31] Literally as well as metaphorically, as entertainment and sport were the two fields in which black Americans were allowed to partake. With Ronald Regan's election, politics and entertainment merged, and as well as B-movie appearances, political bit parts too became possible for a miniscule minority of the black minority. President Obama himself was no great break from elitism. He was educated in the most prestigious private school in Honolulu as a child. See Elliot Major, L. (2008) 'A British Obama would need an elite education', *The Independent*, 27 November.

[32] Ball, S.J. (2008) *The education debate*, Bristol: The Policy Press, p 70.

[33] Timmins, N. (2001) *The five giants: A biography of the welfare state* (new edn), London: HarperCollins, p 380.

[34] Downes, T.A. and Greenstein, S.M. (2002) 'Entry into the schooling market: how is the behaviour of private suppliers influenced by public sector decisions?', *Bulletin of Economic Research*, vol 54, no 4, pp 341-71, at p 349.

[35] Ibid, p 342.

[36] Dorling, D., Shaw, M. and Davey Smith, G. (2006) 'Global inequality of life expectancy due to AIDS', *British Medical Journal*, vol 332, no 7542, pp 662-4, at p 664, figure 4.

[37] Dorling, D. (2006) 'Class alignment', *Renewal: The Journal of Labour Politics*, vol 14, no 1, pp 8-19.

[38] George, S. (2008) *Hijacking America: How the religious and secular right changed what Americans think*, Cambridge: Polity Press, p 213.

[39] Until 2008 spending in the US was always greater for incumbent Republicans compared to Democrats, and higher in years of rising incomes. The two parties only came close when postwar spending was lowest in 1952. See Bartels, L.M. (2008) *Unequal democracy: The political economy of the new gilded age*, Princeton, NJ: Princeton University Press, p 119.

[40] Goldberg, D.T. (2009) *The threat of race: Reflections on racial neoliberalism*, Oxford: Blackwell, p 70.

[41] Perelman, M. (2006) 'Privatizing education', *Monthly Review*, vol 57, no 10.

---

[42] Irvin, G. (2008) *Super rich: The rise of inequality in Britain and the United States*, Cambridge: Polity Press, p 158; quoting Jonathan Kozol in *Harpers Magazine*, September 2005, pp 48-9, in turn quoting from the headteacher who called the pupils he created 'robots'.

[43] See Giroux, H.A. and Saltman, K. (2008) 'Obama's betrayal of public education? Arne Duncan and the corporate model of schooling', *Truthout* (www.truthout.org/121708R). .

[44] Tomlinson, S. (2007) 'Learning to compete', *Renewal: A Journal of Social Democracy*, vol 15, nos 2/3, pp 117-22, at p 120. The 57 varieties include numerous types of specialist school, 'beacons', 'academies' and many other flavours of division.

[45] Goldberg, D.T. (2009) *The threat of race: Reflections on racial neoliberalism*, Oxford: Blackwell, p 78.

[46] Seton-Rogers, S. (2003) 'Watson, Crick, and who?', *web Weekly: News from the Harvard Medical Community*, 7 April.

[47] 'Lab suspends DNA pioneer Watson', 19 October 2007, BBC News, http://news.bbc.co.uk/2/hi/science/nature/7052416.stm

[48] Connelly, M. (2008) *Fatal misconception: The struggle to control world population*, Cambridge, MA: Harvard University Press, p 272; Shockley's prize was given to him and two others for the invention of the transistor, the key to early computing.

[49] 'Francis Crick's controversial archive on first public display', see www.wellcome.ac.uk/News/Media-office/Press-releases/2003/WTD002850.htm

[50] Not simply as a result of having no great prizes, but perhaps also as a product of a little more understanding and acceptance of humanity, is the arrangement of prestige in academic journals and departments in the social sciences, arts and humanities, which is far less hierarchical than is often found in other academic disciplines. Of course generalisations such as this are not rules. The only living person to have received two Nobel prizes, Fred Sanger, appears a remarkably humane biochemist despite leading quite a closeted life. Linus Pauling similarly showed it was possible to be more than just a chemist, and won two prizes. These were for such different things that he is the only person counted twice in Figure 4 (this volume).

[51] The Post-Autistic Economics Network and the Association of Heterodox Economists have pointed out how ridiculous traditional economics has become. Orthodox economists produce 'dictionaries' of their subject where almost 90% of the 'great economists' listed are men from just eight US Ivy League universities. Just as it is a little unfair on those with autism to link them to those who have chosen to be economists so too it is a little unfair on the

'mad' (who are often far more sane) to repeat the oft-told retort that only the mad and traditional economists believe that growth is forever possible; even prize winners such as Joe Stiglitz now criticise economics as it is traditionally taught. For these stories and more see Scott Cato, M. (2009) *Green economics: An introduction to theory, policy and practice*, London: Earthscan, pp 25 and 31.

[52] Rogoff, K. (2002) 'An open letter to Joseph Stiglitz', International Monetary Fund (www.imf.org/external/np/vc/2002/070202.htm); see also Kay, J. (2004) *The truth about markets: Why some nations are rich but most remain poor* (2nd edn), London: Penguin, p 381 for references to economists slandering one another.

[53] Irvin, G. (2008) *Super rich: The rise of inequality in Britain and the United States*, Cambridge: Polity Press, p 157.

[54] Mayer, S.E. (2001) 'How did the increase in economic inequality between 1970 and 1990 affect children's educational attainment?', *American Journal of Sociology*, vol 107, no 1, pp 1-32.

[55] In Britain in 1997 Gordon Marshall the then head of the nation's Economic and Social Research Council and his colleagues suggested that there was the possibility: '... that children born to working-class parents simply have less natural ability than those born to higher-class parents', documented in S. White (2007) *Equality*, Cambridge: Polity Press, at p 66. It may be a tad cruel to the facially disfigured, but it is now often stated that the lie that the upper classes have better genes is simply propagated by ignorant chinless wonders whose only valid claim to special genetic inheritance is their lack of chin. Faced with increasing vocal and sustained opposition to their claims to be innately superior, those who have been told they are superior often retreat into self-supporting social bubbles for security. Within such comfort bubbles it is easier to believe statements such as that children born to working-class parents simply have less natural ability than children born to upper-class parents.

[56] '... children of different class backgrounds tend to do better or worse in school – on account, one may suppose, of a complex interplay of sociocultural and genetic factors' (Goldthorpe, J. and Jackson, M. [2007] 'Education-based meritocracy: the barriers to its realization', *Economic Change, Quality of Life and Social Cohesion*, 6th Framework Network [www.equalsoc.org/uploaded_files/regular/goldthorpe_jackson.pdf], p S3).

[57] See note 28 above.

[58] Identifying potential 'Oxbridge material' was an old term used in England for such practices before they became institutionalised. The idea that different people are made of different mental 'material' was most commonly espoused in the era of 1920s and 1930s eugenics when those who advocated the inheritability of intelligence wrote that it '... is seen with especial clearness in these numerous cases – like the Cecils, or the Darwins – where intellectual

ability runs in families' (Wells, H.G., Huxley, J. and Wells, G.P. [1931] *The science of life*, London: Cassell and Company Limited, p 823). That the offspring of such families do not now dominate intellectual life provides an extra spoonful of evidence to add to the great pile built up since the 1930s that now discredits eugenics and other such '… foolish analogies between biology and society [whereby the world's richest man] … Rockefeller was acclaimed the highest form of human being that evolution had produced, a use denounced even by William Graham Sumner, the great "Social Darwinist"' (Flynn, J.R. [2007] *What is intelligence? Beyond the Flynn effect*, Cambridge: Cambridge University Press, pp 147-8).

[59] The number of women expected to be awarded prizes in every decade from 1901 onwards has always been less than five, so the statistical test that is taught to novice students of probability cannot be applied. However, in an exact test, if the process is random, and on average 4.9% of prizes were awarded to women each year before 1950, then over the 15 years 1948–62 (inclusive) and the five prizes then available, the chance that not a single woman would be awarded a prize in any year is $(1-0.049)^{(15*5)}=0.023$ or 2.3% (if all prize giving is independent).

[60] Walter Lippmann, who was also an early critic of IQ testing, quoted in Kamin, L.J. (1981) 'Some historical facts about IQ testing', in S. Raby (ed) *Intelligence: The battle for the mind*, London: Pan Books, pp 90-7, at p 90. Just as Albert Einstein came to regret the work he had done that was later used to develop the nuclear bomb, so Walter Lippmann regretted that which his early work was later used to produce.

[61] Howe, M.J.A., Davidson, J.W. and Sloboda, J.A. (1999) 'Innate talents: reality or myth?', in S.J. Ceci and W.M. Williams (eds) *The nature–nurture debate: The essential readings*, Oxford: Blackwell, pp 258-90.

[62] Timmins, N. (2001) *The five giants: A biography of the welfare state* (new edn), London: HarperCollins, p 380. Note that there were also a few technical schools, but they never caught on so are not mentioned further here apart from saying that they were early evidence of beliefs in a continuum.

[63] A significant few had been deemed not educable until the Education Act of 1981 decreed that none were to be obviously warehoused (or 'garaged') any longer, all having a right to some kind of education.

[64] Wilkinson, R.G. and Pickett, K. (2009) *The spirit level: Why more equal societies almost always do better*, London: Allen Lane, p 238.

[65] Gillborn, D. and Youdell, D. (2000) *Rationing education: Policy practice, reform and equity*, Buckingham: Open University Press.

[66] Hirschfield, P.J. (2008) 'Preparing for prison? The criminalization of school discipline in the USA', *Theoretical Criminology*, vol 12, no 1, pp 79-101, at pp 79, 82.

[67] Orr, D. (2008) 'Proof that we fail too many children', *The Independent*, 19 March.

[68] Rwanda only ranks similarly to the US if those awaiting trial for war crimes are included; for the ranking by civilian crimes see the Worldmapper website, in particular, www.worldmapper.org/posters/worldmapper_map293_ver5.pdf

[69] The likelihood of children from different areas getting to university and to different types of university is mapped in Thomas, B. and Dorling, D. (2007) *Identity in Britain: A cradle-to-grave atlas*, Bristol: The Policy Press, which uses data from studies that show that in absolute terms almost all the extra places went to children resident in the already most 'privileged' areas. In January 2010 the Higher Education Funding Council for England published research showing a reverse in the trend. See Dorling, D. (2010) 'Expert opinion', *The Guardian*, 28 January, p 10.

[70] Ball, S.J. (2008) *The education debate*, Bristol: The Policy Press, p 180, criticising and quoting from p 20, para 1.28 of the 2005 White Paper on *Higher standards: Better schools for all*, Department for Education and Skills, emphasis added.

[71] Stanton, A. (2007) *Mr Gum and the biscuit billionaire*, London: Egmont, p 66. Incidentally it has been convincingly argued that J.K. Rowling, the author of *Harry Potter*, based her main character on Tony Blair and that Harry's fortunes mirrored his, so all is still far from utopia in the world of children's stories. 'Rowling is Blair's triumph (single mum becomes billionaire) and dark mirror' (Kelly, S. [2008] 'Novelising New Labour', *Renewal*, vol 16, no 2, pp 52-9, at p 58).

[72] Gillborn, D. and Youdell, D. (2000) *Rationing education: Policy practice, reform and equity*, Buckingham: Open University Press, p 221.

[73] Ball, S.J. (2008) *The education debate*, Bristol: The Policy Press, p 173, referring to *The Independent on Sunday*'s release of an unpublished Department for Education and Skills report, during December 2006.

[74] Wilkinson, R.G. and Pickett, K. (2009) *The spirit level: Why more equal societies almost always do better*, London: Allen Lane, p 115.

[75] McCarthy, M. (2008) 'The big question: is it time the world forgot about cannabis in its war against drugs?', *The Independent*, 3 October. Jonathan Adair Turner, who also goes by the title of Baron Turner of Ecchinswell, was a banker who was a Conservative student, but joined the British Social Democratic Party when it was formed, and then became a favourite of the Labour government.

This was all possible without the need for him to alter a single conviction, such was the shift in British politics from 1979 to 1997.

[76] Crim, K. (2005) 'Notes on the intelligence of women', *The Atlantic*, 18 May. Although Larry was taken to task, within just four years he was appointed to advise President Obama on economics. It is reported that in April 2009 he fell asleep on the job (http://thinkprogress.org/2009/04/23/summers-sleep/). Apparently he uses diet coke to try to stay awake. For some advice Larry was given of how to stay awake and be smarter see www.huffingtonpost.com/2009/04/23/larry-summers-falls-aslee_n_190659.html

[77] It is now largely accepted that fertility decline in the world is approaching replacement levels, according to UN central population projections (see www.worldmapper.org on the 2050 projection and technical notes available there). The driving force in this has not been the availability of contraceptives; these have been necessary but are not sufficient. Fertility falls when elitism is overcome enough for women to be allowed to learn and to gain just enough personal power to decide more for themselves. As a result we are now some way past the point where 'Nearly half of the world's population ... lives in countries with fertility at or below replacement levels' (Morgan, S.P. and Taylor, M.G. [2006], 'Low fertility at the turn of the twenty-first century', *Annual Review of Sociology*, vol 32, no 1, pp 375-99, at p 375). And, as fertility falls faster during economic slumps, we may be even further past that point than we currently realise. The date of 2052 is given as this article suggests that it will be just after the mid-century when, worldwide, human population stops rising. It may be earlier. It is unlikely to be later.

[78] Fertility in China fell from 6.4 children per woman to 2.7 in just that one decade immediately preceding the introduction of the one child policy: Connelly, M. (2008) *Fatal misconception: The struggle to control world population*, Cambridge, MA: Harvard University Press, p 570.

[79] Wilkinson, R.G. (2009) 'Rank', D. Dorling, York, personal communication.

Chapter 4

[1] Wilkinson, R.G. and Pickett, K. (2009) *The spirit level: Why more equal societies almost always do better*, London: Allen Lane, p 143.

[2] Alesina, A., Tella, R.D. and MacCulloch, R. (2004) 'Inequality and happiness: are Europeans and Americans different?', *Journal of Public Economics*, vol 88, pp 2009-42.

[3] Wolff, J. and de-Shalit, A. (2007) *Disadvantage*, Oxford: Oxford University Press, p 110, using arguments from Bradshaw, J. and Finch, N. (2003) 'Overlaps in dimensions of poverty', *Journal of Social Policy*, vol 32, no 4, pp 513-25.

[4] Dorling, D., Rigby, J., Wheeler, B., Ballas, D., Thomas, B., Fahmy, E., Gordon, D. and Lupton, R. (2007) *Poverty, wealth and place in Britain, 1968 to 2005*, Bristol: The Policy Press.

[5] Irvin, G. (2008) *Super rich: The rise of inequality in Britain and the United States*, Cambridge: Polity Press, p 189. A fifth of the entire population had outstanding debt on credit cards by 2007; they were no longer a middle-class-only niche: ONS (Office for National Statistics) (2008) *Wealth and Assets Survey: Initial report*, London: ONS.

[6] The 1968/69 Poverty Survey of Britain showed this to be the case. See Dorling, D., Rigby, J., Wheeler, B., Ballas, D., Thomas, B., Fahmy, E., Gordon, D. and Lupton, R. (2007) *Poverty, wealth and place in Britain, 1968 to 2005*, Bristol: The Policy Press.

[7] Ballas, D. and Dorling, D. (2007) 'Measuring the impact of major life events upon happiness', *International Journal of Epidemiology*, vol 36, no 6, pp 1244–52, table 3, which suggests that in essence bad and good holiday experiences tend to balance out, and that holidays not taken with family tend to be associated with a slightly more positive outcome.

[8] In 1759 Adam Smith wrote about the linen shirt and shoes and has been endlessly quoted thereafter. In 1847 Karl Marx wrote on how homes would appear as hovels if a castle was built nearby. In 1901 Seebohm Rowntree wrote on the necessity of being able to afford a stamp to write a letter to a loved one.

[9] Karl Polanyi's writing of 1944 quoted in Magdoff, H. and Magdoff, F. (2005) 'Approaching socialism', *Monthly Review*, vol 57, no 3.

[10] Almond, S. and Kendall, J. (2001) 'Low pay in the UK: the case for a three sector comparative approach', *Annals of Public and Cooperative Economics*, vol 72, no 1, pp 45–76, at p 45.

[11] Offer, A. (2006) *The challenge of affluence: Self-control and well-being in the United States and Britain since 1950*, Oxford: Oxford University Press, pp 234, 292.

[12] Frank, R.H. (2007) *Falling behind: How rising inequality harms the middle class*, Berkeley, CA: University of California Press, p 4.

[13] Burns, J. (2007) *The descent of madness: Evolutionary origins of psychosis and the social brain*, Hove: Routledge, pp 99, 136, 184–5.

[14] GLA (Greater London Authority) (2002) *London divided: Income inequality and poverty in the capital*, London: GLA; p 11 of the summary reported that some 20% of children were living in families that could not save £10 a month nor afford to take a holiday other than by visiting and staying with family.

[15] Ibid, see p 64.

[16] Raymond Baker, director of the Global Financial Integrity and an expert on money laundering, quoted in Mathiason, N. (2007) 'Tax evasion taskforce to probe UK: international group will track $1trillion of illicit funds', *Observer*, 1 July.

[17] Shah, H. and McIvor, M. (2006) *A new political economy: Compass Programme for Renewal*, London: Lawrence & Wishart, p 110.

[18] Take, for instance, the Enlightenment taste for ranking races: 'Immanuel Kant could wedge "the Arab", "possessed of an inflamed imagination", between the basest of (Southern) Europeans and the far East, but significantly above "the Negroes of Africa"' (Goldberg, D.T. [2009] *The threat of race: Reflections on racial neoliberalism*, Oxford: Blackwell, p 163).

[19] See Chapter 3, note 58, page 333, this volume.

[20] Karl Pearson, the man who gave it that name, apparently thought of calling it 'normal' to try to end the dispute between those who termed it 'Gaussian' and those who called it 'Laplacian'. Ending that dispute would in hindsight not appear to have been his only motive in choosing such a loaded term.

[21] Over time the curve tends to move up the grades. Students perform better at tests when teachers can teach better to the test, which they can with each year that passes and, as there are always pressures on those who mark to be more generous as compared with last year, especially if their students are supposed to be especially able, markers have a tendency to become more lenient over time. A department in an elitist university in Britain may now award as many first class degrees as lower second class degrees. The most elite universities do not subdivide second class degrees, presenting yet another shape to the outcome distribution. In general, as we know more, we have become cleverer, but we still have huge difficulty in trying not to constantly claim that within any generation some of us are much cleverer than others.

[22] Unemployment is only possible in countries that have chosen to afford unemployment benefit. Unemployment rates fall when benefit levels are so low that they are very hard to live on. People will then do any work, no matter how demeaning, and will more often turn to crime. The rates of unemployment in a country, and who is unemployed, are thus the results of choices made as to how many jobs to provide for whom, and how punitive a rate of benefit to set. Often fewer jobs are provided for younger adults, who consequently experience higher unemployment and crime rates (Gordon, D. [2008] 'Unemployment', D. Dorling, Bristol, personal communication).

[23] Known more commonly as a chi-squared test, usually attributed to Karl Pearson although Stephen Stigler's law of eponymy, that 'no scientific discovery is named after its original discoverer', may well apply (Bibby, J. [2009] 'Karl Pearson', D. Dorling, York, personal communication).

[24] The chances are at least ten times less likely than the chance of tossing a coin 100 times and counting exactly 50 heads and 50 tails. The chance of that is about 8% (not to be confused with the chance of counting exactly 50 heads then exactly 50 tails, which is extremely small). I'm unsure how many times precisely as my computer dislikes calculating factorials over 170. The figure of 8% is calculated as $100!/50!/50!/2^{100}$.

[25] MacKenzie, D. (1999) 'Eugenics and the rise of mathematical statistics in Britain', in D. Dorling and S. Simpson (eds) *Statistics in society*, London: Arnold, pp 55-61.

[26] Pearson, K. (1902) 'On the fundamental conceptions of biology', *Biometrika*, vol 1, no 3, pp 320-44, at p 334.

[27] Cot, A.L. (2005) '"Breed out the unfit and breed in the fit". Irving Fisher, economics, and the science of heredity', *American Journal of Economics and Sociology*, vol 64, no 3, pp 793-826. There have been too few female economists for a test to be undertaken as to whether they would have been drawn to eugenics had they been greater in number. What is important to remember is that some people were more resistant to eugenicists' ideas than others and that presumably remains the case today.

[28] Ellis, L., Hershberger, S., Field, E. et al (2008) *Sex differences: Summarizing more than a century of scientific research*, New York, NY: Psychology Press; see p 405 on autism, p 321 on mathematics, p 324 on science and p 355 on males rating their abilities highly during adolescence.

[29] Livesey, R. (2007) *Socialism, sex, and the culture of aestheticism in Britain, 1880–1914*, Oxford: Oxford University Press, pp 75, 80, 81, referring explicitly to Karl's doubts over women's 'capacity' and his arguments of 1894 with Emma Brook). Note that Karl was not the worse of the eugenists. For that mantle Sir Francis Galton, Charles Darwin's cousin, is widely regarded as a more 'able' contender. Charles Darwin's son (Leonard Darwin) and grandson (Charles Galton Darwin) are also contenders.

[30] Ibid, p 188, quoting from writers in *The new age* editions published in 1911. In this case the so-called 'race' being discussed was the 'British race', a thing we hear little of today thankfully, as Scots and Welsh and Irish balk at being racially incorporated so crudely (and those three five-letter labels are also now very rarely discussed as if they described 'races').

[31] Whereas just as the things which matter with ethnicity are not 'race' differences but the difference that 'race' makes, what matters with sex '... is not the gender difference; it is the difference gender makes' (MacKinnon, C.A. [2006] *Are women human? And other international dialogues*, Boston, MA: Harvard University Press, p 74).

[32] The war made planning for a National Health Service in Britain possible far earlier than might otherwise have been the case, planning that was not simply a theoretical pipedream. See for example Morris, J.N. (2001 [1944]) 'Health, no 6, Handbooks for discussion groups, Association for Education in Citizenship', in G. Davey Smith, D. Dorling and M. Shaw (eds) *Poverty, inequality and health in Britain*, Bristol: The Policy Press, pp 245-62.

[33] Connelly, M. (2008) *Fatal misconception: The struggle to control world population*, Cambridge, MA: Harvard University Press, p 163. Because it was largely used in secret (and in the past), you won't find many mentions of the term 'crypto-eugenics' using Google, but there are some.

[34] Kamin, L.J. (1974) *The science and politics of IQ*, New York, NY: John Wiley & Sons.

[35] Kamin, L.J. (1981) 'Some historical facts about IQ testing', in S. Raby (ed) *Intelligence: The battle for the mind*, London: Pan Books, pp 90-7.

[36] Smith, R. (2007) *Being human: Historical knowledge and the creation of human nature*, Manchester: Manchester University Press, p 89.

[37] 'Questions of nature versus nurture are meaningless.... For human behavioural disorders such as schizophrenia and autism, the inherent plasticity of the nervous system requires a systems approach to incorporate all of the myriad epigenetic factors that can influence such outcomes' (Gottesman, I.I. and Hanson, D.R. [2005] 'Human development: biological and genetic processes', *Annual Review of Psychology*, vol 56, no 1, pp 263-86, at p 263).

[38] Miller, D. (2005) 'What is social justice', in N. Pearce and W. Paxton (eds) *Social justice: Building a fairer Britain*, London, Politico's, pp 3-20, at pp 14-15.

[39] See Chapter 3, note 28, page 330, this volume.

[40] As quoted in White, S. (2007) *Equality*, Cambridge: Polity Press, p 66, which gives the details of who these people were and the wider context. Stuart White's book is also itself an example of welcome evidence that exceptions to this contemporary prejudice exist even within the hallowed halls. See also Chapter 3, note 55, page 333, this volume.

[41] Goldthorpe, J. and Jackson, M. (2007) 'Education-based meritocracy: the barriers to its realization', Economic Change, Quality of Life and Social Cohesion, 6th Framework Network (www.equalsoc.org/uploaded_files/regular/goldthorpe_jackson.pdf), p S3. See also Chapter 3, note 56, page 333.

[42] Tony Blair disguised his geneticist beliefs by talking of them as the 'God-given potential' of children, but it is clear from the policies he promoted, his 'scientific Christianity', and the way he talked about what he thought of his own children's special potential (see Chapter 5, note 18, page 344, this volume),

that his God dealt out potential through genes. For the full wording of his text about children's abilities delivered in 2005 see Ball, S.J. (2008) *The education debate*, Bristol: The Policy Press, p 12.

[43] Dixon, M. (2005) *Brave new choices? Behavioural genetics and public policy: A discussion document*, London: Institute of Public Policy Research.

[44] Bourdieu, P. (2007) *Sketch for a self-analysis* (English edn), Cambridge: Polity Press, pp 8, 9. Pierre Bourdieu does admittedly go on to criticise French colleagues too, particularly over how the support of some for Stalinism and Maoism was only made possible due to their geographical exclusion from more usual places and people.

[45] Gordon, D. (2007) 'Want 1999–2005', D. Dorling, Bristol, personal communication; comparison made between the 1999 Joseph Rowntree Foundation Poverty and Social Exclusion Survey and the 2004–05 equivalent questions asked in the official ONS Family Resources Survey.

[46] Dorling, D. (2008) 'Worlds apart: how inequality breeds fear and prejudice in Britain through the eyes of two very different teenage girls', *The Guardian*, 12 November.

[47] Hills, J. and Stewart, K. (2009) *Towards a more equal society? Poverty, inequality and policy since 1997*, Bristol: The Policy Press.

[48] See Chapter 8, note 26, page 371, this volume.

[49] These are taken from the categories used in Dorling, D., Rigby, J., Wheeler, B., Ballas, D., Thomas, B., Fahmy, E., Gordon, D. and Lupton, R. (2007) *Poverty, wealth and place in Britain, 1968 to 2005*, Bristol: The Policy Press.

[50] The graph was due to appear first in Gordon, D. (2000) 'The scientific measurement of poverty: recent theoretical advances', in J. Bradshaw and R. Sainsbury (eds) *Researching poverty*, Aldershot: Ashgate, pp 37-58, but was not reproduced correctly. Later a full description was provided in Gordon, D. (2006) 'The concept and measurement of poverty', in C. Pantazis, D. Gordon and R. Levitas (eds) *Poverty and social exclusion in Britain: The Millennium Survey*, Bristol: The Policy Press, pp 29-70.

[51] Abdallah, S. (2008) 'Family Resources Survey', D. Dorling, London: New Economics Foundation, personal communication. His analysis of the Family Resources Survey shows that what is called the 'mean average net unequivalised for household structure weekly income' for the five quintile groups in Britain in 2005/06 were: £150.69, £270.31, £398.13, £576.09 and £1,104.09, not that the nine pence matters at that point. Equivalised for household composition there is no meaningful difference in the resulting ratios; the national arithmetic mean income, which also happens to be that which more than 60% of households lived on *less than* in 2005, was £499.15 a week. See

Chapter 2, note 37, page 327, this volume, for the latest international decile ranges and how widely they vary between countries.

[52] George, S. (2008) *Hijacking America: How the religious and secular right changed what Americans think*, Cambridge: Polity Press, pp 209-12.

[53] Kraemer, S. (1999) 'Promoting resilience: changing concepts of parenting and child care', *International Journal of Child and Family Welfare*, vol 3, pp 273-87.

[54] Dorling, D. (2008) 'Cash and the class system', *New Statesman*, 24 July.

[55] The private cars were commandeered. They had only recently become one of the key symbols of status. For a précis of Orwell's account see Harman, C. (2002) *A people's history of the world* (2nd edn), London: Bookmarks, p 500.

[56] Peter Jones talking on the BBC show 'Top Gear' during 2008. For information on the man and his views of his offspring, see www.bbc.co.uk/dragonsden/dragons/peterjones.shtml

[57] Beck, U. (2000) *World risk society* (2nd edn), Cambridge: Polity Press, p 6, on how the richest fifth of people on the planet consume six times more than did their parents.

[58] Wade, R.H. (2007) 'Should we worry about income inequality?', in D. Held and A. Kaya (eds) *Global inequality: Patterns and explanations*, Cambridge: Polity Press, pp 104-31, at p 109.

[59] Frank, R.H. (2007) *Falling behind: How rising inequality harms the middle class*, Berkeley, CA: University of California Press, annual figures derived from graphs on pp 17 and 19.

[60] Between 2000 and 2005, according to George, S. (2008) *Hijacking America: How the religious and secular right changed what Americans think*, Cambridge: Polity Press, p 211.

[61] Dickens, R., Gregg, P. and Wadsworth, J. (2003) 'Introduction', in R. Dickens, P. Gregg and J. Wadsworth (eds) *The labour market under New Labour: The state of working Britain 2003*, Basingstoke: Palgrave Macmillan, pp 1-13, derived from figure 1.2, p 11.

[62] Ibid.

[63] Ibid.

[64] BBC (2008) 'UK income gap "same as in 1991"', 16 December (http://news.bbc.co.uk/2/hi/business/7786149.stm).

[65] George, V. and Wilding, P. (1999) *British society and social welfare: Towards a sustainable society*, London: Macmillan, p 37.

[66] Elliott, L. and Curtis, P. (2009) 'UK's income gap widest since 60s: Labour admits child poverty failure, incomes of poorest fall', *The Guardian*, 8 May.

[67] George, V. and Wilding, P. (1999) *British society and social welfare: Towards a sustainable society*, London: Macmillan, p 110.

[68] Kelsey, J. (1997) *The New Zealand experiment: A world model for structural adjustment?*, Auckland: Auckland University Press, p 333, far from agreeing with, but quoting the views of Alan Gibbs from 1994.

[69] Ibid.

[70] Somers, M.R. and Block, F. (2005) 'From poverty to perversity: ideas, markets, and institutions over 200 years of welfare debate', *American Sociological Review*, vol 70, pp 260-87.

Chapter 5

[1] People who were seen as having the wrong colour skin were more frequently stabbed; see Leech, K. (2005) *Race*, London: SPCK, pp 79-84, 141-5.

[2] Krugman, P. (2007) *The conscience of a liberal*, New York, NY: W.W. Norton, p 160.

[3] So soon after dictatorships were overthrown in Greece (1974), Portugal (1974) and Spain (1975).

[4] Dorling, D. (2001) 'Anecdote is the singular of data', *Environment and Planning A*, vol 33, pp 1335-40, at pp 1336-9, mentions the National Front as viewed by a child.

[5] The National Front vote collapsed in 1979 as far-right voters voted with the Conservative Party.

[6] Ballescas, R.P. (2003) 'Filipino migration to Japan, 1970s to 1990s', in S. Ikehata and L.N. Yu-Jose (eds) *Philippines–Japan relations*, Manila: Ateneo de Manila University Press, chapter 15, at p 563. Indirectly related is Adolf Hitler's description of women's work as *kinder, küche* and *kirche* (children, kitchen and church) from an earlier time of prejudice. Incidentally, in Britain, in more recent years, the work for which migrant labour has been most needed has been described as 'picking, plucking and packing'.

[7] See Hayter, T. (2004) *Open borders: The case against immigration controls*, London: Pluto Press, p 49, on how the 1960s immigration controls inadvertently encouraged immigration. The rise in prejudice ensured that it was soon forgotten that these immigrants were also deliberately brought to Europe to work night shifts in mills and car plants, to drive buses and to be nurses. By 1989 MORI polls in Britain found over 60% of respondents saying there were

too many immigrants. By 2007 that had risen to 68%. It is easy to stoke up prejudices about numbers of people; see Finney, N. and Simpson, L. (2009) *'Sleepwalking to segregation'? Challenging myths of race and migration*, Bristol: The Policy Press – these particular statistics are from p 53.

[8] Krugman, P. (2007) *The conscience of a liberal*, New York, NY: W.W. Norton, p 133. The quote begins 'But for reasons that remain somewhat unclear...'. Migration replacement of fertility decline is a possible reason to explain the trend across most of the rich world; the pull of money and huge demand for service labour are other reasons.

[9] That particular claim, it is suggested on Wikipedia, is made in the biography by Simon Heffer (1999) *Like the Roman: The life of Enoch Powell*, London: Weidenfeld and Nicolson.

[10] Krugman, P. (2007) *The conscience of a liberal*, New York, NY: W.W. Norton, p 210.

[11] Dorling, D. (2007) 'The soul searching within new Labour', *Local Economy*, vol 22, no 4, pp 317-24.

[12] Goody, J. (2006) *The theft of history*, Cambridge: Cambridge University Press, p 15.

[13] Wilkinson, R.G. and Pickett, K. (2009) *The spirit level: Why more equal societies almost always do better*, London: Allen Lane; see Chapter 9 on teenage pregnancies.

[14] Thoburn, J. (2000) *A comparative study of adoption*, Norwich: University of East Anglia, p 5; the number of children placed in non-family care doubled in the US between 1987 and 1999, was higher than in other affluent nations, and more children were consequently adopted. More are also given up for adoption in the US without being placed in care than in Western Europe or Australasia.

[15] See Basic Income Earth Network (www.basicincome.org/bien/) on how all could be paid a living income.

[16] In the few cases where this was not the case it is remarked on as a problem. As the Public Broadcast Service in the US explains to its browsers: 'Slaves were the lowest class in Athenian society, but according to many contemporary accounts they were far less harshly treated than in most other Greek cities. Indeed, one of the criticisms of Athens was that its slaves and freemen were difficult to tell apart' (www.pbs.org/empires/thegreeks/background/32b.html).

[17] James, O. (2009) *Contented dementia*, London: Vermilion, p 23.

[18] Presumably this was also the view of his wife, or she was not strongly enough opposed to prevent the school choice, but that has not been documented. Blair's comments about the work which would be beneath his children are recorded in Steel, M. (2008) *What's going on*, London: Simon & Schuster, p 8. It is now

often repeated on the web: 'There's a great quote in Robin Cook's memoir. He was talking to Blair about [Blair's] son's selective school and Roy Hattersley was there and they said Harold Wilson had sent his children to a comprehensive and one became a headmaster and the other was a professor in the Open University and Blair said, "I rather hope my sons do better than that!"', as recorded by John Paul Flintoff (www.flintoff.org/what-happened-to-meritocracy). Flintoff repeats online Mark Steel's now widely spreading comment: 'For Blair, status and wealth are everything. It's beyond him to think that education might be worthwhile for itself. He can't possibly think along those lines.'

[19] Irvin, G. (2008) *Super rich: The rise of inequality in Britain and the United States*, Cambridge: Polity Press, p 64.

[20] For a few years in the 1970s it was touch and go. Across the Atlantic the population centre of Britain oscillated between moving north or south at this time and voting became much more unpredictable. Thousands of individual decisions swung one way and another in that decade 1968–78. The most equitable year was probably 1976, but even by then the underlying trajectory on inequality had almost certainly shifted direction. It was within those years in the 1970s that the direction of long-term social change turned. See the argument in Section 4.5 of this book (pages 136-7) as to why 1971 is a key date in the US; many other years can also be singled out. In Britain the discussion of Figure 13 in this volume (pages 174-9) suggests the choice was made in 1974. Worldwide the year 1973 is the year nearest to the knife edge, to the point when the pendulum was hovering most still, pulled almost equally in all directions, and the future was most shrouded.

[21] Irvin, G. (2008) *Super rich: The rise of inequality in Britain and the United States*, Cambridge: Polity Press, p 65.

[22] Offer, A. (2006) *The challenge of affluence: Self-control and well-being in the United States and Britain since 1950*, Oxford: Oxford University Press, p 325.

[23] James, O. (2008) *The selfish capitalist: Origins of affluenza*, London: Vermilion, p 152.

[24] Rose, M. (2005) 'The cost of a career in minutes and morbidity', in D. Housten (ed) *Work–life balance*, London: Macmillan, pp 29-54, at p 42.

[25] Rutherford, J. and Shah, H. (2006) *The good society: Compass Programme for Renewal*, London: Lawrence & Wishart, p 37.

[26] Irvin, G. (2008) *Super rich: The rise of inequality in Britain and the United States*, Cambridge: Polity Press, p 87, Figure 4.2; and p 118.

[27] In her television interview for Granada's 'World in Action' ('rather swamped') on 27 January 1978 (www.margaretthatcher.org/speeches/displaydocument. asp?docid=103485). Unlike Enoch Powell she did not even suggest allowing in just enough others to meet what she saw as the country's needs.

[28] James, O. (2007) *Affluenza: How to be successful and stay sane*, London: Vermilion, p 72.

[29] Bauman, Z. (2007) *Consuming life*, Cambridge: Polity Press, p 142. This wording was often used by Goran Persson, Prime Minister of Sweden (1996–2006).

[30] According to Gøsta Esping-Andersen, as described in Irvin, G. (2008) *Super rich: The rise of inequality in Britain and the United States*, Cambridge: Polity Press, p 103.

[31] Many could describe themselves as English in London, but do not because of the connotations in such a mixed city. In cities where people mix less well, such as in some of the towns and cities of Yorkshire, people often do not describe themselves with a single word that says they are from a particular city, but as a 'Yorkshire man', for instance. Levels of tolerance are particularly high in London and are a little lower than average in some parts of Yorkshire. See the survey studied in Kaur-Ballagan, K., Mortimore, R. and Sapsed, E. (2007) *Public attitudes towards cohesion and integration, Ipsos MORI Report for the Commission on Integration and Cohesion*, London: The Commission on Integration and Cohesion, p 50. This survey predated the rise in BNP votes in Yorkshire.

[32] Pálsson, G. (2002) 'The life of family trees and the book of Icelanders', *Medical Anthropology*, vol 21, pp 337-67, at p 345.

[33] The figures for Japan are now widely known following the publication of Wilkinson, R.G. and Pickett, K. (2009) *The spirit level: Why more equal societies almost always do better*, London: Allen Lane. This book also includes the original argument that equality reduces ethnicity (p 178). Similarly statistics of a 3.5:1 inequality ratio for Iceland can be derived from Statistics Iceland (2007) 'Risk of poverty and income distribution 2003-2004' (www.statice.is/ Pages/444?NewsID=2600).

[34] Mazumdar, P.M.H. (2003) 'Review of Elof Axel Carlson. The unfit: a history of a bad idea', *Bulletin of the History of Medicine*, vol 77, no 4, pp 971-2.

[35] Connelly, M. (2008) *Fatal misconception: The struggle to control world population*, Cambridge, MA: Harvard University Press, pp 347-8.

[36] Goldberg, D.T. (2009) *The threat of race: Reflections on racial neoliberalism*, Oxford: Blackwell, p 26, referring to the work of Ruthie Gilmore on racism as premature mortality. Her definition can even be extended to patterns in murder. See Dorling, D. (2005) 'Prime suspect: murder in Britain', in P. Hillyard,

C. Pantazis, S. Tombs, D. Gordon and D. Dorling (eds) *Criminal obsessions: Why harm matters more than crime*, London, Crime and Society Foundation, pp 23–38, on how supposedly individually motivated murder reflects wider changes in prejudice over time, with rates reducing for women and rising for the poor, as the status of both groups changes.

[37] Hayter, T. (2004) *Open borders: The case against immigration controls*, London: Pluto Press, p 103.

[38] According to the 2001 Census; see Thomas, B. and Dorling, D. (2007) *Identity in Britain: A cradle-to-grave atlas*, Bristol: The Policy Press, p 46.

[39] Green, R. (2007) 'Managing migration impacts', Presentation to the Migration Impacts Forum, 17 October, on Community Cohesion by Rodney Green, Chief Executive, Leicester City Council, London: Home Office, p 6. Last found (11/10/09) at: www.communities.gov.uk/documents/communities/pdf/communitycohesion.

[40] Cohen, S. (2006) *Standing on the shoulders of fascism: From immigration control to the strong state*, Stoke-on-Trent: Trentham Books, p 114.

[41] Cohen, N. (2004) *Pretty straight guys*, London: Faber and Faber, p 74.

[42] Dorling, D. (2008) 'London and the English desert: the grain of truth in a stereotype', *Geocarrefour*, vol 83, no 2, pp 87–98.

[43] Figures from Krugman, P. (2007) *The conscience of a liberal*, New York, NY: W.W. Norton, p 16; extra math(s) is derived: $17/(44-17)\times(10-1)$.

[44] Dorling, D. (2006) 'Commentary: the fading of the dream: widening inequalities in life expectancy in America', *International Journal of Epidemiology*, vol 35, no 4, pp 979–80; Dorling, D. (2006) 'Inequalities in Britain 1997–2006: the dream that turned pear-shaped', *Local Economy*, vol 21, no 4, pp 353–61.

[45] Galbraith, J.K. (1992 [1954]) *The great crash 1929*, London: Penguin, p 194 on the unsoundness of the economy.

[46] Short, J.R., Hanlon, B. and Vicino, T.J. (2007) 'The decline of inner suburbs: the new suburban gothic in the United States', *Geography Compass*, vol 1, no 3, pp 641–56, at p 653.

[47] Kesteloot, C. (2005) 'Urban socio-spatial configurations and the future of European cities', in Y. Kazepov (ed) *Cities of Europe: Changing contexts, local arrangements, and the challenge to urban cohesion*, Oxford: Blackwell, pp 123–48, at p 141.

[48] For John McCain, it was at least seven but may have been as many as 11. All 11 'family' properties were listed by the *New York Times* (www.nytimes.com/ref/us/politics/mccain-properties.html) on 23 August 2008 (by reporter David

M. Halbfinger). David Cameron and his wife owned at least four in 2009, maybe more. David asked the reporter who revealed this please '... not to make me sound like a prat for not knowing how many houses I've got'. *The Times* newspaper revealed this in 2009 (www.timesonline.co.uk/tol/news/politics/article6267193.ece?token=null&offset=84&page=8).

[49] Frank, R.H. (2007) *Falling behind: How rising inequality harms the middle class*, Berkeley, CA: University of California Press, p 136.

[50] Even if you say you believe in inheritance because you believe that your offspring are somehow inferior, incapable of surviving without your help, they would do far better under such circumstances to live in a society that was more equal, where inheritance of wealth was less tolerated. This would be one of those societies that already exist where the living look out for each other more, rather than just for themselves or their families. Such societies are found in most rich countries such as Finland, Sweden, Austria, Korea, Belgium, France, Ireland and Greece. In more unequal societies those few fortunate 'inferior' ones who have to rely on the generosity of their dead relatives live hoping not to be duped out of their inheritance by their unscrupulous and not so financially fortunate neighbours. If you believe in inheritance, even though you do not see your offspring as superior, you still help create division, and help create and maintain suspicion, mistrust and racism.

[51] The story is well known but usually still told as a valiant feat of exploration. The exact date is debated as the date line was not in existence at this time and Cook had travelled from the East.

[52] James I also ruled over Wales, which had been overrun by the English conquest in 1282–83, was treated as a principality from 1301, but was in effect a colony, and had its law replaced by English law in 1536. The idea of Britishness would not even begin to become popular until another century had passed and the Kingdom of Great Britain was created in 1707. Britishness as an identity was not widespread until a century later again, when its rise in popularity was brought about to help with wars against France. The 'British race' is in fact a very recent invention. The Britons originally all spoke Welsh.

[53] Taken from an assessment by three Harvard economists that more calmly says 'a major reason' but which does think of race as widely defined. The quotation is from Krugman, P. (2007) *The conscience of a liberal*, New York, NY: W.W. Norton, p 178. It is worth noting that it could similarly be argued that race is the reason for much of the absence of a Japanese welfare state because pay is so equal due to assumptions of racial unity.

[54] Gordon, D. (2009) 'Global inequality, death, and disease', *Environment and Planning A*, vol 41, no 6, pp 1271-2.

[55] As the medical geographer Peter Haggett used to describe the process whereby sexual diseases were spread (Haggett, P. [1996] 'Sex', D. Dorling, Bristol, personal communication).

[56] Krugman, P. (2007) *The conscience of a liberal*, New York, NY: W.W. Norton.

[57] The rich have always known this. However, when three decades later even the poorest were recorded as saying they looked 'for the image not the face', the brands of clothes each other wore, it caused some shock; see Lawson, N. (2009) *All consuming*, London: Penguin, p 56.

[58] Frank, R. (2007) *Richi$tan*, New York, NY: Random House, p 231.

[59] In Britain prenuptial agreements, contracts drawn up prior to marriage to prevent the sharing of wealth if the marriage is dissolved, were described as a 'valuable weapon in the armoury of the wealthy' by one lawyer on Valentine's Day 2009 (http://business.timesonline.co.uk/tol/business/law/columnists/article3368933.ece, as reported in *The Times*, 14 February 2009), and it was later announced on 5 July 2009 in the case of one woman, Katrin, who had married a banker, that the agreements were binding under British law: 'Nicolas was then a banker at JP Morgan, earning about US$500,000 a year. As Katrin has argued during her legal battle, he too stands to inherit a substantial amount of money. His father is a former vice-president of IBM. She has said his parents are worth £30m; he says £6m'. In this particular relationship it was Nicolas who was the 'poor' one; she was said to be 'worth' between £55 million and £100 million (http://business.timesonline.co.uk/tol/business/law/article6634106.ece). Despite her wealth she is reported to have ended up sleeping on a mattress on the floor of her flat at one point when Nicolas would not move out of the bedroom. It does not sound as if she was particularly happy. The point of recounting this tale is to remember how little great riches increase happiness.

[60] Only one dollar in twenty that North Americans give to charity goes to charities that carry out work for 'public and societal benefit'; see Edwards, M. (2008) *Just another emperor? The myths and realities of philanthrocapitalism*, London: Demos and The Young Foundation.

[61] Goldberg, D.T. (2009) *The threat of race: Reflections on racial neoliberalism*, Oxford: Blackwell, p 238.

[62] This version of her words is taken from the *Daily Mail* and was printed just a few days before the 30th anniversary of her first general election victory; see Phibbs, H. (2007) 'Harman's crazy class war will make us all poorer', *Daily Mail*, 27 April.

[63] Margaret Thatcher first became well known as the government minister who took free milk away from all British school children in 1971; presumably she thought most were not destined to grow tall and hence all did not need to be given milk, that milk should be only for those whose parents could afford

it. An argument was put forward that parents should be responsible for the nutrition of their own children – it was not the state's responsibility. But the state continued to provide free school meals to those deemed poor enough and religious instruction to all who did not opt out. The British state provides mostly free healthcare, just as it once gave children free milk. Where the line is drawn depends on what is thought to be fine for some to go without.

[64] Connelly, M. (2008) *Fatal misconception: The struggle to control world population*, Cambridge, MA: Harvard University Press, pp 258-61.

[65] Krugman, P. (2007) *The conscience of a liberal*, New York, NY: W.W. Norton, p 170.

[66] Goldberg, D.T. (2009) *The threat of race: Reflections on racial neoliberalism*, Oxford: Blackwell, p 337; emphasis in original.

[67] Wars provide a fog that allows other atrocities to take place. Among the many reasons to try to avoid war this one is not often stated. Even if a war may appear just, in taking part in that war the smokescreen in which genocide is possible is created. In 1935 Adolf Hitler explained that 'if war came, he would take up and carry out this question of euthanasia, because it was easier to do so in wartime' (Glover, J. [2001] *Humanity: A moral history of the twentieth century*, London: Pimlico, p 352).

[68] Ibid, p 333. Recent reports suggest that this one Ron was two different men with the same name (see the Ron Ridenhour entry in Wikipedia as of 16 August 2009 in which the doubts are highlighted). If it were two different men then the cause for optimism is ratcheted up a fraction higher as such behaviour, even at that time, was less rare than we thought.

[69] Abhorrent enough for those in power to do something to curb it, which they did by passing the Police and Criminal Evidence Act 1984 and installing CCTV in police stations and vans.

[70] Wilkinson, R.G. (2007) 'Commentary: the changing relation between mortality and income', *International Journal of Epidemiology*, vol 36, no 3, pp 492-4, 502-3, at p 493; referring to the evidence collected by an historian of childhood, DeMause, L. (ed) (1974) *The history of childhood*, London: Condor.

[71] Both the examples of racism being attractive in circumstances of inequality, and of a poor family where the parents were jailed when video evidence was found of their teaching their toddlers to fight each other to harden them, are discussed in detail in Wilkinson, R.G. and Pickett, K. (2009) *The spirit level: Why more equal societies almost always do better*, London: Allen Lane.

[72] The sad personal details of the lives of many men at the head of British industry are described in Peston, R. (2008) *Who runs Britain? How the super-rich are changing our lives*, London: Hodder & Stoughton, pp 46, 82-3, 129, 201-2.

———

[73] Spinney, L. (2004) 'Snakes in suits', *New Scientist*, 21 August.

[74] Moran, M. (2008) 'Representing the corporate elite in Britain: capitalist solidarity and capitalist legacy', in M. Savage and K. Williams (eds) *Remembering elites*, Oxford: Blackwell, pp 64–79, at p 74.

[75] Reiner, R. (2007) *Law and order: An honest citizen's guide to crime and control*, Cambridge: Polity Press, p 6.

[76] Bauman, Z. (2007) *Consuming life*, Cambridge: Polity Press, p 118, quoting from Orwell's 1953 collection of essays.

[77] Offer, A. (2006) *The challenge of affluence: Self-control and well-being in the United States and Britain since 1950*, Oxford: Oxford University Press, p 95.

[78] Pogge, T.W. (2007) 'Why inequality matters', in D. Held and A. Kaya (eds) *Global inequality: Patterns and explanations*, Cambridge: Polity Press, pp 132–47.

[79] Leech, K. (2005) *Race*, London: SPCK. See introductory pages.

Chapter 6

[1] Peston, R. (2008) *Who runs Britain? How the super-rich are changing our lives*, London: Hodder & Stoughton, p 336.

[2] It was said that he had himself become 'a market force' through his pronouncements that year: Treneman, A. (2009) 'Appalling delivery, rambling replies but the Robert Peston show is a masterclass', *The Times*, 5 February.

[3] 'Today Programme', 2 May 2009, BBC Radio 4.

[4] Quote from a poorly titled article: Toynbee, P. (2007) 'Balls's bold plan to end child poverty could revive Labour', *The Guardian*, 11 December, written three days after this article on the most expensive of drinks: Chakrabortty, A. (2007) 'If I had a little money...', *The Guardian*, 8 December.

[5] The chief vice of the affluent has switched from smoking to drinking because of health concerns; and more now avoid cocaine. It was during Herbert Spenser's tour of the US that the cigarette story was first told; see James, O. (2008) *The selfish capitalist: Origins of affluenza*, London: Vermilion, p 193.

[6] ONS (Office for National Statistics) (2008) *Wealth and Assets Survey: Initial report*, London: ONS.

[7] Ibid. It is worth speculating on why ONS chose this particular headline at this time. Later, on 10 December 2009, when the full results were released, their headline was 'Household wealth in GB £9 trillion in 2006/08'.

[8] This is calculated as 4% divided by (4%+2%) and assumes equal numbers of children in each household type with children.

[9] Foster, J.B. (2006) 'The optimism of the heart: Harry Magdoff (1913–2006)', *Monthly Review*, vol 57, no 8 (www.monthlyreview.org/mrzine/foster020106. html), quoting figures revealed by Harry Magdoff, chief statistician of the New Deal Works Progress Administration in the 1940s, and an American socialist.

[10] Frank, R.H. (2007) *Falling behind: How rising inequality harms the middle class*, Berkeley, CA: University of California Press, p 90.

[11] James, O. (2008) *The selfish capitalist: Origins of affluenza*, London: Vermilion, p 153.

[12] PwC (PricewaterhouseCoopers) (2006) *Living on tick: The 21st century debtor*, London: PwC.

[13] Edwards, S. (2008) 'Citizens Advice response to latest repossession figures', Creditman.biz report on remarks of Citizens Advice Head of Consumer Policy, Sue Edwards, London: Citizens Advice Bureau.

[14] BBC (2009) 'Personal insolvency at new record', 7 August (http://news.bbc. co.uk/1/hi/business/8189053.stm).

[15] Frank, R. (2007) *Richi$tan*, New York, NY: Random House, p 153.

[16] The figures for British university students are given in GLA (Greater London Authority) (2002) *London divided: Income inequality and poverty in the capital*, London: GLA, p 80.

[17] Press Association (2008) 'Watchdog to investigate "payday" loans', *The Guardian*, 28 July.

[18] Yates, M.D. (2006) 'Capitalism is rotten to the core', *Monthly Review*, vol 58, no 1.

[19] Irvin, G. (2008) *Super rich: The rise of inequality in Britain and the United States*, Cambridge: Polity Press, p 183.

[20] The cover of the May/June 2009 issue of the journal in which these claims were made had the by-line: 'One repossession claim every half hour: non-high street lenders only want to get their money back'. See *Roof*, vol 34, no 3, and for more details of the wider losses, Dorling, D. (2009) 'Daylight robbery', p 11 of that issue.

[21] Offer, A. (2006) *The challenge of affluence: Self-control and well-being in the United States and Britain since 1950*, Oxford: Oxford University Press, p 90.

[22] Foster, J.B. (2006) 'The household debt bubble', *Monthly Review*, vol 58, no 1 (www.monthlyreview.org/0506jbf.htm), reporting on data released in the

biennial *The state of working America*, written by economists at the Economic Policy Institute (www.epinet.org) in Washington, DC: Mishel, L., Bernstein, J. and Allegretto, S. (2005) *The state of working America: 2004/005*, Ithaca, NY: Cornell University Press.

[23] George, V. and Wilding, P. (1999) *British society and social welfare: Towards a sustainable society*, London: Macmillan, p 147.

[24] Pogge, T.W. (2007) 'Why inequality matters', in D. Held and A. Kaya (eds) *Global inequality: Patterns and explanations*, Cambridge: Polity Press, pp 132–47, at p 143).

[25] Cohen, G.A. (2002) *If you're an egalitarian how come you're so rich?*, Cambridge, MA: Harvard University Press.

[26] Frank, R. (2007) *Richi$tan*, New York, NY: Random House, p 34.

[27] Blastland, M. and Dilnot, A. (2007) *The tiger that isn't: Seeing through a world of numbers*, London: Profile Books, p 17.

[28] Nast, H.J. (2006) 'Critical pet studies?', *Antipode*, vol 38, no 5, pp 894–906, at p 900 and p 903, n 1. Pets also rose to the fore in their importance to the rich during the last gilded age. For this and how pet cemeteries arose see the work of Philip Howell (2002) 'A place for the animal dead: pets, pet cemeteries and animal ethics in late Victorian England', *Ethics, Place and Environment*, vol 5, pp 5–22.

[29] Edwards, M. (2008) 'Just another emperor? The myths and realities of philanthrocapitalism', London: Demos and The Young Foundation, p 91, using as his source the work of Kevin Philips.

[30] A hedge fund manager interviewed in November 2005 and reported in Peston, R. (2008) *Who runs Britain? How the super-rich are changing our lives*, London: Hodder & Stoughton, p 205.

[31] Kitson, M. (2005) 'Economics for the future', *Cambridge Journal of Economics*, vol 29, no 6, pp 827–35, at p 827.

[32] The paper is referred to and discussed further in Irvin, G. (2008) *Super rich: The rise of inequality in Britain and the United States*, Cambridge: Polity Press, p 127.

[33] Offer, A. (2006) *The challenge of affluence: Self-control and well-being in the United States and Britain since 1950*, Oxford: Oxford University Press; paraphrasing and quoting both Thomas Malthus and Adam Smith on p 53.

[34] Ibid. It has been suggested that the population rise that caused Thomas Malthus such consternation was partly created by the greed that drove the enclosures of the Commons. Personal communication with Molly Scot Cato,

referring to Neeson, J.M. (1996) *Commoners: Common right, enclosure and social change in England, 1700–1820*, Cambridge: Cambridge University Press.

[35] Patel, R. (2008) *Stuffed and starved: From farm to fork, the hidden battle for the world food system*, London: Portobello, p 85; see also his n 34 on p 334 for a short essay on Thomas Malthus's mistakes, including how they were partly an English reaction to the French revolution, reflecting an old English fear of, and fascination with, 'the untamed and fecund flesh of the destitute' French revolutionaries.

[36] There are already studies showing that economics students find moral behaviour hard and that less morally inhibited students perform better in learning the subject. See Zsolnai, L. (2003) 'Honesty versus cooperation: a reinterpretation of the moral behavior of economics students', *American Journal of Economics and Sociology*, vol 62, no 4, pp 707-12, and Frank, R.H., Gilovich, T. and Regan, D.T. (1993) 'Does studying economics inhibit cooperation?', *Journal of Economic Perspectives*, vol 7, no 2, pp 159-71.

[37] Prendergast, R. (2006) 'Schumpeter, Hegel and the vision of development', *Cambridge Journal of Economics*, vol 30, no 2, pp 253-75, at p 254, n 1. In this context it is also worth noting that John Maynard Keynes was director of the British Eugenics Society, now known as the Galton Institute, from 1937 to 1945.

[38] Frank, R.H. (2008) *The economic naturalist: Why economics explains almost everything*, London: Virgin Books, p 101. Contrast this book to Frank's masterpiece of a year earlier (*Falling behind: How rising inequality harms the middle class*, Berkeley, CA: University of California Press, cited in notes 10 above and 52 below) for a good example of great variance within a single person's capabilities.

[39] Harford, T. (2009) *Dear Undercover Economist: The very best letters from the 'Dear Economist' column*, London: Little Brown, p 15, letter to Cecilia.

[40] Goldberg, D.T. (2009) *The threat of race: Reflections on racial neoliberalism*, Oxford: Blackwell, p 373), referring to Hannah Arendt's description of the thoughtless man, that 'greatest danger to humankind'.

[41] Collier, P. (2007) *The bottom billion: Why the poorest countries are failing and what can be done about it*, Oxford: Oxford University Press, p 90.

[42] Magnason, A.S. (2008) *Dreamland: A self-help manual for a frightened nation*, London: Citizen Press Ltd, p 53. The 'dreamland' in the title of this book refers to Iceland. Note that Milton Friedman's influence on Icelandic politics following his 1984 visit is now seen as pivotal among the antecedents of the 2008 financial crash there.

[43] The New Testament (Mark 8:36); for a full explanation see Cohen, G.A. (2002) *If you're an egalitarian how come you're so rich?*, Cambridge, MA: Harvard University Press, p 181.

[44] Pogge, T.W. (2007) 'Why inequality matters', in D. Held and A. Kaya (eds) *Global inequality: Patterns and explanations*, Cambridge: Polity Press, pp 132-47, at pp 139-40.

[45] Prentice, C. (2009) '"Econocide" to surge as recession bites', 11 March (http://news.bbc.co.uk/2/hi/business/7912056.stm), quoting Manhattan psychotherapist Jonathan Alpert.

[46] Bertrand, E. (2006) 'The Coasean analysis of lighthouse financing: myths and realities', *Cambridge Journal of Economics*, vol 30, no 3, pp 389-402

[47] Bruni, L. (2000) 'Ego facing alter: how economists have depicted human interactions', *Annals of Public and Cooperative Economics*, vol 71, no 2, pp 285-313.

[48] Kay, J. (2004) *The truth about markets: Why some nations are rich but most remain poor* (2nd edn), London: Penguin, p 361.

[49] Wintour, P. (2009) 'Labour stakes its reputation on second gamble', *The Guardian*, 19 January.

[50] Kay, J. (2004) *The truth about markets: Why some nations are rich but most remain poor* (2nd edn), London: Penguin, p 162. The argument presented is that you should only go to an economist to learn about the economy because you would not go to a DIY dentist to have your teeth fixed. As most people in the world, and increasing numbers even in rich countries, cannot afford to go to dentists due to the inequalities created by free market economics, and as so many dentists, following their accountant's advice, are concentrating now on cosmetic work rather than ending pain, this is hardly a convincing analogy. Worldwide most people who want their teeth fixed have to go to a DIY dentist. Orthodox economists have not improved that situation.

[51] John Kay is the author of a book that explicitly says it is aimed downmarket (of John) at the supposedly 'normally intelligent people': Kay, J. (2009) *The long and the short of it: Financial investment for normally intelligent people who are not in the industry*, London: Erasmus Press. He also provides a good example of how orthodox economists, when they have their arguments upset, complain in aggrieved tones in public; see Kay, J. (2009) 'The spirit level (review)', *The Financial Times*, 23 March.

[52] Offer, A. (2006) *The challenge of affluence: Self-control and well-being in the United States and Britain since 1950*, Oxford: Oxford University Press, pp 284, 285. See also Frank, R.H. (2007) *Falling behind: How rising inequality harms the middle class*, Berkeley, CA: University of California Press, who explains 'The price of the median house has escalated not just because houses have gotten bigger, but also because of the higher premium that desirable locations now command' (p 56).

[53] Tatch, J. (2007) 'Affordability – are parents helping?', *Housing Finance*, no 3, pp 1-11, at p 6, chart 6.

[54] Offer, A. (2006) *The challenge of affluence: Self-control and well-being in the United States and Britain since 1950*, Oxford: Oxford University Press; see p 190 on bathtubs and p 196 on Robert and Helen Lynds' quote from 1929.

[55] I am grateful to Bob Hughes for this argument. He draws on articles including: Fisher, F.M., Grilliches, Z. and Kaysen, C. (1962) 'The cost of automobile model changes since 1949', *Journal of Political Economy*, vol 70, no 5, October, discussed in Baran, P. and Sweezy, P.M. (1966) 'Monopoly capital: an essay on the American economic and social order', *Monthly Review*, pp 138-41.

[56] Crawford, E. (2007) *Beyond 2010 – A holistic approach to road safety in Great Britain*, London: Parliamentary Advisory Council for Transport Safety, p 80.

[57] Baggini, J. (2008) *Welcome to Everytown: A journey into the English mind* (2nd edn), London: Granta, p 98; £5,539 to be exact, £427 more than average housing costs. These are mean averages; the median would be lower, the mode lower still.

[58] Frank, R. (2007) *Richi$tan*, New York, NY: Random House, p 137 (prices given on p 123).

[59] Frank, R.H. (2008) *The economic naturalist: Why economics explains almost everything*, London: Virgin Books, p 145 (see also note 38 above).

[60] Baggini, J. (2008) *Welcome to Everytown: A journey into the English mind* (2nd edn), London: Granta, p 107.

[61] According to one multi-billionaire quoted in Frank, R. (2007) *Richi$tan*, New York, NY: Random House, p 134.

[62] Shah, H. and McIvor, M. (2006) *A new political economy: Compass Programme for Renewal*, London: Lawrence & Wishart, p 48.

[63] That seven-fold ratio is found in Sheffield where it is partly also caused by almost all affluent children under the age of 10 no longer being allowed to play on pavements or walk to neighbours' homes. A similar ratio was reported nationally in evidence given in 2008 to the House of Commons Transport Committee (2009) *Ending the scandal of complacency: Road safety beyond 2010: Further government response to the Committee's Eleventh Report of Session 2007-08*, London: The Stationery Office. In this report MPs said 'We urge the Government to renew its focus on tackling the appalling level of child road traffic deaths associated with deprivation'. In April 2009 the government responded that 'We are proposing to amend our guidance on speed limits, recommending that local highway authorities over time, introduce 20 mph zones or limits into streets which are primarily residential in nature' (see pp 2 and 14 for the Committee's concerns and the government response in www.publications.parliament.uk/pa/cm200809/cmselect/cmtran/422/422. pdf). Evidence that the major single cause of mortality in Britain for those

under the age of 35 is road traffic accidents was given in Dorling, D. (2008) 'Supplementary memorandum, ending the scandal of complacency', House of Commons Transport Committee, *Ending the scandal of complacency: Road safety beyond 2010*, Eleventh Report of Session 2007–08, pp EV 323-4. For more of the underlying studies see Graham, D., Glaister, S. and Anderson, R. (2005) 'The effects of area deprivation on the incidence of child and adult pedestrian casualties in England', *Accident Analysis & Prevention*, vol 37, no 1, pp 125-35.

[64] Dorling, D. (2006) 'Infant mortality and social progress in Britain, 1905–2005', in E. Garrett, C. Galley, N. Shelton and R. Woods (eds) *Infant mortality: A continuing social problem*, Aldershot: Ashgate, pp 213-28.

[65] 'What's going on' is one of the favourite lyrics of celebrity, from Marvin Gaye asking 'why there's so many of you dying (brother)', to the 4 Non-Blondes 'praying for a revolution'. It has always been a popular question to ask why social inequality persists and what might be done to increase justice.

[66] Frank, R. (2007) *Richi$tan*, New York, NY: Random House, pp 49, 143.

[67] Blastland, M. and Dilnot, A. (2007) *The tiger that isn't: Seeing through a world of numbers*, London: Profile Books, p 112; £7,500 is derived by dividing £150 billion by the authors' 20 million homeowner estimate.

[68] Smith, S.J. (2007) 'Banking on housing? Speculating on the role and relevance of housing wealth in Britain', Paper prepared for the Joseph Rowntree Foundation 'Inquiry into Home Ownership 2010 and Beyond', Durham: University of Durham, p 22.

[69] Frank, R. (2007) *Richi$tan*, New York, NY: Random House, p 132.

[70] Diamond, J. (2006) *Collapse: How societies choose to fail or survive* (2nd edn), London: Penguin, p 61. See also Chapter 5, note 48, this volume (page 347), for the 4th and 11th home-owning tendencies of two leading politicians.

[71] Connelly, M. (2008) *Fatal misconception: The struggle to control world population*, Cambridge, MA: Harvard University Press, pp 70, 90, 411.

[72] Although only for a certain elite, according to Major-General Hugh Stott of the Indian Medical Service in a letter to the *British Medical Journal* published on 13 December 1958 (vol 2, p 1480).

[73] Hughes, B. (2008) 'Land', D. Dorling, Oxford, personal communication; see 'Country for sale', *Guardian Weekend*, 26 April 2008 (www.guardian.co.uk/world/2008/apr/26/cambodia) and on the Virgin Islands: www.thepetitionsite.com/takeaction/119884382?z00m=15374441

[74] Frank, R. (2007) *Richi$tan*, New York, NY: Random House, p 131). When a wardrobe is this large it becomes potentially so much more than a receptacle for the storage of clothing. Most wardrobes do not have many other uses, but

these monster closets could each be a very large sitting room, 20 ft by 20, four decent-sized bedrooms, and much more besides.

[75] Berg, M. (2004) 'Consumption in eighteenth- and early nineteenth-century Britain', in R. Floud and P. Johnson (eds) *The Cambridge economic history of modern Britain: Volume 1: Industrialisation, 1700–1860*, Cambridge: Cambridge University Press, pp 357-87, at pp 377-9.

[76] James, O. (2007) *Affluenza: How to be successful and stay sane*, London: Vermilion, p 35.

[77] Bauman, Z. (2007) *Consuming life*, Cambridge: Polity Press, p 101.

[78] Baggini, J. (2008) *Welcome to Everytown: A journey into the English mind* (2nd edn), London: Granta, p 225.

[79] Bauman, Z. (2007) *Consuming life*, Cambridge: Polity Press, p 13, reporting a teacher's description.

[80] Wilkinson, R.G. and Pickett, K. (2009) *The spirit level: Why more equal societies almost always do better*, London: Allen Lane, p 117, quoting Gillian Evans, in turn quoting an anonymous teacher.

[81] Bauman, Z. (2006) *Liquid fear*, Cambridge: Polity Press, p 162.

[82] George, S. (2008) *Hijacking America: How the religious and secular right changed what Americans think*, Cambridge: Polity Press, p 248 and the footnote on that page referring to Mark Buchanan's 2007 article, 'Are we born prejudiced?', *New Scientist*, 17 March.

[83] Zsolnai, L. (2003) 'Honesty versus cooperation: a reinterpretation of the moral behavior of economics students', *American Journal of Economics and Sociology*, vol 62, no 4, pp 707-12. See also note 36 above.

[84] Frank, R.H., Gilovich, T. and Regan, D.T. (1993) 'Does studying economics inhibit cooperation?', *Journal of Economic Perspectives*, vol 7, no 2, pp 159-71.

[85] George, V. and Wilding, P. (1999) *British society and social welfare: Towards a sustainable society*, London: Macmillan, p 132; the fraction is derived from table 5.1.

[86] Keister, L.A. and Moller, S. (2000) 'Wealth inequality in the United States', *Annual Review of Sociology*, vol 26, no 1, pp 63-81. The ratio of 1:1,600 is derived from calculating the fraction 40/(1/40).

[87] See Chapter 5, note 38, page 347, this volume.

[88] ONS (Office for National Statistics) (2008) *Wealth and Assets Survey: Initial report*, London: ONS, Table 2 and p 3 of press release.

[89] Williams, P. (2008) *Please release me! A review of the equity release market in the UK, its potential and consumer expectations*, London: Council of Mortgage Lenders, p 26.

[90] Wyly, E.K., Pearce, T., Moos, M. et al (2009) 'Subprime mortgage segmentation in the American urban system', *Tijdschrift voor Economische en Sociale Geografie*, vol 99, no 1, pp 3-23, at p 3. For those interested see also: Wyly, E.K., Atia, M. and Hammel, D.J. (2004) 'Has mortgage capital found an inner-city spatial fix?', *Housing Policy Debate*, vol 15, no 3, pp 623-85; Wyly, E.K., Atia, M., Foxcroft, H., Hammel, D.J. and Phillips-Watts, K. (2006) 'American home: predatory mortgage capital and spaces of race and class exploitation in the United States', *Geografiska Annaler B*, vol 88, no 1, pp 105-32; and Wyly, E.K., Atia, M., Lee, E. and Mendez, P. (2007) 'Race, gender, and statistical representation: predatory mortgage lending and the US community reinvestment movement', *Environment and Planning A*, vol 39, pp 2139-66.

[91] Kloby, J. (2002) 'Wealth gap woes', *Monthly Review*, vol 53, no 8.

[92] Scott Cato, M. (2009) *Green economics: An introduction to theory, policy and practice*, London: Earthscan, pp 126-7.

[93] Ibid, which provides an excellent introduction to how the majority have been deceived.

[94] Diamond, J. (2006) *Collapse: How societies choose to fail or survive* (2nd edn), London: Penguin, p 150. The term 'pueblo people' is also used and continues to be used today by some groups as, although civilisations die out, whole peoples rarely do in their entirety.

[95] Berg, M. (2004) 'Consumption in eighteenth- and early nineteenth-century Britain', in R. Floud and P. Johnson (eds) *The Cambridge economic history of modern Britain: Volume 1: Industrialisation, 1700–1860*, Cambridge: Cambridge University Press, pp 357-87, at p 366.

[96] Cockshott, W.P. and Cottrell, A. (1983) *Towards a new socialism*, Nottingham: Spokesman, p 23.

[97] Offer, A. (2006) *The challenge of affluence: Self-control and well-being in the United States and Britain since 1950*, Oxford: Oxford University Press, p 94.

[98] Diamond, J. (2006) *Collapse: How societies choose to fail or survive* (2nd edn), London: Penguin, p 75.

[99] Magnason, A.S. (2008) *Dreamland: A self-help manual for a frightened nation*, London: Citizen Press Ltd, p 274.

[100] Liu, J., Daily, G.C., Ehrlich, P.R. et al (2003) 'Effects of household dynamics on resource consumption and biodiversity', *Nature*, vol 421, 30 January, pp 530-3.

[101] Buonfino, A. and Thomson, L. (2007) *Belonging in contemporary Britain*, Report for the Commission on Integration and Cohesion, London: Commission on Integration and Cohesion, p 5; unclaimed bodies information from personal communication, John Mohan, University of Southampton, work in progress; finding mortality rates to be especially high for young men with few friends living in bedsits in the largest cities, exactly how high to be determined.

[102] Dorling, D. and Gunnell, D. (2003) 'Suicide: the spatial and social components of despair in Britain 1980-2000', *Transactions of the Institute of British Geographers*, vol 28, no 4, pp 442-60.

[103] Calcott, A. and Bull, J. (2007) *Ecological footprint of British city residents*, CarbonPlan, Godalming: World Wildlife Fund UK (www.wwf.org.uk/filelibrary/pdf/city_footprint2.pdf), p 8.

[104] See Chapter 5, note 15, page 344, this volume for links to resources that show how basic incomes for all are possible.

[105] James, O. (2007) *Affluenza: How to be successful and stay sane*, London: Vermilion; a remix of pp 158-9, with the final sentence from p 148 (having consulted the author about taking such liberties – or 'making posies', see page 10, this volume).

Chapter 7

[1] The strongest evidence comes from the US where, using data from 2002–06 and having taken into account absolute income, it was recently found that for the odds of reporting poor health, '... regardless of how the reference group was defined, there was a "dose–response" relationship; with individuals in the highest quintile of relative deprivation more likely to report poor health than individuals in the next highest quintile and so on' (Subramanyam, M., Kawachi, I., Berkman, L. et al [2009] 'Relative deprivation in income and self-rated health in the United States', *Social Science & Medicine*, vol 69, pp 327-34, at p 329). This study concerns reporting ill health of all kinds. Among younger adults in affluent countries the majority of serious poor health is poor mental health.

[2] Burns, J. (2007) *The descent of madness: Evolutionary origins of psychosis and the social brain*, Hove: Routledge, p 74. The reference here is to Erich Fromm's *In fear of freedom* (1942) and ends with the suggestion that following industrialisation and individualisation, we are now '... witnessing the psychological consequences of human isolation and dislocation'.

[3] Ibid, p 197.

[4] CEPMHPG (Centre for Economic Performance's Mental Health Policy Group) (2006) *The depression report: A New Deal for depression and anxiety*

disorders, London: CEPMHPG, London School of Economics and Political Science. The figure is derived by doubling 16.4% given in a table at the end of that source based on the survey of 2000. If this appears too crude a method, as in some families more than one adult will be suffering poor mental health and in others there will be only one adult, then take Oliver James' estimate of 23% of individuals suffering emotional distress in Britain, based in turn on World Health Organization estimates and then, clearly, at least a third of families are affected (James, O. [2008] *The selfish capitalist: Origins of affluenza*, London: Vermilion, p 1; James, O. [2009] 'Distress', D. Dorling, Oxfordshire, personal communication).

[5] As revealed by the most comparable World Health Organization psychiatric surveys reported in Wilkinson, R.G. and Pickett, K. (2009) *The spirit level: Why more equal societies almost always do better*, London: Allen Lane, p 67.

[6] The statistics for Britain in this paragraph and the previous one are derived from the Office for National Statistics (ONS): ONS (2001) *Psychiatric morbidity*, London: ONS; ONS (2003) *Better or worse: National statistics*, London: ONS; ONS (2005) *Mental health in children and young people in Great Britain*, London: ONS; MIND (2009) *Statistics 1: How common is mental distress?* (www.mind.org. uk/help/research_and_policy/statistics_1_how_common_is_mental_distress); National Statistics Online (2004) *Mental disorder more common in boys*, London: National Statistics Online; and MHF (Mental Health Foundation) (2005) *Lifetime impacts: Childhood and adolescent mental health, Understanding the lifetime impacts*, London: MHF. They were kindly made available by Dan Vale ([2008] 'Mapping needs', Project seminar presentation, The Young Foundation, 24 June, D. Dorling, London, personal communication).

[7] Collishaw, S., Maughan, B., Goodman, R. et al (2004) 'Time trends in adolescent mental health', *Journal of Child Psychology and Psychiatry*, vol 45, no 8, pp 1350-62.

[8] West, P. and Sweeting, H. (2003) 'Fifteen, female and stressed: changing patterns of psychological distress over time', *Journal of Child Psychology and Psychiatry*, vol 44, no 3, pp 399–411, at pp 406, 409.

[9] Costello, E.J., Erkanli, A. and Angold, A. (2006) 'Is there an epidemic of child or adolescent depression?', *Journal of Child Psychology and Psychiatry*, vol 47, no 12, pp 1263-71.

[10] The one in 25 estimate can be reached either by extrapolating backwards or by taking the lowest rates recorded in the past which both produce similar results as the extrapolation is based on those rates.

[11] In fact they found that 'Only fathers' educational attainment and family financial status remained significant (odds ratios: 3.28–5.30 for grade school of fathers and 2.62–2.78 for being worse off economically)' (Doi, Y.,

Roberts, R., Takeuchi, K. et al [2001] 'Multiethnic comparison of adolescent major depression based on the DSM-IV criteria in a US–Japan study', *Journal of the American Academy of Child and Adolescent Psychiatry*, vol 40, pp 1308-15, at p 1308).

[12] Offer, A. (2006) *The challenge of affluence: Self-control and well-being in the United States and Britain since 1950*, Oxford: Oxford University Press, p 348.

[13] Twenge, J.M. (2000) 'The age of anxiety? Birth cohort change in anxiety and neuroticism, 1952-1993', *Journal of Personality and Social Psychology*, vol 79, no 6, pp 1007-21, at p 1018.

[14] ONS (Office for National Statistics (2008) *Sustainable development indicators in your pocket 2008: An update of the UK government strategy indicators*, London: Department for Environment, Food and Rural Affairs, p 130. The equivalent ONS publication of a year earlier had broken down these statistics by social grade AB, C, D and E (p 125), but not by age, the publication of a year later reported the responses to different questions (p 137), and so comparisons over time for children from this source are not yet possible (in the 2008 study children could say it was 'a bit true' that they were happy, but that option was removed from the later survey and apparent happiness rose by 10%!). For adults by social grade in England stark differences in well-being were reported in 2007. Only those in the best-paid work, grades AB, reported much net happiness and feeling engaged with what they were doing. Those in the worst-paid work, grade E, most often felt unhappy, not engaged, unsafe, depressed, lonely and that everything was an effort. Most probably because they were and it was.

[15] Nancy Shalek (president of Shalek Advertising Agency), as quoted in Kasser, T. (2002) *The high price of materialism*, Cambridge, MA: The MIT Press, p 91.

[16] McChesney, R.W. and Foster, J.B. (2003) 'The commercial tidal wave', *Monthly Review*, vol 54, no 10.

[17] In comments reported in association with the publication of Department for Children, Schools and Families (2007) *The Children's Plan: Building brighter futures*, London: The Stationery Office. Ed Balls was the relevant government minister in charge of this department at the time. In subsequent years he did nothing to reduce the exposure of children to advertising.

[18] Baggini, J. (2008) *Welcome to Everytown: A journey into the English mind* (2nd edn), London: Granta, p 224, relying in turn on a National Consumer Council survey of 2005 referenced on p 274. The same report revealed that some 78% of children in Britain say they 'love shopping'.

[19] Rowan Williams was elected Archbishop of Canterbury in 2003. These words are from the press release to a report from the Children's Society written in his name: Williams, R. (2008) 'Good childhood inquiry reveals mounting

concern over commercialisation of childhood' (www.childrenssociety.org.uk/
whats_happening/media_office/latest_news/6486_pr.html), referencing in
turn: Schor, J. (2004) *Born to buy: The commercialized child and the new consumer
culture*, New York: Scribner; and NCC (National Consumer Council) (2007)
Watching, wanting, wellbeing, London: NCC.

[20] Or, to quote verbatim, 'marinated in the most aggressive advertising and
marketing environment ever known', according to Anya Kamenetz, the
author of *Generation debt*, one of many recent popular books about the evil
of advertising, quoted in Harris, J. (2007) 'The anxious affluent: middle class
insecurity and social democracy', *Renewal: A Journal of Social Democracy*, vol
15, no 4, pp 72-9, at p 75.

[21] Trotter, C. (2007) *No left turn: The distortion of New Zealand's history by greed,
bigotry and right-wing politics*, Auckland: Random House, p 124, noting the
observation was made first by John Dewey.

[22] Bauman, Z. (2007) *Consuming life*, Cambridge: Polity Press, pp 46-7; emphasis
as in the original.

[23] As explained by Sebastian Kraemer, and as clearly evident in the current
economic recession/depression. For a summary of the odds of unemployment
making you ill, the efficiency of the various alternatives and Kraemer's
explanation, see Dorling, D. (2009) 'Unemployment and health (editorial)',
British Medical Journal, vol 338, p b829.

[24] Navarro, V. (2003) 'The inhuman state of US health care', *Monthly Review*,
vol 55, no 4.

[25] Research reported in Edwards, M. (2008) *Just another emperor? The myths and
realities of philanthrocapitalism*, London: Demos and The Young Foundation, p 51.

[26] The dissection of meaning of the private hospital receipt is one of the most
striking and memorable of illustrations included in Edward Tufte's book
Envisioning Information (published by the Graphics Press in 1990). It is not
hard to understand that a medical system that aims to give the best care at the
lowest cost, and one in which profit is not allowed, is both likely to do the
least harm, and most likely to treat you quickly and appropriately when you
actually most need treatment. There are no private accident and emergency
wards in the UK; it is not in the interest of private hospitals to provide such
facilities, ones where the need is so clear and the scope for profiteering so low.

[27] Goldberg, D.T. (2009) *The threat of race: Reflections on racial neoliberalism*,
Oxford: Blackwell, p 88).

[28] DH (Department of Health) (2008) *Tackling health inequalities: 2007 status
report on the programme for action*, London, Health Inequalities Unit, DH, p 46,
and with Professor Michael Marmot, chair of the Scientific Reference Group

on Health Inequalities, suggesting on p 5 that 'action on inequalities in health in England conforms rather well to evidence-based policy making'.

[29] Kelsey, J. (1997) *The New Zealand experiment: A world model for structural adjustment?*, Auckland: Auckland University Press, p 359, quoting in turn and in part, from Prue Hyman.

[30] Whyte, D. (2007) 'Gordon Brown's charter for corporate criminals', *Criminal Justice Matters*, vol 70, pp 31-2. Original source: HM Government (2007) *Regulators' compliance code: Draft code of practice laid before Parliament under section 23(4) of the Legislative and Regulatory Reform Act 2006 for approval by resolution of each House of Parliament*, London: Cabinet Office Better Regulation Executive.

[31] Robert Townsend Farquhar, in the 19th century, arguing in favour of wages in place of slavery for islanders in the Caribbean and Indian Ocean, and quoted in Hudson, M. (2004) 'Scarcity of what and for whom?', *Monthly Review*, vol 56, no 7.

[32] Trotter, C. (2007) *No left turn: The distortion of New Zealand's history by greed, bigotry and right-wing politics*, Auckland: Random House, p 57, quoting a director of the London docks speaking during the 1889 strike.

[33] Offer, A. (2006) *The challenge of affluence: Self-control and well-being in the United States and Britain since 1950*, Oxford: Oxford University Press, p 295, where Avner Offer makes all these points in regard to the US but not China, although the connections are clear, and that is without mentioning how frequently the death penalty is applied in both countries, including for executing children.

[34] Elliot, L. and Atkinson, D. (2007) *Fantasy Island: Waking up to the incredible economic, political and social illusions of the Blair legacy*, London: Constable and Robinson, p 229.

[35] Franz Münterfering, the SPD (*Sozialdemokratische Partei Deutschlands*, the Social Democrat Party) chairman, as quoted in *Bild* and reported in Peston, R. (2008) *Who runs Britain? How the super-rich are changing our lives*, London: Hodder & Stoughton, p 210.

[36] Daniel Loeb, chief executive of the hedge fund 'Third Point', as reported in Peston, R. (2008) *Who runs Britain? How the super-rich are changing our lives*, London: Hodder & Stoughton, p 211.

[37] DeVerteuil, G. (2007) 'Book review: *Fragments of inequality: Social, spatial, and evolutionary analyses of income distribution*. Sanjoy Chakravorty', *Annals of the Association of American Geographers*, vol 97, no 1, pp 219-20, at p 219, according in turn to a recent study by Andrew Beveridge, published in the *New York Times* and referenced by Roberts, S. (2005) 'In Manhattan, poor make 2 cents for every dollar of the rich', the *New York Times*, 4 September. Note that following

the widely reported success of the Namibian basic income project in Otjivero, conditions are becoming slightly less desperate there.

[38] Jackson, T. (2001) 'Website of the week: health inequalities', *British Medical Journal*, vol 322, no 7286, p 622.

[39] Cole, M. (2007) 'Learning without limits: a Marxist assessment', *Policy Futures in Education*, vol 6, no 4, pp 453-63.

[40] Offer, A. (2006) *The challenge of affluence: Self-control and well-being in the United States and Britain since 1950*, Oxford: Oxford University Press, p 287.

[41] Guy, M. (2007) *Public health annual report 2005/06: Focusing on the health of older people*, London: Westminster Primary Care Trust, figures given in accompanying press release.

[42] Ibid, p 22.

[43] The NHS reports for Westminster do suggest such a concentration, although for a wider view see: Parr, H. (2008) *Mental health and social space: Towards inclusionary geographies?*, Oxford: Blackwell p 9. It is also partly the story of *Largactil* as told in Section 7.5, pages 302-3, this volume.

[44] Connelly, M. (2008) *Fatal misconception: The struggle to control world population*, Cambridge, MA: Harvard University Press, p 29; emphasis in original.

[45] Ibid, p 32. A photograph of the mutilated children of the Congo, with their severed hands, was one of the first photographs of genocide survivors to be distributed worldwide. That circulation continues today: http://en.wikipedia. org/wiki/File:MutilatedChildrenFromCongo.jpg

[46] Hall, E. and Drake, M. (2006) 'Diarrhoea: the central issue', in E. Garrett, C. Galley, N. Shelton and R. Woods (eds) *Infant mortality: A continuing social problem*, Aldershot: Ashgate, pp 149-68, at p 149.

[47] Brown, D. (2008) 'Life expectancy drops for some US women', *Washington Post*, 22 April.

[48] http://voltagecreative.com/blog/wp-content/uploads/2008/11/bailout-pie.png. With thanks to ideas merchant Molly Scott Cato for passing on this example.

[49] According to *The Economist*, 'Sea of troubles', 1 August 2009, pp 51-2, which predicted that worldwide shipping supply would soon exceed market need by 50% to 70%.

[50] Seager, A. (2009) 'Industry shows unprecedented fall in demand for power, says Drax', *The Guardian*, 5 August, p 22.

[51] Master's courses in Business Administration (MBAs) became successful because they nurtured short-term bird-brained arguments. 'Profit matters more than anything else, especially in the short term', is one such argument. These were the kinds of arguments that those hiring business graduates wanted to hear and so such arguments had to be generated with the greatest ferocity by business schools trying to place themselves on the very highest perches in the aviary.

[52] Staley, O. (2009) 'Harvard begins case study as tainted MBAs reveal damaged brand', *Bloomberg News*, 2 April. This report was in turn quoting the words of Louis Lataif, reported to be a 1964 graduate of Harvard Business School.

[53] Offer, A. (2006) *The challenge of affluence: Self-control and well-being in the United States and Britain since 1950*, Oxford: Oxford University Press, p 47. On p 53 Avner Offer explains how recently more and more people have come also to behave like those who run corporations: 'Consumption surveys indicate much higher levels of "hand to mouth" consumption than either exponential or hyperbolic models suggest, but the hyperbolic model comes closer to reality, and reality is much less prudent even than the hyperbolic model'.

[54] According to the *New York Times* of 16 January 1910. See also Hudson, M. (2004) 'Scarcity of what and for whom?', *Monthly Review*, vol 56, no 7. In this article Michael Perelman is quoted with reference to the price of passenger pigeons not rising at all as supply fell.

[55] CGD (Commission on Growth and Development) (2008) *The growth report: Strategies for sustained growth and inclusive development*, Washington DC: The International Bank for Reconstruction and Development and The World Bank, on behalf of CGD, pp 1, 12. The one concession made to their critics here is the admission that resources are, eventually, finite, although a few still talk of mining the moon!

[56] Abnormalities of the prefrontal cortex are usually referred to among other conditions causing some people who do well in business to prosper partly because they behave psychopathically. See Spinney, L. (2004) 'Snakes in suits', *New Scientist*, 21 August. The article also reports the 1977 work of Cathy Spatz Widom which discovered that for psychopaths in everyday life, the kind who can be found in boardrooms, the '... main difference she noted between her respondents and convicted criminals who were typically studied at that time was that they were better educated'.

[57] Shah, H. and McIvor, M. (2006) *A new political economy: Compass Programme for Renewal*, London: Lawrence & Wishart, p 143. See also Chapter 6, note 34, page 353, this volume for one suggestion as to why the populations of Europe rose when they did with such global consequences.

[58] Gordon, M.J. and Rosenthal, J.S. (2003) 'Capitalism's growth imperative', *Cambridge Journal of Economics*, vol 27, pp 25–48, pp 33, 43; they do mention

that this was initially Rosa Luxemburg's suggestion, made long before the events she foretold.

[59] Elliot, L. and Atkinson, D. (2007) *Fantasy Island: Waking up to the incredible economic, political and social illusions of the Blair legacy*, London: Constable and Robinson, p 235.

[60] Beck, U. (2000) *World risk society* (2nd edn), Cambridge: Polity Press, p 6.

[61] Rutherford, J. and Shah, H. (2006) *The good society: Compass Programme for Renewal*, London: Lawrence & Wishart, p 85.

[62] Pitts, M., Dorling, D. and Pattie, C. (2007) 'Oil for food: the global story of edible lipids', *Journal of World-Systems Research*, vol 13, no 1, pp 12-32, at p 28.

[63] Brunner, E. (2006) 'Oily fish and omega 3 fat supplements', *British Medical Journal*, vol 332, pp 739-40.

[64] Diamond, J. (2006) *Collapse: How societies choose to fail or survive* (2nd edn), London: Penguin, p 368.

[65] Rose, S., Lewontin, R.C. and Kamin, L.J. (1990) *Not in our genes: Biology, ideology and human nature*, London: Penguin, p 174.

[66] The proprietary form in which *Diazepam* was first marketed by the (now) pharmaceutical giant, Roche; see James, O. (2007) *Affluenza: How to be successful and stay sane*, London: Vermilion, p 204.

[67] Masters, R.D. (2001) 'Biology and politics: linking nature and nurture', *Annual Review of Political Science*, vol 4, no 1, pp 345-69, p 346. Often children are prescribed *Ritalin* because schools will not include them if they are not dosed up.

[68] Dumit, J. (2005) 'The depsychiatrisation of mental illness', *Journal of Public Mental Health*, vol 4, no 3, pp 8-13, at p 11.

[69] James, O. (2008) *The selfish capitalist: Origins of affluenza*, London: Vermilion, p 205.

[70] DH (Department of Health)(2008) *Tackling health inequalities: 2007 status report on the programme for action*, London, Health Inequalities Unit, DH, p 80.

[71] About the number that the non-psychiatric prison population reached by 2005. For earlier figures see Timmins, N. (2001) *The five giants: A biography of the welfare state* (new edn), London: HarperCollins, pp 210-11.

[72] I am very grateful to my father, who was a GP prescribing in Britain in these years, for parts of this history. He suggests that so many mistakes were made over the use of medication because doctors often assumed that if patients kept asking for a drug it was because it was doing good, rather than because the drug was causing dependence and addiction. The staff in prisons, old people's

homes, hospitals, children's units and certain schools found it easier to cope with doped-up 'inmates'. Often in research the wrong questions were asked, or even the wrong people. Relatives and friends were often not asked if the medication had done any good, even the patients themselves were often not asked if they felt that they were back to normal. For other sources of background information see Dorling, D. (2007) 'Guest editorial: the real mental health bill', *Journal of Public Mental Health*, vol 6, no 3, pp 6-13.

[73] Dufour, D.-R. (2008) *The art of shrinking heads: On the new servitude of the liberated in the age of total capitalism* (translation), Cambridge: Polity Press, p 72.

[74] Reported by the Canadian Broadcasting Corporation: CBC (2008) 'Use Ritalin only as last resort for kids with ADHD, guidelines say', 24 September (www.cbc.ca/health/story/2008/09/24/adhd-guide.html).

[75] NHS Quality Improvement Scotland (2007) *NHS quality improvement Scotland: Clinical indicators 2007*, Glasgow: NHS Quality Improvement Scotland, pp 6, 10, 12, 24.

[76] See note 2, page 360 above.

[77] Offer, A. (2006) *The challenge of affluence: Self-control and well-being in the United States and Britain since 1950*, Oxford: Oxford University Press, p 9.

Chapter 8

[1] Bauman, Z. (2008) *The art of life*, Cambridge: Polity Press, p 6.

[2] In place of that conspiracy of the rich, and for a neat two-page recipe, should you wish to know what's going on (as defined in Chapter 6, note 65, page 357, this volume) see Wallerstein, I. (2005) 'The actor and world-systems analysis: comments on Blau and Wieviorka', *Contemporary Sociology*, vol 34, no 1, pp 9-10.

[3] Stephens, L., Ryan-Collins, J. and Boyle, D. (2008) *Co-production: A manifesto for growing the core economy*, London: New Economics Foundation, pp 7-8.

[4] The insertion of the word 'apparently' is all that is needed to begin the process of dismantling the logic of this well-known argument attributed originally to John Rawls. The quotation is taken from Arneson, R.J. (2009) 'Justice is not equality', in B. Feltham (ed) *Justice, equality and constructivism: Essays on G.A. Cohen's 'Rescuing justice and equality'*, Chichester: Wiley-Blackwell, pp 5-25, at p 25.

[5] DCSF (Department for Children, Schools and Families) (2007) *The Children's Plan: Building brighter futures*, London: The Stationery Office, pp 73-4 (emphasis added here); hopefully they did not mean opportunities when they wrote outcomes! However, the DCSF are as fallible as the rest of us.

[6] Rutherford, J. and Shah, H. (2006) *The good society: Compass Programme for Renewal*, London: Lawrence & Wishart, p 51, referring in turn to the Welsh government statement.

[7] Shuayb, M. and O'Donnell, S. (2008) *Aims and values in primary education: England and other countries*, Primary Review Research Survey 1/2, Cambridge: University of Cambridge Faculty of Education, p 22.

[8] Haydon, D. and Scraton, P. (2008) 'Conflict, regulation and marginalisation in the North of Ireland: the experiences of children and young people', *Current Issues in Criminal Justice*, vol 20, no 1, pp 59-78, quoted in last sentence of the article.

[9] Krugman, P. (2007) *The conscience of a liberal*, New York, NY: W.W. Norton, p 211.

[10] Ibid, p 215, on an unnamed Texas legislator (identified on the web as Debbie Riddle); poll figures are given on p 202. On 7 September 2009 Debbie gave instructions to her friends and neighbours on how to avoid their children ever having to hear President Obama speaking (http://debbieriddle.org/2009/09/your-children-do-not-have-to-hear-obamas-speach/).

[11] Dufour, D.-R. (2008) *The art of shrinking heads: On the new servitude of the liberated in the age of total capitalism* (translation), Cambridge: Polity Press, pp 168-9. The quotation continues: 'Descartes's capitalist Amsterdam has now conquered the world. It is not just that everyone in this planetary city is now involved in trade; trade is now involved in everyone in the sense that it shapes us all'.

[12] Harris, R. (2004) 'Government and the economy, 1688–1850', in R. Floud and P. Johnson_(eds) *The Cambridge economic history of modern Britain: Volume 1: Industrialisation, 1700–1860*, Cambridge: Cambridge University Press, pp 204-37, at p 217.

[13] Dixon, T. (2005) *The invention of altruism: Making moral meanings in Victorian Britain*, Oxford: Oxford University Press, p 213, quoting Thomas Paine's *Rights of man*, part I, p 94.

[14] Du Boff, R.B. (2004) 'US hegemony: continuing decline, enduring danger', *Monthly Review*, vol 55, no 7, www.monthlyreview.org/1203duboff.htm

[15] Leonhardt, D. (2009) 'A bold plan sweeps away Reagan ideas', *New York Times*, 27 February. Note that as the year 2009 progressed the plan began to look a little less bold when the President began to associate himself more closely with those associated with bankers and their ideology. In October 2009 he was awarded the Nobel Peace prize, not for what he had done, but in a move widely reported as being encouragement to be more progressive in future, both at home and abroad.

¹⁶ OMB (Office of Management and Budget) (2009) *Inheriting a legacy of misplaced priorities, A new era of responsibility: Renewing America's promise*, Washington: The White House (http://budget2010.org/inheriting-a-legacy-of-misplaced-priorities.html), p 9.

¹⁷ Thanks to Dave Gordon for passing on a version of this summary; see Figures 9 and 11 at www.whitehouse.gov/omb/assets/fy2010_new_era/ Inheriting_a_Legacy1.pdf

¹⁸ Grimshaw, A.D. (2002) 'A review essay on "In search of politics"', *Contemporary Sociology*, vol 31, no 3, pp 257-61, at p 259. The text missing from the quote is '(and here Bauman adopts Jacques Attali's metaphor)'.

¹⁹ The Companies and Remuneration Bill had its third reading in the House of Lords on 13 July 2009 and then went for consideration to the Commons. In the strange world of 2009 politics, many of their Lordships were more opposed to high rates of inequality than were the party who once represented the interests of the poorest of labouring commoners. There was little expectation that the Commons would accept the Bill and make it law, but then these were the strangest of times and that strangeness was changing the nature of the art of the possible. When Britain was last bankrupt, in 1945, the only secure and cheap way to provide security for all, including many of the affluent, and a health service for all, was to introduce a welfare state and National Health Service. Being less rich creates more possibilities.

²⁰ The key person proposing the amendment was Lord Taverne, and the Chancellor who delivered the budget was Alistair Darling. On the amendment see www.equalitytrust.org.uk/node/121 and on the Bill see www.mirror.co.uk/news/columnists/maguire/2009/04/29/harriet-harman-s-equality-bill-points-to-the-route-for-a-better-britain-115875-21316506/

²¹ Irvin, G. (2008) *Super rich: The rise of inequality in Britain and the United States*, Cambridge: Polity Press, p 209.

²² This list is taken from Steel, M. (2008) *What's going on*, London: Simon & Schuster, p 247, and Kelsey, J. (1997) *The New Zealand experiment: A world model for structural adjustment?*, Auckland: Auckland University Press, pp 370-1.

²³ This itself is, of course, just another of those lessons so easily forgotten by humans given that our brains have not evolved to cope with so much to remember. For four versions of the chant being remembered and repeated see Field, P. (1999) 'The anti-roads movement: the struggle of memory against forgetting', in T. Jordan and A. Lent (eds) *Storming the millennium: The new politics of change*, London: Lawrence & Wishart, pp 68-79, at p 74. Patrick Field quotes Milan Kundera, as recorded in turn by Neil Goodwin in *Life in the fast lane* on the M11 road protests. And see also Bauman, Z. (2007) *Consuming life*, Cambridge: Polity Press, p 84, also referring to Milan Kundera's novel *Slowness*.

[24] When the best-off tenth of skilled manual men earned 2.55 times the amount earned by the worst-off tenth; see Section 4.5, at page 140, for the ratio series. Overall wage inequality rates are, and were, much higher with mostly men in managerial positions at the top and mostly women in care work at the bottom by 1996.

[25] Machin, S. (2003) 'Wage inequality since 1975', in R. Dickens, P. Gregg and J. Wadsworth (eds) *The labour market under New Labour: The state of working Britain 2003*, Basingstoke: Palgrave Macmillan, ch 12, at p 191.

[26] The man best known for saying this, Lord Peter Mandelson, enjoyed annoying members of his own political party by making such statements. In 2009 he suggested that 'anti-elitism of some parts of the left on education policy has often been a dead end', presumably to cause more annoyance, as almost everyone is anti-elitist today; see BBC (2009) 'Fee rise "must aid poor students"', 27 July (http://news.bbc.co.uk/2/hi/uk_news/education/8169838.stm). On the same day a key government adviser, Sir Jonathon Porritt, working on a completely different area of policy, resigned, citing Mandelson as the problem: 'Lord Mandelson had been particularly hostile to the concept of sustainable development' (BBC [2009] 'Porritt parting shot at ministers', 27 July (http://news.bbc.co.uk/1/hi/uk/8169627.stm)). One week later it was revealed that Mandelson was trying to find a job for a friend of his (Trevor Phillips) who might otherwise become a Conservative Party adviser given how easy it was to switch sides by 2009 (according to www.dailymail.co.uk/news/article-1203653/Mandelson-tried-persuade-Trevor-Phillips-quit-promising-Ministerial-post.html). Neither Lord Mandelson, nor Sir Jonathan Porritt, nor Mr Phillips held any elected post, but all were in government in one way or another, and this series of spats typified the dying days of New Labour.

[27] See Figure 12, Chapter 5, page 170 for the effects of an economic crash within a period of such inequality reduction. I am grateful to my grandfather, Eric Charlesworth, for telling me these stories in 2009. He was born in 1916.

[28] O'Grady, F. (2007) 'Economic citizenship and the new capitalism', *Renewal: A Journal of Social Democracy*, vol 15, nos 2/3, pp 58-66, at pp 62-3.

[29] Burns, J. (2007) *The descent of madness: Evolutionary origins of psychosis and the social brain*, Hove: Routledge, p 182.

[30] Bauman, Z. (2008) *The art of life*, Cambridge: Polity Press, p 39; emphasis in original.

[31] Baggini, J. (2008) *Welcome to Everytown: A journey into the English mind* (2nd edn), London: Granta, p 181.

[32] Wilkinson, R.G. and Pickett, K. (2009) *The spirit level: Why more equal societies almost always do better*, London: Allen Lane, pp 260-1.

[33] Marx (1907 [1852]) *The Eighteenth Brumaire of Louis Bonaparte*, Chicago, IL: Charles H. Kerr: see Chapter 2, note 27, page 325, this volume,.

[34] Shah, H. and Goss, S. (2007) *Democracy and the public realm: Compass Programme for Renewal*, London: Lawrence & Wishart, p 17; Mohandas Gandhi's words used in the sentence before are quoted on p 11.

[35] Connelly, M. (2008) *Fatal misconception: The struggle to control world population*, Cambridge, MA: Harvard University Press, p 380.

[36] Magnason, A.S. (2008) *Dreamland: A self-help manual for a frightened nation*, London: Citizen Press Ltd, p 279.

[37] Kelsey, J. (1997) *The New Zealand experiment: A world model for structural adjustment?*, Auckland: Auckland University Press, p 393; and see pp 394–8 for just one set of ideas on the way to do the right thing.

[38] Krieger, N. (2000) 'Passionate epistemology, critical advocacy, and public health: doing our profession proud', *Critical Public Health*, vol 10, no 3, pp 287–94, at p 292, who does indeed provide a very good guide to being on the side of the angels.

[39] Ritzer, G. (2004) *The globalization of nothing*, London: Sage Publications, p 216.

Index

Note: The letters f, t and n following page numbers indicate figures, tables and notes.

children
  ability 40, 46, 47t, 51
  anti-depressants, use of 304
  anxiety, rise in 305
  becoming sensitised 220
  capabilities of 311
  competition 278–84
  depression 306
  encouragement 51, 88
  greed, effect of 214–15
  imprisonment 80
  mental health problems 271–2
  mortality rates 29
  neglect, effect on 42
  poverty 117–18
  praise 54
  ranking by 'ability' 36, 37–9
  road deaths 243, 356n
  testing 46, 76, 77, 85, 105–6, 328n, 338n
  see also child poverty; education; schools
Children's Plan (2007) 311
children's stories 83–4
Chile 127, 199, 256
China 88, 127, 167, 300
Chinese week 151
Chlorpromazine 302
choices, curtailment of 159, 160
'choose life' 326n
Churchill, Winston 75–6
cities, changes to 182–3
Citizens Advice Bureau 216
citizens' incomes 267
city living 266, 267
city traders 287
civil rights 63, 64, 146, 316
class 194
Clinton, Bill 139, 181
clothing 240, 253
cognitive behaviour therapies 301
cognitive capabilities 51
cohesion 181–4
Cold War 203
collective actions 24
colonialism 65, 198
comfort bubbles 333n
commercialisation 279
common goods 244
communism 112, 123, 137
  fear of 76

communist witch hunts 80
community cohesion 183, 184
community spirit 184
commuting 125, 182
company insolvencies 216
compassion 19
competition 25, 85, 278–84
complacency 137
comprehensive schools 59, 72
comprehensive universities 58
compulsive disorders 271
conduct problems 272
confidence 85
congestion 237, 242
Congo 138, 290, 365n
conscientious objection 203
Conservative government 59, 78, 120
Conservative Party 139, 174, 178, 343n
  voting concentration 175f, 177–8
conspiracy 307–8
consumer society 280, 117, 119
consumerism 20, 118, 133, 134
consumption 130, 133, 298–9, 366n
contempt of those taking most 319
contraception 56, 141, 201, 290
Cook, James 185
Cook, Robin 156, 345n
Cookson, Catherine 190
cooperation 30, 43
copyright 31
corporate thinking 293–5
corruption 101–2
cortisol 85
cosmetic surgery 253–4
cost of living 259
Council of Mortgage Lenders 260
counter-culture 84
counting beans 234
credit card debt 95, 216, 337n
credit cards 215
Crick, Francis 68, 332n
crime 338n
criminality 80, 84
critical acumen 45
crypto-eugenics 112–15, 340n
Cuba 130
cultural evolution 22
cultural norm 141
culture 284–91
cultures 22, 23